AI in Education, Governance, and Leadership:

Adoption, Impact, and Ethics

Bosede Iyiade Edwards
Universiti Sains Malaysia, Malaysia

Hassan Abuhassna
Sunway University, Malaysia

Damola Olugbade
University of South Africa, Pretoria, South Africa

Olayinka Anthony Ojo
University of Bolton, UK

Wan Ahmad Jaafar Wan Yahaya
Universiti Sains Malaysia, Malaysia

IGI Global
Scientific Publishing
Publishing Tomorrow's Research Today

Vice President of Editorial Melissa Wagner
Director of Acquisitions Mikaela Felty
Director of Book Development Jocelynn Hessler
Production Manager Mike Brehm
Cover Design Jose Rosado

Published in the United States of America by
IGI Global Scientific Publishing
701 East Chocolate Avenue
Hershey, PA, 17033, USA
Tel: 717-533-8845
Fax: 717-533-7115
Website: https://www.igi-global.com E-mail: cust@igi-global.com

Library of Congress Cataloging-in-Publication Data

Names: Edwards, Bosede, 1971- editor | Abuhassna, Hassan, 1986- editor | Olugbade, Damola, 1989- editor | Ojo, Olayinka, 1975- editor | Yahaya, Wan Ahmad Jaafar Wan, 1968- editor
Title: AI in education, governance, and leadership : adoption, impact, and ethics / [edited by] Bosede Iyiade Edwards, Universiti Sains Malaysia, Malaysia, Hassan Abuhassna, Sunway University, Malaysia, Damola Olugbade, University of South Africa, Pretoria, South Africa, Olayinka Anthony Ojo, University of Bolton, UK, Wan Ahmad Jaafar Wan Yahaya, Universiti Sains Malaysia, Malaysia.
Description: Hershey, PA : IGI Global Scientific Publishing, 2026. | Includes bibliographical references (pages 283-318) and index. | Summary: "This book will explore the transformative impact of emerging technologies, especially artificial intelligence (AI) on teaching, learning, and educational outcomes across diverse educational contexts"-- Provided by publisher.
Identifiers: LCCN 2025027497 (print) | LCCN 2025027498 (ebook) | ISBN 9798337355504 hardcover | ISBN 9798337355511 paperback | ISBN 9798337355528 ebook
Subjects: LCSH: Artificial intelligence--Educational applications | Artificial intelligence--Moral and ethical aspects | Education--Effect of technological innovations on | Educational leadership
Classification: LCC LB1028.43 .A39727 2026 (print) | LCC LB1028.43 (ebook)
LC record available at https://lccn.loc.gov/2025027497
LC ebook record available at https://lccn.loc.gov/2025027498

British Cataloguing in Publication Data
A Cataloguing in Publication record for this book is available from the British Library.

Table of Contents

Detailed Table of Contents

respondents. The reliability and validity of the instrument were established (0.75-0.89). The descriptive statistics of frequencies, percentages, means, and standard deviations were used to analyze the data collected. The findings revealed that the current level of impact of AI on teaching/learning among lecturers in special education, and usage was not encouraging enough. It is therefore recommended that training and retraining of lecturers on the use of AI and technological devices should be organized periodically through conferences, workshops and seminars in order to enhance the impact and usage of AI generally among lecturers and those in the field of special education.

As artificial intelligence (AI) continues to revolutionize education, its integration into public sector auditing training represents a critical frontier. This chapter systematically reviews the literature on AI-driven simulations in public sector audit education, analyzing their efficacy, applications, and inherent challenges. A comprehensive screening of 871 studies from Web of Science and Scopus yielded 11 peer-reviewed articles, which were thematically analyzed to identify key findings. The review highlights the transformative potential of AI simulations in fostering critical skills, bridging theory-practice gaps, and enhancing decision-making in audit training. It also addresses barriers to adoption, including technical, financial, and institutional constraints, while underscoring the importance of ethical and cultural considerations. By offering actionable insights, this chapter contributes to advancing the discourse on AI's role in audit education, with implications for educators, policymakers, and practitioners.

The integration of Artificial Intelligence (AI) and Deep Learning (DL) into education is advancing rapidly, but their impact requires further research. This study combines bibliometric analysis and a systematic literature review, guided by the PRISMA framework, to explore this area. The bibliometric analysis examines publication trends, key countries, institutions, journals, leading authors, and important keywords, providing a macro-level overview. The literature review analyzes 27 high-quality academic articles, revealing that AI and DL have significant potential in education, such as personalized learning, real-time feedback, emotion prediction, and improving the overall learning experience. However, challenges like immature technology, high costs, limited human-computer interaction, data security, and ethical concerns remain. This study highlights both the vast potential and the hurdles of AI and DL in education, pointing to the need for continued research to overcome these issues and maximize their benefits in educational contexts.

Artificial intelligence (AI) enhances students' learning motivation through personalized learning systems and intelligent tutoring in education. It provides students with immediate feedback and support to help them overcome their learning difficulties. In addition, the interactive learning environment created by AI further stimulates students' interest and engagement in learning.The impact of AI on student motivation to learn is crucial for improving the teaching system. In this paper, the PRISMA statement template is used for bibliometric analysis, and the Scopus database is used to analyze the publications from 2014 to 2023. 216 papers are retrieved to obtain insights on artificial intelligence and student motivation. The selection criteria are specific inclusion and exclusion criteria that analyze the distribution of publications from 2014 to 2023, the most important countries, research keywords and subject areas, and the most relevant authors and journals.These results offer insightful information about the field's current research interests.

AI in education has transformed teaching, learning, and assessment. It raises difficult ethical issues pertaining to equity, privacy, algorithmic prejudice, and academic integrity. This article examines ethical issues, theoretical frameworks, stakeholder

Preface

INTRODUCTION

The convergence of artificial intelligence (AI) with education, governance, and leadership represents one of the most transformative developments of our time. As digital ecosystems become more sophisticated, AI technologies are reshaping how individuals learn, how institutions function, and how leaders make decisions. This edited volume, *AI in Education, Governance, and Leadership: Adoption, Impact, and Ethics*, explores these developments from a multidisciplinary lens, combining empirical research, bibliometric analysis, and practical insights. The goal is not only to examine how AI is currently being used across these sectors, but also to spark deeper discourse on its ethical, social, and institutional implications.

Our contributors—academics and practitioners from across the globe—bring together their diverse expertise to offer a comprehensive understanding of AI's impact across educational institutions, public governance, and leadership paradigms. This volume delves into current trends, case studies, and theoretical frameworks that inform how AI is adopted, the value it adds, and the risks it poses. These chapters collectively address the necessity of aligning technological advancement with ethical and socially responsible practices. We place special emphasis on inclusivity, accessibility, and accountability—factors that are increasingly central to the responsible integration of AI technologies.

As editors, we recognize the importance of contextualizing AI not as a monolithic solution, but as a tool whose outcomes depend significantly on how it is implemented, regulated, and evaluated. The ethical dimension, particularly in education and leadership, is essential to this volume. Through systematic reviews and global case studies, this book aims to inform researchers, policymakers, technologists, and educators about the real-world applications and challenges associated with AI, helping guide the development of robust, human-centered AI strategies for the future.

CHAPTER OVERVIEWS

Chapter 1: The Impact of AI on Higher Education Trends and Educational Horizons

This chapter provides a bibliometric analysis of over 1,500 articles, showcasing how AI is reshaping global higher education systems. It emphasizes the need for international collaboration and technological evolution in educational reform.

Chapter 2: Impact of Artificial Intelligence on Teaching Learning Among Lecturers in Special Education

Using a quantitative approach, the authors investigate how AI is being adopted—or underutilized—by special education lecturers. The findings suggest that periodic training is essential to increase AI integration and effectiveness.

Chapter 3: Enhancing Public Sector Audit Education Through AI-Driven Simulations

This systematic review explores the use of AI simulations in public sector auditing education, revealing their effectiveness in bridging theory and practice, while also highlighting barriers such as cost and institutional resistance.

Chapter 4: Transforming Education in the Digital Age

A combination of bibliometric and systematic review methods provides insights into how deep learning and AI are changing the educational landscape. Opportunities and challenges are clearly delineated, from personalized learning to ethical hurdles.

Chapter 5: A Bibliometric Analysis of Artificial Intelligence Impact on Student Motivation in Education

This chapter analyzes over 200 publications to investigate the relationship between AI and student motivation. It shows that personalized learning and interactive environments significantly contribute to higher engagement levels.

Chapter 6: Ethical Frameworks in Artificial Intelligence for Education

Through systematic review and bibliometric analysis, this chapter identifies prevailing ethical concerns and theoretical underpinnings relevant to AI in education, including bias, data privacy, and the erosion of academic integrity.

Chapter 7: Ethical Framework for AI in Education: Navigating Challenges and Building Solutions

This chapter builds on the previous one by proposing actionable solutions and policy strategies for the ethical deployment of AI, emphasizing collaboration among stakeholders to ensure fair and transparent implementation.

Chapter 8: Students Data Security Metrics and the Ethical Implication for AI Deployment

Focusing on Nigerian university students, this chapter presents empirical research on data privacy awareness and ethical perceptions of AI, advocating for curriculum reforms to address these growing concerns.

Chapter 9: Exploring the Role of AI in Enhancing Values-Based Leadership and Its Impact on Workplace Engagement

This chapter connects AI technologies to leadership theory and employee engagement, revealing a shift toward AI-human hybrid decision-making models, and emphasizing the need for ethical leadership integration.

Chapter 10: Adoption Factors of AI Tools in the Recruitment Process Using UTAUT Model

By applying the UTAUT model, this chapter examines the behavioral factors influencing AI adoption in recruitment, identifying both drivers and barriers such as perceived risk, usability, and organizational support.

CONCLUSION

As we stand at the intersection of technological progress and societal transformation, it becomes increasingly clear that AI's influence on education, governance, and leadership is not just a trend—it is a paradigm shift. The chapters presented in this volume reflect the rapid evolution of AI technologies, while also critically examining their broader implications. Across sectors and geographies, a recurring theme emerges: the need to balance innovation with responsibility, efficiency with ethics, and automation with humanity.

We hope this volume contributes meaningfully to ongoing conversations in policy circles, academic institutions, and professional communities. The diversity of methodologies and regional perspectives included here offers a holistic view of AI's promise and pitfalls. Whether AI is used to personalize student learning, streamline recruitment, or transform leadership models, the decisions we make today will shape its long-term role in society.

Finally, as editors, we envision this book as a catalyst for more inclusive, ethical, and human-centered AI development. Let this be a call to action for scholars, practitioners, and policymakers to engage deeply with both the opportunities and the responsibilities that AI presents. It is only through such reflective and collaborative efforts that AI can truly serve the public good in education, governance, and leadership.

Bosede Iyiade Edwards
Universiti Sains Malaysia, Malaysia

Hassan Abuhassna
Sunway University, Malaysia

Damola Olugbade
University of South Africa, Pretoria, South Africa

Olayinka Anthony Ojo
University of Bolton, UK

Wan Ahmad Jaafar Wan Yahaya
Universiti Sains Malaysia, Malaysia

Chapter 1
The Impact of AI on Higher Education Trends and Educational Horizons

Ting Li
https://orcid.org/0009-0000-1348-5121
Universiti Teknologi Malaysia, Malaysia & Zao Zhuang University, China

Sanitah Binti Mohd Yusof
Independent Researcher, Malaysia

Hassan Abuhassna
https://orcid.org/0000-0002-5774-3652
Sunway University, Malaysia

Qi Pan
https://orcid.org/0009-0006-2431-7725
Universiti Teknologi Malaysia, Malaysia & Zao Zhuang University, China

ABSTRACT

In the 21st century, artificial intelligence (AI) is rapidly transforming all areas of life, including education, where it has the potential to trigger a fourth revolution. This review uses a bibliometric analysis, guided by the PRISMA framework, to examine the use of AI in higher education. The study analyzed 1,520 articles from the Scopus database, narrowing it down to 373 relevant papers. The results reveal a significant increase in publications since 2020, highlighting global interest in AI's role in higher education. The research shows the multidisciplinary nature of AI, with contributions from various countries, institutions, and authors, with Chan, C.K.Y. being the most prolific author. AI's growing presence in education signals its importance for global educational reform, underscoring the need for continued

DOI: 10.4018/979-8-3373-5550-4.ch001

research and international collaboration to enhance educational resources and student learning. The study recommends further technological development and knowledge expansion to maximize AI's potential in education.

1. INTRODUCTION

In the 21st century, artificial intelligence (AI) develops rapidly and penetrates every area of our lives. The integration of AI and higher education is changing the way that teachers and students collaborate in the classroom, prompting the development of human-AI synergy in classroom instruction (Crompton & Burke, 2023; Wang et al., 2024). According to Chen et al. (2020), teaching and learning in higher education needs cognitive abilities, learning, adaptability, and decision-making capabilities, which are consistent with the characteristics of AI. By ways of personalized learning, teaching support, management optimization, real-time evaluation and feedback, transcultural combination, and collaborative learning, AI adapts to the different needs of higher education(Chen et al., 2020; Popenici & Kerr, 2017; Tapalova & Zhiyenbayeva, 2022). Many studies have proven the effectiveness of AI in higher education. For example, AI helps educators develop and introduce personalized methods to acquire new knowledge and establish abilities (Tapalova & Zhiyenbayeva, 2022), improve teaching efficiency(Allen et al., 2021) and plays an important role in building personalized learning systems for students(Zhai et al., 2021).

However, the integration of AI and higher education faces technological educational and social challenges. For instance, the ethical problem of data collection use, and dissemination(Pedro et al., 2019), the assessment of AI technology in education(Zawacki-Richter et al., 2019), educators' skills acquisition in AI education(Chatterjee & Bhattacharjee, 2020), ethical issues when design and implement AI(Akgun & Greenhow, 2022). Nevertheless, the current education reform provides many opportunities for the development of AI applications in higher education (Zhai et al., 2021).

Given these challenges and opportunities, the researchers use bibliometric analysis to map the AI-driven collaborative teaching paradigm and identify emerging technologies that support human-AI synergy in the classroom. This analysis determines top countries, top researchers, top journals, and development trends in the academic field. This study aims to clarify the future agenda to improve teaching and learning approaches in higher education, which helps to understand the core theme of this volume: creative approaches to human-AI synergy in classroom instruction. Furthermore, bibliometric analysis has been widely used in the education area. For example, Abuhassna (2024) used a systematic literature review and bibliometric analysis to identify the integration of instructional design models (IDMs) and learning theories. Abuhassna et al. (2023) analyzed the role of the Technology Acceptance Model (TAM) in the acceptance of online learning platforms based on bibliometric analysis. Abuhassna et al. (2024) examined the correlation between e-learning platforms and student performance after the COVID-19 pandemic. Therefore, the researcher of this study will follow their steps, and examine the use of AI in higher education.

2. LITERATURE REVIEW

2.1 Previous Bibliometric Review and Research Gap

Based on bibliometric analysis, many publications have been produced on artificial intelligence research in education. To gain a comprehensive understanding of the diversity in AI research and how various countries or districts, authors, educational institutions, or universities respond to AI in education in terms of research and scientific publications, it is essential to evaluate this field and its challenges. Since 2020, numerous bibliometric analyses have been published. Table 1 shows that several review articles have conducted scientific econometric analyses across various fields, including education, medical education, engineering education, and language education. However, few bibliometric reviews focus on higher education.

Table 1. Review articles in the area of AI and higher education

Reference	Software	Area of Focus	Duration	Articles	Databases
Yu and Yu (2023)	VOS viewer	Education	2011-2021	880	Web of Science
Bahroun et al. (2023)	VOS viewer	Medical education and engineering education	2000-2019	207	Scopus
Moreno-Guerrero et al. (2020)	Science Mapping Analysis Tool (Sci MAT)	Education	1956-2019	379	Web of Science
Chankoson et al. (2022)	Cite Space	Education	2003-2020	518	CNKI
Fitriani et al. (2023)	VOS viewer	Education	2014-2020	842	Scopus, Web of Science
Tozzi et al. (2023)	Biblioshiny	Medical Education	2018-2023	3253	Web of Science
Jaleniauskienė et al. (2023)	Vos Viewer	Language education	2018-2022	2609	Web of Science
Harto et al. (2022)	Vos Viewer	Leadership Education	1978-2021	96	Scopus Google Scholar

continued on following page

Table 1. Continued

Reference	Software	Area of Focus	Duration	Articles	Databases
Ilham et al. (2023)	Vos Viewer	Education	2014-2022	1178	Scopus
Song and Wang (2020)	Cite Space and Alluvial	Education	2000-2019	8660	Scopus
Prahani et al. (2022)	VOS viewer	AI education	2011-2021	457	Scopus
Baek and Doleck (2020)	Biblioshiny	Education	2015-2019	135	Web of Science
Bozkurt and Sharma (2023)	t-SNE analysis, text mining, and social network analysis	Education	2022-2024	513	Scopus
Pradana et al. (2023)	VOS viewer	Education	2022-2023	93	Web of Science

Most previous studies have relied on the Scopus Citation Database or the Web of Science (WOS) Citation Database. Furthermore, Vos Viewer is the most used software in bibliometric analysis. Through the analysis and examination of these researchers' work, it is possible to identify diverse perspectives. Yu and Yu (2023) examined the essence and principles of AI ethics in education, and indicated that the use of AI has triggered the revolution of education. Bahroun et al. (2023) demonstrated GAI's transformative impact on medical education and engineering education. Besides, this paper pointed out future research directions in this area, such as GAI-enhanced curriculum design and its long-term influence on learning outcomes. Another study conducted by Moreno-Guerrero et al. (2020) indicated that there is an evolution in AI research in the educational field, focusing on the performance and impact of AI in the educational processes. Chankoson et al. (2022) intuitively revealed the research progress and trends on the application of AI in education in the Chinese context. Fitriani et al. (2023) emphasized the utilization and acknowledgment of the Internet of Things (IoT) and Artificial intelligence (AI) in education. Tozzi et al. (2023) showed positive attitudes to the implementation of emerging technologies, including AI, in specific (pediatric) educational programs and recommended solving gender and age differences in technology adoption. Jaleniauskienė et al. (2023) overviewed the latest research related to the use of artificial intelligence in language education. Harto et al. (2022) agreed that AI can help leadership education, and artificial intelligence is a keyword that appears in most leadership education publications. Ilham et al. (2023) explored three main clusters of AI in education, including the use of AI in general learning, medical education, and higher education. Song and Wang (2020) established five core clusters for educational artificial intelligence (EAI), including intelligent tutoring systems, learning systems, students, labeled training data, and pedagogy. Prahani et al. (2022) found that Holmes, W. was the top-cited author in the area. They pointed out that the study trends are 1) it's an application to students; 2) the subject of education in engineering educations; 3) teaching methods; 4) e-learning based education; 5) education system; 6) curriculum. Baek and Doleck (2020) found that the researchers largely focused on students and learning, and supported international collaboration to improve this field. Bozkurt and Sharma (2023) focused on the trends and patterns of generative AI research in educational praxis and argued that the trending research topics include emotional intelligence, AI literacy, and prompt engineering. Pradana et al. (2023) observed the use of OpenAI ChatGPT in education and concluded that keywords like "challenge," "teaching," and "knowledge" have not been thoroughly researched.

According to the existing literature review,AI has increasingly emerged as having strategic value for education(Seldon & Abidoye, 2018), especially in educational reform, which provides more chances for the development of the application of AI in higher education(Zhai et al., 2021). While there are various review studies on the application of AI in education, there is a lack of reviews in the context of higher education. By incorporating higher education into a comprehensive discussion of AI applications, this study aims to address this gap.

Obviously, the existing bibliometric reviews present macro trends and suggestions in the field of artificial intelligence in education. Most publications do not explore the applications of generative artificial intelligence, chatbots, or intelligent tutoring systems in higher education in depth. In order to present a more comprehensive application of these technologies in teaching, we need to conduct a complementary review of recent empirical and applied research.

2.2 Empirical Studies on Application of Generative AI, Chatbots, and ITSs in Higher Education

To better understand the meaning, feasibility, and challenges of applying AI in the context of higher education, the researchers analyzed the publications that are highly cited. Many studies agree with that the popularity of GenAI has exploded in the past two years (Smutny & Schreiberova, 2020), but the adoption of these technological tools has been splintered in higher education(Hashmi & Bal, 2024). Empirical evidence shows that scholars have concentrated on exploring the application of generative artificial intelligence (AI), educational chatbots, and intelligent tutoring systems (ITSs) in higher education.

On the one hand, many researchers have developed and assessed the application of GenAI and chatbots. Many studies indicate that generative AI has massive potential to improve learners engagement via interactivity and real-time feedback. For instance, Ilieva et al. (2023) found that generative artificial intelligence (AI) technology can help students-teachers interact online by transforming pedagogical activities and guiding both students and instructors interactively. Meanwhile, Many studies support that Chatbots are viewed as an Internet of Things (IoT) interface that could revolutionize teaching and learning, which supports students learning, language practice, and offers teaching assistance(Kumar, 2021). For instance, Smutny and Schreiberova (2020) examined educational chatbots for Facebook Messenger to support learning, and concluded that quizzes or a Question & Answer module can help during the learning process for users. Kumar (2021) presented that educational chatbots were found to improve learning performance and teamwork with a practical impact. Ruan et al. (2021) showed that conversational interfaces may benefit foreign learners' oral language learning, particularly under casual learning settings after examining the conversational interfaces may benefit foreign learners' oral language learning, particularly under casual learning settings they developed. Additionally, the effect of intelligent tutoring systems (ITSs) on higher education has been confirmed. For instance, Castro (2019) supported that digital tools or platforms with human-to-machine interaction capabilities may enhance automated processes for blended learning delivery modes. In this context, intelligent tutoring systems. Besides, Cai et al. (2021) suggested that personalized conversational agents are promising tools to complement existing online resources for math education, which reinforced the view above.

On the other hand, some studies uncover that there was an imbalance of available tools with regard to supported languages, genres, and pedagogical focus (Cai et al., 2021). For instance, Kumar (2021) found that affective-motivational learning outcomes such as perception of learning, need for cognition, motivation, and creative self-efficacy were not influenced by educational chatbots. Zhang et al. (2024) also showed that chatbots might reduce writing self-efficacy.

In summary, while empirical studies have presented promising applications of generative AI, educational chatbots, and intelligent transportation systems (ITS) in higher education, they tend to focus on the positive impact of learning outcomes in isolation. Therefore, it is essential to review and examine more systematic and quantitative research in this field.

This study uses bibliometric analysis, which attempts to provide better educational experiences and propose comprehensive teaching strategies. This bibliometric evaluation aimed to solve the following research inquiries:

1. What is the distribution of AI and higher education publications by year for the last decade?"
2. What are the most relevant journals and authors in AI and higher education?
3. What are the most productive countries in AI and higher education?
4. Which educational institutions have made the most significant contributions to the study of AI in higher education?

5. Which authors have produced the most substantial contributions to the field of AI in higher education?
6. What are the primary research keywords for the last decade of AI and higher education?
7. Which topic area is the most critical in terms of AI in higher education?

3. MATERIALS AND METHODS

3.1 Research Design

This study uses a bibliometric analysis approach to evaluate the research landscape of artificial intelligence (AI) in higher education. The researchers employed the Systematic Reviews and Meta-Analyses (PRISMA) framework (Page et al., 2021) and VOS Viewer software (Soegoto et al., 2022) to conduct research design and data analysis. By following the PRISMA template, the researchers transparently reported the reasons for the evaluation, what the authors did, and their findings (Page et al., 2021). As Soegoto et al. (2022) explained, VOS Viewer helps researchers conduct data analysis and visualization.

This bibliometric survey complies with the Preferred Reporting Items for Systematic Reviews and Meta-Analyses (PRISMA) framework. The researchers followed the PRISMA guidelines to retrieve data to ensure the quality of the review (Haddaway et al., 2022; Page et al., 2021). The main objective is to map the research landscape thoroughly to investigate the state of the use of AI in higher education. The study includes a thorough review of the top countries, educational institutions, journals, and authors in this field. It also discovers prevalent trends and primary research terms. Building on similar prior research, this analysis emphasizes the value of bibliometric reviews to advance knowledge in this academic field.

This study employed Vos Viewer to conduct data visualization and analysis. As Soegoto et al. (2022) explained, Vos Viewer was extensively employed for data visualization and analysis, along with the PRISMA framework for bibliometric analysis. Vos Viewer makes building and observing bibliometric networks easier. These networks, which are supported by co-authorship, citations, and bibliographical links, may include journals, publications, researchers, or individual works. Vos Viewer helps us map and analyze complex AI research networks, identify prominent journals, publications, and authors, visualize trends, and discover academic topics. Its interactive graphical user interface and powerful data processing capabilities make in-depth data analysis possible to identify trends and patterns in AI research in higher education. In addition, Vos Viewer's analysis of the geographic distribution of publications and institutional-author collaborations improves understanding of the research dynamics of AI and higher education.

3.1.1 Identification

3.1.1.1. Database Selection

The Scopus database was carefully selected as the primary source for this review on June 7, 2024, based on its extensive coverage, high-quality data, and powerful analytical capabilities.

3.1.1.2. Search Strings

The search methodology was carefully designed to ensure a comprehensive search of relevant studies. Structured search queries (e.g., queries using TI-TLE-ABS-KEY) included specific criteria such as "(AI AND higher education)". This study included publications published between 2014 and 2023, focusing on specific subject areas such as arts and humanities, computer science and social sciences. The search was strictly limited to articles and journal publications in English. The specific inclusion and exclusion criteria is shown in table 2.

Table 2. Inclusion and exclusion criteria.

Inclusion Criteria	**Exclusive Criteria**
Studies in AI and higher education	Studies outside the specified subject areas
Publications from the years 2014 to 2023	Publications before 2013 and those from 2024
Publications published in English	Publications in other languages
Journal articles	Conference papers, books, book chapters, blogs
Journals as the source type	All other sources

3.1.2. Screening and Selection

The initial database search used the main keyword "AI and higher education" and retrieved 1,520 articles. Based on the inclusion and exclusion criteria mentioned above, the number of relevant articles was narrowed down to 373. During the screening process, 1,147 papers that did not meet the criteria were excluded.

3.1.3. Inclusion and Reporting

Figure 1 shows the details and results of this bibliometric analysis following the PRISMA framework. The following part will address the research questions and present systematic and comprehensive results.

Figure 1. Prisma framework.

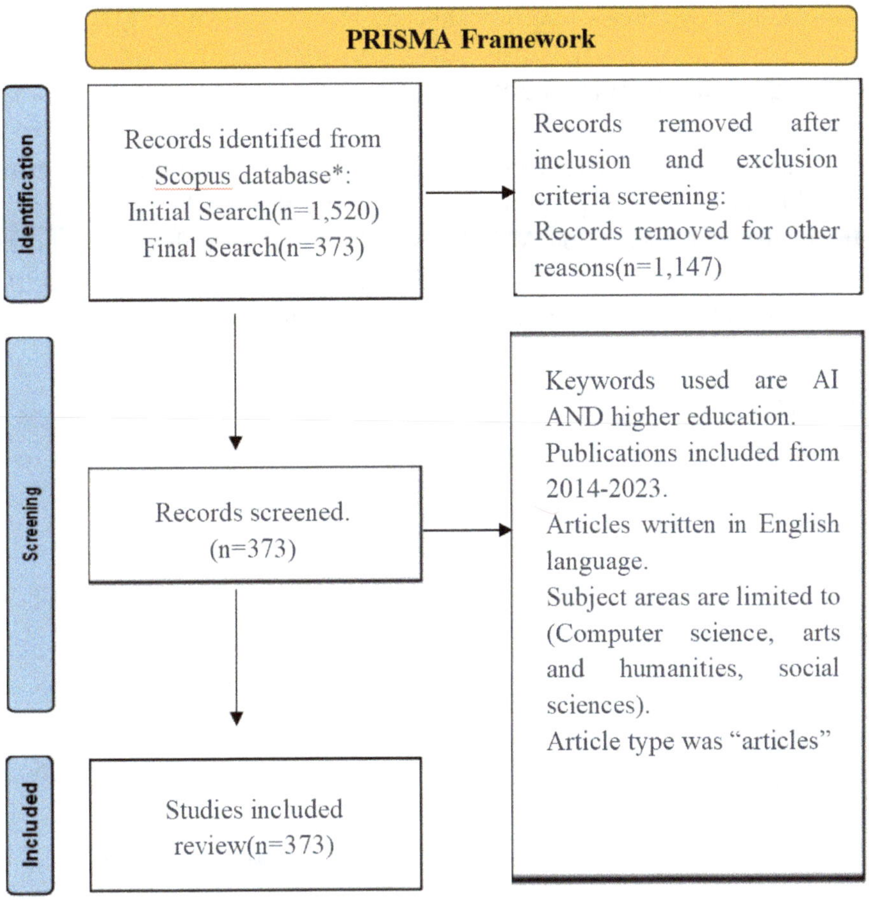

4. RESULTS

This section presents the bibliometric analysis results of the relationship between AI and higher education. This study covers the literature from the past decade, exploring the discipline from several perspectives. These aspects include major subject areas, publishing trends, influential scholars, and main research keywords. This review aims to portray the development of AI research, discover the key factors guiding scholarly investigation, and offer an in-depth analysis to explore the impact of AI on higher education in a worldwide view.

4.1. The Distribution by Years

This part will answer the following research question: " What is the distribution of AI and higher education publications by years for the last decade?" There is a notable increase in research on AI in higher education. Even though publication remained modest between 2014 and 2019, there is a marked surge from 2022-2023, indicating a significant rise in interest and attention in this field, as shown in Figure 2.

Figure 2. Distribution by years

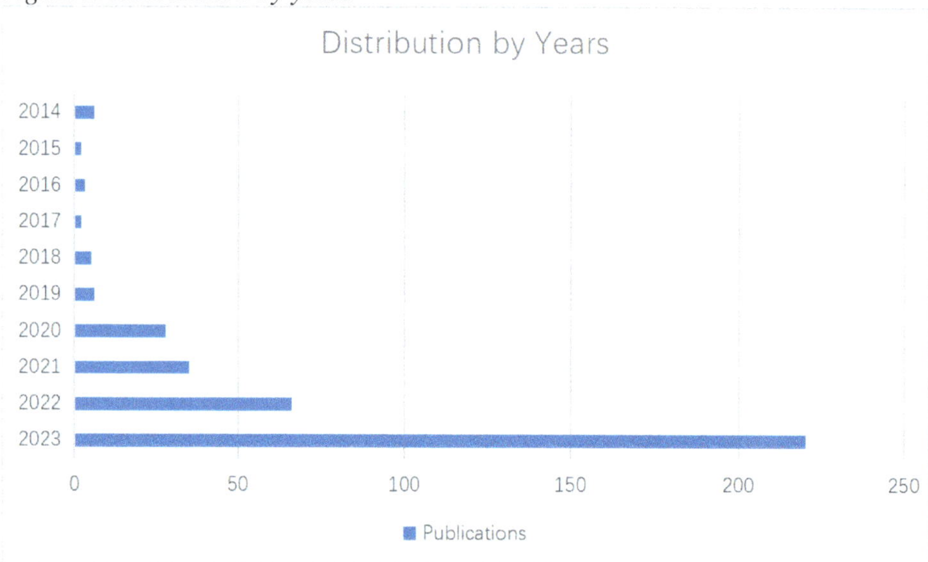

Specifically, from 2014 to 2019, the number of publications remained at a low level. However, 2020, the number of publications started to increase from 2020. Interestingly, the growth was particularly notable in 2023, with the number of publications reaching a peak of 219, exceeding all previous years combined. The observed trend, especially the increasing trend after 2020, indicates that people take AI more seriously. This may be attributed to the global shift to online education, which has been necessitated by the COVID-19 pandemic and AI technological developments. The data points to growing curiosity among academic and applied communities about the impact of AI on higher education, marking the emergence of a booming research field.

4.2. The Most Relevant Journals

To address the second research inquiry, what are the most relevant journals and authors in AI and higher education? According to the data provided, a large number of publications that make great contributions to this subject are shown in Table 3.

Table 3. The top 10 journals in AI and higher education research

Journal	*TP	*TC	Cite Score	Most cited article	Times cited	Publisher
Education Sciences	3334	15,882	4.8	E-learning critical success factors during the COVID-19 pandemic: A comprehensive analysis of e-learning managerial perspectives	312	Multidisciplinary Digital Publishing Institute (MDPI)
Journal Of Applied Learning And Teaching	232	2,081	9.0	COVID-19: 20 Countries' higher education intra-period Digital Pedagogy Responses	1235	Kaplan Singapore
Sustainability Switzerland	55,991	381,357	6.8	Impacts of the COVID-19 pandemic on the life of higher education students: A global perspective	1053	Multidisciplinary Digital Publishing Institute (MDPI)
Education And Information Technologies	1,767	17,613	10.0	A review of the use of virtual reality head-mounted displays in education and training	732	Springer Nature
International Journal Of Educational Technology In Higher Education	238	4,594	19.3	Systematic review of research on artificial intelligence applications in higher education – where are the educators?	888	Springer Nature
Computers And Education Artificial Intelligence	183	3,080	16.8	Vision, challenges, roles, and research issues of Artificial Intelligence in Education	337	Elsevier
Journal Of University Teaching And Learning Practice	314	1,133	3.6	Academic Integrity considerations of AI Large Language Models in the post-pandemic era: ChatGPT and beyond	145	Open Access Publishing Association

continued on following page

Table 3. Continued

Journal	*TP	*TC	Cite Score	Most cited article	Times cited	Publisher
International Journal Of Emerging Technologies In Learning	1,683	8,389	5.0	Augmented Reality and Virtual Reality in Education. Myth or reality?	214	International Association of Online Engineering
Frontiers In Education	2,789	7,992	2.9	A Critical Review of Research on Student Self-Assessment	237	Frontiers Media SA
International Journal Of Artificial Intelligence In Education	125	1,393	11.1	The Behavior of Tutoring Systems	605	Springer Nature

*TP=Top Publication, *TC=Top Citation

The journals that are most relevant to AI and its impact on higher education are shown in Table 3. The data indicates several significant articles. "Education Sciences," a scholarly journal published by the Multidisciplinary Digital Publishing Institute (MDPI), is renowned for its remarkable total of 3,334 articles, 15,882 citations, and a citation score of 4.8. With 312 citations, its most-cited piece examines e-learning success factors. Meanwhile, the "Journal of Applied Learning and Teaching," published by Kaplan Singapore, shows a great impact with a total of 232 articles, 2,081 citations, and a cite score of 9.0. The article that has the most citations, 1,235, refers to digital pedagogy in higher education. The journal "Sustainability Switzerland," which is likewise distributed by the Multidisciplinary Digital Publishing Institute (MDPI), is well-known for its 55,991 articles, 381,357 citations, and 6.8 cite score. With 1,053 citations, its renowned paper on the life of higher education students has attracted attention. "Education And Information Technologies" by Springer Nature has compiled 1,767 articles with a total of 17,613 citations, and a citation score of 10.0. Cited 732 times, the journal's most-cited piece explores the use of virtual reality head-mounted displays in education and training. Likewise, the "International Journal of Educational Technology in Higher Education", another publication by Springer Nature, has 238 articles and 4,597 citations, with a cite score of 19.3. Among these, a systematic review of artificial intelligence applications in higher education is particularly remarkable, having been cited 888 times.

With a cite score of 16.8, the "Computers And Education Artificial Intelligence" published by Elsevier, contributes 183 articles and 3,080 citations. Cited 337 times, its linchpin piece investigates the issues of Artificial Intelligence in Education. The Science and Information Organization's "Journal Of University Teaching And Learning Practice" by Open Access Publishing Association has a citation score of 3.6, published 314 articles and cited 1,133 times. With 145 citations, the most-cited paper concentrates on AI large language models.

Furthermore, the "International Journal Of Emerging Technologies In Learning" by the International Association of Online Engineering, has a citation score of 5.0, published 1,683 articles, and cited 8,389 times. Cited 214 times, a prominent paper from this journal shows augmented reality and virtual reality in education. "Frontiers In Education," a Frontiers Media SA publication, receives a cite score of 2.9, with 2,789 articles and 7,992 citations. Its most-cited paper, which has been cited 237 times, examines student self-assessment. Finally, "International Journal Of Artificial Intelligence In Education" by Springer Nature, has 125 publications, cited 1,393 times and has a citation score of 11.1 and a 605-times-cited important paper on the behavior of tutoring systems.

4.3. The Most Significant Countries

Regarding the third research inquiry, what are the most productive countries in AI and higher education? According to the data presented, we can observe the distribution of publications by nation as shown in Figure 3.

Figure 3. Distribution of publications by nation

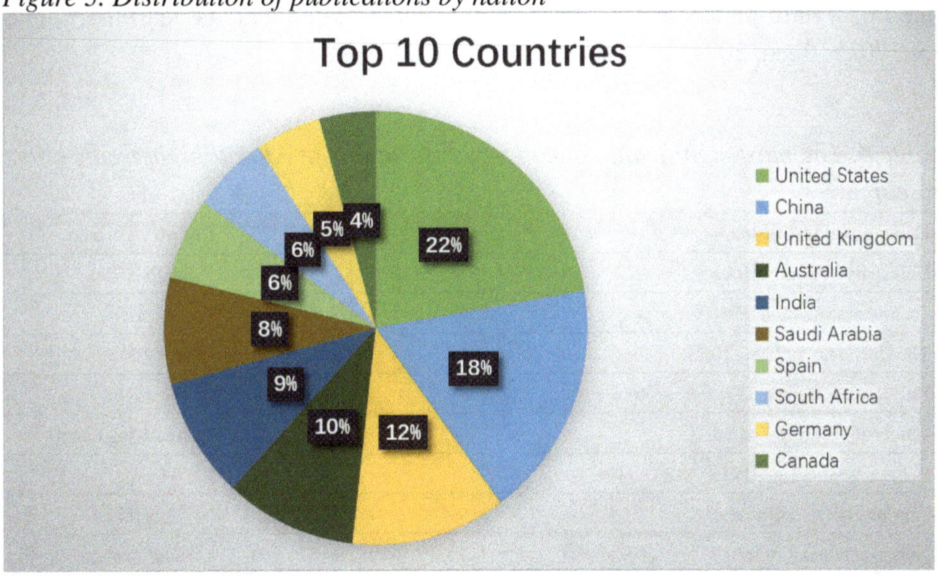

The United States, with 62 articles, emerges as the frontrunner in this field of study (figure 3), indicating significant attention and funding in AI and higher education. China is closely behind with 49 articles, which present its considerable dedication to the development of AI and its impact on higher education. The United Kingdom's extensive work in this field, including 33 publications, indicates the

UK's contribution to AI and higher education. A substantial interest in Australia is shown in 28 articles, which mostly concern the use of AI on teachers' behavior and pedagogy. India, with 24 publications, appears as a significant contributor, proving the use of AI in learners in higher education. Saudi Arabia's growing emphasis on various AI technologies in higher education is shown by its 22 articles, which is particularly significant in a nation with such diverse students. In 17 articles, Spain illustrates the importance and challenges of AI in higher education. South Africa focuses its research on ChatGPT in education via its 16 papers. The 14 papers published in Germany demonstrate that a rising regional interest in using AI to improve education is on the rise. Canada's devotion to the creation and investigation of the use of AI and its impacts on students is shown by its 12 publications.

Collectively, these countries shown in Figure 3 make up the majority of AI and higher education research. The distribution reflects the extensive and multifaceted nature of research interest in this field. For example, in the Unite States, universities are using Khan Academy, AI-driven adaptive learning to support SEM education(Tassell et al., 2024). In the meantime, Edmodo, as Technology-Based Formative Assessment, was widely used to enhance students' learning outcome and boost student engagement(Nuraini et al., 2025). In China, institutions have adopted intelligent tutoring systems (ITS) to support large-scale language learning(Lai & Lin, 2025; Shen, 2024).

Table 4. The most significant educational institutions in AI and higher education research

Educational institution	TP	Country/District
University of South Africa	7	South Africa
Tecnológico de Monterrey	7	Mexico
The University of Hong Kong	6	Hong Kong
University of Tasmania	6	Australia
University College London	6	United Kingdom
Beijing Normal University	6	China
CQUniversity Australia	6	Australia
King Abdulaziz University	5	Saudi Arabia
University Business Academy in Novi Sad	4	Serbia
The University of Sheffield	4	United Kingdom

TP= Total publication

The University of South Africa has produced the most total publications (TP) in South Africa, with a total of 7 (Table 4), underscoring its contribution to research on AI and higher education. Seven articles from the Tecnológico de Monterrey, located in Mexico, show the country's dedication to AI research. The University of Hong Kong has published six articles, which has had a significant influence on this area. This illustrates the institution's commitment to the research on AI and higher education. The University of Tasmania, situated in Australia, demonstrates the country's efforts on AI research. With a notable six publications, University College London in the United Kingdom distinguishes itself in Europe, demonstrating its dedication to the development of AI. The publications' distribution by countries are shown in Figure 4.

Figure 4. The geographical distribution of publications

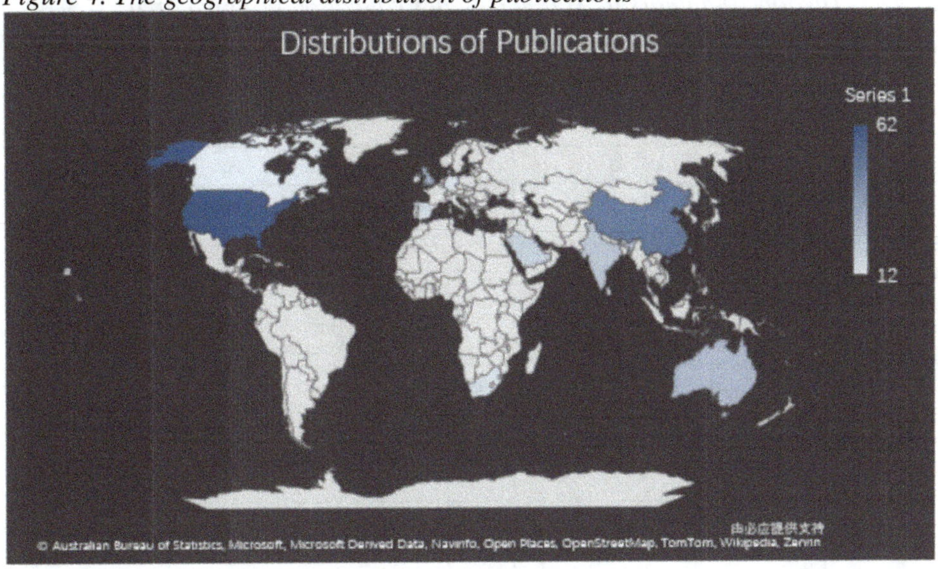

The Beijing Normal University in China has published six articles, which revealed its important position in this field. Six publications from CQ University Australia, which is situated in Australia, depict the dedication to AI research. Five articles from the King Abdulaziz University in Saudi Arabia signify a growing emphasis on research in AI and higher education. The four papers of the University Business Academy in Novi Sad, located in Serbia, show the nation's dedication to AI research. The University of Sheffield, which is located in the United Kingdom, produced four papers, increasing Europe's contribution to this field.

Overall, these academic institutions emphasize the worldwide scope of AI research in higher education in different nations or districts. The variety of views not only improves the development of this field but also provides significant support for the improvement of education systems in various countries.

4.5. The most Prolific Authors

In response to the fifth research question, " Which authors have produced the most substantial contributions to the field of AI in higher education?" An analysis of the data presented reveals the authors in AI in the higher education research area, as shown in Table 5.

Table 5. The top 10 authors in AI in the higher education research area

Author	Year of first publication	*TP	h-index	*TC	Current affiliation	Country/District
Chan, C.K.Y.	2005	83	19	1,232	The University of Hong Kong	Hong Kong
Cowling, M.	2003	45	11	721	CQ University Australia	Australia
Crawford, J.	2017	50	16	2,221	Tasmanian School of Business and Economics	Australia
Rudolph, J.	2019	41	10	1,993	Kaplan Higher Education Singapore	Singapore
Tan, S.	2020	25	10	701	Kaplan Higher Education Singapore	Singapore
Bozkurt, A.	2015	77	24	2,026	Anadolu Üniversitesi	Turkey
Chiu, T.K.F.	2014	72	26	2,226	Chinese University of Hong Kong	Hong Kong
Cukurova, M.	2015	100	20	1,400	University College London	United Kingdom
Ilić, M.P.	2015	21	9	295	University Business Academy in Novi Sad	Serbia
Kuleto, V.	2012	15	7	266	Information Technology School	Serbia

*TP= Total publications, *TC= Total citations

Table 5 shows the most prolific authors. For instance, Chan published her first paper in 2005, with a total of 83 papers and an h-index of 19, with a total of 1,232 citations. Chan is affiliated with the University of Hong Kong and has become an authority in the field through her extensive research. Since Cowling started his academic career in 2003, he has accumulated 45 publications till now, with 721 citations and an h-index of 11. His partnership with CQ University in Australia indicates that his reputation in the field is increasing. Since Crawford started his academic research in 2017, he has published 50 papers to date, with 2,221 citations, and h-index of 16. His collaboration with Tasmanian School of Business and

Economics in Australia signifies his influential reputation in the area. Rudolph has accumulated 41 papers, with 1,993 citations, and an h-index of 10 since his starting in 2019. His affiliation with Kaplan Higher Education Singapore demonstrates the significant developments that the country has achieved in this field. Twenty-five articles of Tan Shannon were cited 701 times with h-index of 10. Her association with Kaplan Higher Education Singapore indicates the growing academic focus on AI and its impact on higher education.

Since Bozkurt started his studies in 2015, he has published 77 publications, with 701 citations and an h-index of 24. His cooperation with Anadolu University in Turkey demonstrates his rising progress in the area. Chiu T.K.F., who started his academic career in 2014, published 72 papers, with 2,026 citations, and an h-index of 26. He contributes to enhance China's position in the field of AI research through partnership with the Chinese University of Hong Kong. Cukurova started his scholarly pursuits in 2015, publishing a total of 100 publications. These works have been cited 1400 times, with an h-index of 20. He has made an important contribution to the area through University College London in the United Kingdom. Twenty-one papers authored by Ilić have been cited 295 times, with an h-index of 9 since 2015. This underscores Ilić's devotion to the area via his association with the University Business Academy in Serbia. Since his first publication in 2012, Kuleto has added up to 266 citations and fifteen publications, which is reflected in his h-index of seven. The Information Technology School in Serbia is with is his affiliated school.

These research and publications reflect the internationalization trend in the area of the use of AI in higher education. Particularly, the growth of emerging scholars will bring more developments and advancements to this area.

4.6. The Primary Research Keywords and Trends

Regarding the sixth question, " What are the primary research keywords for the last decade of AI and higher education?" The data indicates the primary research terms and their frequency of appearance, as shown in Figure 5.

Figure 5. The primary research keywords and their occurrences (Visualized using VOSviewer)

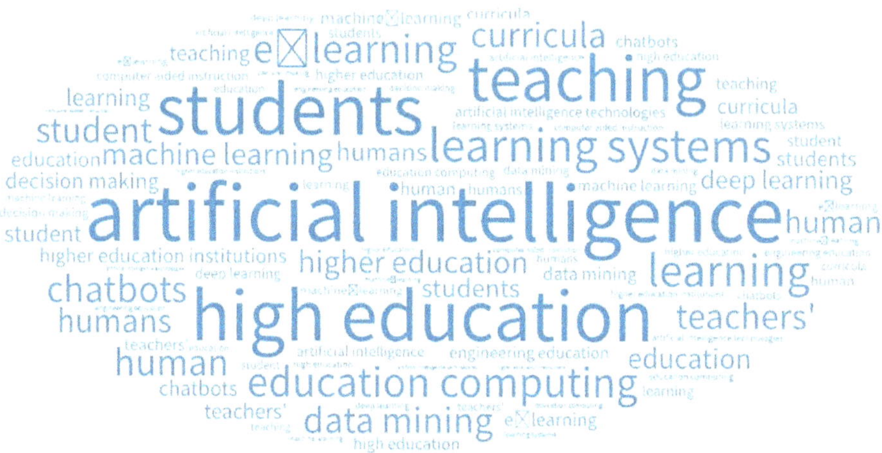

Visualized by the relationship between keywords and the size of the frequency of occurrence, figure 5 shows the critical research terms in the field of the impact on higher education. For instance, the term "artificial intelligence" became the most frequently used keyword, appearing 174 times, proving its importance in the field of education. The term "higher education" was also frequently used, reaching 135 times, which highlights the main focus of the research domain. The terms "ChatGPT", "chatbots", and "AI", which represent artificial intelligence, appeared 56, 54 and 52 times respectively, showing a growing research focus on generative AI and conversational agents in educational contexts. These terms reflect an increasing interest in dialog-based AI tools that support student learning and facilitate teacher-AI collaboration. The terms such as "learning system" and "decision making" appeared frequently, suggesting the hot spots in the development of intelligent tutoring systems (ITS) that can dynamically respond to learners' needs. These terms have assumed a strategic position in recent research exploring human-AI synergy models in higher education. The prominence of hot words such as "machine learning", "deep learning", and "e-learning" in the list, all appearing 23 times, indicates the close integration of technology and education and the trend of innovative research. Overall, the distribution of research keywords and their occurrences shows the interdisciplinary nature. Generative AI, chatbots, and intelligent tutoring systems are becoming key tools in changing classroom instruction and educational experiences.

4.7. The Most Important Subject Area

Regarding the seventh inquiry, which topic area is the most critical in terms of AI in higher education? According to the data presented, Social Sciences emerge as a significant area of study, with a considerable collection of 287 publications. The importance of this demonstrates that social science has a substantial interest in sociological, behavioral, and pedagogy, and artificial intelligence is crucial to the development of the sociology of education, education policy, and the application of learning theories.

Figure 6. The most important subject area

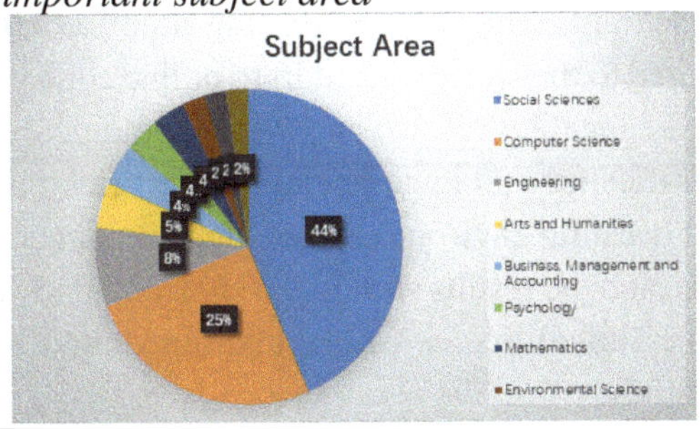

The most important subject area is shown in Figure 6. Computer Science published 166 articles, which indicates that artificial intelligence technology and information systems are very important for the development and advancements of this field. Engineering is another interesting and important area with 53 publications, since it involves the development of algorithms, and application systems for the application of AI in higher education. The Arts and Humanities and Business, Management, and Accounting, which published 31 and 28 articles respectively, provide significant devotion to the research of the use of artificial intelligence in higher education. Psychology's 24 articles indicate an interest in the cognitive and motivational aspects of artificial intelligence in higher education. Advanced comprehension of the application of artificial intelligence may be received from the areas of Mathematics and Environmental Science, which published 23 and 16 publications respectively.

5. DISCUSSION

The bibliometric study provided a comprehensive view of the dynamic field of AI and its impact on higher education. The findings indicate how the field has grown and developed, with contributions from many countries and institutions, as well as a growing focus among academics.

5.1. Trends in Publication and Geographic Distribution

The scholarly publications on the use of artificial intelligence in higher education began to increase significantly in 2020 and reached a new peak in 2023. This indicates that academic fields are paying increasing attention to this area. The above change may be attributed to the worldwide shift to online education, which has been necessitated by global education reform and AI technological developments. This surge reflects the significance and huge potential of artificial intelligence in transforming teaching and learning environments of higher education. These papers are distributed worldwide, and the results shows that substantial investment in countries or districts such as the United States, China, and the United Kingdom proves the global nature of this study.

However, the impact of different educational and cultural environments of artificial intelligence on the advancement of higher education is an interesting phenomenon, which shows the advantages and challenges of different countries in this field and provides rich views and insights. In the United States, recent studies contribute to artificial intelligence (AI) student assistants in the classroom, and the application of AI (such as ChatGpt) in education. These efforts aim to enhance classroom personalization and develop human-AI interaction models in teaching and learning. In China, recent research focuses on the implementation of intelligent tutoring systems (ITS) and generative AI technologies, particularly in online and language education. This reflects the country's emphasis on the application of digital transformation in education. The United Kingdom contributes to discussions on AI ethics and human-AI collaborative instructional design.

These trends indicate that different countries have implemented different policies to form different human-computer collaboration models, from ITS-based automation to generative AI and chatbot-assisted teaching. These changes have also triggered thinking about education reform and provided valuable educational experience for teaching innovation.

5.2. Influential Journals and Educational Institutions

This study identifies renowned academic publications and institutions that are conducting cutting-edge research on artificial intelligence in higher education. These information facilitate scholars who wish to participate in frontier research in this specific field. For instance, Education Sciences, Journal of Applied Learning and Teaching, and Sustainability Switzerland have published many studies on intelligent tutoring systems (ITS), agent-based learning, and the behavioral dynamics of AI-supported instruction. These journals contribute to ITS technologies and human-AI synergy. Education and Information Technologies, and the International Journal of Educational Technology in Higher Education, have published highly cited studies on generative AI applications, and chatbot teaching practices. These efforts reflect a growing interest in AI-driven personalized learning and real-time classroom support.

In addition, journals like Computers and Education Artificial Intelligence and Journal of University Teaching and Learning Practice, contribute to AI ethic, challenges and roles of artificial intelligence (AI). These studies enriched the educational experiences and helped shape the emerging framework of human-machine collaborative teaching models. These journals' citation influence and thematic alignment reflect their importance in prompting educational innovation at the intersection of pedagogy and AI technologies.

Additionally, the significance of several educational institutions demonstrates not only distinct priorities in applying specific AI technologies to classroom practice and human-AI collaborative innovation, but also an important force in shaping forthcoming policies and methodologies. Scholars, with cooperation and exchanges with these institutions, can improve the further development of the use of artificial intelligence in higher education. For instance, the University of South Africa focuses on intelligent tutoring systems to enhance distance learning through real-time feedback. At Tecnológico de Monterrey, the researchers highlight the integration of generative AI tools into collaborative learning, supporting students' success through AI-assisted teaching tasks. University of Hong Kong explores how AI tools (ChatGPT) can be applied to writing for language instruction, aiming to align machine and human feedback. The University of Tasmania investigates AI-supported reflection mechanisms, promoting student-AI-teacher feedback loops. At University of Tasmania, the researchers focus on the design of human-AI synergy models, especially in the areas of ethics and teacher roles. From these findings, these institutions contribute to the area of AI-driven model in higher education and human-AI synergy in educational practice.

5.3. Prolific Authors and Research Keywords

The ongoing research and publications of prolific scholars in the field of integrating artificial intelligence with higher education indicate that they make significant contributions to the field. Particularly, there are some progresses on generative AI, chatbots, and intelligent tutoring systems (ITS). The research of these scholars is not only the basis for understanding this area, but also the important force for future advancement. For instance, Chan,C.K.Y, and CowlingM. who is from the University of HongKong and CO University Australia respectively, contribute to generative AI, and AI assistance. Crawford.J, who is from Tasmanian School of Business and Economics, explores the AI ethics (ethical ChatGpt). Their publications of these prolific authors provides foundational insights and practical models for AI-supported instruction.

Furthermore, the keywords obtained from primary sources can help identify the main research topic and development trends in this field. For example, "artificial intelligence (AI)", "students learning", and "higher education", indicate the focus of classroom-level applications. When juxtaposed with terms like "ChatGPT", "Generative AI", and "deep learning" representing artificial intelligence and the educational dimension of "teaching" and "education", the prominence of buzzwords such as "machine learning", "deep learning", and "e-learning" indicates the close integration of technology and education and innovative research trends. These research keywords reflect a shift from exploring AI as an independent tool to exploring how it can be used with educators to enhance learning personalization, achieve human-AI collaboration, and co-design instructional strategies. Overall, the outputs of key researchers and keyword trends indicate that the co-worker between human-AI synergy and education, is developing rapidly and the results are becoming more mature.

Some empirical studies have also proved this trend mentioned previously. A study of AMINA (2024)demonstrated that Grammarly assists students with academic writing by offering real-time AI-generated feedback to promote students' autonomy. Another research conducted by Saqr et al. (2024) stated that AI tools, such as Blackboard, Moodle, and Edmodo, help teachers manage classroom communication and recommend personalized content, and boost student engagement. Moreover, Khan Academy adjusted the level of problem difficulty based on learner performance through AI algorithms, realizing students' self-paced learning(Soojin, 2024). These examples show that AI is becoming a real partner in classroom-based instruction by offering students personalized support, timely feedback, and adaptive learning content.

Moreover, as human-AI teaching models continue to develop, the ethical issues, like data security, AI bias, and teachers' role, should be considered(Airaj, 2024). Therefore, institutions should establish clear and detailed ethical rules to highlight the flowchart of data collection and protect staff and student information. While AI was widely implemented in many learning activities, teachers remain irreplaceable in the learning process. Therefore, the targeted teaching training programs are necessary to reduce instructors' resistance and support effective AI integration into educational practice.

5.4. Subject Areas and Their Implications

This study covers a wide array of topics, showing the multidisciplinary nature of the integration of AI and higher education. Social sciences and computer science, which account for 44% and 25% of the total respectively, indicate that technological progress and the integration between educational theory and practice. Furthermore, the articles published in this field by disciplines such as engineering, arts and humanities, business, management and accounting, and psychology, demonstrate that interdisciplinary approaches are significant for developing appropriate and effective AI learning environments for higher education.

In conclusion, this bibliometric study results not only provide scholars with a comprehensive status analysis and knowledge resources, but also guide practice for education policymakers, politicians, and technicians. To ensure that the digital learning environment is productive and conducive to the advancement of higher education, it is necessary to keep pace with the continuous progress of artificial intelligence and its applications.

5.5. Summary of the Results of This Review

Table 5 presents a comprehensive summary extracted from this research article, providing a detailed analysis of the development, consequences, and potential future directions of the impact of AI on higher education. To fully understand the scholarly attention, geographical distribution, main authors, and specific topic focus in this area, the data is divided into several important parts, including findings, implications, trends, and plans. The findings reflect an increased interest in emerging technologies and their integration into classroom practice, particularly the development of technologies such as ChatGPT, chatbots, and intelligent tutoring systems. Artificial intelligence technologies are reshaping classroom structures, teaching content, learning assessments, and how teachers and students interact. Research hotspots identified in the bibliometric results, such as personalized learning and adaptive learning, indicate that AI tools integrate into instruction design. The study aims to depict the present state of research and predict the future development path of this field, as shown in Table 6.

Table 6. A thorough examination of the use of AI on higher education: Principal discoveries and prospects for the future

Aspect	Findings	Implications	Trends	Future Agenda
Publications	An enormous surge of publications after 2020, and reached a new peak in 2023. In 2023, the number of publications reached 218.	An increasing concern in academic circles about the use of AI in higher education is evident.	Consistent yearly expansion of publications, especially with a research boom surging after 2020	Ongoing investigation to understand and improve the impact of the impact of AI on higher education, such as teaching and learning in higher education.
Journals	"Education Sciences," "Journal Of Applied Learning And Teaching," and "Sustainability Switzerland " are all significant journals.	Academics in pursuit of the most recent developments in the use of AI in higher education must check out these journals.	Extensive contributions from various journals, with a focus on the use of AI in education.	Further research into development and the use of AI to improve teaching and learning in the classroom.
Countries/ districts	The country with the most contributions is the United States, China, and the United Kingdom.	Indicating the impact of AI from different educational fields and cultural backgrounds on higher education.	Increasing contributions from several countries or districts on a global scale.	More collaborative research to improve AI techniques for use in higher education worldwide.
Educational Institutions	University of South Africa and Tecnológico de Monterrey are important funders of this cause.	The importance of educational institutions in the development of research and the use of AI in higher education is emphasized.	Some countries have conducted extensive research on the use of AI in higher education, such as South Africa and Mexico.	It is important to encourage more educational institutions all around the world to participate in research through international cooperation.

continued on following page

Table 6. Continued

Aspect	Findings	Implications	Trends	Future Agenda
Authors	This subject has both recognized and new scholars, such as Chan, Cecilia Ka Yuk, and Cowling, Michael.	In the field of the use of AI in higher education, this study attaches importance to the contribution and accomplishments made by individual scholars.	Both experienced researchers and newcomers contributed to the area.	It is important to support and recognize researchers to encourage further advancements in the use of AI in higher education.
Keywords	The most frequently appearing keywords include "artificial intelligence," "higher education," "chatbots," "ChatGPT," "education," and "machine teaching," "deep teaching,"	It reflects the use of AI in higher education, especially the impact of ChatGPT on education. And the emphasis on student-centered teaching approaches.	This reflects the importance of higher education on AI technology, pedagogy, and student-centered perspectives.	Further research frontier tools and analytical methods in the field of AI in higher education.

As shown in Table 6, this study mainly demonstrates the relevance of AI and higher education. The study highlights the dynamic and evolving nature of AI's impact on higher education. The considerable increase in publications and international devotion since 2020 indicates the rising significance and dynamic nature of AI for higher education development, especially in the wake of the COVID-19 pandemic. The involvement of multiple countries or districts, educational institutions, and researchers emphasizes the broad and multidisciplinary nature of the field. Learning in AI environments, which blends pedagogical principles, technological advances, and student-centered approaches, is an important area of research and implementation. The work from leading educational institutions and prominent authors reinforces the trend of human-AI collaboration in teaching environments. These results suggest that the development of artificial intelligence technology will be closely related to educational applications, namely, educational innovation will also rely on the development and updating of artificial intelligence technology. In the future, it is expected that more focus will be placed on applying emerging technologies, developing global partnerships, and conducting multidisciplinary research to improve the positive impact of AI on higher education. This phenomenon establishes a good foundation for future research and advancement in the field of digital education.

6. CONCLUSIONS

6.1 Conclusion of the findings

The bibliometric analysis adopted in this research provides a thorough and inclusive examination of the dynamic correlation between artificial intelligence and higher education. It indicates a considerable increase in academic research in this area, which shows the expanding significance of the use of artificial intelligence in higher education. Certain topic areas and keywords indicate the interdisciplinary nature of the research, which reveals how AI intersects with pedagogy, and technological innovation. The funding for research in this field comes from many funding countries and different educational institutions around the world, showing the global nature of this field. The international collaboration among scholars, technicians, and researchers establishes the foundation for further research in this field. In an era of rapid development of digital platforms, ongoing research is crucial for innovating educational methods and improving student learning experiences.

These findings suggest that generative AI, chatbots, and intelligent tutoring systems are emerging themes in this field. These themes reflect the technological innovation, and demonstrate the transformation of teaching tools in teaching. With the development of the digital era and the reform in higher education, future research will go beyond technical performance and focus more on exploring human-computer collaborative models. Specifically, future research will focus on the application of AI tools in teaching design, such as teacher collaboration, content co-creation, teaching feedback, and adaptive learning. Exploring how such models can improve learning outcomes, teacher autonomy, and student engagement across disciplines and cultures is crucial for the next stage of human-AI collaborative teaching frameworks. In this context, this study provides a foundational basis for supporting the innovation and application of AI in future higher education.

6.2 Recommendations for Educators: Human-AI Synergy in Practice

Based on the findings of this bibliometric analysis, the following recommendations are proposed to guide educators in the responsible and effective integration of AI technologies. Instructors should start with a simple application with AI, such as automated feedback or generating teaching content, which allows instructors to integrate AI tools into the classroom without high risk. Second, AI should be embedded into existing learning activities, like using Grammarly to revise students' writing tasks. Third, educators should guide students' critical thinking when interpreting

AI-generated results. Finally, targeted teacher training programs are also crucial to enhance the meaningful application of AI in education.

REFERENCES

Abuhassna, H. (2024). *From Theory to Practice: The Impact of E-Learning on Student Performance, Trends, and Educational Horizons*. Qeios.

Abuhassna, H., Adnan, M. A. B. M., & Awae, F. (2024). Exploring the synergy between instructional design models and learning theories: A systematic literature review. *Contemporary Educational Technology*, *16*(2), ep499. DOI: 10.30935/cedtech/14289

Abuhassna, H., Yahaya, N., Zakaria, M., Zaid, N. M., Samah, N. A., Awae, F., Nee, C. K., & Alsharif, A. H. (2023). Trends on using the technology acceptance model (TAM) for online learning: A bibliometric and content analysis. *International Journal of Information and Education Technology (IJIET)*, *13*(1), 131–142. DOI: 10.18178/ijiet.2023.13.1.1788

Airaj, M. (2024). Ethical artificial intelligence for teaching-learning in higher education. *Education and Information Technologies*, *29*(13), 17145–17167. DOI: 10.1007/s10639-024-12545-x

Akgun, S., & Greenhow, C. (2022). Artificial intelligence in education: Addressing ethical challenges in K-12 settings. *AI and Ethics*, *2*(3), 431–440. DOI: 10.1007/s43681-021-00096-7 PMID: 34790956

Allen, B., McGough, A. S., & Devlin, M. (2021). Toward a framework for teaching artificial intelligence to a higher education audience. [TOCE]. *ACM Transactions on Computing Education*, *22*(2), 1–29. DOI: 10.1145/3485062

Amina, F. (2024). Exploring EFL Students 'Perceptions on the use of Grammarly as an AI Writing Tool to Enhance Academic Writing Proficiency The Case Study of Master Two English Students at Mohammed Kheider University.

Baek, C., & Doleck, T. (2020). A bibliometric analysis of the papers published in the journal of artificial intelligence in education from 2015-2019.

Bahroun, Z., Anane, C., Ahmed, V., & Zacca, A. (2023). Transforming education: A comprehensive review of generative artificial intelligence in educational settings through bibliometric and content analysis. *Sustainability (Basel)*, *15*(17), 12983. DOI: 10.3390/su151712983

Bozkurt, A., & Sharma, R. C. (2023). Challenging the status quo and exploring the new boundaries in the age of algorithms: Reimagining the role of generative AI in distance education and online learning. *Asian Journal of Distance Education*, *18*(1).

Cai, W., Grossman, J., Lin, Z. J., Sheng, H., Wei, J. T.-Z., Williams, J. J., & Goel, S. (2021). Bandit algorithms to personalize educational chatbots. *Machine Learning*, *110*(9), 2389–2418. DOI: 10.1007/s10994-021-05983-y

Castro, R. (2019). Blended learning in higher education: Trends and capabilities. *Education and Information Technologies*, *24*(4), 2523–2546. DOI: 10.1007/s10639-019-09886-3

Chankoson, T., Chen, F., Wang, Z., Wang, M., & Sukpasjaroen, K. (2022). Knowledge mapping for the study of Artificial Intelligence in Education Research: Literature reviews. *Journal of Intelligence Studies in Business*, *12*(3), 27–37. DOI: 10.37380/jisib.v12i3.896

Chatterjee, S., & Bhattacharjee, K. K. (2020). Adoption of artificial intelligence in higher education: A quantitative analysis using structural equation modelling. *Education and Information Technologies*, *25*(5), 3443–3463. DOI: 10.1007/s10639-020-10159-7

Chen, L., Chen, P., & Lin, Z. (2020). Artificial intelligence in education: A review. *IEEE Access : Practical Innovations, Open Solutions*, *8*, 75264–75278. DOI: 10.1109/ACCESS.2020.2988510

Crompton, H., & Burke, D. (2023). Artificial intelligence in higher education: The state of the field. *International Journal of Educational Technology in Higher Education*, *20*(1), 22. DOI: 10.1186/s41239-023-00392-8

Fitriani, A., Rosidah, R., & Zafrullah, Z. (2023). Biblioshiny: Implementation of artificial intelligence in education (1976-2023). *Journal of Technology Global*, *1*(01), 11–25.

Haddaway, N. R., Page, M. J., Pritchard, C. C., & McGuinness, L. A. (2022). PRISMA2020: An R package and Shiny app for producing PRISMA 2020-compliant flow diagrams, with interactivity for optimised digital transparency and Open Synthesis. *Campbell Systematic Reviews*, *18*(2), e1230. DOI: 10.1002/cl2.1230 PMID: 36911350

Harto, B., LN, S. Y., Rukmana, A. Y., Komalasari, R., & Dwijayanti, A. (2022). Bibliometric analysis of transforming leadership education with artificial intelligence. In 1st Virtual Workshop on Writing Scientific Article for International Publication Indexed SCOPUS (pp. 385-390).

Hashmi, N., & Bal, A. S. (2024). Generative AI in higher education and beyond. *Business Horizons*, *67*(5), 607–614.

Ilham, R., Muhammad, I., Aji, L. J., Rizal, S. U., & Özbilen, F. M. (2023). Artificial intelligence research in education: A bibliometric analysis. *Journal of Education Global*, *1*(1), 45–55.

Ilieva, G., Yankova, T., Klisarova-Belcheva, S., Dimitrov, A., Bratkov, M., & Angelov, D. (2023). Effects of generative chatbots in higher education. *Information (Basel)*, *14*(9), 492. DOI: 10.3390/info14090492

Jaleniauskienė, E., Lisaitė, D., & Daniusevičiūtė-Brazaitė, L. (2023). Artificial intelligence in language education: A bibliometric analysis. *Sustainable Multilingualism*, *23*(1), 159–194. DOI: 10.2478/sm-2023-0017

Kumar, J. A. (2021). Educational chatbots for project-based learning: Investigating learning outcomes for a team-based design course. *International Journal of Educational Technology in Higher Education*, *18*(1), 65. DOI: 10.1186/s41239-021-00302-w PMID: 34926790

Lai, C.-H., & Lin, C.-Y. (2025). Analysis of Learning Behaviors and Outcomes for Students with Different Knowledge Levels: A Case Study of Intelligent Tutoring System for Coding and Learning (ITS-CAL). *Applied Sciences (2076-3417)*, *15*(4).

Moreno-Guerrero, A.-J., López-Belmonte, J., Marín-Marín, J.-A., & Soler-Costa, R. (2020). Scientific development of educational artificial intelligence in Web of Science. *Future Internet*, *12*(8), 124. DOI: 10.3390/fi12080124

Nuraini, F. I., Sodiq, J., & Prastikawati, E. F. (2025). Edmodo as Technology-Based Formative Assessment: How It Enhances Reading Comprehension. *International Journal of Research in Education*, *5*(1), 81–92. DOI: 10.26877/ijre.v5i1.1368

Page, M. J., McKenzie, J. E., Bossuyt, P. M., Boutron, I., Hoffmann, T. C., Mulrow, C. D., Shamseer, L., Tetzlaff, J. M., Akl, E. A., & Brennan, S. E. (2021). The PRISMA 2020 statement: an updated guideline for reporting systematic reviews. *bmj, 372*.

Pedro, F., Subosa, M., Rivas, A., & Valverde, P. (2019). Artificial intelligence in education: Challenges and opportunities for sustainable development.

Popenici, S. A., & Kerr, S. (2017). Exploring the impact of artificial intelligence on teaching and learning in higher education. *Research and Practice in Technology Enhanced Learning*, *12*(1), 22. DOI: 10.1186/s41039-017-0062-8 PMID: 30595727

Pradana, M., Elisa, H. P., & Syarifuddin, S. (2023). Discussing ChatGPT in education: A literature review and bibliometric analysis. *Cogent Education*, *10*(2), 2243134. DOI: 10.1080/2331186X.2023.2243134

Prahani, B., Rizki, I., Jatmiko, B., Suprapto, N., & Tan, A. (2022). Artificial intelligence in education research during the last ten years: A review and bibliometric study. [iJET]. *International Journal of Emerging Technologies in Learning, 17*(8), 169–188. DOI: 10.3991/ijet.v17i08.29833

Ruan, S., Jiang, L., Xu, Q., Liu, Z., Davis, G. M., Brunskill, E., & Landay, J. A. (2021). Englishbot: An ai-powered conversational system for second language learning. *Proceedings of the 26th International Conference on Intelligent User Interfaces*

Saqr, R. R., Al-Somali, S. A., & Sarhan, M. Y. (2024). Exploring the acceptance and user satisfaction of AI-driven e-learning platforms (Blackboard, Moodle, Edmodo, Coursera and edX): An integrated technology model. *Sustainability, 16*(1), 204.

Seldon, A., & Abidoye, O. (2018). *The fourth education revolution*. Legend Press Ltd.

Shen, S. (2024). Application of large language models in the field of education. *Theoretical and Natural Science, 34*(1), 147–154. DOI: 10.54254/2753-8818/34/20241163

Smutny, P., & Schreiberova, P. (2020). Chatbots for learning: A review of educational chatbots for the Facebook Messenger. *Computers & Education, 151*, 103862. DOI: 10.1016/j.compedu.2020.103862

Soegoto, H., Soeryanto Soegoto, E., Luckyardi, S., & Abhi Rafdhi, A. (2022). A bibliometric analysis of management bioenergy research using vosviewer application. *Indonesian Journal of Science and Technology, 7*(1), 89–104. DOI: 10.17509/ijost.v7i1.43328

Song, P., & Wang, X. (2020). A bibliometric analysis of worldwide educational artificial intelligence research development in recent twenty years. *Asia Pacific Education Review, 21*(3), 473–486. DOI: 10.1007/s12564-020-09640-2

Soojin, K. (2024). The Meaning of Personalized Learning Structures in AI-based Educational Platforms: From the Perspective of Learned Curriculum. *Educational Technology International, 25*(2), 297–329.

Tapalova, O., & Zhiyenbayeva, N. (2022). Artificial intelligence in education: AIEd for personalised learning pathways. *Electronic Journal of e-Learning, 20*(5), 639–653. DOI: 10.34190/ejel.20.5.2597

Tassell, J., Novak, E., Gordon, A., Vondrova, N. a., & Denning, S. (2024). Studying the Impact of Khan Academy as a Personalized Learning Platform with Pre-Service Elementary Teachers of Mathematics in the Czech Republic. EdMedia+ Innovate Learning

Tozzi, A. E., Gesualdo, F., Pandolfi, E., Ferro, D., Cinelli, G., Bozzola, E., Aversa, T., Di Mauro, A., Mameli, C., & Croci, I. (2023). Prioritizing educational initiatives on emerging technologies for Italian pediatricians: Bibliometric review and a survey. [PubMed]. *Italian Journal of Pediatrics, 49*(1), 112.

Wang, D., Tao, Y., & Chen, G. (2024). Artificial intelligence in classroom discourse: A systematic review of the past decade. *International Journal of Educational Research, 123*, 102275. DOI: 10.1016/j.ijer.2023.102275

Yu, L., & Yu, Z. (2023). Qualitative and quantitative analyses of artificial intelligence ethics in education using VOSviewer and CitNetExplorer. *Frontiers in Psychology, 14*, 1061778. DOI: 10.3389/fpsyg.2023.1061778 PMID: 36968737

Zawacki-Richter, O., Marín, V. I., Bond, M., & Gouverneur, F. (2019). Systematic review of research on artificial intelligence applications in higher education–where are the educators? *International Journal of Educational Technology in Higher Education, 16*(1), 1–27. DOI: 10.1186/s41239-019-0171-0

Zhai, X., Chu, X., Chai, C. S., Jong, M. S. Y., Istenic, A., Spector, M., Liu, J.-B., Yuan, J., & Li, Y. (2021). A Review of Artificial Intelligence (AI) in Education from 2010 to 2020. *Complexity, 2021*(1), 8812542. DOI: 10.1155/2021/8812542

Zhang, R., Zou, D., & Cheng, G. (2024). Self-regulated digital game-based vocabulary learning: Motivation, application of self-regulated learning strategies, EFL vocabulary knowledge development, and their interplay. *Computer Assisted Language Learning*, •••, 1–43. DOI: 10.1080/09588221.2024.2344555

Chapter 2
Impact of Artificial Intelligence on Teaching Learning Among Lecturers in Special Education

Oyeyemi Omolayo Oladimeji
https://orcid.org/0000-0002-9753-7175
Federal College of Education Special, Oyo, Nigeria

Oluwatoyin Racheal Ogunwale
Federal College of Education Special, Oyo, Nigeria

ABSTRACT

This study investigated the impact of Artificial Intelligence on teaching learning activities among lecturers in special education. Three research questions guided the study. A quantitative research design was adopted. The population comprised 20 academic staff in the field of special education. A self designed questionnaire tagged Impact of Artificial Intelligence (IAI) were used to collect data from the respondents. The reliability and validity of the instrument were established (0.75-0.89). The descriptive statistics of frequencies, percentages, means, and standard deviations were used to analyze the data collected. The findings revealed that the current level of impact of AI on teaching/learning among lecturers in special education, and usage was not encouraging enough. It is therefore recommended that training and retraining of lecturers on the use of AI and technological devices should be organized periodically through conferences, workshops and seminars in order to enhance the impact and usage of AI generally among lecturers and those in the field of special education.

DOI: 10.4018/979-8-3373-5550-4.ch002

INTRODUCTION

Artificial Intelligence Software is becoming pronounced and worldwide appreciated, especially in the field of special education. It is an embodiment of instructional and communication Technological devices and gadget that improves the effectiveness and work in such a way that add value to life. AI are seen as disruptive technological devices that can significantly improve special education practices. They serve as interface between teachers and learning and creates an opportunity for improvement in individualized learning. This emphasizes its usefulness and relevance in the field of special education. Whether we believe it or not, we are all making use of AI in one way or the other. This shows that there is a need for constant usage and development in line of its appropriate usage in any field we find ourselves, especially among students with special education needs and disability. Lametti (2022) opined that several people across the world are making use of Artificial Intelligence. Every individual utilizes AI daily either by surfing the net, shopping or travelling Mathew et al (2023). Artificial Intelligence can be defined as systems of machines and computers that collaboratively work together in order to logically follow the pattern of human cognition (Tai 2020). Artificial Intelligence is defined as computers that are utilized and subjected to performance of mental activities and assignment that are often performed by human beings in education (Baker and Smith 2022).

The impact of Artificial Intelligence (AI) on teaching/learning among special education teachers vary widely based on several factors, including access to technology, training opportunities, and the specific educational environment. Artificial Intelligence (AI) is one of the fast-growing technologies that brings about improvement in lectures and teachers' performance in teaching learning activities (Cleopas 2023). Research indicates that while many teachers acknowledge the potential of AI, their level of proficiency and comfort with these tools often depends on prior training, institutional support, and the availability of resources (Al-Azawei, Serenelli, and Lundqvist 2017). Artificial Intelligence (AI) has emerged as a transformative force across various sectors, including education, with notable potential in Nigeria (Eze, -Nwankwo, Akintoye, and Ogbu 2021). Its capacity to personalize learning, automate administrative tasks, and support diverse learning needs offers significant opportunities to enhance educational practices in the country (Adebayo, 2022). In special education, (AI) could play a pivotal role in providing customized educational resources, improving communication, and promoting an inclusive learning environment (Ogunyemi, Adeyemi, Bello, & Yusuf 2023).

However, the successful integration of AI in Nigerian educational settings largely hinges on educators' knowledge and their ability to effectively utilize these technologies (Ibrahim and Sulaimon 2023). Artificial Intelligence has the potential to enhance teaching learning, especially in the field of special education. It has the capability to provide personalized learning experiences, by focusing on learners' individual needs. It helps teachers to identify areas of weakness in each learner with the view of providing extra support where necessary. Barua et al (2022) posited that Artificial Intelligence is useful in providing support for students with disabilities in diverse ways.

Numerous AI-based tools have been developed to cater for the unique needs of teaching in the academic setting and in the field of special education. These tools harness advanced algorithms and data processing capabilities to streamline tasks, offer personalized learning experiences, and provide valuable insights for research endeavors. Some of these AI-based tools include Intelligent Tutoring Systems (ITS): Intelligent Tutoring Systems utilize (AI) algorithms to adapt to individual learning needs. These systems provide personalized feedback and guidance to students, aiding in their academic progress. For lecturers, ITS can be a valuable tool for tailoring teaching materials based on individual student requirements (VanLehn, - Zheng, Zheng, and Zhang 2021).

Plagiarism Detection Software is an AI-powered plagiarism detection tool crucial in maintaining academic integrity. These tools employ advanced algorithms to compare submitted work with vast databases, identifying instances of plagiarism and ensuring the authenticity of research outputs (Sallam and Hossain, 2018, Anih 2019). Automated Grading Systems: Automated grading systems, driven by AI, can efficiently assess assignments, exams, and coursework. These systems not only save time for lecturers but also provide consistent and unbiased evaluations, fostering fairness in the assessment process (Zafar, Rehman and Amin2018). Other AI-based tools still include predictive analytics tools; this tool utilizes AI algorithms to analyze historical data and predict student performance trends.

Lecturers can leverage these insights to identify at-risk students early, enabling targeted interventions to support their academic success (Romero and Ventura, 2010). Another AI tool or software is Research Topic Recommendation Systems. This AI-based recommendation system analyzes academic literature, citation patterns, and emerging trends to suggest relevant research topics. Lecturers can use these tools to stay abreast of current developments and discover novel avenues for their research endeavors (Ren, Shen and Zhang 2012). However, despite the promising potential of AI tools in academics, as listed above, the extent of utilization of these tools is still a subject under investigation.

In this context, the utilization of AI-based tools for teaching and research refers to the effective and efficient application of these technological solutions in educational and research settings. It involves leveraging AI tools to enhance teaching methodologies, streamline research processes, and ultimately improve the overall quality of education (Anderson and Dron 2011). The utilization of these AI-based tools is paramount, because it enhances Personalization, take for instance, AI-based tools, such as Intelligent Tutoring Systems (ITS), enable personalized learning experiences by adapting to individual student needs. This personalized approach enhances student engagement and comprehension. It also enables efficiency in Grading and Assessment, like, Automated grading systems, powered by AI streamline the assessment process for lecturers. This not only saves time but also ensures consistency and objectivity in evaluations. More also in research for instance, it provides Advanced Data Analytics, Predictive analytics tools utilize AI algorithms to analyze historical data, providing insights into student performance trends. Lecturers can proactively identify students at risk and tailor interventions accordingly. AI-based tools as well provide Innovative Research Insights; AI facilitates more efficient literature reviews and research topic selection.

Recommendation systems help researchers stay abreast of emerging trends, fostering innovative and impactful research (Siemens 2013). In no doubt, the utilization of AI-based tools in teaching and research holds immense importance for advancing education and knowledge creation. Not only that, in education, numerous global systems have embraced digital technology-based approaches such as e-learning, distance education, e-assessment, artificial intelligence, cloud computing, and gamification for instructional delivery and assessment (Ukeh and Nwankwo, 2023; Anih and Ukeh, 2023; Okechukwu and Ukeh 2022; Ukeh 2020). Nevertheless, despite all this above-mentioned importance associated with utilizing various type of AI-based tools, lecturers in Nigerian universities, seem not to have fully embraced these technologies.

However, be it as it may, one cannot out rightly say for sure that Lecturers in most tertiary institutions are not effectively utilizing AI-based tools in teaching learning processes and mostly in conducting consistent research without proper empirical and statistical evidence. On this note it is worthwhile to state that, the primary concern of these researchers is to indeed ascertain the extent to which the lecturers in tertiary institutions in Nigeria are consistent with the use of AI-based tools in teaching. The study therefore investigated the current situation as touching the impact of AI on teaching learning among the lecturers in special education, explore available tools for teaching and research, and address the significant barrier hindering their widespread utilization.

The integration of Artificial Intelligence (AI) in education is a rapidly evolving trend that holds the promise of transforming traditional teaching and learning paradigms in Nigeria (Eze Nwankwo, Akintoye, and Ogbu 2022). AI encompasses a variety of technologies, including machine learning, natural language processing, and intelligent tutoring systems, which can adapt to individual learning needs, automate administrative tasks, and offer innovative forms of educational support (Adebayo, 2024). This technological shift is poised to impact Nigerian educational practices significantly, providing opportunities for personalized learning and streamlined administrative processes (Ibrahim and Sulaimon 2023). In the context of special education, particularly for students with hearing impairments, AI presents significant potential to address specific challenges. For example, AI-driven applications can provide real-time translation of spoken language into text, enhance communication through sign language recognition, and personalize learning experiences based on individual needs and progress (Ogunyemi, Adeyemi, Bello and Yusuf 2023). These technologies can bridge communication gaps, support comprehension, and offer tailored instructional materials that are challenging to develop manually (Zhang 2020). Despite these promising advancements, there is limited empirical research focused on how educators in specialized institutions are leveraging on AI.

Teachers play a crucial role in implementing these technologies effectively, and their knowledge and attitudes towards AI can significantly impact its integration and utility in the classroom.

CREATIVE HUMAN-AI SYNERGY IN INSTRUCTIONAL PRACTICE AMONG LECTURERS IN SPECIAL EDUCATION

The combination of human ingenuity and artificial intelligence (AI) has brought in a new era of instructional innovation. In special education, learner needs require adaptive and personalized strategies, therefore the synergy between human lecturers and AI technologies holds transformative potential. Creative human-AI synergy in instructional practice simply means collaborative interaction where educators and intelligent systems work together, enhance, and deliver learning experiences. This synergy is not about replacing teachers but enhancing their capabilities to better meet the unique needs of learners with special needs and disabilities. (Holmes et al. 2021).

There are several ways or samples of how AI tools could be synergistically integrated into classroom instructions for students with special needs and disabilities. Some of them are explained below:

1) Personalized Reading Support via Text-to-Speech and AI Narration

Scenario:

A student with dyslexia or visual impairment that struggles with decoding printed text could be assisted using AI tools such as Microsoft Immersive Reader or NaturalReader AI and Speechify (for AI voice personalization). The Human-AI Synergycould simply mean that the lecturer selects reading materials and aligned it with the student's IEP goals, while the AI reads the text aloud, highlights words in sync, and offers picture dictionaries, the lecturer therefore, supplements the reading by asking questions from students by tailoring vocabulary practice based on the AI-generated word difficulty analysis.

2) AI-Supported AAC (Augmentative and Alternative Communication) for Non-Verbal Students

Scenario:

Non-verbal students require assistance to communicate during classroom discussions. Some of the AI Tools that could be of great assistance for such students are Proloquo2Go (AI-supported speech generation) and CoughDrop or Talkitt AI for motor-impaired speech recognition. Human-AI Synergy could be that the lecturer configures the AAC app with subject relevant to vocabulary development and symbol. During these activities, students use the tool to positively contribute their ideas, views and respond to questions, or request for assistance. The lecturer therefore builds peer inclusion by facilitating structured interaction between AAC users and peers.

3) Behavior Monitoring and Emotional Recognition for Students with Autism

Scenario:

A student with Autism Spectrum Disorder (ASD) that lacks speech exhibits behavioral challenges that negatively impedes learning could be assisted with AI tools like Motional (emotion recognition AI) or AI-based facial recognition software like Affectiva and Nudgespot Classroom Assistants. These tools could be synergistically integrated by the lecturer in the following ways

- The AI monitors facial expressions or physiological signals could be used to detect the level of emotional distress the student is going through.
- When the level of stress has been detected, the system automatically alerts the teacher, who then initiates calming strategies or sensory breaks.
- Over time, the lecturer reviews AI logs to identify triggers and adjust the classroom environment to soothe the emotional behavior of the affected student.

Statement of the Problem

Despite the growing potential of artificial intelligence (AI) and technological devices to enhance the learning experience for students with special education needs and disabilities, there is limited research examining the impacts of these tools on teaching/learning among teachers in the field of special education. There is need for awareness, sufficient and repeated training and retraining of teachers on the impact of AI and technological devices on education of students with disabilities. There is a need for students also to know the importance and benefit attached to consistent exposure to AI-powered educational tools. This study therefore addressed the gap in understanding the impact of AI on teaching learning among the teachers of students with special needs and disabilities and the challenges they encounter while using the devices.

Purpose of the Study

The purpose of this study is to investigate the impact of Artificial Intelligence on teaching learning among lecturers in special education. In specific terms this study aimed:

1. To assess the level of knowledge of artificial intelligence (AI) among the lecturers of students with special needs and disabilities in the Federal College of Education (Special), Oyo.
2. To evaluate the extent to which artificial intelligence (AI) technologies are used in their teaching / learning processes.
3. To identify the challenges and barriers to the adoption of artificial intelligence (AI) tools in special education settings.

Research Questions

The following research questions were raised and answered in the study:

1. What is the current level of knowledge about artificial intelligence (AI) among lecturers of students with special education needs and disabilities at the Federal College of Education (Special), Oyo?
2. How frequently and effectively do these teachers use artificial intelligence (AI) technologies in their teaching
3. What are the main challenges and barriers faced by these educators in using AI tools?

Research Design

This study adopted a quantitative research design to objectively assess the impact of artificial intelligence (AI) on teaching/learning, its knowledge and utilization among teachers. Structure survey research was conducted in analyzing numerical data, which facilitates statistical analysis and generalization of findings.

Population and Sample

The target population for this study consists of all lecturers of students with special education needs and disabilities in Federal College of Education Special, Oyo. This group is selected because they directly interact with AI tools and technologies in their teaching learning processes. A sample of 20 teachers was selected using stratified random sampling to ensure representation from different departments and levels of teaching experience. The sample size is determined to balance statistical reliability and manageability of data collection and analysis. Also, the sample size of 20 lecturers was used because the school is not only for students with disabilities, hence very few samples size of 20 lecturers in the school of special education. There are very many lecturers but in other fields.

Data Collection and Instrument

The primary instrument for data collection was a structured questionnaire designed to assess various aspects of the impact of artificial intelligence (AI) on teaching, its knowledge and usage.

The questionnaire was tagged: questionnaire on impact of artificial intelligence on teaching/learning among teachers of students with special needs and disabilities. This questionnaire was divided into two sections, section A and B. Section A contain the personal data of the respondent which includes: age, gender, level/qualification and years of teaching experience; while section B contain statement on impact of AI on teaching learners with disabilities, the knowledge and usage of artificial intelligence among teacher of students with special educational needs and disabilities. The questionnaire was validated through a pilot test with a small group of teachers not included in the main study. The test re-test method was used to obtain the reliability of the instrument. The questionnaire was administered on five (5) lecturers of students with special needs and disabilities, who are not part of the actual respondents but share similar characteristics with the actual respondents. The instrument was re-administered to the same group of respondents after two weeks to ascertain the reliability.

Data Analysis

Data collected was analysis using frequencies, percentages, means, and standard deviations to summarize responses related to artificial intelligence (AI) knowledge and usage.

RESULTS AND DISCUSSION

Table 1. Gender of the respondents

GENDER	FREQUENCY	PERCENTAGE
MALE	10	50%
FEMALE	10	50%
TOTAL	20	100%

Figure 1. Age of the respondence

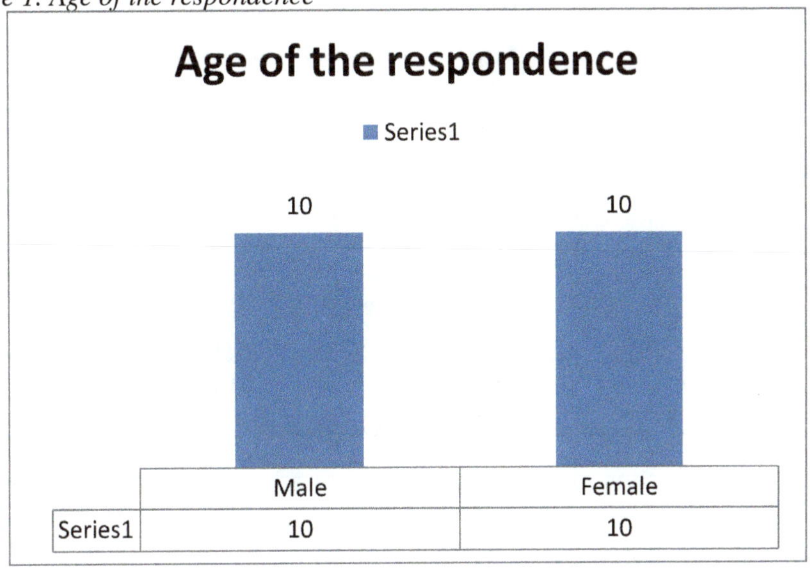

The data presented above describes the characteristics of the respondents used for this study. in terms of gender, 10 (50%) of the respondents were male and 10 (50%) were females. this implies that male and female participant participated equally in the study.

Table 2. Age of the respondents

AGE	FREQUENCY	PERCENTAGE
25 – 30 YEARS	5	25%
31 – 45 YEARS	10	50%
46 – 50 YEARS	3	15%
51 YEARS AND ABOVE	2	10%
TOTAL	20	100%

Figure 2. Series 1

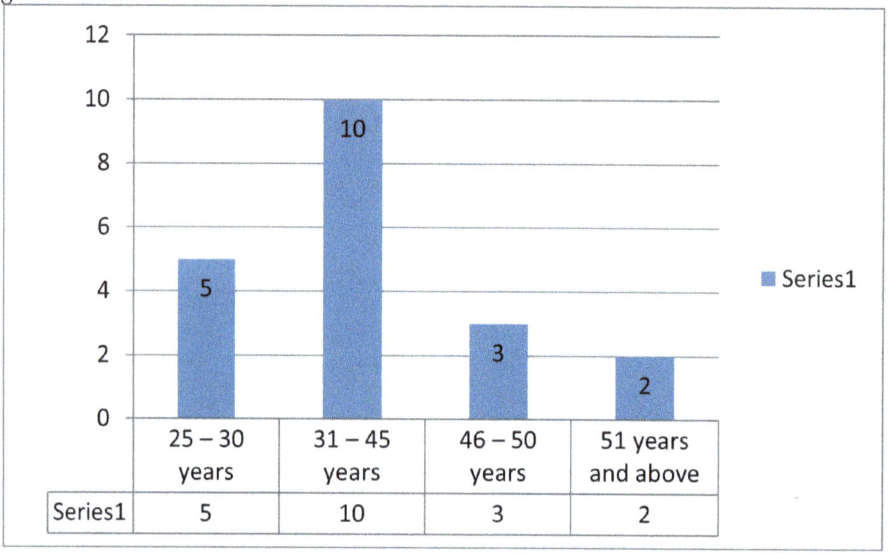

In the above chart, the age range of the respondents are presented with 5 (25%) of the respondents aged 25-30 years, 31-45 years being 10 (50%), 3 (15%) being 46-50 years, lastly, 51 years and above being 2 (10%), this implies that majority of the respondents that participated in this study are in the age range of 31-45 years.

Research Question 1: What is the current level of impact of Ai on teaching learning among lecturers in special education, the knowledge about artificial intelligence (ai) and it' s usage

Table 3. Research Question 1

Variable	N	M	SD	A	T-CAL	T-TAB	REMARK
Artificial Intelligence							
Current Level of Impact of AI on Teaching	20	16.5	1.816	0.05	7.2908	2.013	Rejected
Usage and Knowledge							

The artificial intelligence (Mean=15.5; S.D =1.816) the current level of impact of AI on teaching/learning among lecturers in special education, knowledge and usage (mean = 3.5, S.D =0.8366) was significant (t (20) = 7.2908; $p<0.05$). This implies that, the current level of impact of AI on teaching/learning among lecturers in special education and knowledge about artificial intelligence (AI) and usage should be improved. Many factors could be responsible for this. It could be availability or accessibility. Where they are available, many lecturers lack the knowledge and the technical know-how of such devices.

Research Question 2: What is the frequency of artificial intelligence (AI) usage?

Table 4. Research Question 2

VARIABLE			N		M	SD	A	T-CAL	T-TAB	REMARK
	ARTIFICIAL INTELLIGEN CE				19.					
			20			1.975				
					5		0.05	8.0645	2.013	REJECTED
	FREQUENCY	20		0.5		0.316				

Table 5. Research Question 3

VARIABLE	N		M		SD	A		T-CAL	T-TAB	REMARK
ARTIFICIAL	20		19.25	1.962						
INTELLIGENCE							8.2815		2.013	REJECTED
						0.05				
CHALLENGES	20		0.75		0.387					
AND BARRIERS										

Artificial Intelligence (Mean = 19.25; S.D = 1.962) the challenges and barriers (Mean = 0.75, s.d = 0.387) was significant (t (20) =8.2815; p<0.05). which implies that there are challenges and barriers in using artificial intelligence (AI) tools. This means that even though the teachers are using AI, there are challenges that could have been responsible for the short falls encountered despite the frequency of the usage as seen in the previous research question.

Discussion of Findings

The findings from this study were discussed based on the result of the analysis. This study investigated the impact of AI on teaching learning among the lectures in special education; the knowledge and frequency of usage of artificial intelligence were also ascertained. The first research question states that what is the current level of impact of on teaching/learning among lecturers in special education, the knowledge they have acquired about AI and its usage as related to their profession? The result shows that the current level of impact of AI was significant, meaning that lecturers should brace up and be intentional about knowing more on the importance of AI, going for training and retraining as earlier mentioned so that learners with special needs will not be left out in the world of technology. This result corroborates the assertion of López, Ruiz, & Turner (2023) who averred that while there is general awareness of AI concept such as machine learning and natural language processing, many teachers lack practical knowledge regarding their applications in special education. This lack of understanding can hinder teachers' ability to select and implement appropriate AI tools that could enhance learning outcomes for students with special needs and disabilities. There is need for lecturers in special education to improve their knowledge of and the ability to effectively use AI technologies which are especially crucial to diverse and individualized needs of learners with disabilities. Teachers are to be exposed to the key reasons why AI usage and understanding are vital for educators in this field, some of which are for personalized and differentiated instruction

AI systems which are capable of analyzing student performance data and tailoring instructional materials to suit each learner's pace, strengths, and needs. In special education, where no two students may have the same learning profile, lecturers should have the understanding of the ability of AI to deliver adaptive learning experiences which can greatly improve student outcomes. They should take cognizance of the fact that AI can help tailor learning to individual student needs by offering customized resources and real-time feedback, particularly beneficial in the context of inclusive education (Luckin et al., 2016).

Another key importance of AI to be addressed and known among lecturers is that AI enhances accessibility among students with special needs and disabilities. AI-powered tools such as text-to-speech, speech-to-text, image recognition, and real-time captioning remove barriers to learning for students with sensory, communication, or physical disabilities. Lecturers who are knowledgeable in these tools can facilitate a more inclusive classroom environment. Lecturers should consistently make judicious use of AI technological devices because AI-driven assistive technologies significantly enhance accessibility for students with disabilities, promoting equity in education" (Al-Azawei et al., 2016).

This result is also in tandem with the position of Smith & Johnson (2022) who emphasized that teachers often receive minimal training focused on the integration of technology into special education curricula. This gap indicates a pressing need for targeted professional development that empowers educators with the skills necessary to harness AI effectively. Understanding the specific AI knowledge among special educators can take inclusive education to another dimension. The second research question says what is the frequency of AI usage among the special educators? The result shows that the frequency of usage was significant. However, the frequencies of AI usage among teachers are critical indicators of how well these technologies are being integrated into educational practices. Frequent use of AI can lead to personalized learning experiences, which are particularly beneficial for students with special needs and disabilities. This result negates the recent research by Brown & Thompson (2023), which reveals that while some teachers incorporate AI tools like speech recognition software and adaptive learning platforms, the frequency of their usage is often inconsistent. This inconsistency may stem from a lack of training, resources, or time to explore and implement these technologies in the classroom. Kim, Nguyen, & Brown (2022) found that teachers who frequently utilize AI tools report enhanced engagement and better learning outcomes for their students. Their study suggests that consistent use of AI not only improves instructional practices but also supports the diverse learning needs of students with hearing impairments. A focused evaluation of the specific AI technologies employed could provide valuable insights into usage patterns and informing future initiatives aimed at improving AI integration.

Implication of the Study

The findings of the study on the use of Artificial Intelligence (AI) among students with special needs and disabilities have significant implications for inclusive education. AI has the potential to enhance and transform how students with diverse learning needs access and engage with instructional content. Through adaptive learning systems, real-time feedback, and assistive technologies such as speech recognition, text-to-speech, and behavioural and emotion tracking, Consistent use of AI give room for more personalized and accessible learning environment which fosters improved academic outcomes and promotes greater independence and classroom participation among students with disabilities. The study suggests that leveraging these tools effectively and creating an effective human-AI synergy can help bridge learning gaps and support the individual education plans (IEPs) that are central to special education.

However, the successful integration of AI also depends on the preparedness of educators and institutions. Special education lecturers must be equipped with AI literacy to utilize these tools ethically and efficiently, ensuring they complement rather than replace human interaction. Policymakers and educational leaders are therefore urged to establish guidelines that promote responsible AI use, while also providing adequate infrastructure and professional development opportunities. In essence, the implications of the study highlight that AI, when thoughtfully and properly utilized and applied can significantly enhance inclusion, personalization, and equity in the education of students with special needs and disabilities.**Top of FormBottom of Form**

CONCLUSION

This study was carried out to investigate the impact of Artificial Intelligence on teaching learning among the lecturers in special education, the knowledge and the frequency of usage of these technological devices and software were also investigated. It has been discovered that most often, teachers do not often useAI and they are not with adequate understanding of the usage of AI. It becomes therefore difficult for them to integrate AI into the classroom activities especially among students with special education needs and disabilities. This is now calling the attention of old and young, teachers and students to the understanding of the fact that AI are increasingly being considered as potent instruments that cannot be pushed aside in educational trend especially in special education. Issues on the knowledge, usage and consistent training and retraining for teachers to effectively handle and use AI in their individual field should be reflected upon and see as part of challenges confronting the field of special education.

Recommendations

Based on the findings of this study the following recommendations were made to improve the knowledge and usage of AI among the special educators.

1. There should be Targeted Professional Development: comprehensive training programs that focus on AI applications and usage in special education, emphasizing practical, hands-on experiences should be implemented for effective classroom usability.
2. Training and re-training: There should be established mentorship and coaching systems where experienced educators can guide less experienced teachers and lecturers in utilizing AI technologies effectively especially in the field of special education.
3. Collaborative Learning Environments: There is need to cultivate a culture of collaboration among teachers to share best practices, resources, and experiences related to AI integration and usage.
4. Access to Resources: There is need to ensure that both educators and students have access to the necessary technological devices, tools and infrastructural facilities, including reliable internet and updated hardware. This will facilitate constant usage and awareness of the importance of artificial intelligence in the education of students with special needs and disabilities.
5. Awareness Campaigns: There is need to create awareness and the need to stage programs highlighting the conduct and benefits of AI in special education and to motivate teachers to explore these new inventions and other technological devices that can promote inclusive educational system.

REFERENCES

Adebayo, A. A. (2024). Artificial Intelligence and Lecturers' Effectiveness in Ogun State Owned Universities. *FUOYE International Journal of Business and Economics Education, 1*(1), 188–198.

Al-Azawei, A., Serenelli, F., & Lundqvist, K. (2016a). Extending the technology acceptance model to assess the impact of assistive technology on students with disabilities. *Computers & Education, 95*, 58–67.

Al-Azawei, A., Serenelli, F., & Lundqvist, K. (2016b). Universal Design for Learning (UDL*): A content analysis of peer-reviewed journal papers from 2012 to 2015.The Journal of Scholarship of Teaching and Learning, 16*(3), 39–56. DOI: 10.14434/josotl.v16i3.19295

Baker, T., & Smith, L. (2022). Educ-AI-tion rebooted? Exploring the future of artificial intelligence in schools and colleges. Retrieved from Nesta Foundation. http://media.nesta.org.uk

Barua, P. D., Vicnesh, J., Gururajan, R., Oh, S. L., Palmer, E., Azizan, M. M., & Acharya, U. R. (2022). Artificial Intelligence Enabled Personalized Assistive Tools to Enhance Education of Children with Neuro developmental Disorders: A Review. *International Journal of Environmental Research and Public Health, 19*(3), 1–26. DOI: 10.3390/ijerph19031192 PMID: 35162220

Cleopas, B. C. (2023). Advent of artificial intelligence: Prospect and Challenges in Nigeria education system. *Education Research,* 06 (06), 01-09. Retrieved from http://media.nesta.org.uk

Holmes, W., Bialik, M., & Fadel, C. (2021). *Artificial intelligence in education: Promises and implications for teaching and learning*. Center for Curriculum Redesign.

Lametti, D. (2022). A.I could be great for college essays. https://slate.com/technology/2022/12/-college-essay-plagiarism.html

Luckin, R., Holmes, W., Griffiths, M., & Forcier, L. B. (2016). *Intelligence unleashed: An argument for AI in education*. Pearson.

Mathew, T. M., Eleazar, V., Lisa, D., James, B., & Jose, B. (2023).. . *Journal of Special Education Technology, 38*(3), 404–416. DOI: 10.1177/01626434231165977

Ogunyemi, Adeyemi, M. B., Bello, M. A., & Yusuf, T. (2023). AI-based personalized learning in Nigerian educational settings: Opportunities and challenges. *Journal of Educational Technology Development and Exchange, 15*(1), 77–92.

Smith, R., & Johnson, K. (2022). Real-time transcription technologies and their impact on students with hearing impairments. *Journal of Educational Technology Systems, 48*(2), 189–204. DOI: 10.2190/ET.43.2.f

Tai, M. C. (2020). The impact of artificial intelligence on human society and bioethics. *Tzu* 15. *Chiba Medical Journal, 32*(4), 339–343. PMID: 33163378

VanLehn, Zheng, L., Zheng, D., and Zhang, Z. (2021). Educators' attitudes towards AI in education: A comprehensive review. *Educational Technology Research and Development, 69*(2), 751–773.

Zawacki-Richter, O., Marín, V. I., Bond, M., & Gouverneur, F. (2019). Systematic review of research on artificial intelligence applications in higher education – Where are the educators? *International Journal of Educational Technology in Higher Education, 16*(1), 39. DOI: 10.1186/s41239-019-0171-0

Zhang, X., Yang, D., & Li, X. (2020). Advances in deep learning for speech recognition: A review. *IEEE Transactions on Neural Networks and Learning Systems, 31*(7), 2458–2474.

Chapter 3
Enhancing Public Sector Audit Education Through AI–Driven Simulations:
A Systematic Review

Olugbade Damola
https://orcid.org/0000-0003-3938-6273
University of South Africa, South Africa

Audrey Hlabisang Legodi
https://orcid.org/0000-0001-5311-7307
University of South Africa, South Africa

ABSTRACT

As artificial intelligence (AI) continues to revolutionize education, its integration into public sector auditing training represents a critical frontier. This chapter systematically reviews the literature on AI-driven simulations in public sector audit education, analyzing their efficacy, applications, and inherent challenges. A comprehensive screening of 871 studies from Web of Science and Scopus yielded 11 peer-reviewed articles, which were thematically analyzed to identify key findings. The review highlights the transformative potential of AI simulations in fostering critical skills, bridging theory-practice gaps, and enhancing decision-making in audit training. It also addresses barriers to adoption, including technical, financial, and institutional constraints, while underscoring the importance of ethical and cultural considerations. By offering actionable insights, this chapter contributes to advancing the discourse on AI's role in audit education, with implications for educators, policymakers, and practitioners.

DOI: 10.4018/979-8-3373-5550-4.ch003

INTRODUCTION

As public accountability demands grow, the need for skilled public sector auditors has never been greater. Yet, traditional training methods struggle to keep pace with today's complex audit environments. Could artificial intelligence (AI) be the catalyst for transforming how we prepare tomorrow's auditors? The integration of artificial intelligence in public sector audit education has emerged as a promising avenue to enhance educational outcomes and bridge the gap between theoretical knowledge and practical application. AI-driven simulations, in particular, offer an innovative approach to delivering real-world, scenario-based experiences that traditional audit education methods often lack. These tools provide opportunities for learners to engage with complex audit scenarios, fostering critical skills such as ethical sensitivity and decision-making, which are essential for navigating the contemporary public sector audit environment.

Despite their potential, the adoption of AI-driven simulations in audit education remains underexplored. Bhavani (2020) identified 92 AI-based simulations implemented in management education; however, only a small subset is tailored for audit-specific training. Among these, 62 were developed by private firms, and 30 were offered by universities globally, highlighting a significant gap in resources dedicated to audit education. This gap underscores the need for targeted investment and research to develop AI tools that address the unique challenges of public sector auditing. While existing studies affirm the potential of AI-driven simulations, many rely on limited case samples or lack longitudinal data, raising questions about the generalizability and sustained impact of their findings.

Audit committees play a pivotal role in ensuring transparency, accountability, and compliance within public sector governance (Ellwood & García-Lacalle, 2016). Preparing auditors to fulfill these roles necessitates rigorous training that combines theoretical frameworks with hands-on experiences (Aslan, 2021). Traditional pedagogical approaches often fail to replicate the nuanced decision-making and regulatory complexities encountered in public sector auditing (García-García et al., 2024; Gilbertson & Herron, 2014). AI-driven simulations offer a transformative solution by creating interactive environments that mirror real-world audit tasks, thus enabling students to develop the critical thinking and ethical reasoning skills required for professional practice. For instance, the National Audit Office (NAO) has conducted training sessions for its employees on artificial intelligence, illustrating practical applications of AI in audit work and highlighting its benefits and associated risks. In addition to academic studies, practical implementations of AI in audit education and training are emerging across professional contexts. For instance, Kingston Smith, a UK-based auditing firm, employs MindBridge's AI platform to analyze transaction data, identify risks, and flag anomalies, enhancing audit efficiency by modeling financial risks across entire datasets. Similarly, Guaranty Partners offers a professional course titled AI-Powered Internal Auditing: Tools and Techniques, designed to train auditors in applying AI to internal audit tasks such as data analytics, automation, and risk assessment, while also addressing implementation challenges and future trends. To cap it up, recent advances in AI-enhanced learning environments have shown promising results in improving educational access and outcomes in underserved regions. For example, Olugbade (2025) demonstrates how mobile technologies and AI can democratize education in rural Nigeria, fostering more inclusive and equitable learning experiences. Similarly, Edwards, Olugbade, and Ojo (2024) found that AI chatbots can support cognitive load management and improve both learning outcomes and student attitudes in middle school vocational education settings.

This study aims to evaluate the effectiveness of AI-driven simulations in public sector audit education by examining their impact on bridging the gap between theoretical knowledge and practical application. It seeks to identify the primary challenges and limitations that hinder the implementation of AI-driven tools in audit training, focusing on technical, financial, and institutional barriers. Furthermore, the research explores the specific AI-enabled features that enhance learning outcomes for future auditors, such as adaptive feedback, scenario-based learning, and data-driven decision-making. Additionally, the study investigates the ethical, cultural, and practical considerations involved in adopting AI simulations, particularly how these tools can be tailored to diverse regulatory environments to ensure equitable and context-sensitive application. Through this comprehensive analysis, the study contributes valuable insights into the transformative potential of AI-driven simulations for advancing public sector audit education. To achieve these objectives, the review addresses the following research questions (RQs):

> RQ1: What evidence exists on the efficacy of AI-driven simulations for public sector audit training?
> RQ2: What are the primary challenges in implementing AI-driven simulations within public sector audit education?
> RQ3: How do AI-based tools impact the development of critical skills needed for effective audit committee participation?
> RQ4: What ethical and cultural considerations are involved in adopting AI simulations across diverse public sector contexts?

By investigating these questions, this chapter aims to contribute to the discourse on the integration of AI in public sector audit education. It offers insights for researchers, educators, and policymakers, emphasizing the potential of AI-driven simulations to transform audit training practices. The subsequent sections detail the study's methodology (Section 3), present findings (Section 4), discuss implications (Section 5), provide a conclusion (Section 6), and outline actionable recommendations (Section 7).

METHODOLOGY

This chapter employs a systematic review approach, adhering to the Preferred Reporting Items for Systematic Reviews and Meta-Analyses (PRISMA) guidelines to ensure transparency, rigor, and replicability throughout the research process. By systematically synthesizing relevant literature, this method provides a comprehensive overview of the role of AI-driven simulations in public sector audit education, evaluating their efficacy, identifying challenges, and exploring opportunities for future application.

DATA COLLECTION

The literature review focused on peer-reviewed studies published in reputable academic journals and conference proceedings. The initial search encompassed two major academic databases, Web of Science (WoS) and Scopus, ensuring a broad and multidisciplinary scope. Keywords such as "AI-driven simulations," "audit education," "public sector auditing," and "AI in education" were used in various combinations to retrieve relevant articles. The search yielded an initial pool of 871 studies, as seen in Figure 1.

To refine the selection, inclusion and exclusion criteria were applied. Articles were included if they focused on AI applications in audit education, particularly those relevant to the public sector. Studies unrelated to auditing or those lacking empirical evidence were excluded. After title and abstract screening, 38 studies were shortlisted for full-text review.

Figure 1. PRISMA Flow Diagram of the Systematic Review Process for AI-Driven Simulations in Public Sector Audit Education

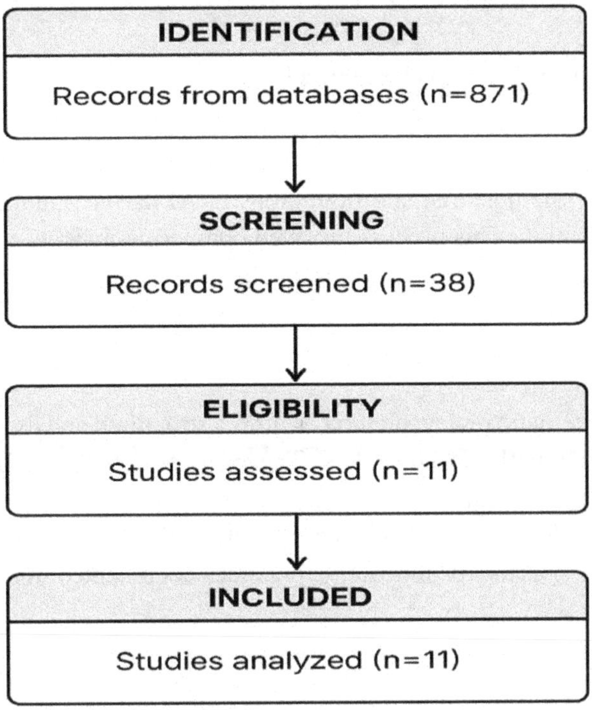

Following a detailed assessment of their relevance, 11 studies as shown in table 1 were identified as suitable for this review.

THEMATIC ANALYSIS

The selected studies were subjected to a thematic analysis to extract key insights and identify recurring patterns. The analysis categorized findings into four core themes:

1. Effectiveness of AI-Driven Simulations: Examining their ability to enhance learning outcomes, improve engagement, and develop critical skills.
2. Challenges in Implementation: Identifying barriers such as financial constraints, technical limitations, and institutional resistance.
3. AI-Enabled Features for Enhanced Learning: Investigating specific features such as adaptive learning algorithms, scenario-based training modules, and ethical decision-making frameworks.

4. Ethical and Cultural Considerations: Exploring issues related to bias, transparency, and the contextual relevance of AI tools in diverse regulatory environments.

SYNTHESIS AND INTERPRETATION

The findings from the thematic analysis were synthesized to provide an integrated understanding of the potential and limitations of AI-driven simulations in public sector audit education. This process involved comparing insights across studies to highlight commonalities, contradictions, and gaps in the existing research.

Limitations

While the systematic review method ensures a structured and thorough analysis, certain limitations must be acknowledged. The reliance on studies available in English and indexed in specific databases may have excluded relevant research published in other languages or less accessible sources. Additionally, the focus on peer-reviewed articles may have overlooked innovative practices documented in gray literature.

Table 1. Summary of Reviewed Studies on AI-Driven Simulations in Public Sector Audit Education

Title	Authors	Year	Citation	Publisher	Contributions
AI competencies for internal auditors in the public sector	Aldemİr, C., & Uçma Uysal, T.	2024	12	Taylor & Francis	The article explores AI's integration in internal auditing, emphasizing the need for auditors to develop technological competencies. It highlights AI's potential in automating tasks like fraud detection and underscores the importance of balancing technological tools with human expertise. The research advocates for continuous professional education to equip auditors with AI skills, ultimately arguing that effective auditing requires a synergy between advanced AI technologies and professional judgment.
Artificial Intelligence in Auditing: A Conceptual Framework for Auditing Practices	Leocádio, D., Malheiro, L., & Reis, J.	2024	1	MDPI	AI integration in auditing practices transforms roles, enabling proactive real-time monitoring and informed decision-making in risk analysis, financial management, and regulatory compliance.
The impact of artificial intelligence on information audit usage: Evidence from developing countries	Almaqtari, F. A., Farhan, N. H., Al-Hattami, H. M., Elsheikh, T., & Al-dalaien, B. O. A. (2024)	2024	5	Elsevier	The study explores Information audit adoption in Egypt and Jordan, examining artificial intelligence's impact. Through surveying 443 participants, researchers found internal factors and AI significantly influence technology adoption. Key insights include positive correlations between intention and actual usage of Information audit technologies, with AI dimensions like cloud computing enhancing perceived benefits. The research offers practical recommendations for firms, auditors, and policymakers to support technological integration in the Middle Eastern context.
Framework for Integrating Generative AI in Developing Competencies for Accounting and Audit Professionals	Anica-Popa, I., Vrîncianu, M., Anica-Popa, L., Cismasu, I., & Tudor, C.	2024	4	MDPI	Integrating Generative AI into accounting and auditing systems can revolutionize lifelong learning and skills development, assisting decision-making and enhancing data analysis and risk management.

continued on following page

Table 1. Continued

Title	Authors	Year	Citation	Publisher	Contributions
Leveraging artificial intelligence (AI) in public sector financial risk management: Innovations, challenges, and future directions	Bouchetara, M., Zerouti, M., & Zouambi, A. R.	2024	4	Taylor & Francis	The paper explores AI's transformative potential in enhancing financial risk management within the public sector, highlighting machine learning technologies' ability to process vast data, recognize patterns, and predict complex financial risks like credit, market, liquidity, and operational challenges. By examining AI's application in predictive modeling, scenario analysis, and decision-making optimization, the study critically analyzes both the opportunities and challenges of integrating advanced technologies into public financial systems.
Current auditor expertise and future relevance of innovative audit technology: evidence from Indonesia public sector auditor	Yahya, M. R., Jalaluddin, & Batara, G.	2024	4	Taylor & Francis	The study examines technology adoption in Indonesia's supreme audit institution (BPK-RI) during the COVID-19 pandemic, focusing on auditors' expertise levels across 18 innovative audit technologies. Using surveys and statistical analysis, the research reveals that cloud computing, self-service reports, and scanbots are considered most relevant, while auditors' knowledge remains moderate. The findings highlight a significant expertise gap in digital audit technologies, underscoring the critical need for targeted educational initiatives and policy interventions to enhance auditors' technological capabilities.
The Role of IT Governance in the Integration of AI in Accounting and Auditing Operations	Almaqtari, F. A.	2024	3	MDPI	A comprehensive study reveals that IT governance is crucial for successfully integrating AI technologies in accounting and auditing, demonstrating significant improvements in operational efficiency and decision-making processes. The findings not only contribute to academic literature but also provide practical insights for organizational leaders, IT specialists, and policymakers on navigating the complex landscape of AI adoption in financial operations.

continued on following page

Table 1. Continued

Title	Authors	Year	Citation	Publisher	Contributions
Leveraging AI for Enhanced eGovernment: Optimizing the Use of Open Governmental Data	Carayannis, E. G., Askounis, D., Andoutropoulou, M., & Zotas, N.	2024	1	Springer	The paper investigates AI's transformative potential in eGovernment, focusing on its ability to optimize open governmental data and drive transparency, innovation, and economic growth. By examining pioneering government implementations of AI technologies, the study explores both the significant opportunities and challenges in adopting artificial intelligence within the public sector.
Adoption of artificial intelligence in auditing: An exploratory study	Seethamraju, R., & Hecimovic, A.	2022	3	Sage	AI adoption in auditing can improve audit quality and deliver value-adding services, but requires a rethink of audit practice due to perceived lack of control in AI 'black-box' environments.
Auditing the AI auditors: A framework for evaluating fairness and bias in high stakes AI predictive models.	Landers, R., & Behrend, T.	2022	188	American Psychologist	Psychological audits can effectively evaluate the fairness and bias of AI systems, benefiting from psychology's expertise across disciplines.
Ethics-based auditing to develop trustworthy	Mökander, J., & Floridi, L.	2021	182	Springer	Ethics-based auditing can improve decision-making, user satisfaction, growth potential, law-making, and relieve human suffering in AI.

RESULTS

The systematic review yielded several significant findings concerning the role of AI-driven simulations in public sector audit education. The analysis identified key themes related to their effectiveness, challenges in implementation, AI-enabled features that enhance learning, and ethical and cultural considerations. These findings provide a comprehensive understanding of the current state of research in this field.

Effectiveness of AI-Driven Simulations in Audit Training

AI-driven simulations have demonstrated significant potential in enhancing learning outcomes for public sector audit education. Studies highlighted that these tools provide immersive, scenario-based learning environments that enable students to engage with complex, real-world audit tasks. This hands-on approach fosters critical thinking, problem-solving, and decision-making skills—core competencies required for effective public sector auditing. Furthermore, AI simulations were shown to enhance cognitive understanding by visualizing complex data and facilitating personalized feedback through adaptive learning systems. Several studies also emphasized the ability of AI simulations to improve knowledge retention and student engagement, particularly in subjects requiring high levels of practical application, such as auditing.

Challenges in Implementing AI-Driven Simulations

Despite their potential, the integration of AI-driven simulations into public sector audit education faces several challenges. Technical and financial barriers were prominent, with many institutions lacking the resources to invest in the necessary technology and infrastructure. Public sector training programs often operate under strict budget constraints, limiting their ability to adopt advanced AI tools. Additionally, the effectiveness of these simulations depends heavily on educator readiness and proficiency with AI technologies. However, a lack of professional development opportunities and the steep learning curve associated with mastering AI tools have hindered widespread adoption. Cultural and institutional resistance, stemming from preferences for traditional teaching methods and concerns over job security, further complicates integration efforts.

AI-Enabled Features Enhancing Learning Outcomes

The review identified several AI-enabled features that significantly enhance the learning experience in audit education. Adaptive learning algorithms emerged as a critical feature, allowing simulations to tailor feedback and tasks to individual learners' progress and skill levels. Scenario-based training modules were particularly effective in replicating real-world audit tasks, providing students with opportunities to develop practical competencies. Data-driven decision-making scenarios were another standout feature, enabling students to work with large datasets and practice analyzing and interpreting complex information—a key requirement for modern audit committee responsibilities. Ethical and compliance-based modules integrated into simulations further prepared students to navigate the ethical dilemmas they are likely to encounter in their professional roles.

Ethical and Cultural Considerations

The findings also underscored the importance of addressing ethical and cultural considerations in the design and implementation of AI-driven simulations. Bias and transparency in AI algorithms were significant ethical concerns, with the potential to create inequitable learning opportunities if not carefully managed. Additionally, the cultural relevance of simulation scenarios was critical to their effectiveness. Studies emphasized the need for AI tools to be tailored to the unique regulatory and cultural contexts of diverse public sector environments. For example, simulations designed for Nigeria and South Africa would need to align with the specific ethical considerations and auditing frameworks of these regions.

The results of this systematic review highlight the transformative potential of AI-driven simulations for public sector audit education. While these tools offer considerable benefits in terms of skill development, engagement, and preparedness, their successful implementation requires addressing significant challenges, including financial constraints, educator readiness, and ethical design considerations. By focusing on these areas, institutions can maximize the impact of AI-driven simulations, equipping future auditors with the competencies needed to navigate the complexities of public sector governance.

DISCUSSION

The findings of this systematic review underscore the transformative potential of AI-driven simulations in public sector audit education, while also highlighting several critical challenges and considerations. This section contextualizes the results within the broader landscape of public sector auditing and AI adoption, drawing on existing literature to analyze the implications of these findings.

Enhancing Learning Outcomes Through AI-Driven Simulations

AI-driven simulations have demonstrated the capacity to bridge the gap between theoretical knowledge and practical application in audit education. By offering scenario-based training environments, these tools enable students to engage with real-world tasks, developing critical skills such as ethical reasoning, decision-making, and problem-solving. This aligns with studies that emphasize the role of AI in enhancing cognitive and practical competencies through immersive learning experiences (Bhavani, 2020; Anica-Popa et al., 2024). Furthermore, the ability of adaptive algorithms to provide personalized feedback supports the development of a learner-centered approach, which is crucial for fostering deep engagement and retention of knowledge.

However, the findings also suggest that the effectiveness of these simulations is contingent on their design and contextual relevance. For instance, simulations tailored to reflect specific regulatory and cultural frameworks, such as those in Nigeria and South Africa, are more likely to resonate with students and produce meaningful learning outcomes. This observation reinforces the need for culturally sensitive AI designs, as highlighted in research by Almaqtari et al. (2024) and Mökander & Floridi (2021).

Addressing Challenges in Implementation

The review identified significant barriers to the adoption of AI-driven simulations in public sector audit education, including technical, financial, and institutional constraints. Public sector institutions often operate under strict budget limitations, making it challenging to invest in the necessary technology and infrastructure. This is consistent with findings by Bouchetara et al. (2024), who noted that financial constraints remain a pervasive issue in integrating advanced technologies in public sector training.

Educator readiness also emerged as a critical factor influencing the successful implementation of AI simulations. The steep learning curve associated with mastering AI tools, coupled with limited professional development opportunities, poses a significant challenge. Gilbertson and Herron (2014) argue that overcoming this barrier requires targeted training programs to equip educators with the skills needed to effectively integrate AI tools into their curricula.

Cultural and institutional resistance further complicates adoption efforts. Preferences for traditional teaching methods and concerns about job security and data privacy often hinder the acceptance of AI-driven approaches. Addressing these challenges requires strategic interventions, such as fostering collaboration between educators and technology providers to build trust and demonstrate the value of AI tools in enhancing educational outcomes.

Ethical and Cultural Considerations

The ethical implications of AI-driven simulations warrant careful consideration. Bias in AI algorithms can inadvertently reinforce inequities, undermining the fairness and inclusivity of these tools. Mökander & Floridi (2021) highlight the importance of designing transparent and accountable AI systems to mitigate these risks. Additionally, ensuring cultural relevance in simulation scenarios is critical for their effectiveness. For example, tailoring simulations to align with the auditing frameworks and ethical norms of specific regions can enhance their applicability and impact.

Implications for Policy and Practice

The integration of AI-driven simulations in public sector audit education has significant implications for policymakers, educators, and practitioners. Policymakers must prioritize funding and infrastructure development to support the adoption of advanced educational technologies. Collaborative partnerships with technology providers and international organizations can help address financial and technical barriers. Educators, on the other hand, should focus on building their capacity to effectively use AI tools, leveraging targeted training programs and continuous professional development.

Practitioners and institutions must also adopt a proactive approach to addressing ethical concerns and ensuring the cultural relevance of AI-driven simulations. Developing guidelines for ethical AI design and implementation can promote trust and accountability, while localized content development can enhance the applicability of simulations in diverse regulatory environments (Almaqtari et al., 2024).

The discussion highlights the dual potential and challenges of integrating AI-driven simulations into public sector audit education. While these tools offer significant benefits in terms of skill development and engagement, their successful implementation requires addressing financial, technical, and cultural barriers. By adopting a holistic approach that combines investment in technology, educator training, and ethical design practices, stakeholders can unlock the full potential of AI-driven simulations to transform audit education and prepare future auditors for the complexities of public sector governance.

Recommendations

Based on the findings of this study, several actionable recommendations are proposed to advance the integration of AI-driven simulations in public sector audit education. First, fostering strategic partnerships with technology providers and international organizations is essential. Such collaborations can facilitate access to AI-driven tools through mechanisms like grants, sponsorships, or cost-sharing models, thereby alleviating financial barriers that many public sectors institutions face.

Second, targeted training programs for educators should be prioritized. Equipping audit educators with the necessary skills to incorporate AI-based instructional strategies into their teaching practices will ensure a smoother integration of simulations into existing curricula. This professional development is critical to maximizing the potential of AI technologies in audit education.

Third, the development of localized content is paramount. AI-driven simulations must be tailored to reflect the regulatory and cultural contexts of specific regions to enhance their relevance and applicability. By aligning simulation scenarios with local public sector auditing frameworks and ethical considerations, these tools can provide more meaningful and impactful learning experiences.

Finally, it is vital to establish ongoing evaluation frameworks to monitor and assess the effectiveness of AI-driven simulations. Regular evaluations can help ensure that these technologies meet educational objectives, provide actionable insights for improvement, and adapt to evolving pedagogical needs over time.

CONCLUSION

AI-driven simulations hold significant promise for transforming public sector audit education by bridging the gap between theoretical knowledge and practical application. These tools offer a dynamic, practice-oriented approach that fosters critical skills such as ethical reasoning, decision-making, and problem-solving. The findings of this systematic review underscore the potential of AI simulations to enhance learning outcomes and better prepare students for the complexities of public sector auditing.

However, the successful integration of AI-driven simulations is not without challenges. Financial constraints, technical barriers, and cultural resistance present significant hurdles that must be addressed. Furthermore, the ethical design of these tools, including the mitigation of biases and the alignment of content with local regulatory and cultural contexts, remains crucial to ensuring their effectiveness and equity.

To fully harness the benefits of AI-driven simulations, a multifaceted approach is needed. Investments in infrastructure, educator training, and strategic partnerships can facilitate their adoption, while ongoing evaluation frameworks will ensure their continual improvement and relevance. By addressing these challenges and leveraging the unique capabilities of AI, public sector audit education can evolve to meet the demands of modern governance, equipping future auditors with the competencies needed to excel in their roles.

REFERENCES

Aldemİr, C., & Uçma Uysal, T. (2024). AI competencies for internal auditors in the public sector. EDPACS, 69(1), 3-21. https://doi.org/DOI: 10.1080/07366981.2024.2312001

Almaqtari, F. A. (2024). The Role of IT Governance in the Integration of AI in Accounting and Auditing Operations. *Economies*, *12*(8), 199. DOI: 10.3390/economies12080199

Almaqtari, F. A., Farhan, N. H., Al-Hattami, H. M., Elsheikh, T., & Al-dalaien, B. O. A. (2024). The impact of artificial intelligence on information audit usage: Evidence from developing countries. *Journal of Open Innovation*, *10*(2), 100298. DOI: 10.1016/j.joitmc.2024.100298

Anica-Popa, I., Vrîncianu, M., Anica-Popa, L., Cismasu, I., & Tudor, C. (2024). Framework for Integrating Generative AI in Developing Competencies for Accounting and Audit Professionals. *Electronics (Basel)*, *13*(13), 2621. Advance online publication. DOI: 10.3390/electronics13132621

Aslan, L. (2021). *The Evolving Competencies of the Public Auditor and the Future of Public Sector Auditing*. Contemporary Issues in Public Sector Accounting and Auditing., DOI: 10.1108/S1569-375920200000105008

Bhavani, G. (2020). Artificial Intelligence: Simulations in Audit Education. 2020 11th International Conference on Computing, Communication and Networking Technologies (ICCCNT), 1-5. https://doi.org/DOI: 10.1109/ICCCNT49239.2020.9225523

Bouchetara, M., Zerouti, M., & Zouambi, A. R. (2024). Leveraging artificial intelligence (AI) in public sector financial risk management: Innovations, challenges, and future directions. *EDPACS*, *69*(9), 124–144. DOI: 10.1080/07366981.2024.2377351

Carayannis, E. G., Askounis, D., Andoutropoulou, M., & Zotas, N. (2024). Leveraging AI for Enhanced eGovernment: Optimizing the Use of Open Governmental Data. *Journal of the Knowledge Economy*, •••, 1–36. DOI: 10.1007/s13132-024-02317-w

Edwards, B. I., Olugbade, D., & Ojo, O. A. (2024). Facilitating Cognitive Load Management and Improved Learning Outcomes and Attitudes in Middle School Technology and Vocational Education Through AI Chatbot. *Journal of Technical Education and Training*, *16*(3), 114–131. DOI: 10.30880/jtet.2024.16.03.009

Ellwood, S., & García-Lacalle, J. (2016). Examining Audit Committees in the Corporate Governance of Public Bodies. *Public Management Review*, *18*(8), 1138–1162. DOI: 10.1080/14719037.2015.1088566

García-García, R., García-Caballero, C., Villarreal-Lara, R., & Mirón-Mérida, V. (2024). On-site inspection as a tool for developing auditing skills in engineering: Integrating continuous education contents into higher education programs. *Frontiers in Education*, *9*, 1416110. Advance online publication. DOI: 10.3389/feduc.2024.1416110

Gilbertson, D., & Herron, T. (2014). Including audit regulation in the accounting curriculum. *Research in Accounting Regulation*, *26*(1), 118–131. DOI: 10.1016/j.racreg.2014.02.013

Guaranty Partners Trainings. (n.d.). AI-powered internal auditing: Tools and techniques. https://guarantypartnerstrainings.com/course/ai-powered-internal-auditing-tools-and-techniques/

Landers, R., & Behrend, T. (2022). Auditing the AI auditors: A framework for evaluating fairness and bias in high stakes AI predictive models. *The American Psychologist*. Advance online publication. DOI: 10.1037/amp0000972 PMID: 35157476

Leocádio, D., Malheiro, L., & Reis, J. (2024). Artificial Intelligence in Auditing: A Conceptual Framework for Auditing Practices. *Administrative Sciences*, *14*(10), 238. Advance online publication. DOI: 10.3390/admsci14100238

Mökander, J., & Floridi, L. (2021). Ethics-Based Auditing to Develop Trustworthy AI. *Minds and Machines*, *31*(2), 323–327. DOI: 10.1007/s11023-021-09557-8

National Audit Office. (2022, May 9). NAO employees learn about artificial intelligence. https://www.nao.gov.bh/en/article/nao-employees-learn-about-artificial-intelligence

Olugbade, D. (2025). Democratizing Education in Rural Nigeria Through AI and Mobile Technologies as a Transformative Pathway to Inclusive Learning. In M. Sanmugam, B. Edwards, N. Mohd Barkhaya, & Z. Khlaif (Eds.), Fostering Inclusive Education with AI and Emerging Technologies (pp. 233-250). IGI Global. https://doi.org/DOI: 10.4018/979-8-3693-7255-5.ch010

Seethamraju, R., & Hecimovic, A. (2022). Adoption of artificial intelligence in auditing: An exploratory study. *Australian Journal of Management*, *48*(4), 780–800. DOI: 10.1177/03128962221108440

Yahya, M. R., Jalaluddin, , & Batara, G. (2024). Current auditor expertise and future relevance of innovative audit technology: Evidence from Indonesia public sector auditor. *Asia Pacific Journal of Public Administration*, *46*(4), 1–17. DOI: 10.1080/23276665.2024.2312139

Chapter 4
Transforming Education in the Digital Age: An Analysis of Artificial Intelligence and Deep Learning Through Bibliometric and Systematic Literature Review

Qi Pan
https://orcid.org/0009-0006-2431-7725
University Technology Malaysia, Malaysia

Nurul Farhana Jumaat
Independent Researcher, Malaysia

Hassan Abuhassna
https://orcid.org/0000-0002-5774-3652
Independent Researcher, Malaysia

Liu Tao
Zaozhuang University, China

ABSTRACT

The integration of Artificial Intelligence (AI) and Deep Learning (DL) into education is advancing rapidly, but their impact requires further research. This study combines bibliometric analysis and a systematic literature review, guided by the PRISMA framework, to explore this area. The bibliometric analysis examines publication trends, key countries, institutions, journals, leading authors, and important keywords, providing a macro-level overview. The literature review analyzes 27 high-quality

DOI: 10.4018/979-8-3373-5550-4.ch004

academic articles, revealing that AI and DL have significant potential in education, such as personalized learning, real-time feedback, emotion prediction, and improving the overall learning experience. However, challenges like immature technology, high costs, limited human-computer interaction, data security, and ethical concerns remain. This study highlights both the vast potential and the hurdles of AI and DL in education, pointing to the need for continued research to overcome these issues and maximize their benefits in educational contexts.

1. INTRODUCTION

Education is undergoing a remarkable transformation in the digital era. Artificial intelligence (AI) and deep learning (DL) are widely used in several areas, especially in education, where they are gradually transforming traditional teaching models and learning experiences(Sarker, 2021). Many researchers in education have tried to integrate AI and DL into education to maximize their potential to enrich instructional strategies, provide personalized learning, and improve students' learning outcomes(Grassini, 2023). Natural language processing (NLP) is one of the major technologies of AI, which allows machines to understand and produce human language to provide real-time feedback and personalized tutoring for language instruction(T. Alqahtani et al., 2023). Moreover, to realize students' best learning outcome, another technology, Intelligent Tutoring Systems (ITS), has been developed to manage instructors' teaching content and difficulty based on students' interactions and performance (Alam, 2023). In addition, convolutional neural networks (CNNs) are a powerful instrument to help create virtual labs to improve students' learning experience (Ching et al., 2018).

Based on these technological foundations, AI-powered tools have been integrated into real classrooms in recent years. For example, Chatbots are used to provide personalized learning(Gudoniene et al., 2024). Moreover, adaptive learning platforms like Duolingo and Squirrel AI dynamically further adjust content and difficulty to suit the continuous needs of learners(Coşulean, 2024; Wang, 2025). In addition, AI-driven feedback systems and automated grading tools assist educators in managing instructional load and offering timely support(Vetrivel et al., 2025). In this case, students' learning habits, abilities, and preferences can be identified by these advanced technologies. Therefore, it is possible to provide students with customized personalized learning content and teaching methods. These technologies are likely to improve teaching quality and efficiency (L. Chen et al., 2020). For educators, the implementation of AI and DL can not only enrich learning content but also leverage their potential for prediction to help educators better monitor students' learning during the learning process. In this way, instructors are likely to know better students' needs and adjust their instructional strategies timely manner. To sum up, it can be concluded that AI and DL have broad prospects for application in education to bring out a smarter and more effective learning experience (Paek & Kim, 2021).

Besides that, many studies have proposed that the implementation of AI and DL must face several challenges or issues, such as Technical issues(Oche et al., 2021), high costs(Ramessur et al., 2021), ethical issues(Groumpos, 2023), data security(Wellnhofer, 2022), etc. Considering this, it is crucial to identify the current status, impact, and challenges of AI and DL in education, as well as provide suggestions for future development to optimize their implementation. Therefore, a systematic literature review is needed to evaluate their impacts and propose constructive recommendations for future agenda.

From a methodology perspective, the innovation of this study is to combine bibliometric analysis and systematic literature review (SLR) utilizing the PRISMA framework proposed by Moher et al. (2009). Following the previous studies, many scholars have implemented these methodologies to make a significant contribution to this field. For example, Abuhassna, Adnan, et al. (2024) have combined bibliometrics and a systematic literature review to examine the relevant literature about the integration of instructional design models and learning theories. This analysis provided robust evidence for how instructional design models and learning theories can be integrated effectively. Additionally, Abuhassna, Awae, et al. (2024) have also used this approach to provide a comprehensive understanding of the application of artificial intelligence (AI) and deep learning (DL) in education, and also proposed future research directions and suggestions. In another study, Abuhassna, Alnawajha, et al. (2024) looked into the integration of the ADDIE model with technology into instructional design. They discussed its impact, advantages as well as technologies and platforms used, and proposed future suggestions for future research. Therefore, building on these foundations, we will use this dual-method approach to delve deeper into the role of AI and DL in education to strengthen our understandings and applications.

The bibliometric analysis helped us identify the main trends, hot spots, and key contributors in the field, while the systematic literature review further validated and enriched these findings, providing deep insights into the application of AI and DL in education. Through this innovative research design, this paper can comprehensively evaluate the impact of AI and DL technologies in education and offer new perspectives and in-depth analysis for future development in educational technology.

To achieve the objective of this study, this review will be structured into two main phases: a bibliometric analysis and a systematic literature review. The following questions are posed for the first phase of this review (the bibliometric analysis):

(1) What are the top publication years, countries or districts, educational institutions, journals, authors, subject areas, and keywords for integrating Artificial Intelligence (AI) and Deep Learning (DL) in education?

The questions below are used to address the second phase of this review(the systematic literature review):

(2) What are the applications of AI and ML in education, and what impact do they have?
(3) What variables does research focus on in AI and DL in education?
(4) What are the findings or trends in AI and DL research in education?
(5) What are the primary challenges or limitations of AI and DL research in education?
(6) What are the future directions for AI and DL research in education?

2. MATERIALS AND METHODS

2.1 Research Design

The objective of this review is to understand comprehensively the issues and hot points of the integration of AI/DL into education. To achieve this, bibliometric analysis and systematic literature review were implemented. Firstly, we used bibliometric analysis to conduct a quantitative analysis of relevant literature in the past ten years(2014-2023) based on the Scopus database. We outlined the research hotspots and development trends by counting the top publication years, countries or districts, educational institutions, authors, journals, and keywords.

With this strong foundation, the researchers conducted a systematic literature review to dive further into specific issues in this area. After specifying the research objectives, we developed comprehensive inclusion and exclusion criteria to search and screen the relevant literature. Based on a deep analysis of this literature, we gain a thorough understanding of the integration of AI/DL into education and the challenges they face. The systematic literature review not only enables us to evaluate and enrich the findings of Bibliometric analysis, provides profound insights into research issues relevant, but also highlights the future research direction in this field.

To make sure this review is comprehensive and systematic, we implemented a standardized reporting process named the PRISMA framework(Moher et al., 2009). PRISMA FRAMEWORK is the preferred tool for researchers to conduct systematic literature reviews, as it provides scientific and rigorous guidelines to improve the quality and validity of literature reviews. Figure 1 enlists the PRISMA FRAMEWORK employed in this study.

2.2 Search Strategy

Scopus was selected as the database for this study. Because it is one of the largest databases that covers a wide range of academic journals, conference papers, and documents from different disciplines. The search for articles on this research started in June 2024. The keywords such as "Artificial intelligence", "Deep learning", and "education" were all implemented. The initial draft of this study included 1183 articles found. Then, a list of Boolean operators was used to obtain a more accurate result, such as TITLE-ABS-KEY ("AI" AND "deep learning" AND "education") AND PUBYEAR > 2013 AND PUBYEAR < 2024 AND (LIMIT-TO (SUBJAREA, "COMP") OR LIMIT-TO (SUBJAREA, "SOCI") OR LIMIT-TO (SUBJAREA, "ARTS")) AND (LIMIT-TO (LANGUAGE, "English")) AND (LIMIT-TO (DOCTYPE, "ar")). Through this phase, 693 articles were found in this research.

Then, we conducted a bibliometric analysis based on these 693 articles to identify the trends and research patterns in this field. In addition, to ensure the distribution and application of research findings, in the meantime to enhance the clarity and significance of literature reviews. We added inclusion criteria as "AND (LIMIT-TO (OA, "all"))", which resulted in 137 articles found in the Scopus database. We tried to download these 137 articles, and at last, only 62 articles were downloaded successfully, and 75 articles were excluded. We do the first quality assessment on these 62 articles. The publications that were not related to artificial intelligence, deep learning, and education, or that any of the above three keywords were missing, were excluded. Through this phase, 27 articles were retained and 35 articles were excluded. Therefore, in this study, 27 papers were used in the systematic literature review. Table 1 outlines the specific inclusion and exclusion criteria for this study.

Figure 1. Prisma framework

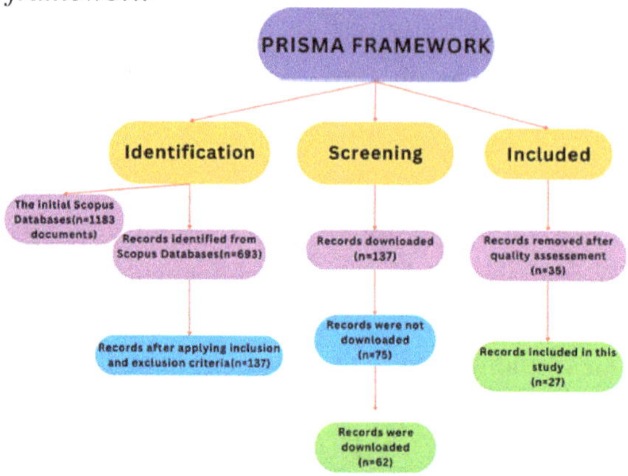

Table 1. The inclusion and exclusion criteria

Inclusion Criteria	Exclusion Criteria
Publication from 2014 to 2023	Publications before 2013 were not accepted, and as 2024 is not yet over, publications in 2024 were also not accepted.
Articles only	Conferences, blogs, theses, and book chapters
Written in English.	Studies that do not specifically focus on AI and DL in education will be excluded.
Subject area (social science, computer, and arts).	Any other subject area.

2.3 Data Synthesis and Analysis

After selecting articles from the Scopus database, we will do data synthesis and analysis. This phase aims to identify the main themes, research types, trends, limitations, and future directions related to the impact of the integration of AI/DL into education. The steps taken in this phase will be detailed as follows:

Method:

In this study, we employed content analysis to identify and classify the main aspects of the integration of AL/DL into education.

Process:

1. Publications Review

We conducted a thorough review of the articles included in this study to find out the research objectives, challenges, and limitations considering the integration of AL/DL into education.

2. Classification

We categorized the themes, trends, difficulties, and future agendas according to their types.

Outcome:

The result of this analysis not only provides the challenges or strengths of the impact of AI/DL on education but also draws a blueprint for future research.

2.4 Research Questions

The results of this review are used to address the research questions outlined in the introduction.

3. RESULTS

To achieve the objective of our study, we employ bibliometric analysis and a systematic literature review (SLR). The combination of these two analyses can propose not only a broad perspective of this field but also offer an in-depth analysis of this topic.

The bibliometric analysis helps us identify the main trends and patterns in the research field, highlighting the research dynamics and hot spots. Following this, we conducted a systematic literature review to further delve into these identified topics, allowing us to analyze the details of relevant literature.

This combination of two methods ensures that our study is coherent and systematic. Bibliometric analysis reveals the broad overview and background of this topic, while the systematic literature review offers detailed insights to enrich our findings. Through these methods, we can validate and expand our conclusions drawn from each method.

3.1 The First Phase (Bibliometric Analysis)

Artificial intelligence (AI) and deep learning (DL) are changing traditional teaching models and making education more personalized and efficient(L. Chen et al., 2020). Considering this, it's very important to understand comprehensively AI and deep learning in education to understand the critical insights that can impact the future development of education in a technology-driven world. In the continuously developing area of AI and Deep learning in education, to achieve this objective, bibliometric analysis becomes an essential instrument to evaluate the academic landscape in this field. It involves a systematic approach to assessing the body of work on AI and DL in education to identify the research topic and development direction. In addition, bibliometric analysis highlights the productive journals or authors by conducting citation counts. Besides that, it illustrates collaborative networks between academics and institutions. With these approaches, bibliometrics reveals the development context of this field and outlines a blueprint for the future development of AI and DL in education.

In this first phase of bibliometric analysis, VOSviewer software was used to identify the top publication years, countries or districts, educational institutions, authors, journals, and keywords related to the integration of AI/DL into education.

3.1.1 What are the Top Publication Years, Countries or Districts, Educational Institutions, Journals, Authors, Subject Areas, and Keywords for Integrating Artificial Intelligence (AI) and Deep Learning (DL) in Education?

1) The top publication years in the field of integration of AL/DL into education

According to the results presented in Figure 2, Before 2019, the publications in this field were relatively low, indicating that the integration of artificial intelligence and deep learning received less attention in the education field. However, the quantity of publications on AL/DL integration into education increased significantly in recent years, particularly in 2023, when the number of publications reached a peak of 289, highlighting that the integration of AL/DL into education has emerged as a prominent research field.

Figure 2. Publication distributions by years in the field of integration of AL/DL into education

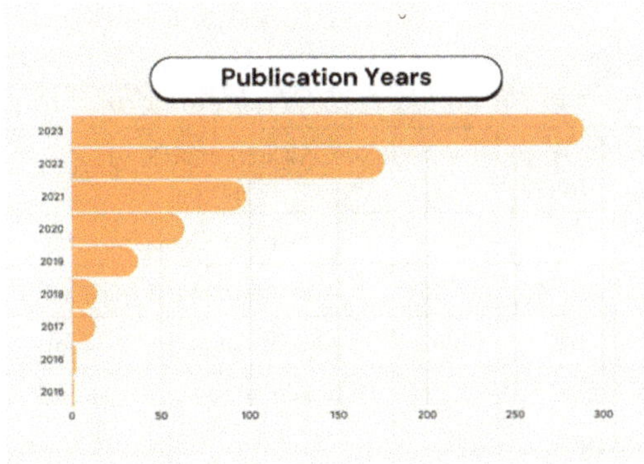

2) The top educational institutions in the field of AI/DL integration into education

Figure 3 lists the top 10 productive educational institutions in the field of AI/DL integration with education. Among these educational institutions, Zhejiang University and University College Dublin have a significant impact on the academic landscape, as presented by their publications of 7. Other prominent educational institutions, including King Abdulaziz University and the Sri Lanka Institute of Information Technology, also have notable contributions with 6. Following closely are the University of Hong Kong, University of Toronto, Chandigarh University, and Uttaranchal University, with publications of 5. The work of these educational institutions plays an important role in integrating AI and DL into education and has led to more personalized and effective learning experiences.

Figure 3. Top 10 educational institutions in the field of AI/DL integration into education

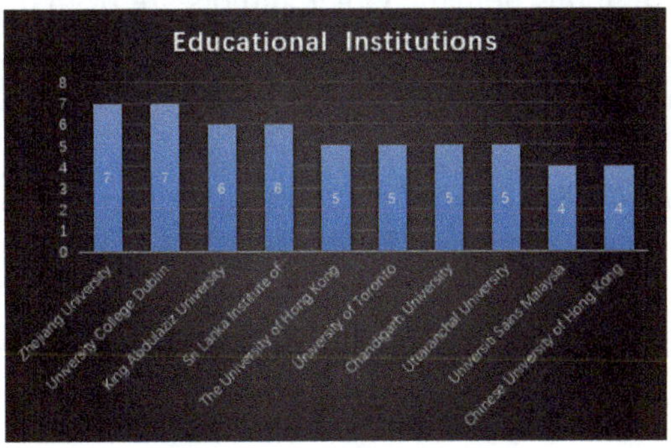

(3) *The top authors in the field of AI/DL integration with education in China.*

Table 2. The top authors in the field of AI/DL integration into education

Author	TP	H-Index	TC	Current affiliation	Country/Districts
Becker, Brett A.	122	27	2514	University College Dublin	Ireland
Denny, Paul C.	152	33	3745	The University of Auckland	New Zealand
Prather, James	34	17	1002	Abilene Christian University	United States
Shaik, Thanveer Basha	15	6	189	University of Southern Queensland	Australia
Bosch, Jan	454	53	10538	Chalmers University of Technology	Sweden
Chatterjee, Indranath	45	8	189	Manchester Metropolitan University	United Kingdom
Cho, Gyusung	45	6	192	TongMyong University	South Korea
Dann, Christopher Ewart	25	4	88	University of Southern Queensland	Australia
Dzhusupova, Rimma	7	4	24	Technische Universiteit Eindhoven	Netherlands
Finnie-Ansley, James	7	5	318	The University of Auckland	New Zealand
Hwang, Gwojen	572	80	24288	National Taiwan University of Science and Technology	TaiWan

Table 2 shows the notable authors of AI/DL integration. This review analyzed 10 outstanding authors who have made important contributions to the rapidly expanding field of AI/DL integration in education. Among these authors, Becker, Brett A., stands out with numerous publications of 122, an H-index of 27, and a total citation of 2514. His affiliation with University College Dublin in Ireland illustrates his expertise in this domain. Other authors are from different universities and academic organizations. Their continuous work defines the landscape of AI/DL integration into education.

(4) *The top journals that focus on AI/DL integration into education*

Table 3. The top journals that focus on AI/DL integration into education

Journal	TP	TC	Cite score	Publisher
Lecture Notes in Computer Science	76955	203812	2.6	Springer Nature
Communications in Computer and Information Science	21959	23780	1.1	Springer Nature
IEEE Access	49687	484743	9.8	IEEE
Lecture Notes in Networks and Systems	41485	35811	0.9	Springer Nature
LNICST	6071	3929	0.6	Springer Nature
Sensors	35041	256060	7.3	MDPI
Advances in Intelligent Systems and Computing	29624	26852	0.9	Springer Nature
Sustainability (Switzerland)	55991	381357	6.8	MDPI
International Journal of Advanced Computer Science and Applications	4997	11686	2.3	Science and Information Organization
Applied Sciences	44530	237130	5.3	MDPI

Table 3 lists a comprehensive analysis of the top 10 journals of AL/DL integration in education. Lecture Notes in Computer Science stands out with the highest total publication of 76955, reflecting its important position in this area. The other two journals, IEEE Access from IEEE and Sustainability from MDPI, with 484743 and 381357 total citations, respectively, also have a significant role in AL/DL integration in education. These journals, as well as others on the table, illustrate diverse contributions and significant influence in the development of AI/DL integration into education.

(5) *The countries or districts focus on AI/DL integration into education.*

Figure 4. Top 10 countries in publications on AL/DL integration into education

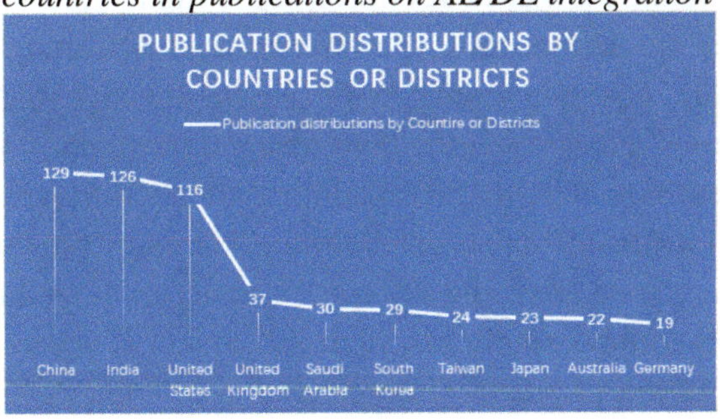

Figure 4 illustrates the publication distributions by countries or districts in the field of integration of AL/DL into education. Among these countries, China stands out with 129 papers, illustrating that it is very advanced in this field. India follows closely, with 126 publications, indicating that it also has high interest and investment in AL/DL integration into education. The United States ranks third with 116 papers. It proves that its research in this field is also very important. In general, some Asia countries, like China, India, South Korea, and Japan, are major countries that contribute to this field. In addition, the United States and the UK, as important Western countries, have also shown continued research interest in this field. Figure 5 shows the leading countries in publications on AL/DL integration into education.

Figure 5. Publication distributions by countries

(6) *The top keywords used in publications in the field of AI/DL integration with education*

Figure 6 displays the most used keywords in the field of AI/DL integration into education. An in-depth analysis of the keywords in AL/DL integration reveals the phrases that play the most important role in shaping this dynamic and developing field. "Deep learning" emerges as the dominant subject among these terms, This means that deep learning not only receives more attention in research but also has strong correlations with other topics. In addition, "learning systems" closely follow, demonstrating research on "learning systems" also occupies an important position. Moreover, some other important terms, such as "students", show that many studies focus on the integration of AL/DL into education to enhance students' learning experience. At last, "Artificial intelligence" with 90 occurrences, and a total link strength of 648, indicating the increasing acceptance of artificial intelligence as a popular technology in the domain of education.

Figure 6. The most used keywords in the field of AL/DL integration into education

3.2 The Second Phase (the Systematic Literature Review, SLR)

The second phase(Systematic literature review) provided comprehensive new insights into the integration of AI/DL into education. These insights include common themes, significant findings, emerging trends, primary challenges, and future agendas.

3.2.1 What are the Applications of AI and ML in Education, and What Impact Do They Have?

This part focuses on the applications of AI/DL and their impact on education. The most important results are shown in Table 4.

Table 4. Applications of AI and DL and Their Impact on Education

Studies	AI and DL application	Impact on Education
Li and Mohamad (2023)	Latent Dirichlet Integrated Deep Learning (LDiDL)	This paper discusses the LDiDL model to assess and enhance students' English Oral proficiency. This study demonstrates that the LDiDL model is a potential AI tool based on deep learning to improve learning outcomes and provide personalized learning.
Shu and Gu (2023)	The Edu-Metaverse is based on smart education	This paper examines the Edu-Metaverse model in education. This method aims to enhance students' learning outcomes.
Koć-Januchta et al. (2022)	AI-enriched biology book	It examines how AI-enriched biology books have been used in education. This method optimizes cognitive load for deeper learning in higher education.

continued on following page

Table 4. Continued

Studies	AI and DL application	Impact on Education
Fahd and Miah (2023)	Big Data Analytical Solution (BDAS)	Big Data Analytical Solution (BDAS) was used in this study. This may predict student success factors and improve students' learning.
N. D. Alqahtani et al. (2023)	Hybrid AI Approach(CNN-SVM and CNN-RF)	Hybrid models (CNN-SVM and CNN-RF) are dyslexia detection which were used in this study to provide more informed and timely educational interventions.
Z. Chen et al. (2020)	Hybridized Deep Neural Network (HDNN) in education 4.0	This study highlighted the importance of Hybridized Deep Neural Network (HDNN) in education 4.0 to improve student performance analysis and promote personalized learning.
Babu et al. (2023)	Metaheuristic Optimization-based Feature Subset Selection with an Optimal Deep Learning Model (MOFSS-ODL)	This article introduced the MOFSS-ODL model in education to improve students' learning outcomes by predicting student performance and providing personalized feedback.
Shi et al. (2023)	Smart Classroom Teaching Model	This research proposed a Smart Classroom Teaching Model to provide a personalized learning experience and enhance teaching effectiveness.
Winiarti et al. (2022)	Convolutional Neural Network (CNN) method based on AI/DL	This research demonstrated the implementation of the Convolutional Neural Network (CNN) method based on AI/DL in cultural education and preserving traditional knowledge.
Chaudhry et al. (2023)	Evaluation Approach in Higher Education(ChatGPT)	This paper highlights the importance of AI tools, such as ChatGPT, in educational practice.
Lee and Kim (2023)	Metaverse-based education	It introduces Metaverse-based Education aims to encourage student engagement and immersive learning
Shiao et al. (2023)	Dropout risk prediction model	The dropout risk prediction model was used in this study to identify high-risk students and to reduce the dropout rate.
Trabelsi et al. (2023)	Real-Time Attention Monitoring System: YOLOv5 Model	A new monitoring system: the YOLOv5 Model was employed in education to evaluate student engagement, to help teachers provide personalized instructions
Yang (2022)	Natural Language Processing (NLP), Character-level recurrent neural network with Back Propagation neural network (Cha_RNN_ BPNN)	This study elaborates on Character-level recurrent neural networks with Back Propagation neural networks (Cha_RNN_BPNN) to enhance English language education and improve students' learning outcomes
Xu et al. (2023)	Agar phantom model and deep learning technique	This article presents an AI based on a deep-learning model using the Agar phantom model to assist medical students learn ultrasound quickly and safely.
Alhazmi et al. (2023)	XLNet neural network model	The XLNet neural network model was implemented in this research to analyze students' emotions, guiding students' improvement in learning.
Latif et al. (2023)	The Internet of Things (IoT)-Based AI-Powered Braille Learning System	This paper presents the Internet of Things (IoT)- based AI-powered Braille Learning System to help visually impaired people in education and communication.
Rathod et al. (2022)	LIRIS Children Spontaneous Facial Expression Video Database, a dataset of emotions, LIRIS-Mesh, Authors-Mesh, and explainable artificial intelligence (XAI)	This study creates the LIRIS Children Spontaneous Facial Expression Video Database to identify children's emotions in online learning and to further improve teacher-student interaction.
Albdrani and Al-Shargabi (2023)	Chatgpt with 5Es model	This study highlights the importance of ChatGPT in education with its potential for personalized learning and timely feedback.
AL-Ghamdi et al. (2022)	Artificial Intelligence-Based Cybersecurity Intrusion Detection Model(AICIDHEI) technique.	This research introduces the AICIDHEI technique, which integrates AI and DL for higher education security and efficiency.
Gomaa et al. (2023)	Transformer-Based Embeddings and BI-LSTM Network	The study introduces Transformer-Based Embedding and BI-LSTM Networks in education for short answer scoring and accurate assessment.

continued on following page

Table 4. Continued

Studies	AI and DL application	Impact on Education
Michel-Villarreal et al. (2023)	Artificial intelligence, deep learning, and ChatGPT	This study emphasizes the importance of ChatGPT in higher education and calls for more research and guidelines on ChatGPT.
Kumar et al. (2023)	Deep-learning-based Automatic Essay Scoring (AES)	This study exposes the Deep-learning-based Automatic Essay Scoring (AES) in essay scoring.
Alghamdi and Ragab (2022)	SRODL-LAC technique, median filtering (MF), Densely Connected Networks (DenseNet-77), Search and rescue optimization (SRO) algorithm	SRODL-LAC technique based on an AI biometric system was employed in Higher education to ensure cybersecurity and service quality.
Omarov et al. (2023)	PoseNet-enabled deep neural network	It proposes a PoseNet-enabled deep neural network based on an AI-driven system to identify the issues in physical education and to improve personalized and effective physical learning.
Aljohani et al. (2022)	A framework to predict future skills needs based on AI and big data.	This research elaborates a framework based on AI and big data to predict future skills needed in the Saudi education job market, aiming to align education with industry needs in Saudi Arabia.

Table 4 outlines the application of AI/DL and its impact on education. In summary, AI/DL is transforming the education field by providing personalized learning, encouraging student engagement, and predicting the needs of future education. Moreover, by identifying and monitoring students' emotions and behaviors, the application of AI/DL in education not only helps teachers provide timely feedback and support but also enhances their learning outcomes and efficiency. For example, an intelligent tutoring system, such as Squirrel AI, offers personalized and timely feedback through analysis of learners' data (Cai & Liu, 2024). Additionally, ChatGPT assists educators in generating lesson content, providing feedback, reducing preparation time, and realizing adaptive instruction(ElSayary, 2024). Furthermore, AI chatbots like Edmodo Assistant facilitate conversational support, helping students solve problems independently and promoting self-directed learning (Alisoy & Sadiqzade, 2024). These AI-powered tools explained how artificial intelligence makes instruction more personalized, responsive, and effective.

To further understand the overall impact of AI/DL in education, it is necessary to understand the new opportunities created by AI techniques for educational development. This will be explained in detail in the next part.

3.2.2 What Variables Does Research Focus on Regarding AI and DL in Education?

The applications of AI/DL in education have created lots of possibilities to enrich students' learning experiences and improve their learning outcomes. This section takes a comprehensive exploration of the variables related to AI/DL applications in education, as outlined in Table 5.

Table 5. Variables related to AI/DL applications in education

Studies	AI and DL variables	AI and DL impact
Li and Mohamad (2023)	Students' English proficiency assessment	Using the LDiDL framework based on AI to evaluate Students' English oral proficiency and provide personalized suggestions.
Shu and Gu (2023)	Students learning outcome	Using an Edu-Metaverse-backed smart education model based on AI and DL to improve student learning outcomes.
Koć-Januchta et al. (2022)	Students' three sub-types of cognitive load and their relationship with learning gain, self-regulated learning, and usability perception	Exploring the impact of the AI-enriched biology book, which integrates AI and DL, on students' cognitive load as well as their relationship with learning gain, self-regulated learning, and usability perception
Fahd and Miah (2023)	Students success factors	Developing an AI tool to predict students' success factors and to provide personalized learning.
N. D. Alqahtani et al. (2023)	Identification of Dyslexia via Handwriting Image Analysis.	AI might be used to resolve special issues, for example, detecting Dyslexia by analyzing handwriting images.
Z. Chen et al. (2020)	Students performance	These references belong to AI-driven tests and data analysis for predicting students' performance and providing personalized learning.
Babu et al. (2023)	Students Academic Performance	AI is expected to be used in higher education to improve students' academic performance.
Shi, Muhammad Umer, & Shi (2023)	Effectiveness of college-level English education	AI may be used to optimize the effectiveness of blended learning in college-level English education.
Winiarti et al. (2022)	To identify the type of building using deep learning and AI	AI will likely be used not only to identify and classify traditional Indonesian architectural styles but also to enhance students' understanding of their history and culture as an educational tool.
Chaudhry et al. (2023)	Student's Performance in Higher Education	It is possible to use AI and DL in higher education, especially ChatGPT, to predict and enhance student performance.
Lee and Kim (2023)	Learners' focus and immersion	AI may be used to improve and optimize learners' focus and immersion.
Shiao et al. (2023)	Students drop out and learning outcomes	This might demonstrate the use of AI to reduce students' dropouts and enhance their learning outcomes.
Trabelsi et al. (2023)	Students' emotions, attendance, and attention levels	AI might be used to monitor and assess students' engagement and attention in learning.
Yang (2022)	Students' English learning outcomes	This might include investigating how learners can benefit from NLP, especially in English learning

continued on following page

Table 5. Continued

Studies	AI and DL variables	AI and DL impact
Xu et al. (2023)	Students ultrasound skills	This reference examines how AI/DL is incorporated into the training of ultrasound-guided technology to Enhance the speed and accuracy of learners' acquired skills
Alhazmi et al. (2023) and Rathod et al. (2022)	Students' emotions	Using AI/DL to analyze students' emotions to enhance the quality of education is certainly involved in these articles.
Latif et al. (2023)	Arabic and English bilingual individuals' learning outcomes	Applications of AI/DL in education can improve Arabic and English bilingual individuals quality of life
Albdrani and Al-Shargabi (2023)	Students learning	The significance of AI in providing personalized learning is the focus of this study.
Pucchio et al. (2022)	Students' perceptions of AI	How students perceive the use of AI in the learning environment is the concern of this study.
AL-Ghamdi et al. (2022) and Alghamdi and Ragab (2022)	Intrusion detection in higher education	In higher education, AI/DL can tackle intrusion detection to ensure the security of educational networks.
Gomaa et al. (2023)	Short Answer Grading	Short Answer Grading systems powered by AI are meant to enhance accuracy and efficiency, save teacher time, and improve learning outcomes.
Michel-Villarreal et al. (2023)	Challenges and Opportunities of Generative AI	This article highlighted the impact of AI on higher education.
Kumar et al. (2023)	Effectiveness of Automatic Essay Scoring (AES)	The optimization of AES based on AI is the focus of this study
Omarov et al. (2023)	Athletes' technique and performance	Using AI techniques in physical education to improve students' performance is involved.
Aljohani et al. (2022)	Student satisfaction, retention, and employability,	This reference belongs to AI-based analysis of big data to predict the future market's demand for sustainable skills.

The results of the table above highlight the various applications of AI/DL in education, including students' learning outcomes, students' engagement, language proficiency, and security of educational networks. In addition, the potential of AI to provide personalized learning, predict students' performance, and optimize instructional support demonstrates that the integration of AI/DL into education is revolutionary.

To deepen our understanding with a thorough perspective, we should explore how AI techniques are transforming the educational environment nowadays. Based on an in-depth analysis of the significant impact of AI/DL applications on education, we can find out their potential not only to improve students' learning outcomes but also to establish a new paradigm for teaching and learning.

3.2.3 What are the Significant Findings or Emerging Trends in AI and DL Research in Education?

Based on the review paper, we can have a comprehensive understanding of how AI/DL is transforming the learning environment by emphasizing the significant findings or emerging trends of the integration of AI/DL into education. The applications of AI/DL are advancing the development and innovation of educational technology. In the Li and Mohamad (2023) study, a framework named LDiDL, an AI tool based on a deep learning model, can be used to provide accurate assessments of English speaking proficiency and improve English learners' learning outcomes. An Intelligent education platform of AI, such as Edu-Metaverse, is illustrated in the study of Shu and Gu (2023), which has significantly improved English learners' performance and virtual technologies. The study of Koć-Januchta et al. (2022) proposed AI textbooks based on a deep learning model to reduce students' cognitive load. And AI tools, such as the BDAS technique, have achieved more accuracy in predicting students' academic performance(Fahd & Miah, 2023).

Moreover, the applications of AI/DL have made great progress in the special education domain. For example, the CNN-SVM model(N. D. Alqahtani et al., 2023), which integrates AI and DL, has achieved a significant accuracy rate of 99.33% in identifying children's dyslexia. This technique has the potential to identify the difficulties during children's learning, provide appropriate instructional support, and ultimately improve their reading skills. Considering the history and cultural education, the Convolutional Neural Network (CNN) method based on the AI/DL model has shown great effectiveness of 97% in recognizing traditional architectural styles. In this way, the AI technique significantly assists the preservation and instruction of traditional culture. In terms of medical education, the AI technique is considered an effective tool due to its ability to provide personalized learning and analyze large amounts of data(Pucchio et al., 2022).

In addition, AI and DL implementation have enriched the educational content and instructional strategies, and in the meantime, boosted the innovation of educational technology. The study of Trabelsi et al. (2023) proposed automatic attention assessment systems to measure students' emotions and attention during learning, meanwhile, the personalized instructional guidance provided by AI based on deep learning aims to reduce students' dropout rate and enhance their engagement in learning(Shiao et al., 2023). The AI-driven Braille learning system based on Internet technology improves Braille learning and visually impaired people's reading abilities and communication(Latif et al., 2023). In terms of data analysis, models such as Character-level recurrent neural networks effectively classify a large amount of discussion forum data and provide in-depth insights into teaching (Yang, 2022). These studies not only improve the personalization and interactivity of education but also provide educators with richer teaching resources and more effective teaching strategies.

Overall, the AI technique is transforming different areas of education. These papers just provided a comprehensive view of AI's impact on the learning environment.

3.2.4 What are the Primary Challenges or Limitations of AI and DL Research in Education?

Although the applications of AI/DL are full of potential in the education domain, they also face some challenges. Shu and Gu (2023) highlight the challenges with technological immaturity, high implementation costs, lack of human-computer interaction, front-line teachers or instructional designers, and lower levels of students' core literacy. According to Koć-Januchta et al. (2022), new limitations for AI textbooks are difficulties in the measurement of cognitive load, difficulties of AI textbook design, students' self-regulation skills, and limitations of instruments' validity and reliability. Reference of N. D. Alqahtani et al. (2023) demonstrates the effectiveness of Dyslexia via Handwriting Image Analysis as well as its limitations, such as limited handwriting datasets for children with dyslexia and research relevance. Section Shi, Muhammad Umer, & Shi(2023) identify the benefits of the Smart Classroom Teaching Model in enhancing English students' learning outcomes, while it also underlines the need for more research to test the reliability of the teaching model. The study of Chaudhry et al. (2023) highlight the need for more research on students' learning affected by AI.

Moreover, Lee and Kim (2023) emphasize AI's potential to improve students' immersion and focus, but the limitation of generalization is the main challenge of this study. Considering the prediction of AI tools, Shiao et al. (2023) underscore AI's development in the future to reduce students' dropout rates and encourage them to learn. Trabelsi et al. (2023) emphasize the need for a larger dataset for deep-learning neural networks to work effectively. Xu et al. (2023) highlight the necessity of clearer pictures and accurate labels for the identification of AI tools. Albdrani and Al-Shargabi (2023) and Michel-Villarreal et al. (2023) stress the potential of ChatGPT but highlight the problems with sample size and technical issues. Pucchio et al. (2022) investigate students' perception of AI but also acknowledge its limitations, with the lack of AI training, educational opportunities, and curriculum being the main challenges. In summary, although AI and DL have great potential in education, their value can only be fully realized by addressing the identified technical and implementation challenges.

3.2.5 What are the Future Directions for AI and DL Research in Education?

Based on examining the significant findings or emerging trends of AI/DL, we can observe that the integration of AI/DL is transforming the education field. This section will try to highlight the potential of AI techniques and propose future directions and recommendations to facilitate their continued development in the education domain.

Li and Mohamad (2023) highlight the importance of NLP models to do language evaluation and enhancing spoken language proficiency. Shu and Gu (2023) call for more Edu-Metaverse-based on smart education should be used at a variety of levels of education. Koć-Januchta et al. (2022) emphasize that the investigation of AI textbooks should be expanded to improve students' learning outcomes. In the digital era, AI techniques such as Big Data Analytical Solutions (BDAS) (Fahd & Miah, 2023), the HDNN model in education 4.0(Z. Chen et al., 2020), MOFSS-ODL(Babu et al., 2023), Chatgpt(Chaudhry et al., 2023), Metaverse-based education, Dropout risk prediction model(Shiao et al., 2023), SRODL-LAC technique(Alghamdi & Ragab, 2022) need to be fully implemented to test their efficiency, in predicting students' performance. According to N. D. Alqahtani et al. (2023), a bigger and more comprehensive dataset is stressed for children with dyslexia. Accordingly, Lee and Kim (2023) suggest that the continuous experiment size should be expanded to realize the generalization of the future study. Considering the potential ability of AI tools to provide personalized learning and guidance, some research, for example, Shiao et al. (2023), Yang (2022), Albdrani and Al-Shargabi (2023), and Michel-Villarreal et al. (2023), suggests that more empirical research needs to be conducted to strengthen the potential of AI techniques. In terms of the automatic scoring system, Gomaa et al. (2023) and Kumar et al. (2023) advise that the accuracy and simplicity of the system to be the focus of future work. The studies of Shiao et al. (2023), Babu et al. (2023), Z. Chen et al. (2020) and Aljohani et al. (2022) propose that the prediction of AI tools needs to be improved in the future.

In conclusion, these studies shed light on the pathway of AI/DL in the future, with ongoing research to improve the accuracy, efficiency, and efficacy of the AI technique. By addressing the challenges faced and expanding the perspectives of empirical research, AI/DL can ultimately transformthe learning environment, which will result in a more personalized, effective, and efficient learning experience.

4. DISCUSSION

This review comprehensively analyzes the current state, applications, impacts, and future trends of integrating artificial intelligence (AI) and deep learning (DL) in education. Firstly, there is a significant increase in papers published on AI/DL in education in 2023. Secondly, leading countries such as China, India, and the United States, as well as major educational institutions, like Zhejiang University and University College Dublin, have made great contributions in this field. In addition, AI/DL technology has the potential to provide personalized learning and data analysis, which in turn improves learning outcomes and educational security. Various case studies have demonstrated the effectiveness of AI in real classroom applications. According to Wang (2025), Squirrel AI has been used to deliver adaptive learning based on student performance to boost learner engagement and achievement. Another study of Attah et al. (2024) showed that Quizalize, an AI-enhanced formative assessment platform, has been adopted to provide automated feedback based on students' performance. During the application of AI/DL in instruction, the teacher plays a crucial role in successful AI integration. Therefore, many studies indicated that targeted professional development is essential to reduce resistance and promote effective application(Shakimova et al., 2024; Tomaskinova & Tomaskin, 2024). For example, Ding et al. (2024) showed that case-based training improved teachers' confidence and readiness to apply AI tools. Moreover, Kayal (2024) emphasized the need for support and pedagogical alignment to ensure meaningful AI integration.

Although AI and deep learning technologies show great potential in education, they also face some challenges. For example, insufficient technological maturity, high cost, and lack of human-computer interaction have limited their widespread use in education. Finally, it proposes future research directions, recommending improvements in the predictive capabilities and personalized guidance of AI technology through empirical research and the expansion of datasets. These steps are aimed at fostering innovation and development in education.

RQ1: What are the top publication years, countries or districts, educational institutions, journals, authors, subject areas, and keywords for integrating Artificial Intelligence(AI) and Deep Learning(DL) in education?

In the first section of this review, we conduct a bibliometric analysis to provide comprehensive insights into the integration of AI/DL into education from a worldwide perspective. Accordingly, the bibliometric analysis aims to address the first research question of this study. The year with the highest number of publications is 2023, indicating that after the COVID-19 pandemic, the integration of AI/DL into education has become a significant research field all over the world. Zhejiang University, University College Dublin, King Abdulaziz University, and Sri Lanka Institute of Information Technology are cutting-edge AI and DL in education, exemplifying their excellent research that is shaping the future of educational technology. Reputable authors, such as Becker, Brett A, with 122 total publications from Ireland, Denny. Paul C, with 152 total publications from New Zealand, their output research has promoted

the comprehension and implementation of AI and DL in education. The top countries, headed by China, with 129 articles, and followed by India and the United States with 126 and 116 articles respectively, are at the forefront of worldwide research in AI and DL in education. The keywords "deep learning" and "Artificial intelligence" reflect not only their substantial impact on the education domain but also their collaborative character, which has strong correlations with other topics, like machine learning, data analysis, personalized learning, educational psychology, prediction of data, and instructional design.

RQ2 and RQ3: What are the applications of AI and ML in education, and what impact do they have? What variables does research focus on regarding AI and DL in education?

In the second phase, a systematic literature review is conducted to further analyze the specific issue of applications of AI and DL in education and also to answer the second research question of this study. The extent of AI techniques in education covers educational network security, learning systems, administrative automation, and smart education, while deep learning in education includes: Convolutional Neural Networks (CNN), Natural language processing(NLP), personalized learning, data analysis, prediction of student performance, etc. The integration of AI and DL has a significant impact on education, such as reducing students' dropout rates, improving learning outcomes, saving teachers' time, enhancing student engagement, and strengthening the security of the learning environment by predicting students' performance, providing personalized learning guidance, advanced analytics, and natural language processing. The integration of AI and DL is employed in various aspects of the education area, predicting that their applications in education are revolutionary.

RQ4: What are the significant findings or emerging trends in AI and DL research in education?

The third research question aims to investigate the integration of AI and DL into education by identifying the main findings and emerging trends. The integration of AI and DL is used to provide an accurate assessment of students' performance, predict students' emotions in learning, and provide timely personalized instructional support. In sum, these studies emphasize their revolutionary impact on different aspects of the education area, like fertilizing and innovating learning content, instructional strategies, and technology.

RQ5: What are the primary challenges or limitations of AI and DL research in education?

To address the fourth research question, this review analyzes the main challenges of applications of AI and DL. Technological immaturity, high costs, limited human-computer interaction, issues with core literacy among students, and limited sample size are the main obstacles to the future development of AI and DL. Besides that, the importance of instruments' validity and reliability is highlighted. Moreover, the need for more AI training and educational opportunities to maximize AI's benefits is stressed. Overall, it is necessary to address these challenges to realize the substantial progress of AI and DL in education.

Some institutions and stakeholders have started to take action to address these issues. For instance, to deal with ethical issues, AI ethics committees have been established in some schools to create clear rules exemplifying the collection and application of student and staff data(Mouta et al., 2025). Moreover, Nigerian universities are turning to free or open-source platforms, sharing digital resources between institutions to reduce the high cost of AI(Peter et al., 2024). At the same time, teacher training programs are being provided to support instructors in integrating AI tools into real teaching practice(Ding et al., 2024; Ismail et al., 2024).

RQ6: What are the future directions for AI and DL research in education?

The sixth research question refers to providing suggestions for the future development of AI and DL. AI is considered an instrument to improve the learning experience and student performance. Therefore, future work should focus on the full implementation of AI tools to test their accuracy and effectiveness in learning. In addition, to improve the accuracy and generalization of AI tools, it is necessary to expand larger data sets and sample sizes. Lastly, more empirical research about AI is needed to improve its potential for predicting data and providing personalized guidance for students. These recommendations highlight the strategies for advancing AI and DL in education, focusing on personalized learning, improvement of accuracy, and practical applications.

5. CONCLUSION

This review implements bibliometric analysis and systematic literature review to identify significant impacts, main challenges, and future agendas of artificial intelligence (AI) and deep learning (DL) in education. The review, it found that there is the highest number of papers published on AI/DL education research in 2023, illustrating the rapid development of artificial intelligence around the world. Moreover, some countries have made significant contributions to this field, like China, India, and the United States. The bibliometric analysis also highlights the development trends and hot topics all over this field, including reputable academic institutions and main research keywords.

AI and deep learning technologies have shown wide applications in the education domain and have brought a transformative impact. Through personalized learning, these technologies can customize students' learning experiences to meet different learning styles and needs. The application of data analysis technology in education makes the collection and analysis of educational data more efficient, thereby helping to accurately evaluate student performance and provide instant feedback. In addition, the advancement of educational network security technology has provided a solid guarantee for ensuring the security of the educational environment. In terms of learning outcomes, AI and deep learning technologies can improve students' academic performance and reduce student dropout rates through personalized teaching support. At the same time, these technologies can also increase students' participation in class, stimulate interest in learning, and thus improve the overall learning effect. By predicting learners' emotions, AI technology can also perform emotion recognition and analysis to provide teachers with targeted teaching plans, thereby further optimizing personalized teaching support. Overall, AI and deep learning technologies are comprehensively transforming the education industry and promoting improvements in education quality and efficiency.

Artificial intelligence (AI) and deep learning (DL) technologies are experiencing rapid development and showing great potential in the field of education. Despite this, the full implementation of the widespread application of AI technology in education still faces many challenges, including immaturity of technology, resource allocation, lack of human-computer interaction, and teacher training, etc. These limit the full development of AI technology.

To solve these problems, corresponding adjustments need to be made in educational practices and policies. In this context, the review proposes future research directions, emphasizing the need to improve the prediction capabilities and personalized guidance of AI technology based on empirical research, as well as expanding datasets to achieve the generalization of AI technology.

To achieve substantial progress and innovation in AI/DL within the education field, the review offers several suggestions for future development. These include improving AI technology, expanding datasets and sample sizes, and enhancing AI training and education opportunities. By implementing these measures, the paper anticipates more in-depth and extensive applications of AI/DL technology in education.

REFERENCES

Abuhassna, H., Adnan, M. A. B. M., & Awae, F. (2024). Exploring the synergy between instructional design models and learning theories: A systematic literature review. *Contemporary Educational Technology*, *16*(2), ep499. DOI: 10.30935/cedtech/14289

Abuhassna, H., Alnawajha, S., Awae, F., Adnan, M. A. B. M., & Edwards, B. I. (2024). Synthesizing technology integration within the Addie model for instructional design: A comprehensive systematic literature review. *Journal of Autonomous Intelligence*, *7*(5), 1546. DOI: 10.32629/jai.v7i5.1546

Abuhassna, H., Awae, F., Adnan, M. A., Daud, M., & Almheiri, A. S. (2024). The Information Age for Education via Artificial Intelligence and Machine Learning: A Bibliometric and Systematic Literature Analysis. *International Journal of Information and Education Technology (IJIET)*, *14*(5), 700–711. DOI: 10.18178/ijiet.2024.14.5.2095

AL-Ghamdi, A. S., Ragab, M., & Sabir, M. F. S. (2022). Enhanced artificial intelligence-based cybersecurity intrusion detection for higher education institutions. *Computers, Materials & Continua*, *72*(2).

Alam, A. (2023). Harnessing the Power of AI to Create Intelligent Tutoring Systems for Enhanced Classroom Experience and Improved Learning Outcomes. In *Intelligent Communication Technologies and Virtual Mobile Networks* (pp. 571–591). Springer. DOI: 10.1007/978-981-99-1767-9_42

Albdrani, R. N., & Al-Shargabi, A. A. (2023). Investigating the Effectiveness of ChatGPT for Providing Personalized Learning Experience: A Case Study. *International Journal of Advanced Computer Science and Applications*, *14*(11). Advance online publication. DOI: 10.14569/IJACSA.2023.01411122

Alghamdi, A., & Ragab, M. (2022). Artificial intelligence Techniques based learner authentication in cybersecurity higher education institutions. *Computers, Materials & Continua*, *72*(2), 3131–3144. DOI: 10.32604/cmc.2022.026457

Alhazmi, S., Khan, S., & Syed, M. H. (2023). Learning-Related Sentiment Detection, Classification, and Application for a Quality Education Using Artificial Intelligence Techniques. *Intelligent Automation & Soft Computing*, *36*(3), 3487–3499. DOI: 10.32604/iasc.2023.036297

Alisoy, H., & Sadiqzade, Z. (2024). Mobile-Assisted Language Learning (MALL): Revolutionizing Language Education. *Luminis Applied Science and Engineering*, *1*(1), 60–72. DOI: 10.69760/lumin.202400002

Aljohani, N. R., Aslam, M. A., Khadidos, A. O., & Hassan, S. U. (2022). A Methodological Framework to Predict Future Market Needs for Sustainable Skills Management Using AI and Big Data Technologies [Article]. *Applied Sciences (Basel, Switzerland)*, *12*(14), 6898. Advance online publication. DOI: 10.3390/app12146898

Alqahtani, N. D., Alzahrani, B., & Ramzan, M. S. (2023). Detection of Dyslexia Through Images of Handwriting using Hybrid AI Approach. *International Journal of Advanced Computer Science and Applications*, *14*(10). Advance online publication. DOI: 10.14569/IJACSA.2023.0141099

Alqahtani, T., Badreldin, H. A., Alrashed, M., Alshaya, A. I., Alghamdi, S. S., bin Saleh, K., Alowais, S. A., Alshaya, O. A., Rahman, I., Al Yami, M. S., & Albekairy, A. M. (2023). The emergent role of artificial intelligence, natural learning processing, and large language models in higher education and research. *Research in Social & Administrative Pharmacy*, *19*(8), 1236–1242. DOI: 10.1016/j.sapharm.2023.05.016 PMID: 37321925

Attah, J. O., Ogunlade, O. O., &Otemuyiwa, B. I. (2024). Effect of Gamification-Based Teaching on Junior Secondary School Student's Academic Performance in Mathematics in Kwara State. *Andragogi: Jurnal Pendidikan dan Pembelajaran*, *4*(2), 153-165.

Babu, I., MathuSoothana, R., & Kumar, S. (2023). Evolutionary Algorithm Based Feature Subset Selection for Students Academic Performance Analysis. *Intelligent Automation & Soft Computing*, *36*(3), 3621–3636. DOI: 10.32604/iasc.2023.033791

Chen, L., Chen, P., & Lin, Z. (2020). Artificial intelligence in education: A review. *IEEE Access : Practical Innovations, Open Solutions*, *8*, 75264–75278. DOI: 10.1109/ACCESS.2020.2988510

Chen, Z., Zhang, J., Jiang, X., Hu, Z., Han, X., Xu, M., Savitha, V., & Vivekananda, G. (2020). Education 4.0 using artificial intelligence for students performance analysis. *Inteligencia Artificial*, *23*(66), 124–137.

Ching, T., Himmelstein, D. S., Beaulieu-Jones, B. K., Kalinin, A. A., Do, B. T., Way, G. P., Ferrero, E., Agapow, P.-M., Zietz, M., Hoffman, M. M., Xie, W., Rosen, G. L., Lengerich, B. J., Israeli, J., Lanchantin, J., Woloszynek, S., Carpenter, A. E., Shrikumar, A., Xu, J., & Greene, C. S. (2018). Opportunities and obstacles for deep learning in biology and medicine. *Journal of the Royal Society, Interface*, *15*(141), 20170387. DOI: 10.1098/rsif.2017.0387 PMID: 29618526

Coşulean, L. (2024). Adaptive learning platforms as a means of individualised learning. In *Probleme de filologie: Aspecte teoretice şi practice Materialele Conferinţei ştiinţifice internaţionale, edi ia a Xa 8 decembrie 2023* (pp. 136-141). Biblioteca Ştiinţifică a Universităţii de Stat Alecu Russo.

Ding, A.-C. E., Shi, L., Yang, H., & Choi, I. (2024). Enhancing teacher AI literacy and integration through different types of cases in teacher professional development. *Computers and Education Open*, *6*, 100178. DOI: 10.1016/j.caeo.2024.100178

ElSayary, A. (2024). An investigation of teachers' perceptions of using ChatGPT as a supporting tool for teaching and learning in the digital era. *Journal of Computer Assisted Learning*, *40*(3), 931–945. DOI: 10.1111/jcal.12926

Fahd, K., & Miah, S. J. (2023). Designing and evaluating a big data analytics approach for predicting students' success factors. *Journal of Big Data*, *10*(1), 159. DOI: 10.1186/s40537-023-00835-z

Gomaa, W. H., Nagib, A. E., Saeed, M. M., Algarni, A., & Nabil, E. (2023). Empowering short answer grading: Integrating transformer-based embeddings and BI-LSTM network. *Big Data and Cognitive Computing*, *7*(3), 122. DOI: 10.3390/bdcc7030122

Grassini, S. (2023). Shaping the future of education: Exploring the potential and consequences of AI and ChatGPT in educational settings. *Education Sciences*, *13*(7), 692. DOI: 10.3390/educsci13070692

Ismail, A., Aliu, A., Ibrahim, M., & Sulaiman, A. (2024). Preparing teachers of the future in the era of artificial intelligence. *Journal of Artificial Intelligence. Machine Learning and Neural Network*, *44*, 31–41.

Kayal, A. (2024). Transformative Pedagogy: A Comprehensive Framework for AI Integration in Education. In *Explainable AI for Education: Recent Trends and Challenges* (pp. 247-270). Springer. DOI: 10.1007/978-3-031-72410-7_14

Koć-Januchta, M. M., Schönborn, K. J., Roehrig, C., Chaudhri, V. K., Tibell, L. A., & Heller, H. C. (2022). "Connecting concepts helps put main ideas together": Cognitive load and usability in learning biology with an AI-enriched textbook. *International Journal of Educational Technology in Higher Education*, *19*(1), 11. DOI: 10.1186/s41239-021-00317-3

Kumar, Y., Parekh, S., Singh, S., Li, J. J., Shah, R. R., & Chen, C. (2023). Automatic essay scoring systems are both overstable and oversensitive: Explaining why and proposing defenses. *Dialogue & Discourse*, *14*(1), 1–33. DOI: 10.5210/dad.2023.101

Latif, G., Brahim, G. B., Abdelhamid, S. E., Alghazo, R., Alhabib, G., & Alnujaidi, K. (2023). Learning at Your Fingertips: An Innovative IoT-Based AI-Powered Braille Learning System. *Applied System Innovation*, *6*(5), 91. DOI: 10.3390/asi6050091

Lee, J., & Kim, Y. (2023). Sustainable educational metaverse content and system based on deep learning for enhancing learner immersion. *Sustainability (Basel)*, *15*(16), 12663. DOI: 10.3390/su151612663

Li, W., & Mohamad, M. (2023). An Efficient Probabilistic Deep Learning Model for the Oral Proficiency Assessment of Student Speech Recognition and Classification [Article]. *International Journal on Recent and Innovation Trends in Computing and Communication*, *11*(6), 411–424. DOI: 10.17762/ijritcc.v11i6.7734

Michel-Villarreal, R., Vilalta-Perdomo, E., Salinas-Navarro, D. E., Thierry-Aguilera, R., & Gerardou, F. S. (2023). Challenges and opportunities of generative AI for higher education as explained by ChatGPT. *Education Sciences*, *13*(9), 856. DOI: 10.3390/educsci13090856

Moher, D., Liberati, A., Tetzlaff, J., &Altman, D. G. (2009). Preferred reporting items for systematic reviews and meta-analyses: the PRISMA statement. *bmj, 339*.

Mouta, A., Torrecilla-Sánchez, E. M., & Pinto-Llorente, A. M. (2025). Comprehensive professional learning for teacher agency in addressing ethical challenges of AIED: Insights from educational design research. *Education and Information Technologies*, *30*(3), 3343–3387. DOI: 10.1007/s10639-024-12946-y

Oche, P. A., Ewa, G. A., & Ibekwe, N. (2021). Applications and challenges of artificial intelligence in space missions. *IEEE Access : Practical Innovations, Open Solutions*, *12*, 44481–44509. DOI: 10.1109/ACCESS.2021.3132500

Omarov, B., Nurmash, N., Doskarayev, B., Zhilisbaev, N., Dairabayev, M., Orazov, S., & Omarov, N. (2023). A Novel Deep Neural Network to Analyze and Monitoring the Physical Training Relation to Sports Activities. *International Journal of Advanced Computer Science and Applications*, *14*(9). Advance online publication. DOI: 10.14569/IJACSA.2023.0140977

Paek, S., & Kim, N. (2021). Analysis of worldwide research trends on the impact of artificial intelligence in education. *Sustainability (Basel)*, *13*(14), 7941. DOI: 10.3390/su13147941

Peter, U. I., Orubebe, E. D., & Oladokun, B. D. (2024). Transforming Education in Nigerian Universities: The Role of Free and Open-Source Software (FOSS) in Teaching and Learning. *Asian Review of Social Sciences*, *13*(1), 39–47. DOI: 10.70112/arss-2024.13.1.4239

Pucchio, A., Rathagirishnan, R., Caton, N., Gariscsak, P. J., Del Papa, J., Nabhen, J. J., Vo, V., Lee, W., & Moraes, F. Y. (2022). Exploration of exposure to artificial intelligence in undergraduate medical education: A Canadian cross-sectional mixed-methods study. *BMC Medical Education*, *22*(1), 815. DOI: 10.1186/s12909-022-03896-5 PMID: 36443720

Ramessur, R., Raja, L., Kilduff, C. L., Kang, S., Li, J.-P. O., Thomas, P. B., & Sim, D. A. (2021). Impact and challenges of integrating artificial intelligence and telemedicine into clinical ophthalmology. *Asia-Pacific Journal of Ophthalmology*, *10*(3), 317–327. DOI: 10.1097/APO.0000000000000406 PMID: 34383722

Rathod, M., Dalvi, C., Kaur, K., Patil, S., Gite, S., Kamat, P., Kotecha, K., Abraham, A., & Gabralla, L. A. (2022). Kids' emotion recognition using various deep-learning models with explainable ai. *Sensors (Basel)*, *22*(20), 8066. DOI: 10.3390/s22208066 PMID: 36298415

Sarker, I. H. (2021). Deep learning: A comprehensive overview on techniques, taxonomy, applications and research directions. *SN Computer Science*, *2*(6), 420. DOI: 10.1007/s42979-021-00815-1 PMID: 34426802

Shakimova, D. D., Lawrence, K. C., & Aubakirova, Z. K. (2024). Professional development training can help teachers to build resistance against teaching associated stress. *Cogent Education*, *11*(1), 2346049. DOI: 10.1080/2331186X.2024.2346049

Shi, L., Muhammad Umer, A., & Shi, Y. (2023). Utilizing AI models to optimize blended teaching effectiveness in college-level English education. *Cogent Education*, *10*(2), 2282804. DOI: 10.1080/2331186X.2023.2282804

Shiao, Y.-T., Chen, C.-H., Wu, K.-F., Chen, B.-L., Chou, Y.-H., & Wu, T.-N. (2023). Reducing dropout rate through a deep learning model for sustainable education: Long-term tracking of learning outcomes of an undergraduate cohort from 2018 to 2021. *Smart Learning Environments*, *10*(1), 55. DOI: 10.1186/s40561-023-00274-6

Shu, X., & Gu, X. (2023). An empirical study of A smart education model enabled by the edu-metaverse to enhance better learning outcomes for students. *Systems*, *11*(2), 75. DOI: 10.3390/systems11020075

Vetrivel, S., Arun, V., Ambikapathi, R., & Saravanan, T. (2025). Automated Grading Systems: Enhancing Efficiency and Consistency in Student Assessments. In *Adopting Artificial Intelligence Tools in Higher Education* (pp. 41-61). CRC Press.

Wang, J. (2025). Revolutionizing Education for Sustainable Development Through Adaptive Learning and Artificial Intelligence. In *Rethinking the Pedagogy of Sustainable Development in the AI Era* (pp. 63–92). IGI Global Scientific Publishing. DOI: 10.4018/979-8-3693-9062-7.ch004

Wellnhofer, E. (2022). Real-world and regulatory perspectives of artificial intelligence in cardiovascular imaging. *Frontiers in Cardiovascular Medicine*, *9*, 890809. DOI: 10.3389/fcvm.2022.890809 PMID: 35935648

Winiarti, S. W., Sunardi, S., Ahdiani, U., & Pranolo, A. (2022). Tradition Meets Modernity: Learning Traditional Building using Artificial Intelligence. *Asian Journal of University Education*, *18*(2), 375–385. DOI: 10.24191/ajue.v18i2.17992

Xu, F. W. X., Choo, A. M. H., Ting, P. L. M., Ong, S. J., & Khoo, D. (2023). Leveraging AI in Postgraduate Medical Education for Rapid Skill Acquisition in Ultrasound-Guided Procedural Techniques. *Journal of Imaging*, *9*(10), 225. DOI: 10.3390/jimaging9100225 PMID: 37888332

Yang, Z. (2022). Natural Language Enhancement for English Teaching Using Character-Level Recurrent Neural Network with Back Propagation Neural Network based Classification by Deep Learning Architectures. *JUCS. Journal of Universal Computer Science*, *28*(9), 984–1000. DOI: 10.3897/jucs.94162

Chapter 5
A Bibliometric Analysis of Artificial Intelligence: Impact on Student Motivation in Education

Liu Dan
https://orcid.org/0009-0007-3685-236X
University of Technology Malaysia, Malaysia

Hasnah Binti Mohamed
University of Technology Malaysia, Malaysia

Hassan Abuhassna
https://orcid.org/0000-0002-5774-3652
Sunway University, Malaysia

ABSTRACT

Artificial intelligence (AI) enhances students' learning motivation through personalized learning systems and intelligent tutoring in education. It provides students with immediate feedback and support to help them overcome their learning difficulties. In addition, the interactive learning environment created by AI further stimulates students' interest and engagement in learning.The impact of AI on student motivation to learn is crucial for improving the teaching system. In this paper, the PRISMA statement template is used for bibliometric analysis, and the Scopus database is used to analyze the publications from 2014 to 2023. 216 papers are retrieved to obtain insights on artificial intelligence and student motivation. The selection criteria are specific inclusion and exclusion criteria that analyze the distribution of publications from 2014 to 2023, the most important countries, research keywords and subject areas, and the most relevant authors and journals.These results offer

DOI: 10.4018/979-8-3373-5550-4.ch005

insightful information about the field's current research interests.

1. INTRODUCTION

Artificial intelligence (AI) technology is rapidly becoming integrated into the education sector, profoundly affecting the way teaching is done and the students' learning experience (Zhai et.al, 2021). With the popularity of AI applications such as intelligent learning systems, personalized learning platforms and educational robots, the learning process for students has become more flexible and interactive (Limna et al., 2022) These technologies can not only provide customized learning resources according to the individual needs of students, but also stimulate students' learning motivation and improve learning results through immediate feedback and adaptive assessment.

With the growing emphasis on integrating customized learning and AI technologies in education, there is an urgent need to examine the current status of research and track growing trends across the almost ten-year study period (Ivanova et al.,2024). Student motivation is a key factor affecting academic success, and AI technology shows significant potential in enhancing student motivation (Dunn & Kennedy, 2019). Through AI-driven adaptive learning systems, students are able to learn at their own pace and enjoy a more personalized and engaged learning experience, thereby maintaining long-term interest in learning. At the same time, AI tools can also make learning content more lively and interesting through innovative means such as augmented reality (AR), gamified learning and virtual reality (VR), and further stimulate the intrinsic motivation of students (Lu et al., 2021).

In addition, AI can enhance students' learning motivation through gamification and interactive technologies. The research of Hellín et al. (2023)has shown that gamified learning elements, such as rewards, challenges, and competition, significantly increase student engagement and motivation. AI can automate and personalize these functions, further improving their effectiveness.However, while AI shows great potential for boosting student motivation, the discussion about its impact is still ongoing.

2. LITERATURE REVIEW

In recent years, the application of artificial intelligence (AI) in the field of education has gradually attracted extensive attention from the academic community (Chen et al., 2022). AI technology has many influence mechanisms when it affects students' learning motivation. Rane et al. (2023) point out that AI technology can personalize the learning experience and help students customize learning according to their own learning pace and interests. This personalized learning path helps improve students' intrinsic motivation. In addition, the AI-driven intelligent tutoring system enhances students' self-efficacy through real-time feedback and guidance, thus stimulating students' learning interest. However, some studies of Sharma (2024), George (2024), and Hossain and Islam (2024) have suggested that over-reliance on technology may lead to dehumanization of the learning process, reducing interpersonal interaction and the emotional support role of teachers.Other studies of Goswami and Sharma (2024) and Bulathwela, Pérez-Ortiz, Holloway, Cukurova, and Shawe-Taylor (2024) have pointed out that unequal access to AI technology could exacerbate educational inequality, especially in low-resource areas, where some students may not enjoy the advantages of this innovative technology.

Between 2014 and 2023, the impact of AI technologies on student motivation is likely to become increasingly significant in teaching and learning. Lee (2023), Hamid et al.(2023) and Jin et al.(2023) have studied the impact of artificial intelligence on student motivation in teaching from different aspects, and have a deep understanding of artificial intelligence's effects on teaching methods and learning. However, despite AI's significant promise for increasing student motivation, its application also faces some challenges (Pedro et al., 2019). Therefore, in research exploring the relationship between AI and student motivation, these factors must be considered to ensure the effectiveness and sustainability of AI technology in education.

3. THE OBJECTIVES OF THE REVIEW

The objectives of this study can be summarized in three main points:

(1) To study the annual changes, growth trends, and evolution of research topics in this field.
(2) To identify the countries, researchers and journals that produce the most and have the greatest influence in this field.
(3) To explore the main research keywords and disciplinary fields related to artificial intelligence and student motivation.

4. THE RESEARCH QUESTIONS OF THE REVIEW

The study also presents a visual analysis of the influence of AI on students' motivation from different topics in an educational context, with data sourced from scopus to answer the following research questions:

(1) What is the distribution and trend of publications on Artificial Intelligence and student motivation from 2014 to 2023?
(2) What are the most influential countries, authors, and journals in the field of student motivation and Artificial Intelligence?
(3) What are the key research keywords and the primary subject areas associated with Artificial Intelligence and student motivation from 2014 to 2023?

5. METHODOLOGY

A bibliometric analysis was used in this study to conduct a systematic literature review (SLR) using the PRISMA declaration form and Preferred Reporting Items for Meta-analysis, which used the PRISMA template to include four processes, specifically for the purposes of identification, screening, and eligibility, and finally to choose which studies were part of the review. Data from the Scopus scientific database were used for bibliometric analysis. The queries passed were related to "artificial intelligence" and student motivation, searching for article titles, abstracts and keywords in Scopus. In order to quantify academic communication, analyze and display the status of present research and trends on student motivation in AI education, the literature was extracted from the Scopus database for detailed bibliometric analysis.

The topics chosen for this study are artificial intelligence and student learning motivation used in the scopus database for retrieval research. The total number of articles in this systematic literature review is 957, and the data was selected by PRISMA statement template. The first stage in the identification process was to identify documents in the database using the keywords "artificial intelligence" and "student learning motivation." These results were then filtered, and 210 were left after limiting the time range, article type, and language to English. Use VOSviewer's software tools for data analysis and visualization. VOSviewer is capable of efficiently analyzing and visualizing bibliometric data, helping researchers extract valuable information from a large number of literature(Bukar et al., 2023). This visual analysis can not only clearly show the correlation between different research topics, but also reveal the research trends and evolution paths in the field, thus providing more in-depth insight and guidance for academic research. The figure 1 shows the PRISMA process.

Figure 1. The PRISMA process

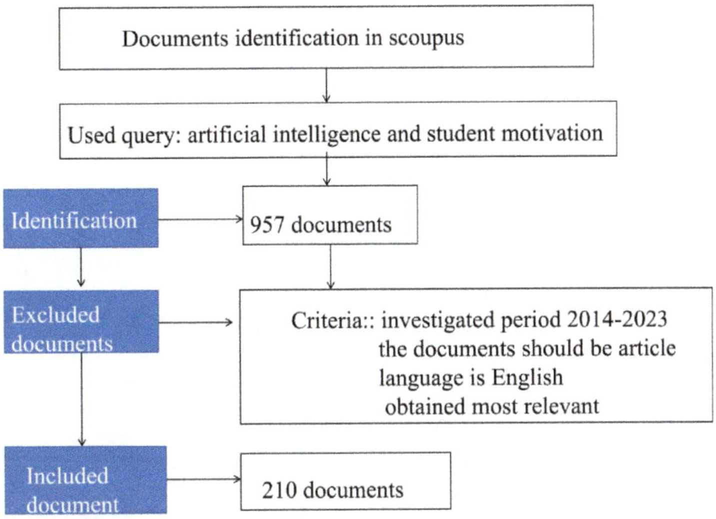

6. RESULT

Research question 1. Answer the distribution of publications on artificial intelligence and student motivation between 2014 and 2023. As shown in Figure 2, overall, the number of publications in this decade has increased. There was only one paper published on the topic in 2014, an increase in 2015, but a decline in 2016. Then there was a gradual rise from 2016 to 2018, but a decline again from 2018 to 2020. Since 2020, the amount of documents has raised significantly, and by 2023, the quantity of documents has increased to 84.

Figure 2. The distribution of publication from 2014 to 2023

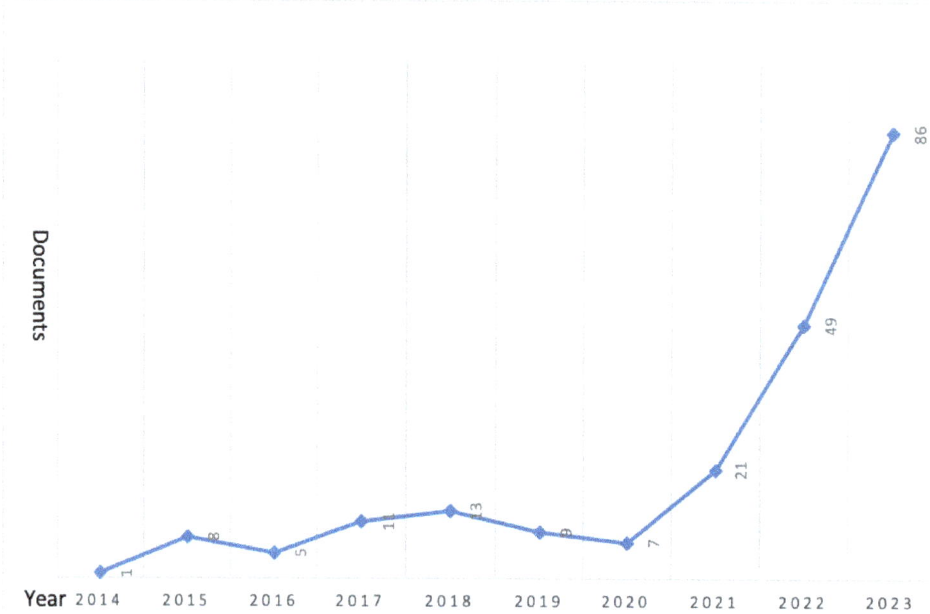

Research question 2. The second research question aimed to determine the most relevant journals, authors and countries in artificial intelligence and student motivation. Figure 3 illustrates the total number of publications (TP) of the primary journals in the study of student motivation and artificial intelligence. Then, the Scopus database selected the ten most highly cited journals in the subject, and analyzed the detailed information of these journals, including total publication volume (TP), citation score, total citations (TC), the most cited article, the number of citations of the article, and the publisher name of the journal.

Figure 3. The pie chart of most relevant journals in artificial intelligence and student motivation research

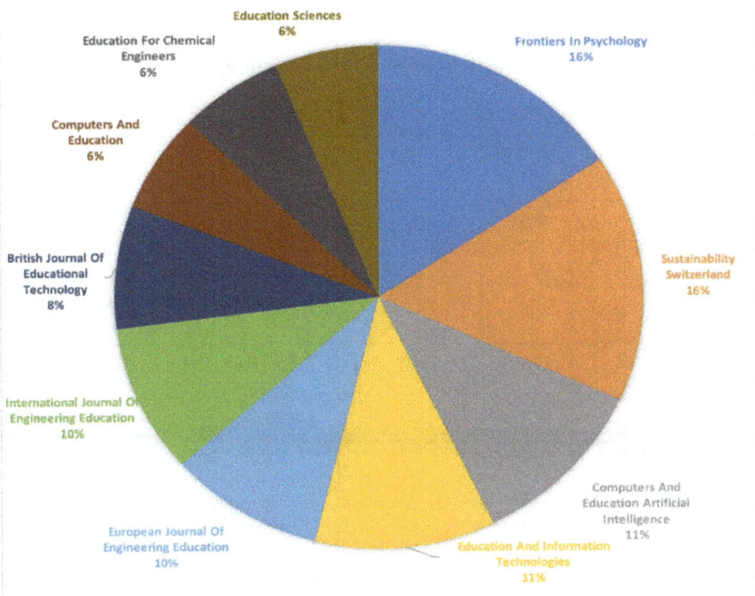

As shown in Table 1, the journal with the most links to AI and learning motivation research is Frontiers in Psychology, with 10 publications and 11,948 citations. "Sustainability (Switzerland)" also published 10 articles, and the number of citations reached 381,357. The most frequently cited article in this journal is Blockchain technology enhances sustainable higher education. This article studies the technology of blockchain and focuses on the influence of motivation on collaborative activity. This has had a beneficial effect on the academic performance of higher education institutions (HEI). There are four publications in the journal of Education Sciences, but the citations reached 15,882 times, and the correlation is also very high.

Table 1. Summarizes the most significant journals on AI and student motivation

No	journals	TP	TC	Cite scores(2023)	Most cited articles	Time cited
1	Frontiers in Psychology	10	119948	5.3	Enhancing academic writing skills and motivation: assessing the efficacy of ChatGPT in AI-assisted language learning for EFL students	23
2	Sustainability (Switzerland)	10	381357	6.8	Blockchain technology enhances sustainable higher education	54
3	Computers and Education: Artificial Intelligence	7	3080	16.8	The effect of generative artificial intelligence (AI)-based tool use on students' computational thinking skills, programming self-efficacy and motivation7	82
4	Education and Information Technologies	7	17613	10	Exploring a self-directed interactive app for informal EFL learning: a self-determination theory perspective	23
5	European Journal of Engineering Education	6	1805	7.3	Activating learning in engineering education using ICT and the concept of 'Flipping the classroom'	58
6	International Journal of Engineering Education	6	1337	2.4	A comparison of flipped and traditional classroom learning: A case study in mechanical engineering	23
7	British Journal of Educational Technology	5	7042	15.6	A reflective thinking-promoting approach to enhancing graduate students' flipped learning engagement, participation behaviors, reflective thinking and project learning outcomes	66
8	Computers and Education	4	20486	27.1	A self-determination theory (SDT) design approach for inclusive and diverse artificial intelligence (AI) education	108
9	Education for Chemical Engineers	4	1548	8.8	Programming skills in the industry 4.0: are chemical engineering students able to face new problems?	46
10	Education Sciences	4	15882	4.8	Needs and performance analysis for changes in higher education and implementation of artificial intelligence, machine learning, and extended reality	32

TP: top publication; TC: top citation

Research Question 2 also involves the most important authors in the area of artificial intelligence and student motivation.The top 10 authors were listed after a search was conducted in the Scopus database.Table 2 presents a list of the most effective authors on AI and student motivation in the field of education, with detailed information about these authors, including author name, first publication year, total publications (TP), H-index, total citations (TC), and affiliation as of right now. According to the Scopus database, the most prolific author is Chai, Ching Sing from the Chinese University of Hong Kong, whose first paper in this field was published in 2021. In total, he has published 264 papers, been cited 9,515 times, and has an H-index of 56. Ranked as the second most productive author is Hwang Gwojen from National Taiwan University of Science and Technology, who has published 582 papers and been cited 25,125 times. His paper ranks first in total citations. Among the top 10 authors, the author with the highest number of citations of relevant papers is an article by Chai, Ching Sing and Chiu, Thomas K.F, Dai and Yun, which is cited 108 times.

Table 2. Summary of the most prolific authors in AI and student motivation

No	Name	TP	TC	H-index	Most cited articles	Time cited	Affiliation
1	Chai, Ching Sing	264	9515	56	A self-determination theory (SDT) design approach for inclusive and diverse artificial intelligence (AI) education	108	Chinese University of Hong Kong
2	Hwang, Gwojen	582	25125	82	A reflective thinking-promoting approach to enhancing graduate students' flipped learning engagement, participation behaviors, reflective thinking and project learning outcomes	66	National Taiwan University of Science and Technology
3	Chiu, Thomas K.F.	75	2622	28	A self-determination theory (SDT) design approach for inclusive and diverse artificial intelligence (AI) education	108	Chinese University of Hong Kong
4	Yueh-Min, Huang Ray	669	11822	55	The exploration of continuous learning intention in STEAM education through attitude, motivation, and cognitive load	38	National Cheng Kung University
5	Chen, Peiying	16	343	9	Impacts of an AI-based chabot on college students' after-class review, academic performance, self-efficacy, learning attitude, and motivation	54	Chihlee University of Technology
6	Chu, Samuel Kai Wah	181	4607	36	Effects of chatbot-assisted in-class debates on students' argumentation skills and task motivation	20	Hong Kong Metropolitan University

continued on following page

Table 2. Continued

No	Name	TP	TC	H-index	Most cited articles	Time cited	Affiliation
7	Dai, Yun	36	605	10	A self-determination theory (SDT) design approach for inclusive and diverse artificial intelligence (AI) education	108	Chinese University of Hong Kong
8	Fonseca, David	205	2206	24	Technological adaptation of the student to the educational density of the course. A case study: 3D architectural visualization	33	Universitat Ramon Llull
9	Ilić, Valentin Kuleto Milena	22	358	9	Blockchain technology enhances sustainable higher education	54	University Business Academy in Novi Sad
10	Khambari, Mas Nida Md	73	298	8	Improvement of Pre-Service Teachers' Practical Knowledge and Motivation about Artificial Intelligence through a Servicelearning-based Module in Guizhou, China: A QuasiExperimental Study	6	Universiti Putra Malaysia

TP: top publication; TC: top citation

Regarding the countries that have contributed the most to AI and learning motivation research, Figure 4 shows a map that identifies the most influential countries in the Scopus database based on total publications (TP). Table 3 summarizes the countries that have made the most significant contributions in this field, and lists analytical indicators such as ranking, country names, total publications (TP), and the most important academic institutions. Table 3 clearly demonstrates that China is the foremost country in the domain of AI and learning motivation research, with a total of 40 papers published, of which Beijing Normal University is the most important research institution in the field. It is followed by the United States with 33 publications, of which the University of Florida is the most important institution. Spain ranks third with 22 papers published, and Universidad Politecnica de Madrid is the most important Spanish institution in this field.

Figure 4. The map of the most important countries in AI and student motivation

Table 3. An overview of the most important countries in AI and student motivation

Rank	Country	TP	Most significant academic institution
1	China	40	Beijing Normal University
2	United States	33	University of Florida
3	Spain	26	Universidad Politécnica de Madrid
4	India	13	Lovely Professional University
5	Saudi Arabia	12	King Faisal University
6	United Kingdom	10	University of Cambridge
7	South Korea	9	Florida State University
8	Malaysia	8	Universiti Sains Malaysia
9	Mexico	8	Tecnológico de Monterrey
10	Australia	5	Western Sydney University

To give a clearer view, Figure 5 depicts the quantity of documents for each nation as a bar chart. In addition to the top three countries mentioned earlier, the top ten countries also include the United Kingdom, Australia, Malaysia, Mexico and other countries, which have also made important contributions to the research in this area.

Figure 5. The bar chart of publication according to the countries

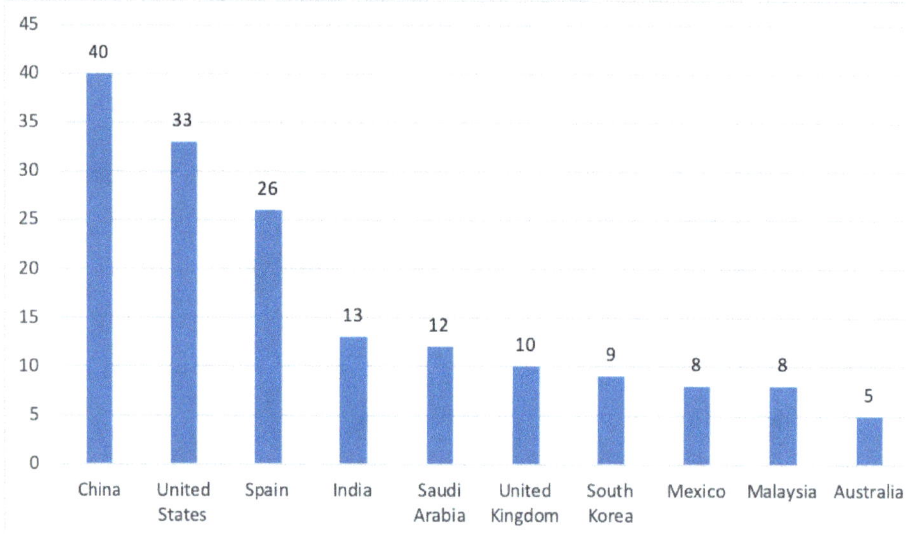

Research question 3. This study used VOSviewer software to analyze the relationship between co-authors and states related to research on artificial intelligence and learning motivation. As shown in Figure 6, The results demonstrated that China and the United States possessed the strongest link strength, with 13 links each. China involved 40 articles, the total number of citations is 398; The United States involved 33 articles with a total of 555 citations. The next strongest countries were the UK, India and Saudi Arabia, each with nine links, with the UK having the highest overall amount of citations at 244. Although Spain has a link strength of 6, its total number of citations is 421. The map also illustrates the relationships between co-authors among other countries.

Figure 6 A map illustrating the collaboration network between countries based on co-authorship

Next, this study examines the co-occurrence of primary research keywords used in the field of artificial intelligence and student motivation during the last decade. Figure 7 depicts the mapping depending on the co-occurrence relationships between all keywords in the Scopus database. The results show that "artificial intelligence" is the keyword with the most frequent co-occurrence rate (Oc = 139) and the highest link strength (560), followed by "student" (Oc = 88) and "motivation" (Oc = 64). In addition, additional keywords with strong co-occurrence rates include "learning system" (Oc = 36), "teaching" (Oc = 36), "education" (Oc = 33), "e-learning" (Oc = 34) and "active learning" (Oc = 28).

Moreover, Figure 8 shows the co-occurrence pattern of author keywords . The most frequent keyword was "artificial intelligence"(Oc=68) and had a total of 50 links to other keywords. This was followed by "motivation" (Oc=23) and "active learning" (Oc=24). Other keywords such as "higher education" (Oc=14), "e-learning" (Oc=11) and "chatgpt" (Oc= 10) were also displayed in the map.

Figure 7. A map illustrating the co-occurrence relationships among all keywords.

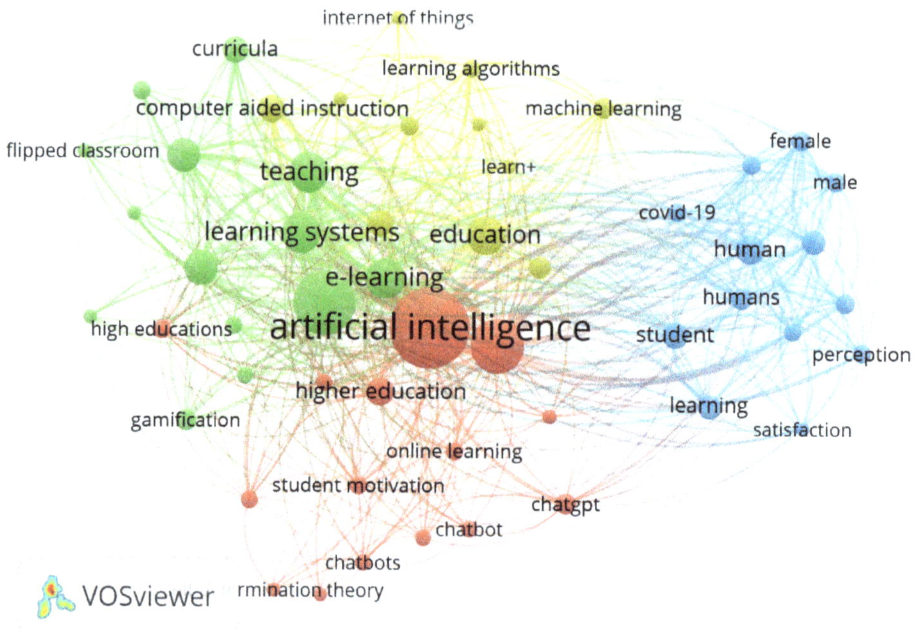

Figure 8. A map showing the co-occurrence relationships among author keywords.

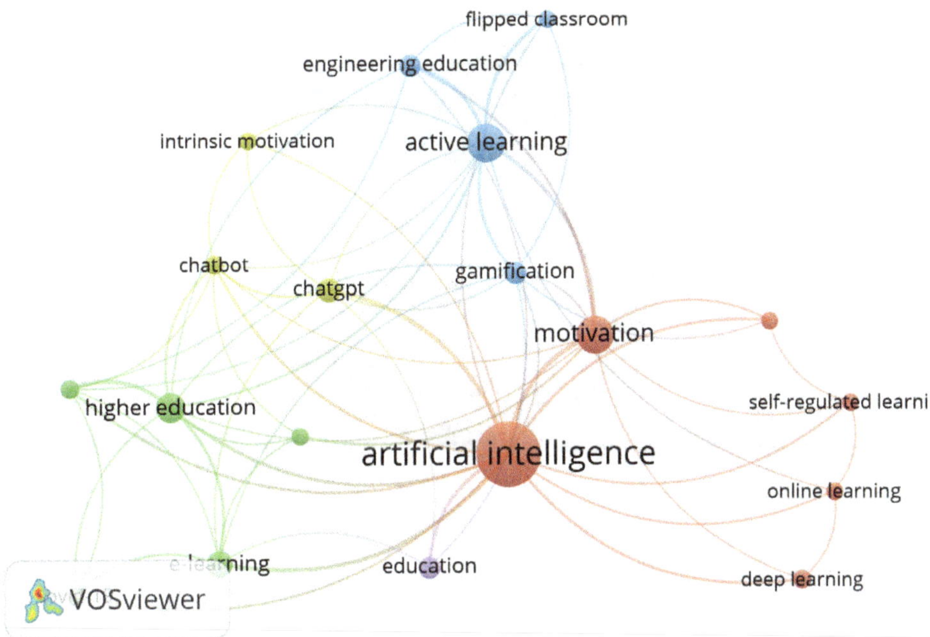

In terms of the most significant subject area in AI and student motivation, the highest percentage (31.8%), including 135 documents, was in social science. Therefore, the social sciences seem to be the subject area most relevant to AI and student motivation. This was followed by 97 papers published (22.8%) from computer science. The fields with the fewest publication were Earth and Planetary Sciences, Economics, Econometrics and Finance, Neuroscience, and Nursing, and only one document for each subject. The remaining data of publication on AI and student motivation according to the subject area is shown in Figure 9.

Figure 9. The pie chart displaying the number of publications by subject area

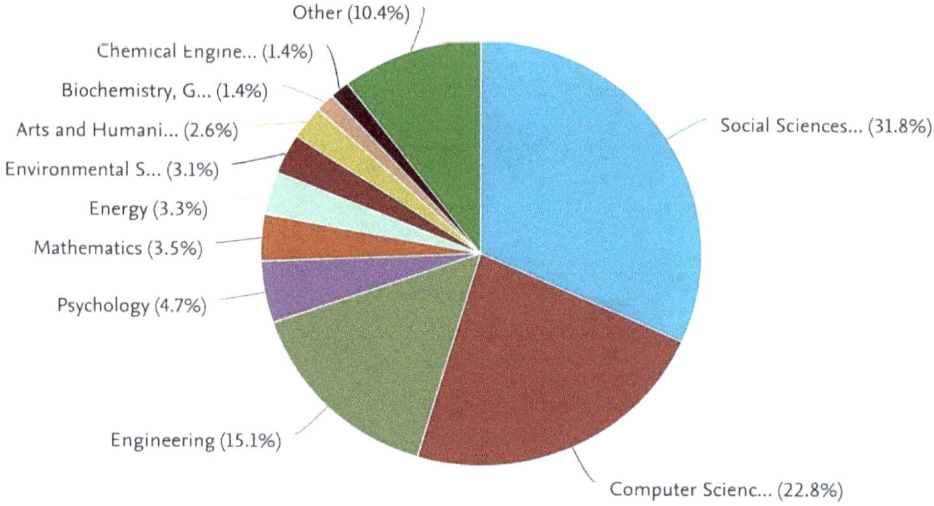

7. DISCUSSION

The application of AI in education, especially in stimulating students' motivation, does not merely rely on its automated functions. More and more teaching practices show that AI tools, such as chatbots and tutoring robots, are collaborating with teachers to provide personalized learning support (Chiu et al.,2024). For instance, in some online learning platforms, AI can not only adjust the content based on students' performance, but also help teachers more accurately identify students' learning difficulties through real-time feedback, thereby jointly enhancing students' learning motivation and classroom participation. Although AI technology has brought significant potential in the field of education, its application is also accompanied by some ethical issues, especially in terms of student data privacy and AI bias (Huang, 2023).

According to the Scopus database literature analysis results, from 2014 to 2023, artificial intelligence (AI) and learning motivation research publications in the field of education show a clear growth trend. It reflects the continuing concern in the field of education about the complex interaction between technological progress and the psychology of learning (Beer & Mulder, 2020). Akyuz (2020) pointed out that initial research has focused on the implementation of AI technology in education area, such as personalized teaching systems and intelligent tutoring tools, to explore its potential impact on student motivation. However, with the development of technology and the advancement of educational theories, the academic community has gradually deepened its attention to this field, and the research content has expanded from the simple application of technology to explore how AI affects students' intrinsic motivation, autonomous learning ability and learning effectiveness (Vistorte et al.,2024). This growth not only reveals the potential of AI to inspire and sustain student motivation, but also reflects the ongoing exploration in educational practice of how to effectively integrate AI technology to promote positive learning experiences. This trend shows that educators and researchers are becoming more aware of the important role of AI in shaping learning motivation and enhancing learning outcomes, while also highlighting the need for careful research on motivation and learning experiences in a rapidly changing technological environment.

In addition, the bibliometric analysis displays that the journal most relevant to AI and student motivation in the field of education is published by Frontiers in Psychology and Sustainability (Switzerland). The most frequently cited articles are Enhancing academic writing skills and motivation: assessing the efficacy of ChatGPT in AI-assisted language learning for EFL students and Sustainability (Switzerland) Published Blockchain technology enhances sustainable higher education. The first article is to evaluate the effects of AI on students' English writing skills and motivation (Bucea-Manea- oniş et al., 2021). The second article uses blockchain technology to focus on the impact of students' motivation on cooperative work. In higher education, student engagement leads to better learning results. Researchers discovered that motivation, teamwork, and student engagement are significant variables in increasing student learning results (Song & Song, 2023). Two articles explore the impact of technology on student motivation from different perspectives. Motivation is a key factor in improving students' learning outcomes, whether in improving motivation in English writing or teamwork and engagement in collaborative work. The most prolific author of this analysis is Chai, Ching Sing, from the Chinese University of Hong Kong, whose article discusses how SDT (Self-determination theory) based needs reinforced by teacher and student traits (gender and achievement level) influence artificial intelligence education at the secondary level in terms of student motivation (Xia et al., 2022).

Moreover, this study also analyzed the main research keywords of artificial intelligence and student motivation in the past decade. According to the results, artificial intelligence, student motivation are the most frequently used keywords within the domain of artificial intelligence and student motivation. These three keywords also have. The combination of artificial intelligence and learning motivation will become an important driving force to improve teaching effectiveness and students' independent learning in the future of higher education. AI technology can not only personalize the learning experience and provide timely feedback on learning progress, but also enhance students' intrinsic learning motivation through interaction and support (Huang et al., 2023). The deployment of AI technology in collaborative learning can promote teamwork and knowledge sharing among students, thus further enhancing students' sense of participation and responsibility (Mora et al.,2020). As these technologies continue to evolve, they will play an integral role in developing students' ability to innovate and adapt to the demands of future jobs.

The study also highlighted social science as the most significant subject area related to AI and student motivation. AI is also involved in the field of computer science. The two fields are closely interlinked. The social sciences focus on human behavior, psychology, and education, and student motivation is one of the core issues. Computer science is responsible for developing and optimizing AI technologies to make them work better in education (Pedro et al, 2019). Therefore, researchers are conducting interdisciplinary research in these two fields to investigate how AI technology can be used to improve students' learning motivation and effectiveness, thereby driving educational innovation. Ouyang et al.(2022) showed that AI technologies can personalize the learning experience and enhance interactive feedback, while the theoretical framework of the social sciences helps explain its impact on student behavior and psychology.

With the development of AI technology, students' learning data is widely collected and analyzed, which may bring the risk of privacy leakage. The algorithms of AI systems may unintentionally exacerbate existing biases (Mensah, 2023). For instance, when evaluating students' abilities, some AI models may make unfair judgments due to deviations in training data. Therefore, while promoting the application of AI, it is necessary to ensure its fairness and transparency and protect students' privacy rights (Khan, 2024). Future research can further explore how AI and teachers can better collaborate in personalized education and how AI can enhance students' intrinsic motivation in different educational environments. Furthermore, with the advancement of AI technology, research on how AI can support teachers in tracking students' emotional changes and learning progress in real time will also be an important direction.

In conclusion, according to the findings of this study, the importance of AI in education for student motivation is reflected in its ability to significantly personalize and optimize the learning experience, thereby enhancing learning motivation. The effective use of AI can offer tailored content and feedback according to each student's ability level, interest and learning progress through an adaptive learning system, avoiding the problem of “sameness” in traditional teaching, and enhancing students' sense of participation and interest in learning (Kabudi et al., 2021). Meanwhile, AI technology can also help students realize their progress faster through instant assessment and data analysis, enhance self-efficacy and accomplishment, and thus stimulate intrinsic motivation. In addition, AI can facilitate collaborative learning and interaction, making the learning process more interesting and challenging, which also helps to cultivate students' motivation to learn in the long run. In the future, AI will become an important tool to enhance student autonomy and stimulate intellectual curiosity, laying the foundation for the full popularization of personalized education.

8. CONCLUSION AND IMPLICATION

With the rapid growth of artificial intelligence in the modern era, we must fully utilize its function in the field of education and activate students' excitement based on their individualized development. A bibliometric analysis of 210 papers on learning motivation and artificial intelligence was done for this study. The decade from 2014 to 2023 has seen an overall uptick in publications related to AI and learning motivation. This means that these two topics have important potential for development. The relevant journals, mostly published by Frontiers in Psychology and Sustainability (Switzerland), have made important contributions to the research on artificial intelligence and student motivation in education. Furthermore, the most prolific author is Chai, Ching Sing, currently associated with the Chinese University of Hong Kong, who first published relevant publications in the field from 2021 onwards, with a total of 9,515 citations. Moreover, the study also showed that China is the most important country in the field of AI and student motivation, with a total of 40 papers published, of which the most prolific institution is Beijing Normal University. In terms of AI and motivation for learning, China and the United States have the highest overall link strength of co- authors, which is very important for the exposure of the significance of applying AI and motivation for learning on a global scale. AI, students, and motivation are the keywords that appear most frequently in most of the publications analyzed in this study. Most journals use these two keywords to study the details of AI and learning motivation analysis research. From the perspective of subject areas, social science and computer science are the most significant subject areas of artificial intelligence and student motivation in education, engineering and psychology, mathematics and other fields are also involved.

From this research can be drawn the importance of artificial intelligence in teaching and learning, through artificial intelligence to enhance students' learning motivation. In the field of education, artificial intelligence significantly enhances students' learning motivation through personalized learning experiences, instant feedback and adaptive learning, gamified learning, the promotion of collaboration and interaction, and the reduction of learning pressure. AI can provide a tailored learning path based on the individual needs of students, and help students correct mistakes in time, see progress, and enhance their sense of accomplishment through real-time feedback. At the same time, AI can also increase the fun and interaction of learning through gamification elements and intelligent matching collaborative learning, reduce pressure, and thus enhance students' self-confidence and long-term learning enthusiasm.

The advantage of this chapter lies in exploring the possibility of enhancing students' motivation through artificial intelligence. This topic holds significant value because the application of artificial intelligence in the field of education is increasing day by day. Understanding its impact on students' motivation is crucial for formulating effective teaching strategies and technologies. From the perspective of the current relevance of educational trends, exploring how artificial intelligence can enhance students' motivation is in line with the current educational reform and future development discussions. By adopting the bibliometric analysis method, the existing research achievements can be systematically reviewed and analyzed, providing a quantitative academic basis for this topic. This advantage enhances the credibility of the chapter. By adopting the bibliometric analysis method, the existing research achievements can be systematically reviewed and analyzed, providing a quantitative academic basis for this topic. This advantage enhances the credibility of the chapter. The combination of artificial intelligence, education and psychology (motivation) has promoted interdisciplinary research. This in-depth exploration can provide a more detailed understanding and reveal how technological progress affects students' behaviors and learning outcomes.

9. LIMITATION AND IMPROVEMENT

This chapter can be improved in the following aspects to better align with the title "Generators, Robots and Counselors: Innovative Approaches of Human-Machine Collaboration in Classroom Teaching". There is a lack of in-depth exploration of human-machine collaboration in the chapter. The collaboration between AI and teachers in enhancing students' motivation should be discussed more clearly, especially how to support teachers in formulating personalized learning paths through AI tutoring systems. There is a lack of discussion on emerging trends of AI in education, such as adaptive learning systems and emotional AI, emphasizing the application of these trends in the classroom. Furthermore, the chapter does not delve deeply into the ethical issues of AI, particularly challenges such as algorithmic bias and data privacy. It is necessary to enhance and explore how to balance the application of technology with ethical requirements. By adding actual case studies to demonstrate the practical application of AI tools in education, it can help readers better understand the actual effect of human-machine collaboration. These improvements will contribute to the depth and practicality of the chapter content, making it more in line with the theme of this book.

REFERENCES

Akyuz, Y. (2020). Effects of intelligent tutoring systems (ITS) on personalized learning (PL). *Creative Education, 11*(06), 953–978. DOI: 10.4236/ce.2020.116069

Beer, P., & Mulder, R. H. (2020). The effects of technological developments on work and their implications for continuous vocational education and training: A systematic review. *Frontiers in Psychology, 11*, 918. DOI: 10.3389/fpsyg.2020.00918 PMID: 32457688

Bucea-Manea- oniş, R., Martins, O. M., Bucea-Manea- oniş, R., Gheorghi ă, C., Kuleto, V., Ilić, M. P., & Simion, V. E. (2021). Blockchain technology enhances sustainable higher education. *Sustainability (Basel), 13*(22), 12347. DOI: 10.3390/su132212347

Bukar, U. A., Sayeed, M. S., Razak, S. F. A., Yogarayan, S., Amodu, O. A., & Mahmood, R. A. R. (2023). A method for analyzing text using VOSviewer. *MethodsX, 11*, 102339. DOI: 10.1016/j.mex.2023.102339 PMID: 37693657

Bulathwela, S., Pérez-Ortiz, M., Holloway, C., Cukurova, M., & Shawe-Taylor, J. (2024). Artificial intelligence alone will not democratise education: On educational inequality, techno-solutionism and inclusive tools. *Sustainability (Basel), 16*(2), 781. DOI: 10.3390/su16020781

Chen, X., Zou, D., Xie, H., Cheng, G., & Liu, C. (2022). Two decades of artificial intelligence in education. *Journal of Educational Technology & Society, 25*(1), 28–47.

Chiu, T. K., Moorhouse, B. L., Chai, C. S., & Ismailov, M. (2024). Teacher support and student motivation to learn with Artificial Intelligence (AI) based chatbot. *Interactive Learning Environments, 32*(7), 3240–3256. DOI: 10.1080/10494820.2023.2172044

Dunn, T. J., & Kennedy, M. (2019). Technology Enhanced Learning in higher education; motivations, engagement and academic achievement. *Computers & Education, 137*, 104–113. DOI: 10.1016/j.compedu.2019.04.004

George, A. S. (2024). Technology Tension in Schools: Addressing the Complex Impacts of Digital Advances on Teaching, Learning, and Wellbeing. *Partners Universal Multidisciplinary Research Journal, 1*(3), 49–65.

Goswami, A., & Sharma, A. (2024). AI for bridging socio-economic inequities in Indian education space. *International Journal of Innovation and Scientific Research, XI*(IV), 890–935. DOI: 10.51244/IJRSI.2024.1104066

Hamid, H., Zulkifli, K., Naimat, F., Yaacob, N. L. C., & Ng, K. W. (2023). Exploratory study on student perception on the use of chat AI in process-driven problem-based learning. *Currents in Pharmacy Teaching & Learning*, *15*(12), 1017–1025. DOI: 10.1016/j.cptl.2023.10.001 PMID: 37923639

Hellín, C. J., Calles-Esteban, F., Valledor, A., Gómez, J., Otón-Tortosa, S., & Tayebi, A. (2023). Enhancing student motivation and engagement through a gamified learning environment. *Sustainability (Basel)*, *15*(19), 14119. DOI: 10.3390/su151914119

Hossain, M. E., & Islam, M. A. (2024). AI and the Future of Education: Philosophical Questions about the Role of Artificial Intelligence in the Classroom. *International Journal of Research and Innovation in Social Science*, *8*(IIIS, 3s), 5541–5547. DOI: 10.47772/IJRISS.2024.803419S

Huang, A. Y., Lu, O. H., & Yang, S. J. (2023). Effects of artificial Intelligence–Enabled personalized recommendations on learners' learning engagement, motivation, and outcomes in a flipped classroom. *Computers & Education*, *194*, 104684. DOI: 10.1016/j.compedu.2022.104684

Huang, L. (2023). Ethics of artificial intelligence in education: Student privacy and data protection. *Science Insights Education Frontiers*, *16*(2), 2577–2587. DOI: 10.15354/sief.23.re202

Ivanova, M., Grosseck, G., & Holotescu, C. (2024, February). Unveiling Insights: A Bibliometric Analysis of Artificial Intelligence in Teaching. *In Informatics* (Vol. 11, No. 1, p. 10). MDPI. DOI: 10.3390/informatics11010010

Jin, S. H., Im, K., Yoo, M., Roll, I., & Seo, K. (2023). Supporting students' self-regulated learning in online learning using artificial intelligence applications. *International Journal of Educational Technology in Higher Education*, *20*(1), 37. DOI: 10.1186/s41239-023-00406-5

Kabudi, T., Pappas, I., & Olsen, D. H. (2021). AI-enabled adaptive learning systems: A systematic mapping of the literature. *Computers and Education: Artificial Intelligence*, *2*, 100017. DOI: 10.1016/j.caeai.2021.100017

Khan, W. N. (2024). Ethical Challenges of AI in Education: Balancing Innovation with Data Privacy. *Journal of AI in Education: Innovations, Opportunities, Challenges, and Future Directions*, *1*(1), 1–13.

Lee, S., & Park, G. (2023). Exploring the impact of ChatGPT literacy on user satisfaction: The mediating role of user motivations. *Cyberpsychology, Behavior, and Social Networking*, *26*(12), 913–918. DOI: 10.1089/cyber.2023.0312 PMID: 38090765

Limna, P., Jakwatanatham, S., Siripipattanakul, S., Kaewpuang, P., & Sriboonruang, P. (2022). A review of artificial intelligence (AI) in education during the digital era. *Advance Knowledge for Executives, 1*(1), 1–9. DOI: 10.1080/13621025.2022.2147262

Lu, A., Wong, C. S., Cheung, R. Y., & Im, T. S. (2021, April). Supporting flipped and gamified learning with augmented reality in higher education. In Frontiers in education (Vol. 6, p. 623745). *Frontiers Media SA*. DOI: 10.3389/feduc.2021.623745

Mensah, G. B. (2023). Artificial intelligence and ethics: a comprehensive review of bias mitigation, transparency, and accountability in AI Systems. *Preprint, November, 10*(1).

Mora, H., Signes-Pont, M. T., Fuster-Guilló, A., & Pertegal-Felices, M. L. (2020). A collaborative working model for enhancing the learning process of science & engineering students. *Computers in Human Behavior, 103*, 140–150. DOI: 10.1016/j.chb.2019.09.008

Ouyang, F., Zheng, L., & Jiao, P. (2022). Artificial intelligence in online higher education: A systematic review of empirical research from 2011 to 2020. *Education and Information Technologies, 27*(6), 7893–7925. DOI: 10.1007/s10639-022-10925-9

Pedro, F., Subosa, M., Rivas, A., & Valverde, P. (2019). Artificial intelligence in education: Challenges and opportunities for sustainable development. DOI: 10.1145/3394332.3402828

Rane, N., Choudhary, S., & Rane, J. (2023). Education 4.0 and 5.0: Integrating artificial intelligence (AI) for personalized and adaptive learning. DOI: 10.2139/ssrn.4638365

Sharma, Y. (2024). Use of Modern Technology to Improve the Quality of Education. [JOIREM]. *Journal Publication of International Research for Engineering and Management, 10*(12).

Song, C., & Song, Y. (2023). Enhancing academic writing skills and motivation: Assessing the efficacy of ChatGPT in AI-assisted language learning for EFL students. *Frontiers in Psychology, 14*, 1260843. DOI: 10.3389/fpsyg.2023.1260843 PMID: 38162975

Vistorte, A. O. R., Deroncele-Acosta, A., Ayala, J. L. M., Barrasa, A., López-Granero, C., & Martí-González, M. (2024). Integrating artificial intelligence to assess emotions in learning environments: A systematic literature review. *Frontiers in Psychology, 15*, 1387089. DOI: 10.3389/fpsyg.2024.1387089 PMID: 38966729

Xia, Q., Chiu, T. K., Lee, M., Sanusi, I. T., Dai, Y., & Chai, C. S. (2022). A self-determination theory (SDT) design approach for inclusive and diverse artificial intelligence (AI) education. *Computers & Education*, *189*, 104582. DOI: 10.1016/j.compedu.2022.104582

Zhai, X., Chu, X., Chai, C. S., Jong, M. S. Y., Istenic, A., Spector, M., Liu, J.-B., Yuan, J., & Li, Y. (2021). A Review of Artificial Intelligence (AI) in Education from 2010 to 2020. *Complexity*, *2021*(1), 8812542. DOI: 10.1155/2021/8812542

Zhang, H., Lee, I., Ali, S., DiPaola, D., Cheng, Y., & Breazeal, C. (2023). Integrating ethics and career futures with technical learning to promote AI literacy for middle school students: An exploratory study. *International Journal of Artificial Intelligence in Education*, *33*(2), 290–324. DOI: 10.1007/s40593-022-00293-3 PMID: 35573722

Chapter 6
Ethical Frameworks in Artificial Intelligence for Education:
A Systematic Review and Practical Insights Through Bibliometric Analysis

Mohammed AlEisaei
https://orcid.org/0009-0007-0484-4605
Sohar University, Oman

Ali Mohammad Jubran
https://orcid.org/0009-0001-5464-363X
Faculty of Education and Arts, Sohar University, Oman & Yarmouk University, Irbed, Jordan

Mohamad Azrien bin Mohamed Adnan
https://orcid.org/0000-0002-3578-3581
Universiti Malaya, Malaysia

Haitham Salim Humaid Al Qurri
Universiti Malaya, Malaysia

ABSTRACT

AI in education has transformed teaching, learning, and assessment. It raises difficult ethical issues pertaining to equity, privacy, algorithmic prejudice, and academic integrity. This article examines ethical issues, theoretical frameworks, stakeholder views, and ethical AI deployment in education through a systematic

DOI: 10.4018/979-8-3373-5550-4.ch006

literature review (SLR). This study synthesises ethical AI research in education by defining major challenges, exploring theoretical and philosophical contributions, analysing educator and student views, and assessing ethical AI integration solutions. The PRISMA framework discovered 414 Scopus articles. After applying inclusion/ exclusion criteria, 37 papers were examined. The study categorises and interprets findings across major themes using bibliometrics. AI biases, data privacy hazards, and critical thinking and academic integrity loss are among the ethical concerns found. Constructivism, sociocultural theories, and multi-theoretical frameworks underpin ethical AI.

INTRODUCTION

The rapid advancement of artificial intelligence (AI) technologies has significantly transformed the educational landscape, offering opportunities for personalized learning, enhanced instructional methodologies, and streamlined administrative processes. From automated grading systems to adaptive learning platforms, AI has the potential to redefine how education is delivered and experienced. However, alongside its promise, AI integration has sparked critical debates surrounding ethical issues such as data privacy, algorithmic biases, equity, and the role of human agency in learning environments. Addressing these concerns requires robust ethical frameworks to guide the responsible adoption of AI in education, ensuring that technological advancements align with core values of equity, inclusivity, and academic integrity (Swindell et al., 2024; Butson & Spronken-Smith, 2024).

One prominent challenge arises from the proliferation of generative AI tools, such as ChatGPT, which allow students to produce human-like text effortlessly. This capability has blurred the lines between original work and machine-generated content, posing significant implications for academic integrity and assessment practices. Institutions are grappling with policy inconsistencies, as some encourage ethical AI use while others ban it outright. These varying approaches underscore the urgent need for clear guidelines to govern AI usage in educational contexts and ensure a consistent understanding among students and educators (Gonsalves, 2024).

AI's ability to handle complex datasets, automate decision-making, and facilitate personalized learning environments has brought numerous benefits but also unique ethical dilemmas. For instance, biases embedded in algorithms can perpetuate inequalities, while the unequal access to advanced AI tools risks exacerbating existing educational disparities. Beyond technical fixes, these challenges demand a critical examination of the societal and cultural implications of AI in education, ensuring that its adoption does not unintentionally reinforce systemic barriers (Swindell et al., 2024; Butson & Spronken-Smith, 2024).

Efforts to navigate these challenges have led to the development of ethical frameworks and structured methodologies for integrating AI in education. Grounded in human-centric approaches and philosophical principles, these frameworks emphasize the importance of ethical considerations alongside technological capabilities. For example, the works of Freire and Bloom advocate for a humanizing use of AI that fosters critical thinking, creativity, and ethical engagement in learning. Similarly, decision-making models such as multi-attribute group decision-making (MAGDM) offer structured approaches for evaluating AI's impact on education, balancing efficiency with ethical responsibility (Swindell et al., 2024; Mahboob et al., 2024).

Despite these advancements, gaps remain in understanding and applying these ethical frameworks effectively. Existing research highlights the potential of AI to enhance educational practices but also warns against its risks if implemented without sufficient ethical oversight. This paper aims to address these gaps by synthesizing current research on AI ethics in education and providing practical insights. The goal is to contribute to the development of strategies that not only harness AI's transformative power but also ensure its implementation upholds principles of transparency, fairness, and integrity. By fostering a critical dialogue on these issues, this study seeks to inform policies and practices that will shape the future of ethical AI integration in education. Thus, the following research questions were developed to achive this study objective:

1. What are the prevailing ethical concerns associated with the use of artificial intelligence in education, and how have these concerns been addressed in recent literature?
2. How do existing ethical frameworks guide the integration of AI technologies in education, and what are their limitations in addressing challenges such as equity, privacy, and academic integrity?
3. What role do philosophical and theoretical perspectives play in shaping ethical frameworks for AI in education, and how can these perspectives inform future practices?
4. How do educators and students perceive the ethical use of AI in teaching, learning, and assessment, and what factors influence their compliance with ethical guidelines?
5. What strategies and methodologies have been proposed to evaluate and enhance the ethical deployment of AI in education, particularly in balancing technological efficiency with equity and inclusivity?

METHODS

This systematic review was conducted in adherence to the PRISMA guidelines (Page et al., 2021) to ensure a rigorous, transparent, and replicable methodology. The review aims to identify and synthesize studies addressing ethical frameworks for artificial intelligence (AI) in education, focusing on the practical and theoretical implications of these frameworks. The systematic search was conducted using the Scopus database, chosen for its extensive indexing of high-quality, multidisciplinary academic literature. The search was performed on 25th November 2024 using carefully selected keywords and predefined filters.

The search strategy employed the query:

TITLE-ABS-KEY (ai AND ethical AND frameworks AND education) AND PUBYEAR > 2018 AND PUBYEAR < 2025 AND (LIMIT-TO (SUBJAREA, "COMP") OR LIMIT-TO (SUBJAREA, "SOCI") OR LIMIT-TO (SUBJAREA, "BUSI") OR LIMIT-TO (SUBJAREA, "ARTS") OR LIMIT-TO (SUBJAREA, "ECON")) AND (LIMIT-TO (DOCTYPE, "ar") OR LIMIT-TO (DOCTYPE, "cp")) AND (LIMIT-TO (LANGUAGE, "English")).

1. This query was designed to capture a comprehensive range of studies published between 2019 and 2024, covering the subject areas most relevant to AI ethics and education. Initial search results yielded 414 documents, which were subjected to a systematic screening and eligibility process as outlined in figure 1. Screening Phase: After removing duplicates, abstracts and titles of the records were reviewed to assess their alignment with the study's scope. This process narrowed the records down to 246 documents.
2. **Eligibility Phase**: Full-text screening of the selected documents was conducted. 71 documents were successfully retrieved for detailed evaluation, while 175 records were excluded due to inaccessibility or incomplete data.
3. **Inclusion Phase**: After thorough examination, 37 documents were included in the final analysis based on their direct relevance to the topic. 34 documents were excluded for focusing on unrelated topics such as cybersecurity, sustainable development, healthcare, and management or entrepreneurship courses.

The step-by-step process is visually summarized in the PRISMA flow diagram (Figure 1). This systematic methodology ensures that only high-quality, directly relevant studies inform the review's findings and insights.

Figure 1. PRISMA framework

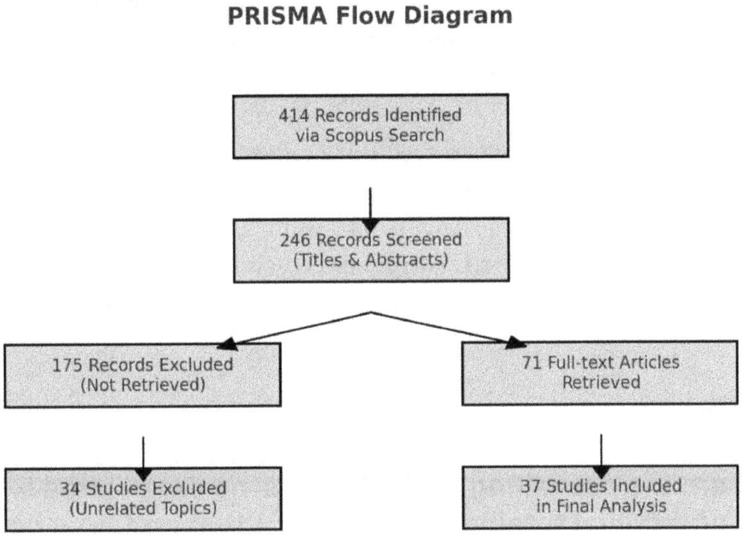

Inclusion and Exclusion Criteria

A clear set of inclusion and exclusion criteria was applied to systematically filter studies and ensure relevance to the research objective. These criteria are detailed in the table below:

Table 1. Inclusion and exclusion criteria

Criteria	Inclusion	Exclusion
Focus	Studies addressing ethical frameworks in the context of AI for education.	Studies focusing on cybersecurity, sustainable development, healthcare, or management unrelated to education.
Publication Period	Published between 2019 and 2024 to reflect recent advancements in the field.	Publications before 2019 or beyond 2024.
Document Type	Articles and conference papers indexed in Scopus.	Non-Scopus indexed publications, reviews, or book chapters.
Subject Areas	Relevant fields, including Computer Science, Sociology, Business, Arts, and Economics.	Irrelevant fields not aligned with the study's educational and ethical focus.
Language	Written in English.	Non-English publications.
Accessibility	Full-text documents retrievable through Scopus or institutional access.	Documents with inaccessible full-text or incomplete records.

Table 1 shows set of inclusion and exclusion criteria was applied to systematically filter studies and ensure relevance to the research objective. The review aimed to ensure all included studies explicitly address the development, application, or evaluation of ethical frameworks for AI in educational contexts. Restricting the timeframe to 2019–2024 ensures that only the most recent and relevant advancements are considered. By narrowing the scope to specific document types and subject areas, the review targeted high-quality, peer-reviewed articles and conference proceedings in fields directly contributing to the discussion on ethics, AI, and education. Including only English publications ensured clarity and accessibility for the analysis, while the exclusion of inaccessible documents minimized biases arising from incomplete data.

RESULTS

1. What are the prevailing ethical concerns associated with the use of artificial intelligence in education, and how have these concerns been addressed in recent literature?

The integration of artificial intelligence (AI) in education has brought forth a myriad of ethical concerns, as highlighted in the reviewed literature. These concerns span across dimensions of equity, access, privacy, biases, accountability, and the implications of generative AI technologies. Fgure 2 shows The integration of artificial intelligence (AI) in education has brought forth a myriad of ethical concerns.

Figure 2. Shows the integration of artificial intelligence (AI) in education has brought forth a myriad of ethical concerns.

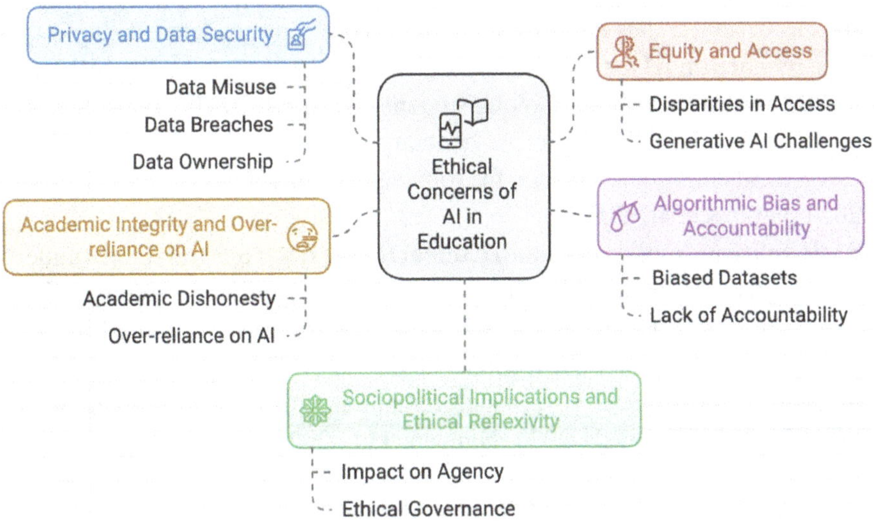

As shown in figure 2 The integration of artificial intelligence (AI) in education has brought forth a myriad of ethical concerns. The researchers divided these into five main domain as follow:

1. **Equity and Access:** Equity in access to AI tools is a recurring concern. Studies emphasize disparities in how AI technologies are distributed and utilized, often disadvantaging underrepresented and resource-constrained communities (Blair Black et al.; Guettala et al., 2024). Similarly, the adoption of generative AI tools raises challenges related to ensuring inclusivity, particularly for diverse linguistic and cultural backgrounds (Lin et al., 2024; Kanont et al., 2024).
2. **Privacy and Data Security:** Data privacy and security are critical issues. Researchers highlight the risks associated with the misuse of personal data and the potential breaches in AI-powered systems (Ibrahim et al., 2024; Luckin et al., 2024). Concerns about data ownership, transparency, and informed consent further complicate the ethical landscape (Holmes et al., 2023; Mökander et al., 2022).
3. **Algorithmic Bias and Accountability:** Algorithmic biases, particularly related to race, gender, and cultural stereotypes, pose significant challenges. Studies identify the perpetuation of inequalities due to biased datasets and insufficient diversity in training data (Ibrahim et al., 2024; Kusuma et al., 2022). The lack of

accountability in automated grading systems and explainable AI (XAI) further exacerbates these concerns (Figueras et al., 2024; Nannini et al., 2024).

4. **Academic Integrity and Over-reliance on AI:** The rise of generative AI tools, such as ChatGPT, has introduced concerns regarding academic dishonesty and over-reliance on AI for learning tasks. Educators worry about diminishing critical thinking and creativity among students (Tarisayi, 2024; Yoon et al., 2024). Additionally, the reliability of AI-generated content and its potential misuse in assessments highlight the need for robust guidelines (Elhersh & Alqawasmeh, 2024; Perkins et al., 2024).
5. **Sociopolitical Implications and Ethical Reflexivity:** Several studies underline the broader sociopolitical implications of AI in education, including its impact on teacher and student agency and the ethical reflexivity required in its integration (Swindell et al., 2024; Mouta et al., 2024). The challenges of balancing innovation with ethical governance remain a critical discussion point in the literature (Mumtaz et al., 2024; Nguyen et al., 2023).

2. How do existing ethical frameworks guide the integration of AI technologies in education, and what are their limitations in addressing challenges such as equity, privacy, and academic integrity?

The reviewed literature highlights various ethical frameworks that have been proposed to guide the integration of AI technologies in education. However, numerous limitations were identified, particularly in addressing critical issues such as equity, privacy, and academic integrity. Figure 3 illustrates the limitations to the existing ethical frameworks guide the integration of AI technologies in education.

Figure 3. The limitations to the existing ethical frameworks guide the integration of AI technologies in education.

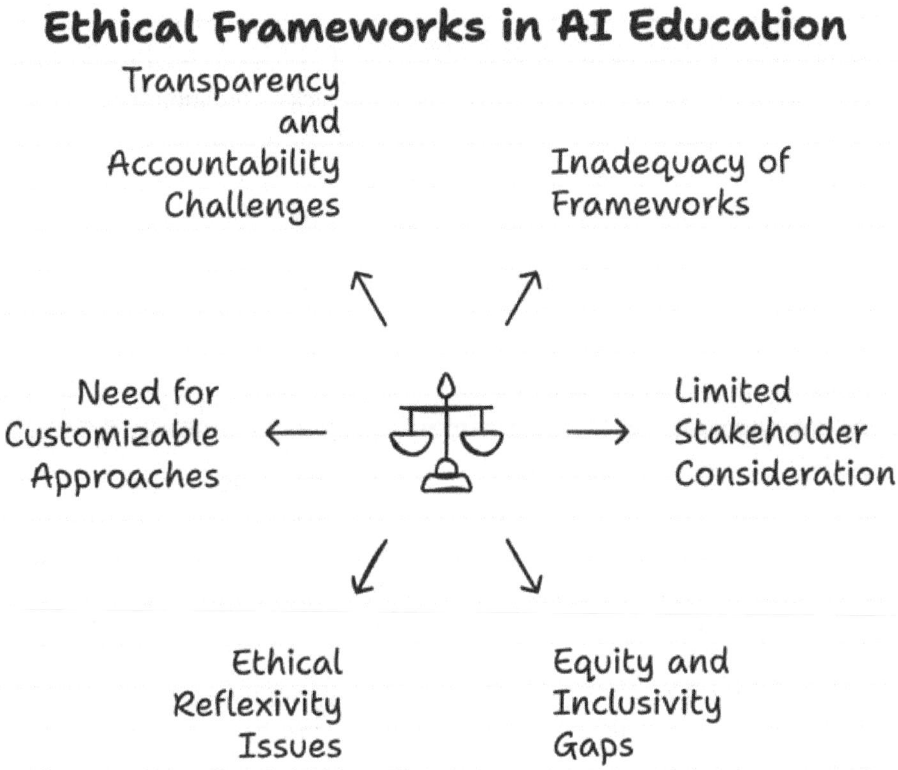

As shown in figure 3, the limitations to the existing ethical frameworks guide the integration of AI technologies in education are elaborated as follow:

1. **Inadequacy of Existing Frameworks:** Many frameworks lack direct AI-specific inclusions and fail to address the nuances of integrating AI technologies in education. For example, ISTE Standards and CAEP guidelines require enhancements to reflect AI's role in modern classrooms (Blair Black et al., 2024). Similarly, AstraZeneca's Principles for Ethical Data and AI emphasize fairness and accountability but lack practical tools for implementation (Mökander et al., 2022). Frameworks such as FATE (Fairness, Accountability, Transparency, Ethics) also need development to address cultural and linguistic diversity in educational contexts (Lin et al., 2024).

2. **Limited Consideration for Stakeholder Needs:** Several frameworks fail to incorporate the perspectives of multiple stakeholders, such as educators, students, and policymakers. For instance, the Golden Triangle Framework emphasizes collaboration between educators, researchers, and developers but needs scalability across varied educational settings (Luckin et al., 2024). Similarly, the AI-ICE framework assesses cognitive engagement but lacks validation for application across different educational levels (Wood & Moss, 2024).
3. **Gaps in Addressing Equity and Inclusivity:** Ethical frameworks often struggle with integrating equity and inclusivity as core principles. The Technology Acceptance Model (TAM) provides theoretical underpinnings but requires adaptation for cultural and contextual relevance (Kanont et al., 2024). Hofstede's cultural dimensions and current AI literacy frameworks fail to address rapidly evolving AI ethics challenges and the diverse cultural contexts in which these technologies are applied (Mumtaz et al., 2024; Taiye et al., 2024).
4. **Insufficient Integration of Ethical Reflexivity:** Some frameworks focus on theoretical principles without providing practical or context-specific implementation guidelines. For example, the "Doing Responsibilities" framework emphasizes shared accountability but lacks mechanisms to integrate nonhuman agents and regulatory aspects (Figueras et al., 2024). Furthermore, ethical customization for adaptive learning systems often remains underdeveloped (Guettala et al., 2024).
5. **The Need for Iterative and Customizable Approaches:** Frameworks like the Delphi-based teacher CPD programs require broader stakeholder inclusion to address ethical challenges in AI-enhanced education effectively (Mouta et al., 2024). Similarly, TAM and UGT frameworks address motivations for AI adoption but lack specificity in ethical and cultural customization (Le et al., 2024).
6. **Challenges in Fostering Transparency and Accountability:** Transparency and accountability are recurring themes in the literature. The AI Assessment Scale (AIAS) offers structured integration of AI tools but requires contextual customization across disciplines (Perkins et al., 2024). Ethical frameworks for explainable AI (XAI) prioritize transparency and fairness but fail to consider the contextual nature of ethical decisions (Nannini et al., 2024).

While existing frameworks provide foundational guidance, they exhibit significant limitations in their scope and adaptability. There is a pressing need for ethical frameworks that integrate stakeholder-driven customization, iterative feedback mechanisms, and practical tools to address challenges related to equity, privacy, and academic integrity. Future efforts should focus on bridging these gaps to foster equitable and ethical AI integration in education.

3. What role do philosophical and theoretical perspectives play in shaping ethical frameworks for AI in education, and how can these perspectives inform future practices?

The reviewed literature underscores the significance of philosophical and theoretical perspectives in shaping ethical frameworks for AI integration in education. These perspectives provide the foundation for addressing ethical challenges and guide the development of practices that prioritize human-centric and culturally sensitive AI applications.

Table 2. The role of philosophical and theoretical perspectives in shaping ethical frameworks for AI in education

Perspective/Theory	Key Features	Examples from Literature
Constructivist Frameworks	Emphasizes collaboration, reflection, and iterative learning in AI integration.	Roy & Putatunda (2023), Perkins et al. (2024), Mohammad Awad AlAfnan (2024).
Sociocultural Perspectives	Focuses on cultural diversity, professional identity, and contextual learning in AI ethics.	Karataş & Yüce (2024), Mumtaz et al. (2024), Yoon et al. (2024).
Humanistic Approaches	Balances technology with ethical considerations, emphasizing socially embedded AI practices.	Cacho (2024), Guettala et al. (2024), Nguyen et al. (2023).
Ethical Design Principles	Incorporates transparency, empathy, and historical context into educational AI applications.	Kusuma et al. (2022), Ibrahim et al. (2024), Holmes et al. (2023).
Multi-Theoretical Frameworks	Combines multiple theories to comprehensively address ethical challenges (e.g., MAGDM, XAI).	Mahboob et al. (2024), Nannini et al. (2024), Taiye et al. (2024).
Dialogic Ethics	Emphasizes shared agency and contextualized understanding of ethical challenges.	Mouta et al. (2024), Figueras et al. (2024).
Posthumanist Perspectives	Explores shared human-nonhuman responsibilities in AI governance.	Figueras et al. (2024).
Practical and Governance Models	Focuses on stakeholder collaboration, interdisciplinary approaches, and practical implementation.	Nguyen et al. (2023), Ibrahim et al. (2024), Holmes et al. (2023).

Table 2 organizes the theoretical and philosophical contributions into key categories, providing a quick reference for the findings. the theoretical and philosophical contributions are categrorized ad follow:

1. **Constructivist and Pedagogical Frameworks:** Constructivist learning theories emerged as a recurring perspective, emphasizing the collaborative and reflective integration of AI. For instance, Roy and Putatunda (2023) advocate for AI as a collaborator rather than a replacement in education. Similarly, Perkins et al. (2024) propose scalable AI assessment frameworks that incorporate iterative and reflexive models. Nancye Blair Black et al. (2024) highlight the TPACK framework and the Theory of Virtuality to support pedagogical integration of AI, while Leelavathi and Surendhranatha (2024) focus on ChatGPT's potential to enhance active learning and critical engagement.
2. **Sociocultural and Humanistic Approaches:** Sociocultural theories play a pivotal role in understanding professional identity formation and diverse cultural contexts in AI ethics. Karataş and Yüce (2024) reflect on sociocultural perspectives in AI-based learning, while Mumtaz et al. (2024) combine Hofstede's Cultural Dimensions Theory with Structural Topic Modeling (STM) to explore cultural differences in AI ethics. Humanistic approaches, such as those discussed by Cacho (2024), balance technological advancements with ethical considerations, emphasizing the need for socially embedded AI practices within academic environments.
3. **Ethical Design and Governance:** Ethical frameworks benefit from design principles that incorporate transparency, empathy, and historical context. Kusuma et al. (2022) integrate these elements into educational AI applications. Meanwhile, Nguyen et al. (2023) highlight interdisciplinary and stakeholder-driven approaches to foster equitable AI integration, stressing the importance of governance frameworks that prioritize fairness and privacy (Ibrahim et al., 2024).
4. **Multi-Theoretical Integrations:** Several studies combine multiple theoretical frameworks to address ethical challenges comprehensively. For example, Mahboob et al. (2024) leverage the Multi-Attribute Group Decision-Making (MAGDM) framework, while Nannini et al. (2024) utilize applied ethics, deontology, consequentialism, and virtue ethics to ground explainable AI (XAI) systems ethically. Yoon et al. (2024) combine the Interactive Proving Experience Framework with sociocultural theories to analyze student-AI collaboration.
5. **Dialogic and Posthumanist Ethics:** Dialogic ethics emphasize shared agency and contextualized understanding of ethical challenges, as proposed by Mouta et al. (2024). Figueras et al. (2024) draw on posthumanist theories to explore shared human-nonhuman responsibilities, advocating for ethical reflexivity in AI adoption.
6. **Practical Implications and Future Directions:** The literature suggests that future frameworks should integrate constructivist and sociocultural perspectives to foster a balanced approach to AI ethics. Holmes et al. (2023) emphasize the

need to differentiate between "doing ethical things" and "doing things ethically" in pedagogy. Embracing interdisciplinary approaches, such as the Soft Systems Methodology (Taiye et al., 2024), can ensure that diverse stakeholder perspectives are incorporated into ethical AI development. Philosophical and theoretical perspectives provide a critical lens for analyzing and addressing ethical challenges in AI integration. By leveraging constructivist, sociocultural, humanistic, and multi-theoretical approaches, educators and policymakers can create ethical frameworks that are adaptable, equitable, and reflective of diverse educational contexts. Future practices should focus on interdisciplinary collaborations and the iterative refinement of these frameworks to address the evolving ethical landscape of AI in education.

4. How do educators and students perceive the ethical use of AI in teaching, learning, and assessment, and what factors influence their compliance with ethical guidelines?

The reviewed studies highlight diverse perceptions among educators and students regarding the ethical use of AI in education. These perceptions are shaped by factors such as transparency, trust, utility, privacy concerns, and the potential impacts on creativity and critical thinking.

Table 3. The diverse perceptions among educators and students regarding the ethical use of AI in education

Perception Theme	Key Insights	Examples from Literature
Utility and Efficiency	Both educators and students recognize AI's potential to enhance efficiency, engagement, and personalization in learning.	Blair Black et al., Mahboob et al. (2024), Luckin et al. (2024).
Concerns Over Integrity	Academic dishonesty, over-reliance, and diminished critical thinking are frequent concerns among educators and students.	Swindell et al. (2024), Roy & Putatunda (2023), Le et al. (2024).
Data Privacy and Fairness	Concerns include risks to data security, algorithmic fairness, and biases in AI systems.	Kusuma et al. (2022), Osamor et al. (2023), Ibrahim et al. (2024).
Perceived Mistrust	Lack of trust in institutional AI policies, ambiguous ethical guidelines, and mixed compliance levels.	Gonsalves (2024), Holmes et al. (2023), Figueras et al. (2024).
Mixed Perceptions by Role	Educators worry about AI's impacts on traditional pedagogy, while students appreciate convenience but fear over-dependence.	Lin et al. (2024), Taiye et al. (2024), Yoon et al. (2024).

continued on following page

Table 3. Continued

Perception Theme	Key Insights	Examples from Literature
Cultural and Contextual Variations	Ethical perceptions vary by region, cultural cluster, and educational context.	Mumtaz et al. (2024), Guettala et al. (2024).
Recommendations for Action	Calls for professional development, structured ethical training, and co-development of guidelines.	Mouta et al. (2024), Mohammad Awad AlAfnan (2024), Perkins et al. (2024).

The perceptions of educators and students regarding the ethical use of AI in education are diverse and multifaceted. Below is an elaboration on the key themes summarized in the table:

1. **Utility and Efficiency:** AI tools are widely appreciated for their ability to enhance efficiency, engagement, and personalized learning experiences. Educators value AI for streamlining administrative tasks and enabling differentiated instruction tailored to individual student needs (Blair Black et al., 2024). Similarly, students recognize AI's adaptability, particularly its ability to provide tailored feedback and real-time support (Luckin et al., 2024; Mahboob et al., 2024).
2. **Concerns Over Integrity:** Despite its benefits, educators and students express significant concerns about academic dishonesty and over-reliance on AI tools. Generative AI, such as ChatGPT, raises ethical dilemmas related to plagiarism and the reduction of critical thinking and creativity in students. For example, Swindell et al. (2024) highlight educators' struggles to balance the efficiency of AI with the need to foster critical thinking and agency in students. Similarly, students worry about the authenticity of AI-generated content and its potential to undermine original thought (Le et al., 2024; Roy & Putatunda, 2023).
3. **Data Privacy and Fairness:** Data security and algorithmic fairness are recurring concerns. Both students and educators emphasize the need for transparency in AI systems to ensure fair treatment and protect personal information (Kusuma et al., 2022; Osamor et al., 2023). For instance, Ibrahim et al. (2024) highlight the challenges of ensuring algorithmic fairness, particularly in systems that rely on biased or incomplete datasets.
4. **Perceived Mistrust:** A lack of trust in institutional AI policies and ambiguous ethical guidelines contribute to mixed perceptions of AI use in education. Gonsalves (2024) identifies students' fear of academic penalties and their mistrust of AI declaration processes. Similarly, Holmes et al. (2023) note that educators and institutions have varying levels of trust in AI, often demanding clearer and more actionable guidelines.

5. **Mixed Perceptions by Role:** Educators and students often perceive AI's role differently. Educators express concerns about AI's impact on traditional pedagogy, fearing it might undermine the development of critical thinking and originality in students (Lin et al., 2024). On the other hand, students value the convenience and efficiency AI offers but are wary of becoming overly dependent on these technologies (Taiye et al., 2024; Yoon et al., 2024).
6. **Cultural and Contextual Variations:** Cultural and contextual differences significantly influence perceptions of AI ethics in education. For example, Mumtaz et al. (2024) report that business students' views on AI ethics vary across cultural clusters, such as Southern Asia and Latin Europe. Guettala et al. (2024) emphasize the need for localized ethical frameworks that consider specific educational and societal contexts.
7. **Recommendations for Action:** To address these concerns, the literature calls for targeted professional development and ethical training programs for educators. Structured initiatives can help teachers and students better understand AI's ethical implications and manage its integration effectively (Mouta et al., 2024). Additionally, co-development of ethical guidelines involving educators, students, and policymakers is critical to fostering transparency and trust in AI systems (Mohammad Awad AlAfnan, 2024; Perkins et al., 2024).

Overall, the perceptions of educators and students highlight both the opportunities and challenges of AI integration in education. While AI tools are valued for their efficiency and personalization capabilities, significant ethical concerns regarding integrity, privacy, and fairness remain. Addressing these concerns requires collaborative efforts, targeted professional development, and the development of transparent and culturally sensitive ethical frameworks.

5. What strategies and methodologies have been proposed to evaluate and enhance the ethical deployment of AI in education, particularly in balancing technological efficiency with equity and inclusivity?

The literature presents a range of strategies and methodologies aimed at promoting the ethical deployment of AI in education. These approaches emphasize the importance of transparency, equity, collaboration, and adaptability to ensure that AI technologies align with ethical standards while enhancing their effectiveness in educational contexts. Table 4 illustrates the strategies and methodologies aimed at promoting the ethical deployment of AI in education.

Table 4. The strategies and methodologies aimed at promoting the ethical deployment of AI in education.

Strategy/Methodology	Key Features	Examples from Literature
Foundational Ethical Frameworks	Frameworks that include AI literacy, transparency, fairness, and community-wide collaboration.	Holmes et al. (2021), Mahboob et al. (2024), Ibrahim et al. (2024).
Iterative and Adaptive Approaches	Emphasizes iterative development, stakeholder feedback, and adaptability of AI systems.	Mouta et al. (2024), Figueras et al. (2024), Guettala et al. (2024).
Stakeholder Involvement	Collaborative approaches engaging educators, policymakers, and students in co-designing AI systems.	Taiye et al. (2024), Luckin et al. (2024), Nannini et al. (2024).
Cultural and Contextual Customization	Tailoring AI tools and guidelines to cultural and contextual needs.	Mumtaz et al. (2024), Le et al. (2024), Tarisayi (2024).
Educational Professional Development	Structured CPD programs to train educators on ethical AI integration.	Karataş & Yüce (2024), Mouta et al. (2024), Elhersh & Alqawasmeh (2024).
Transparency and Accountability	Strategies focusing on transparency, regular audits, and clear ethical guidelines for AI tools.	Perkins et al. (2024), Nannini et al. (2024), Mökander et al. (2022).
AI Tools for Personalized Learning	Using AI tools like ChatGPT to enhance learning while embedding ethical oversight and guidance.	Alshahrani & Qureshi (2024), Leelavathi & Surendhranatha (2024), Wood & Moss (2024).
Compliance and Governance	Policies and governance frameworks promoting balanced technological adoption with ethical integrity.	Cacho (2024), Kanont et al. (2024), Nguyen et al. (2023).

1. **Foundational Ethical Frameworks:** Frameworks such as AIAS (Perkins et al., 2024) and the community-wide framework proposed by Holmes et al. (2021) emphasize integrating ethical considerations like transparency, equity, and inclusivity. These approaches also incorporate multidisciplinary expertise to guide stakeholders in designing trustworthy AI systems.
2. **Iterative and Adaptive Approaches:** Iterative development of AI systems, such as those proposed by Guettala et al. (2024) and Figueras et al. (2024), integrates multi-stakeholder feedback and retrains models to ensure ethical alignment. This approach ensures AI systems can adapt to evolving educational and ethical contexts.
3. **Stakeholder Involvement:** Engaging educators, policymakers, and students in AI co-design processes is critical for aligning technologies with educational needs and ethical principles. Taiye et al. (2024) suggest platforms like CHAT4ISP-AI, which integrate iterative development and stakeholder input, while Luckin et al. (2024) emphasize co-design strategies with educators.

4. **Cultural and Contextual Customization:** Ethical AI deployment requires cultural sensitivity and contextual understanding. For instance, Mumtaz et al. (2024) advocate for culturally tailored ethical guidelines, while Le et al. (2024) focus on integrating cultural contextualization into adoption strategies using frameworks like TAM.
5. **Educational Professional Development:** Professional development programs for educators are necessary to foster ethical reasoning and shared agency in AI integration. Mouta et al. (2024) and Karataş & Yüce (2024) highlight the importance of CPD frameworks that train educators on practical and ethical AI use in classrooms.
6. **Transparency and Accountability:** Clear ethical guidelines and regular auditing processes are crucial for ensuring AI's fairness and reliability. Nannini et al. (2024) propose integrating applied ethics and accountability mechanisms into XAI systems, while Mökander et al. (2022) emphasize risk-based governance tools.
7. **AI Tools for Personalized Learning:** AI tools like ChatGPT and GenAI are proposed for enhancing active learning, critical thinking, and personalization. However, ethical guidelines are needed to address risks like dependency and authenticity concerns (Leelavathi & Surendhranatha, 2024; Alshahrani & Qureshi, 2024).
8. **Compliance and Governance:** Balanced governance frameworks, as proposed by Cacho (2024) and Nguyen et al. (2023), align AI deployment with academic standards while promoting ethical oversight. Such strategies ensure sustainable and equitable adoption of AI in education.

These strategies collectively provide a roadmap for addressing the ethical challenges of AI in education, emphasizing the need for adaptability, inclusivity, and robust stakeholder collaboration.

6. Discussion

The integration of artificial intelligence (AI) in education presents a complex interplay of opportunities and challenges, particularly in addressing ethical concerns, shaping frameworks, and ensuring equitable implementation. This discussion synthesizes the key findings from the study, examining their implications for theory, practice, and future research.

Ethical Concerns in AI for Education

The findings reveal that ethical concerns surrounding AI in education primarily revolve around issues of equity, data privacy, algorithmic bias, and academic integrity. For example, while AI tools are praised for enhancing efficiency and personalization (Luckin et al., 2024; Blair Black et al., 2024), concerns persist regarding their potential to perpetuate inequities and biases, especially in resource-constrained environments (Tarisayi, 2024; Ibrahim et al., 2024). Algorithmic bias, as highlighted by Kusuma et al. (2022), underscores the need for transparent and inclusive datasets to ensure fairness.

Additionally, academic integrity emerged as a critical issue, particularly with generative AI tools like ChatGPT. Educators and students fear the erosion of critical thinking and originality, raising concerns about over-reliance on AI-generated content (Swindell et al., 2024; Roy & Putatunda, 2023). These findings suggest that ethical guidelines must address not only technical issues but also the broader pedagogical implications of AI integration.

The Role of Theoretical Perspectives in Shaping Ethical Frameworks

The study highlights the significance of philosophical and theoretical perspectives in shaping ethical AI frameworks. Constructivist theories, such as those proposed by Roy and Putatunda (2023) and Perkins et al. (2024), emphasize the importance of collaboration and reflection in AI deployment. Similarly, sociocultural and humanistic approaches advocate for culturally sensitive and socially embedded AI practices (Karataş & Yüce, 2024; Cacho, 2024). These theoretical perspectives provide a foundation for addressing the diverse ethical challenges of AI, emphasizing the importance of aligning technological innovation with educational values.

Notably, multi-theoretical approaches, such as the integration of MAGDM and Hofstede's Cultural Dimensions Theory (Mahboob et al., 2024; Mumtaz et al., 2024), highlight the need for interdisciplinary and context-specific frameworks. These approaches underscore the value of combining ethical design principles, such as transparency and empathy, with cultural and contextual customization to create inclusive AI systems.

Perceptions of Educators and Students

The study reveals mixed perceptions among educators and students regarding AI's role in education. While both groups acknowledge the potential of AI to enhance efficiency and engagement, significant concerns remain about its ethical implications. Educators worry about the impact of AI on traditional pedagogy, particularly its potential to undermine critical thinking and creativity (Swindell et al., 2024; Wood & Moss, 2024). Students, on the other hand, value AI for its adaptability and personalized learning capabilities but express concerns about dependency and academic dishonesty (Lin et al., 2024; Le et al., 2024).

Cultural and contextual differences further influence these perceptions. For instance, Mumtaz et al. (2024) note that business students' views on AI ethics vary across cultural clusters, emphasizing the need for localized ethical guidelines. These findings highlight the importance of involving diverse stakeholders in the development of ethical frameworks to ensure that they address the unique needs and concerns of different educational contexts.

Strategies and Methodologies for Ethical AI Deployment

The study identifies a range of strategies and methodologies for evaluating and enhancing the ethical deployment of AI in education. Iterative and adaptive approaches, such as those proposed by Guettala et al. (2024) and Figueras et al. (2024), emphasize the importance of stakeholder feedback and retraining AI models to address evolving ethical challenges. These approaches align with the call for interdisciplinary and collaborative frameworks that integrate diverse perspectives (Nannini et al., 2024; Taiye et al., 2024).

Professional development and ethical training programs for educators also emerge as critical strategies for fostering ethical AI integration. For example, Mouta et al. (2024) propose structured CPD programs to enhance educators' ethical reasoning and collaborative agency. Additionally, governance frameworks that prioritize transparency, fairness, and accountability, such as the AIAS and CHAT4ISP-AI models, provide practical tools for balancing technological efficiency with equity and inclusivity (Perkins et al., 2024; Taiye et al., 2024).

Implications for Theory and Practice

The findings underscore the importance of aligning theoretical frameworks with practical strategies to address the ethical challenges of AI in education. Constructivist and sociocultural theories provide a foundation for developing inclusive and culturally sensitive AI systems, while iterative and adaptive methodologies offer practical solutions for addressing technical and ethical issues. These insights highlight the need for interdisciplinary collaboration and stakeholder involvement in designing ethical AI frameworks.

For practitioners, the findings emphasize the importance of professional development and ethical training programs to equip educators with the skills and knowledge needed to integrate AI effectively. Policymakers and institutions must also prioritize the development of governance frameworks that ensure transparency, accountability, and fairness in AI deployment.

FUTURE RESEARCH DIRECTIONS

This study highlights several areas for future research. First, there is a need for longitudinal studies to evaluate the long-term impacts of AI on teaching, learning, and assessment. Second, future research should explore the effectiveness of professional development programs in fostering ethical AI integration. Third, further investigation is needed to understand the cultural and contextual factors influencing perceptions of AI ethics, particularly in underrepresented and resource-constrained contexts.

CONCLUSION

The integration of AI in education presents both opportunities and challenges, necessitating a balanced approach that prioritizes ethical considerations. By aligning theoretical frameworks with practical strategies and involving diverse stakeholders, the education sector can harness the potential of AI while addressing its ethical implications. This study provides a foundation for future research and practice, emphasizing the importance of transparency, equity, and inclusivity in the ethical deployment of AI in education.

REFERENCES

AlAfnan, M. A. (2024). Integrating AI into learning taxonomies: Ethical challenges and constructivist approaches. *Journal of Educational Technology, 19*(1), 45–78.

Alshahrani, S., & Qureshi, H. (2024). AI in immersive learning: Opportunities and ethical considerations. *Virtual Reality & Learning Journal, 14*(2), 67–89.

Barrera Castro, M.. (2024). Addressing bias in AI-powered personalized learning systems: Ethical challenges. *Computers & Education, 204*, 104801.

Blair Black, N.. (2024). *A framework for approaching AI education in educator preparation programs*. Association for the Advancement of Artificial Intelligence. DOI: 10.1609/aaai.v38i21.30351

Butson, R., & Spronken-Smith, R. (2024). AI and its implications for research in higher education: A critical dialogue. *Higher Education Research & Development, 43*(3), 563–577. DOI: 10.1080/07294360.2023.2280200

Cacho, L. (2024). Integrating AI into the educational policy landscape: Opportunities and challenges. *Education Policy Analysis Archives, 32*(5), 145–163.

Elhersh, A., & Alqawasmeh, F. (2024). Social media sentiment on ChatGPT in education: Ethical implications. *Journal of Social Media Research, 16*(4), 78–98.

Figueras, A.. (2024). Shared responsibilities in AI-enhanced educational tools: Ethical implications. *Learning, Media and Technology, 49*(2), 34–56.

Gonsalves, C. (2024). Addressing student non-compliance in AI use declarations: Implications for academic integrity and assessment in higher education. *Assessment & Evaluation in Higher Education.*

Guettala, A.. (2024). Ethical integration of generative AI in adaptive learning environments. *International Review of Research in Open and Distance Learning, 25*(1), 45–61.

Holmes, W.. (2021). The future of AI in education: Ethical frameworks for innovation. *British Journal of Educational Technology, 52*(4), 901–917.

Hutchinson, D. (2024). AI literacy for school librarians: Ethical considerations and best practices. *School Library Research, 17*(2), 45–68.

Ibrahim, M.. (2024). Addressing algorithmic bias in AI applications for education. *Journal of Learning Analytics, 11*(2), 45–67.

Kanont, J.. (2024). Cultural considerations in AI adoption for equitable education. *Education and Information Technologies*, *29*(4), 901–925.

Karataş, T., & Yüce, S. (2024). Ethical perspectives on integrating ChatGPT in teacher education: Benefits and challenges. Turkish Journal of Educational Technology.

Kusuma, D.. (2022). Ethical design principles for AI-based adaptive learning environments. *Journal of Educational Technology Systems*, *51*(3), 189–207.

Le, M.. (2024). Student motivations and ethical concerns in ChatGPT usage: A TAM and UGT perspective. *International Journal of Educational Technology in Higher Education*, *21*(3), 34–56.

Leelavathi, S., & Surendhranatha, R. (2024). Ethical considerations in the use of AI-assisted tools in management education. *Indian Journal of Management Studies*, *15*(2), 78–98.

Lin, Z.. (2024). AI-enhanced learning environments: Ethical challenges and design solutions. *Computers & Education*, *203*, 104786.

Luckin, R.. (2024). Collaborative frameworks for human-centric AI in education. *Computers in Human Behavior*, *127*, 107820.

Mahboob, A., Ullah, Z., Ovais, A., Rasheed, M. W., Edalatpanah, S. A., & Yasin, K. (2024). A MAGDM approach for evaluating the impact of artificial intelligence on education using 2-tuple linguistic q-rung orthopair fuzzy sets and Schweizer-Sklar weighted power average operator. *Frontiers in Artificial Intelligence*, *7*, 1347626. DOI: 10.3389/frai.2024.1347626 PMID: 38550976

Mökander, J.. (2022). A framework for ethical AI implementation in corporate training environments. *Journal of Business Ethics*, *178*(1), 23–40.

Mouta, H.. (2024). CPD programs for AI ethics: Addressing ethical challenges in AIEd. *Educational Technology Research and Development*, *72*(1), 78–95.

Mumtaz, Z.. (2024). AI ethics through cultural lenses: Frameworks for equitable deployment. *Asian Journal of Educational Research*, *13*(1), 89–107.

Nannini, C.. (2024). Explainable AI in education: An applied ethics approach. *Journal of Educational Technology Research*, *35*(1), 23–45.

Nguyen, V.. (2023). Global standards for ethical AI integration in education: A stakeholder perspective. *International Journal of Educational Development*, *59*(2), 23–41.

Osamor, C. H.. (2023). AI tools in education: Opportunities and ethical challenges. *Journal of Educational Computing Research*, *61*(1), 34–56.

Page, M. J., McKenzie, J. E., Bossuyt, P. M., Boutron, I., Hoffmann, T. C., Mulrow, C. D., & Moher, D. (2021). The PRISMA 2020 statement: An updated guideline for reporting systematic reviews. *BMJ (Clinical Research Ed.)*, *372*(71). Advance online publication. PMID: 33782057

Perkins, M.. (2024). AI in assessments: Ethical integration through the AI Assessment Scale. *Australasian Journal of Educational Technology*, *40*(4), 78–95.

Roy, S., & Putatunda, P. (2023). Pedagogical applications of AI in literature education: Ethical challenges and opportunities. *Humanities and Technology Review*, *15*(2), 78–96.

Soodan, R.. (2024). Leveraging AI for higher education: Addressing privacy and adoption concerns. *AI & Society*, *39*(1), 12–34.

Swindell, A., Greeley, L., Farag, A., & Verdone, B. (2024). Against artificial education: Towards an ethical framework for generative artificial intelligence (AI) use in education. *Online Learning : the Official Journal of the Online Learning Consortium*, *28*(2), 7–27. DOI: 10.24059/olj.v28i2.4438

Taiye, K.. (2024). Ethical dilemmas in generative AI for academic writing: A case for policy frameworks. *Policy Futures in Education*, *22*(3), 123–143.

Tarisayi, K. S. (2024). Generative AI and the ethical dilemmas in resource-constrained educational contexts. *South African Journal of Education*, *44*(1), 56–72.

Wood, T., & Moss, G. (2024). AI in classrooms: Building scaffolds for ethical integration. *Australian Journal of Education*, *68*(1), 45–62.

Yoon, S.. (2024). Ethical AI and academic proofs: A systematic ethical integration framework. *AI & Society*, *40*(2), 56–72.

APPENDIX

Table 5.

	Authors	Ethical Concerns Addressed in AI for Education (RQ1)	Existing Ethical Frameworks and Limitations (RQ2)	Philosophical/ Theoretical Perspectives in AI Ethics (RQ3)	Educators' and Students' Perceptions of AI Ethics (RQ4)	Strategies/ Methodologies for Ethical AI Deployment (RQ5)
1	Nancye Blair Black et al.	Concerns include equity, access, data privacy, and biases in AI tools used for instructional purposes.	Frameworks such as ISTE Standards and CAEP guidelines lack direct AI-specific inclusions and require enhancements.	Highlights the TPACK framework and Theory of Virtuality to address pedagogical integration of AI in EPPs.	Addresses the need for preservice teachers to understand societal implications of AI and develop critical ethical consciousness.	Proposes a seven-strategy framework including foundational AI literacy, exploratory experiences, and cross-curricular integration.
2	Mahboob et al. (2024)	Ethical concerns include fairness, transparency, accountability, privacy, and overcoming biases in AI systems for education.	Current frameworks are limited in addressing multi-stakeholder decision-making and fail to incorporate robust quantitative tools.	Multi-attribute group decision-making (MAGDM) framework using 2-tuple linguistic q-rung orthopair fuzzy sets for ethical AI integration.	Highlights diverse stakeholder perspectives emphasizing the need for transparency and trust in AI applications.	Proposes Entropy-VIKOR methodology to balance technical efficiency with ethical considerations in decision-making processes for AI integration.
3	Gonsalves (2024)	Concerns include non-compliance with AI use declarations, academic integrity challenges, and ambiguity in policy guidelines.	Frameworks like coursework coversheets and institutional guidelines lack clarity and enforcement, reducing effectiveness.	The Theory of Planned Behaviour (TPB) was used to analyze attitudes, subjective norms, and perceived control in AI use compliance.	Students fear academic penalties, lack trust in institutional fairness, and view AI declaration processes as ambiguous and inconsistent.	Proposes clear, consistent policies with transparency, trust-building strategies, and educational workshops on ethical AI usage.
4	Swindell et al. (2024)	Key concerns include generative AI's impact on academic integrity, bias in content generation, and its sociopolitical implications.	Framework highlights gaps in aligning AI technologies with Freire's and Arendt's humanizing educational goals.	Integrates perspectives from Freire, Arendt, Foucault, and Anders to propose human-centric and action-oriented ethical AI practices.	Educators struggle with balancing AI's efficiencies with fostering critical thinking, creativity, and student agency in the classroom.	Proposes a framework combining Revised Bloom's Taxonomy with Arendtian action to ethically integrate AI in learning and foster humanizing outcomes.

continued on following page

Table 5. Continued

	Authors	Ethical Concerns Addressed in AI for Education (RQ1)	Existing Ethical Frameworks and Limitations (RQ2)	Philosophical/ Theoretical Perspectives in AI Ethics (RQ3)	Educators' and Students' Perceptions of AI Ethics (RQ4)	Strategies/ Methodologies for Ethical AI Deployment (RQ5)
5	Butson & Spronken-Smith (2024)	Ethical concerns include data privacy, informed consent, and the methodological biases induced by AI tools in higher education.	Frameworks addressing AI integration lack emphasis on epistemological foundations and often prioritize quantitative over qualitative methods.	Highlights dialectical and epistemological tensions between AI's efficiency and traditional academic methodologies.	Mixed perceptions: educators value AI's efficiency but worry about undermining critical thinking, originality, and academic identity.	Proposes a dialectical framework for reconciling technological adoption with ethical integrity and epistemological rigor.
6	Karataş & Yüce (2024)	Key concerns include academic integrity, data security, and equitable access to AI tools in teacher education.	Existing frameworks inadequately address AI literacy and ethical guidelines in teacher training curricula.	Reflects on the sociocultural and narrative perspectives to understand professional identity formation in AI-based learning.	Preservice teachers value ChatGPT's ability to personalize learning but express concerns over its potential to hinder critical thinking.	Proposes integrating comprehensive AI literacy into teacher education, emphasizing ethical use and practical training for AI tools.
7	Soodan et al. (2024)	Concerns include data privacy, plagiarism risks, job impacts, and the ethical use of AI in academics.	TTF model used to assess the alignment of AI tools with academic tasks; frameworks lack sufficient empirical validation.	Combines Task-Technology Fit (TTF) and social network theories to explore adoption patterns among academics.	Academics appreciate efficiency gains from chatbots but express concerns over privacy and job impacts.	Proposes alignment of chatbot features with academic tasks, user-centered design, and training for adoption; suggests leveraging peer networks for diffusion.
8	Lin et al. (2024)	Concerns include inclusivity for diverse cultural and linguistic backgrounds, data biases, accountability, and academic integrity.	FATE framework (Fairness, Accountability, Transparency, Ethics) lacks full development in addressing cultural and linguistic diversity.	Draws from constructivism to understand students' reflective and meaning-making processes when engaging with AI.	Students appreciate AI's adaptability and personalized learning but express concerns about dependency, bias, and academic dishonesty.	Proposes co-designing AI with students to enhance cultural inclusivity and incorporating ethical standards through improved guidelines and training.
9	Ibrahim et al. (2024)	Algorithmic bias in AI systems, particularly concerning skin color, gender, and age; lack of diverse datasets; risks of misuse.	Ethical frameworks like the FATE model exist but need robust mechanisms to address algorithmic biases and data fairness.	Emphasizes a human-centered approach by integrating fairness, privacy, and transparency principles into AI governance frameworks.	Educators recognize the potential of AI for improving efficiency but stress concerns about ethical implications and algorithmic fairness.	Proposes targeted algorithms to identify and mitigate biases in datasets, emphasizing transparency, fairness, and regular auditing processes.

continued on following page

Table 5. Continued

	Authors	Ethical Concerns Addressed in AI for Education (RQ1)	Existing Ethical Frameworks and Limitations (RQ2)	Philosophical/ Theoretical Perspectives in AI Ethics (RQ3)	Educators' and Students' Perceptions of AI Ethics (RQ4)	Strategies/ Methodologies for Ethical AI Deployment (RQ5)
10	Mökander et al. (2022)	Ethical concerns include balancing innovation with risk management, data privacy, and harmonizing standards across AI systems.	Frameworks like AstraZeneca's Principles for Ethical Data and AI focus on fairness, accountability, and transparency but lack practical tools for implementation.	Emphasizes bioethical principles from classical philosophy as a foundation for AI governance in corporate contexts.	Highlights employee concerns about ethical risks of AI and the need for clear operational guidance to align governance across divisions.	Proposes actionable strategies such as creating compliance tools, AI audits, and risk-based governance to harmonize and operationalize ethics.
11	Osamor et al. (2023)	Concerns include data privacy, plagiarism risks, digital divide, reinforcement of biases, and depersonalization of education.	Emphasizes the need for a comprehensive ethical framework addressing fairness, accountability, and inclusivity in AI tools.	Uses interpretivism to explore subjective perspectives on ethical dilemmas in AI-enabled education.	Students and educators see potential in AI for personalized learning and efficiency but express worries about overreliance and misinformation.	Proposes thematic analysis for identifying and mitigating risks; emphasizes balancing AI's capabilities with human-centered education principles.
12	Leelavathi & Surendhranatha (2024)	Concerns include bias, authenticity, and misinformation in AI-generated content; ethical use of ChatGPT in management education.	Existing frameworks do not fully address AI's role in fostering critical thinking and creativity within educational settings.	Draws on pedagogical theories to highlight ChatGPT's potential in enhancing active learning and fostering critical engagement.	Educators and students value ChatGPT for engagement and creativity but express concerns over authenticity and misuse risks.	Proposes integrating ChatGPT for active learning, critical thinking development, and personalized education, with a focus on ethical guidelines.
13	Tarisayi (2024)	Concerns include academic integrity, reduced critical thinking, misinformation, and equity in resource-constrained contexts.	Socio-technical systems theory suggests a need for policies aligning AI tools with academic and institutional goals.	Utilizes socio-technical systems theory to explore technology's complementary role in academic ecosystems.	Mixed perceptions: some academics view ChatGPT as a threat to integrity, while others recognize its potential for efficiency and personalization.	Advocates for flexible governance frameworks to align AI adoption with academic standards, emphasizing transparency, human oversight, and critical analysis.
14	Kusuma et al. (2022)	Concerns include privacy risks, racial and gender bias in facial recognition systems, and historical bias in data archives.	Operationalized Long et al.'s AI Literacy framework, focusing on transparency, inclusivity, and accountability, but requiring iterative refinement.	Highlights ethical design principles, integrating transparency, empathy, and historical context into educational AI applications.	Users appreciated learning about algorithm limitations but emphasized concerns about data privacy and algorithmic fairness.	Proposes an iterative three-phase ethical design process, incorporating expert consultation and user feedback to refine AI literacy and inclusivity.

continued on following page

Table 5. Continued

	Authors	Ethical Concerns Addressed in AI for Education (RQ1)	Existing Ethical Frameworks and Limitations (RQ2)	Philosophical/ Theoretical Perspectives in AI Ethics (RQ3)	Educators' and Students' Perceptions of AI Ethics (RQ4)	Strategies/ Methodologies for Ethical AI Deployment (RQ5)
15	Mouta et al. (2024)	Concerns include diminished teacher and student agency, privacy risks, and cultural biases in AI systems.	Dialogic ethics-based frameworks address ethical concerns but require broader input from diverse educational stakeholders.	Utilizes dialogic ethics to emphasize shared agency and contextualized understanding of ethical challenges in AI adoption.	Educators highlight the need for professional development focused on ethical reasoning and shared agency to manage AI integration.	Proposes structured CPD programs addressing ethical concerns, collaborative agency, and adaptive pedagogical practices for AI integration.
16	Figueras et al. (2024)	Concerns include accountability gaps, biases in automated grading systems (AGS), data privacy, and the misuse of AGSs.	The 'Doing Responsibilities' framework emphasizes shared and temporal responsibilities but requires integration of regulatory aspects and nonhuman agents.	Draws on posthumanist theories and 'Doing Responsibilities' framework to explore shared human-nonhuman responsibilities.	Educators feel burdened by the accountability gaps in AGSs; students emphasize the need for fairness and transparency in grading systems.	Proposes iterative retraining of ML models, integration of multi-stakeholder feedback loops, and balancing transparency with system adaptability.
17	Nguyen et al. (2023)	Concerns include learner autonomy, data privacy, systemic bias, and inequalities exacerbated by AI technologies in education.	UNESCO's global standards and OECD's principles address high-level ethical considerations but lack detailed, contextualized implementation guidelines.	Highlights interdisciplinary and stakeholder-driven approaches to foster human-centered and equitable AI in education.	Mixed perceptions on balancing opportunities with risks such as surveillance, bias, and diminishing learner autonomy.	Proposes thematic analysis for creating unified ethical principles to guide stakeholders in designing and deploying trustworthy AI systems.
18	Mumtaz et al. (2024)	Cultural influences on perceptions of AI ethics, including biases, academic dishonesty, and varying definitions of ethical behavior.	Existing frameworks like Hofstede's cultural dimensions fail to address rapidly evolving AI ethics challenges in education.	Combines Hofstede's Cultural Dimensions Theory with Structural Topic Modeling (STM) to explore cultural differences in AI ethics.	Business students' perceptions vary significantly by cultural cluster, with marked differences between Southern Asia and Latin Europe on ethical AI usage.	Proposes culturally tailored ethical guidelines, stakeholder-informed policymaking, and the use of Structural Topic Modeling to identify and address cultural variances in ethical AI perceptions.

continued on following page

Table 5. Continued

	Authors	Ethical Concerns Addressed in AI for Education (RQ1)	Existing Ethical Frameworks and Limitations (RQ2)	Philosophical/ Theoretical Perspectives in AI Ethics (RQ3)	Educators' and Students' Perceptions of AI Ethics (RQ4)	Strategies/ Methodologies for Ethical AI Deployment (RQ5)
19	Holmes et al. (2021)	Concerns include fairness, accountability, transparency, inclusion, and unintended consequences in AI deployment.	Recognizes the lack of community-wide frameworks and highlights the necessity for multidisciplinary, robust guidelines.	Differentiates between "doing ethical things" and "doing things ethically" to emphasize moral obligations in pedagogy.	Mixed opinions on the adequacy of ethical considerations, with calls for greater transparency and actionable guidelines.	Proposes a community-wide framework integrating multidisciplinary expertise, iterative design, and inclusion of stakeholder feedback.
20	Wood & Moss (2024)	Concerns include academic dishonesty, overreliance on AI, ethical missteps in GenAI use, and privacy issues in AI-assisted learning.	The AI-ICE Framework assesses cognitive engagement but requires broader validation for varied educational levels.	Combines the ICE Model and AI paradigms to analyze learner-AI interaction, emphasizing ethical and cognitive engagement.	Students appreciated the practical use of GenAI but initially expressed concerns over plagiarism and privacy risks.	Proposes scaffolded integration of GenAI with an emphasis on reflective practice, ethical education, and hands-on experiential learning.
21	Luckin et al. (2024)	Concerns include data privacy, equity, overreliance on AI, lack of transparency, and limited educator involvement in AI development.	The Golden Triangle Framework highlights educator, researcher, and developer collaboration but needs broader scalability.	Emphasizes learner-centered design, contextual engagement, and human-centric approaches to AI integration in education.	Educators express concerns over semi-functional technologies but acknowledge AI's potential for personalized learning and equity.	Proposes iterative co-design between developers and educators, strategic AI governance, and transparent frameworks for AI deployment.
22	Roy & Putatunda (2023)	Concerns include over-reliance on AI, creative limitations, data privacy, and balancing teacher and AI roles in pedagogy.	Indian NEP 2020 framework supports technology-driven learning but lacks specific AI governance guidelines for literature pedagogy.	Draws from constructivist learning theories to advocate for AI as a collaborator rather than a replacement in education.	Students enjoy AI-enhanced activities but raise concerns about creative authenticity and the potential reduction of critical thinking.	Proposes AI tools like ChatGPT and Verse by Verse for activity-based learning, emphasizing collaborative approaches and critical discussions.
23	Taiye et al. (2024)	Concerns include academic integrity, plagiarism risks, and ethical challenges of using generative AI in academic writing.	Current AI literacy frameworks lack a focus on stakeholder-driven customization and iterative feedback.	Uses Soft Systems Methodology (SSM) to navigate and integrate diverse stakeholder perspectives for co-development of AI tools.	Mixed reactions from students and educators on AI's role; students fear over-reliance, while educators highlight ethical dilemmas.	Proposes CHAT4ISP-AI, an AI-enabled platform for academic writing with iterative development, stakeholder input, and ethical customization.

continued on following page

Table 5. Continued

	Authors	Ethical Concerns Addressed in AI for Education (RQ1)	Existing Ethical Frameworks and Limitations (RQ2)	Philosophical/ Theoretical Perspectives in AI Ethics (RQ3)	Educators' and Students' Perceptions of AI Ethics (RQ4)	Strategies/ Methodologies for Ethical AI Deployment (RQ5)
24	Guettala et al. (2024)	Concerns include data privacy, equity in access, algorithmic bias, and pedagogical challenges in adopting generative AI.	Frameworks for integrating generative AI into adaptive learning focus on scalability but often lack ethical customization for varied contexts.	Highlights transition from Education 4.0 (technology-centric) to Education 5.0 (human-centric and socially embedded learning).	Educators acknowledge generative AI's efficiency but raise concerns about reliance, equity, and maintaining emotional learning connections.	Proposes a collaborative educator-technologist model for iterative development of AI systems with a focus on scalability, personalization, and ethical oversight.
25	Kanont et al. (2024)	Concerns include ethical challenges in technology adoption, language barriers, plagiarism, and unintended educational dependency.	The Technology Acceptance Model (TAM) framework provides theoretical underpinnings but requires adaptation for cultural and contextual relevance.	Draws on TAM to assess Expected Benefits, Perceived Ease of Use, and Behavioural Intention in Generative-AI adoption.	Students highlight mixed perceptions, valuing Generative-AI's utility but expressing concerns over ease of use reducing perceived usefulness.	Proposes integrating ethical guidelines, fostering AI literacy, and creating university environments to support innovation and equitable access to Generative-AI.
26	Barrera Castro et al. (2024)	Concerns include data privacy, equity, algorithmic bias, and over-reliance on AI systems in personalized learning.	Frameworks often lack clarity in defining roles of educators versus AI and face challenges integrating ethical customization.	Highlights Education 4.0 principles with a focus on AI as a tool to enhance adaptability and learner engagement.	Students value the tailored content delivery and real-time feedback, but educators emphasize concerns over bias and reliance.	Proposes frameworks focusing on adaptive learning systems, emphasizing AI-based real-time assessment, personalized interfaces, and educator training.
27	Cacho (2024)	Concerns include academic dishonesty, dependence on AI tools, equity in access, and maintaining authentic learning experiences.	The AI Ecological Education Policy Framework offers guidelines but lacks detailed operationalization across diverse settings.	Combines AI Ecological Policy Framework with humanistic approaches to balance technological and ethical considerations in academia.	Students appreciate the utility of generative AI tools but highlight risks of intellectual laziness, while educators emphasize ethical integration.	Proposes balanced guidelines adaptable across institutions, emphasizing ethical AI literacy, inclusivity, and collaborative policy-making with stakeholders.
28	Le et al. (2024)	Concerns include data privacy, over-reliance, academic dishonesty, and equity in the accessibility of ChatGPT in learning.	TAM and UGT frameworks address motivations for AI adoption but lack specific focus on ethical and cultural customization.	Combines Technology Acceptance Model (TAM) and Uses and Gratifications Theory (UGT) to explore motivations for ChatGPT usage.	Students show a preference for ChatGPT's convenience but express concerns over ethical use, particularly regarding over-reliance.	Proposes integrating ethical guidelines and cultural contextualization within TAM and UGT frameworks for improving AI adoption strategies.

continued on following page

Table 5. Continued

	Authors	Ethical Concerns Addressed in AI for Education (RQ1)	Existing Ethical Frameworks and Limitations (RQ2)	Philosophical/ Theoretical Perspectives in AI Ethics (RQ3)	Educators' and Students' Perceptions of AI Ethics (RQ4)	Strategies/ Methodologies for Ethical AI Deployment (RQ5)
29	Nannini et al. (2024)	Concerns include opacity, biases, lack of accountability, and inadequate ethical reflection in Explainable AI (XAI).	Ethical frameworks for XAI often prioritize transparency and fairness but fail to address the contextual nature of ethical decisions.	Uses applied ethics, deontology, consequentialism, and virtue ethics to propose ethical grounding for explainable AI systems.	Highlights a gap in educators' and policymakers' engagement, emphasizing the need for interdisciplinary collaboration.	Proposes integrating stakeholder engagement, interdisciplinary education, and applied ethics into the design and governance of XAI systems.
30	Hutchinson (2024)	Concerns include the role of school librarians in addressing AI ethics, misinformation risks, and the evolving IL landscape.	The FOSIL framework supports inquiry-based learning but requires integration with ethical AI literacy in curricula.	Combines inquiry-based learning with the Framework of Skills for Inquiry Learning (FOSIL) to enhance IL and ethical reasoning.	Librarians and educators express hesitancy but see AI's potential to transform IL and critical thinking instruction.	Proposes integrating AI with inquiry-based learning using FOSIL to foster IL and ethical engagement, alongside librarian involvement.
31	Elhersh & Alqawasmeh (2024)	Concerns include academic integrity, authenticity, reliability of AI-generated content, and ethical considerations in public discourse.	Ethical frameworks lack inclusivity and transparency in addressing nuanced public perceptions of generative AI in education.	Employs thematic analysis and sentiment analysis to examine public discourse, highlighting socio-ethical implications.	Public sentiment on ChatGPT's role in education is predominantly positive but tempered by concerns over academic integrity and data privacy.	Proposes continuous dialogue among educators, policymakers, and developers, leveraging social media analytics for real-time feedback and ethical improvements.
32	Alshahrani & Qureshi (2024)	Concerns include academic integrity, privacy, equity in access, and over-reliance on AI in classrooms.	Ethical frameworks for ChatGPT in education lack specific strategies for balanced integration with traditional pedagogy.	Highlights the need for human-AI collaboration frameworks to ensure balanced pedagogical integration.	Educators view ChatGPT positively for enhancing creativity and engagement but express concerns about privacy and dependency risks.	Proposes integrating ChatGPT with interactive tools such as AR and VR, promoting co-creation with educators to foster personalized and immersive learning environments.
33	Mouta et al. (2024)	Concerns include diminished teacher and student agency, privacy risks, and lack of ethical reflexivity in AI integration.	The Delphi-based framework offers teacher CPD programs but needs broader inclusion of non-expert stakeholder perspectives.	Combines socio-constructivist theories with grounded theory to foster collaborative ethical learning in AIEd development.	Teachers express varying levels of awareness of AIEd ethical challenges, emphasizing the need for structured CPD programs.	Proposes a qualitative Delphi-based CPD framework to promote reflective practices, enhance agency, and address ethical challenges in AIEd.

continued on following page

Table 5. Continued

	Authors	Ethical Concerns Addressed in AI for Education (RQ1)	Existing Ethical Frameworks and Limitations (RQ2)	Philosophical/ Theoretical Perspectives in AI Ethics (RQ3)	Educators' and Students' Perceptions of AI Ethics (RQ4)	Strategies/ Methodologies for Ethical AI Deployment (RQ5)
34	Holmes et al. (2023)	Concerns include privacy, bias, algorithmic accountability, and ethical concerns around informed consent and transparency.	The "Ethics of Learning with AI" framework highlights gaps in addressing contextual ethics for different stakeholders.	Draws on the ethics of data, algorithms, and education to propose a comprehensive ethical lens for analyzing AI deployment.	Mixed reactions from students, teachers, and institutions, focusing on autonomy, trust, and human-centric approaches to AI usage.	Proposes a unified, stakeholder-inclusive framework integrating informed consent, transparency, and human oversight into institutional AI policies and practices.
35	Yoon et al. (2024)	Concerns include students' over-reliance on generative AI, misinterpretation of proofs, and ethical dilemmas in academic integrity.	The SIPE-AI framework offers insights into student interactions with AI in proof construction but needs broader empirical validation.	Combines Interactive Proving Experience Framework with sociocultural theories to analyze student-AI collaboration.	Students acknowledge AI's utility but express mixed views on dependency and ethical issues in incorporating AI-generated proofs.	Proposes targeted teaching interventions to foster critical evaluation skills and develop ethical guidelines for the academic use of generative AI tools.
36	Mohammad Awad AlAfnan (2024)	Focuses on the ethical challenges in integrating AI into learning taxonomies, including issues of bias and accessibility.	Highlights the limitations of traditional taxonomies like Bloom's in addressing AI-specific learning challenges.	Emphasizes constructivist approaches and the need for ethical frameworks like ESD in AI integration.	Suggests educators need tools for incorporating ethics into AI-driven learning processes.	Proposes a new taxonomy emphasizing ethics, adaptability, and practical application.
37	Perkins et al. (2024)	Concerns include academic integrity, the ethical integration of generative AI, equity in access, and varying pedagogical appropriateness.	The AI Assessment Scale (AIAS) provides structured integration but requires further contextual customization across disciplines.	Combines constructivist learning theories and iterative reflexive models to create scalable AI assessment frameworks.	Students and educators recognize potential in AI tools but stress clarity in usage guidelines and ethical practices.	Proposes the AIAS, a five-level framework to integrate AI tools ethically into assessments, focusing on transparency, critical evaluation, and equity.

Chapter 7
Ethical Framework for AI in Education:
Navigating Challenges and Building Solutions

Shaista Ashraf Farooqi
https://orcid.org/0009-0001-2066-5013
Asia e University, Pakistan

ABSTRACT

Artificial Intelligence (AI) is revolutionizing education by enhancing learning and administrative processes. However, ethical concerns such as data privacy, algorithmic bias, transparency, and equity must be addressed. AI relies on vast student data, posing risks of breaches and bias that can reinforce educational disparities. Opaque decision-making further challenges accountability and trust. Ethical frameworks are essential for responsible AI deployment. Privacy measures, explainable AI, and human-centered design ensure fairness, transparency, and inclusivity. Collaboration among educators, policymakers, and developers is crucial to align AI innovation with ethical standards. By addressing these challenges, AI can enhance education while safeguarding fundamental values.

1. INTRODUCTION

The rise of AI technology is changing education for the better. It customizes the student's learning experience, manages administrative work, and offers insights after analyzing data. For example, AI offers real-time lesson modifications, provides timely assessments regarding a student's performance, and performs timely gap analyses. This adds more responsiveness and adjustability in the educational

DOI: 10.4018/979-8-3373-5550-4.ch007

system. Teaching professionals are able to foster and facilitate active participation of learners in the learning process (Zhai et al., 2021).

Nonetheless, the implementation of advanced AI technologies in education raises a number of ethical and practical issues. One of the most notable includes the handling of the school children's personal information. Academic records, behavior patterns, and even emotional states are examples of sensitive information that AI systems could utilize, making the system a potential target for abuse if not monitored correctly. In this regard, schools must adhere to the GDPR (General Data Protection Regulation) and FERPA (Family Educational Rights and Privacy Act) frameworks by employing privacy-centered techniques like user-controlled data anonymization, federated learning, and encryption (Salloum, 2024).

The possibility of lacking transparency and algorithmic discrimination is another challenge they face. Existing data is used with the AI in question. Their biases may be social or cultural. This results in discrimination, posing significant challenges to equity, for example, in accessing assistance or educational resources. Moreover, decision-making in many AI systems can be opaque, and as a result, these systems are often referred to as black boxes. As a result, trust in the society, educators, and learners is lost without transparency in the processes and systems. These gaps can be filled with attention to fairness algorithms and frameworks of bias accountability, XAI tools, together with active educator supervision in AI instruction and review processes (Shahriar et al., 2023).

This chapter attempts to resolve the ethical issues and offer a rationale of AI in education that balances practicality with intricacies. In doing so, it draws on educational literature and practice as well as models concerning the management of private bias, data, transparency, equability of access, and other constituents of performance enhancement. The Framing AI In Education Systems chapter seeks to enhance the education stakeholder's and system contributors' ability to design AI systems which elevate learning in a way that adheres to principles of equity, access, educational inclusion, and responsibility accountability. The blend of technological innovation and ethical boundaries along with policies tailored to the distinct learning settings highlight the responsibility in which AI must be integrated.

Figure 1 outlines the chapter structure as follows: Section 2 reviews the relevant literature; Section 3 details the adopted methodological approach; Section 4 presents the results derived from the applied framework; Section 5 offers a critical analysis of these results; and Section 6 concludes with a summary of key findings and suggestions for future research.

Figure 1. Organizational flow of the chapter

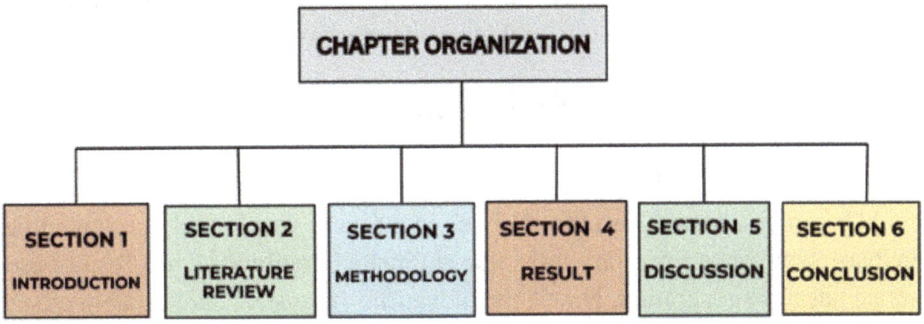

2. LITERATURE REVIEW

With the development and increasingly widespread societal application of information technology, new possibilities for utilizing innovative tools to improve educational processes have opened up. Evidence of this change is the growing importance of Artificial Intelligence (AI) for the enhancement of learning and teaching within institutions. The use of AI based applications enhances the quality of education and enriches the learning experience by personalizing and optimizing curricular content for individual learners (Chen et al., 2020). Such applications perform numerous other educational functions that facilitate the work of educators. These include dynamic content adaptation, sophisticated grading functions, predictive analysis of student performance, progression monitoring, automated report generation, and even more complex tasks such as proactive feedback generation and class activity compilation (Murtaza et al., 2022).

Yet, the literature reviews often mention some aspects of the ethics and the practical ramifications AI has in an academic setting. The implementation of AI technology is often accompanied by massive data collection, which brings up problems concerning privacy, consent, and data protection. To these problems, a solution is offered in the form of institutional guidelines based on legal policies often crafted with privacy bias. More of these problems include unequal access of the AI tools in the institution or region, opaque mechanism, and biased mechanisms of AI. Scholars focus on the requirements of justice, audibility, and AI's capability to foster inclusiveness and equity within protected educational environments (Alawneh et al., 2024).

This review of the literature aims to address such issues as the use of AI in the educational space, the risks it poses, and the solutions provided by scholars and the institutions in the form of privacy and unbiased effectiveness.

2.1 Development of AI in Education

The sheer volume of data in education motivated the gradual emergence of AI, as it could be processed and learnt from. Even in the early years of AI, its capabilities were harnessed for rudimentary tasks like automated grading and test-result-based practice question generation. Now, more advanced AI systems are capable of supporting fully automated learning environments.

Today, AI finds applications in most domains across educational institutions, from schools to universities. AI Personal assistants now verbally respond to students' inquiries and learning management systems (LMS) have integrated features that automatically track progress and resource suggestion. Administrative functions such as managing class schedules and analyzing enrollment data also make use of AI technologies. The importance of AI with regard to devising, implementing, and improving educational designs is increasingly profound with its evolutionary process (Miao et al., 2021).

Figure 2 depicts the applications of AI within education, such as personalized learning, intelligent tutoring systems, automated grading, AI chatbots, predictive analytics, and AI recommendations for courses and prerequisites to improve educational experiences and efficiency.

Figure 2. Various AI applications in education

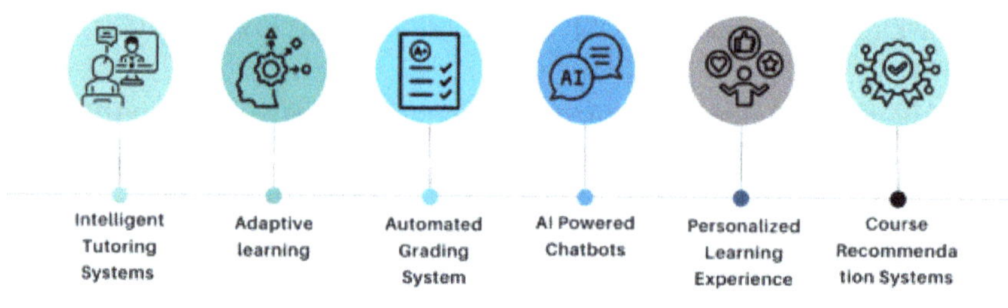

2.1.1 The Application of AI Tools in the Teaching, Learning, and Educational Administration Processes

We are currently in the phase of the implementation of AI into teaching, learning, and the management of education systems. In teaching, AI personalizes instruction through data mining and lesson tailoring. For example, an intelligent tutoring system (ITS) can guide learners through a problem step-by-step, providing hints, partial solutions, or extra examples as necessary. The algorithms employed in these systems are adaptive; they learn from the responses given by students, and the teaching processes can be improved subsequently (Parycek et al., 2024; Chen et al., 2020).

In learning, AI facilitates instant feedback as well as monitoring of progress or milestones achieved. Some AI tools, such as chatbots, can respond to questions released, and so can adaptively learning systems that provide appropriate content based on the user's performance. AI enables active and constructive involvement in learning. AI also fosters flexibility and accessibility supporting virtual learning environments (VLEs) that enable students to access materials at any time and from any location (Zhai et al., 2024).

2.1.2 AI in the Education Sector

AI geared towards education has experienced increased adoption in the past decade. Earlier, AI was shallowly incorporated in the form of simple automation, like in grading and quizzes. Currently, educators are embracing more sophisticated AI that provides tailored curriculums, tracks achievements, and performs administrative functions like the basic automation of repetitive tasks. Research confirms the growing employ of AI technology in all forms of education, including primary schooling and tertiary institutions (Gupta et al., 2024).

The availability of these technologies has substantially increased over time, and research indicates that they are incorporated in widely used functions which facilitate the accomplishing of tasks in a more efficient manner. For example, adaptive learning systems enable students to progress at their individual paces, while predictive analytics identify students who are likely to require intervention so that support can be offered proactively rather than reactively. Other features include simple question answering chatbots, as well as virtual classrooms that provide tailored educational assistance (Zhang & Aslan, 2021).

2.2 AI-Driven Personalization and Adaptive Systems

The most noted utilization of AI is in educational personalization. Often, AI systems will tailor content, pacing, and feedback for each learner based on their unique learning preferences and progress. These systems depend on data from student interactions, including quiz results, task duration, and even the nature of errors committed, to create a profile that will help shape personalized instruction.

Examples of Adaptive Learning Systems make use and apply reinforcement learning, among other things, to modify the complexity of content and suggest tasks depending on how well students are learning. For instance, if a student is struggling with a concept, the system may provide supplementary materials or easier tasks designed to help them gain confidence. This kind of tailoring aids in increasing the students' active participation as well as improving their outcomes (Rane et al., 2023).

Adaptive systems are further augmented by means of NLP through the creation of real-time virtual tutors and chatbots that respond to learner queries instantaneously. To some extent, systems also use behavioral and emotional indicators of learning to modulate the degree of support provided to the learner, thus making online learning more interactive and student-centered (Egunjobi & Adeyeye, 2024).

2.2.1 Machine Learning and Learner Modeling

There is an emerging trend in literature that explores the application of machine learning (ML) in developing learner models for tailored and customized education. These models are generated by evaluating student data which includes, but is not limited to, test results, pacing in learning, and behavioral traits. It is reported that outcome-based prediction, such as performance or dropout rate, is done using supervised learning while clustering of students is done using unsupervised learning (Barbosa, 2023).

With the increased data collected, the learner model can also be modified with the data reflecting the current learning stage of the student. This helps the system adapt content and instruction gradually over time. Research has proven learner modeling to be effective in enhancing engagement and providing appropriate support at different levels (Lang et al., 2025).

2.2.2 Feedback Using NLP with Dynamic Content Adaptation in Real-Time

It is well documented that Natural Language Processing (NLP) technologies are included in the educational AI systems to enhance the interaction and feedback from students. NLP allows systems to processes written or spoken language input, which permits the use of chatbots and virtual tutors to respond to learner queries immediately. Some systems apply sentiment analysis or keyword detection to change content presentation or level of content engagement based on activity values of the learners. This improves responsiveness in learning and helps to sustain motivation among learners, particularly in self-directed or online learning environments (Shaik et al., 2022).

2.2.3 Case Examples (DreamBox, Squirrel AI)

Many authors have focused on some AI-powered educational platforms due to their effectiveness in personalized learning.

- **DreamBox Learning**

To enhance mathematics achievement of K-8 learners, DreamBox Learning has incorporated reinforcement learning techniques to customize instruction and provide feedback on activities in real time. It allows students to set their own pace and controls the rate at which lessons are delivered (Dutta et al., 2024).

- **Squirrel AI**

In China, many learners preparing for various examinations have been supported through the use of Squirrel AI software. This software applies deep learning to diagnose knowledge gaps and provide tailored content using sophisticated learner models (Li et al., 2025).

- **Carnegie Learning**

Carnegie Learning implements AI-driven real-time feedback, teacher dashboards, and other interactive tools that stimulate educator engagement (Alfarra et al., 2024).

- **Century Tech**

Century Tech aids learning personalization through automated pathways and automated wellbeing interaction facilitated by real-time academic data monitoring and automated teacher interactions (Srinivasa et al., 2022).

- **Content Technologies Inc. (CTI)**

Content Technologies Inc. CTI uses Artificial Intelligence technologies for creating customized textbooks and quizzes for their clients as instructional materials which are tailored to each client's preferred style of learning. This is done automatically and cuts work for teachers.

- **Microsoft Immersive Reader**

Microsoft Immersive Reader assists learners with reading disabilities by offering a variety of assistive technologies such as text-to-speech, translation, and visual tracking. It is powered by a Natural Language Processing AI Engine which analyzes content to rephrase sentences and restructure paragraphs to transform them into easier versions while extracting meaningful content (Nair, 2023).

Ethical AI technologies in education are intentionally engineered are listed in Table 1 with their use domains, enabling technologies, and ethical considerations of use.

Table 1. Real-World examples of ethical AI in education

AI Systems	Operational Focus	Ethical Consideration
DreamBox Learning	Personalized with learning for K-12 students	Regular algorithmic audits to identify biases; Compliance with COPPA (Children's Online Privacy Protection Act)
Carnegie Learning	AI-Driven STEM Tutoring	Integration of HITL (Human-in-the-loop) frameworks, allowing educators to monitor and intervene in AI-driven recommendations
Microsoft Education Tools (Immersive Reader)	Enhancing accessibility for students with learning disabilities	Prioritizes inclusivity, adhering to WCAG (Web Content Accessibility Guidelines) and offering customizable accessibility features
OpenEdu Analytics	Ethical data management for educational AI	Ensures compliance with privacy standards while empowering institutions to analyze data responsibly
Squirrel AI	AI-powered adaptive learning for personalized tutoring	Implements AI ethics guidelines to ensure fairness; Data privacy measures to protect student information
Century Tech	AI-Driven personalized learning for schools and institutions	Prioritizes explainability in AI decision-making; Provides teachers with control over AI-driven recommendations

2.3 Institutional Efficiency Through AI

Efficiency in educational institutions is enhanced with AI technologies by automating grading, tracking attendance, and scheduling classes which increases the quality of instructional and student support. Literature cites the use of predictive analytics for the resource management of supporting services to detect students at risk of failing and managing support resources for those students.

2.3.1 Predictive Analytics and Intelligent Automation

Predictive analytics is particularly notable within education technology. Algorithms of such systems analyze students' longitudinal academic records and participation metrics to forecast risks of course failure or dropping out. Predictive analysis is also useful for schools to take preemptive actions by providing tailored guidance, tutoring, or counseling. AI streamlines repetitive tasks as well. It is capable of grading homework, report writing, and scheduling (Aithal, 2023). Course-related information and deadlines can be relayed to students through chatbots powered by AI. In a nutshell, the combination of automation and predictive analytics offers time savings, proactive intervention, and enhanced student-teacher interactions.

2.3.2 LMS integration and AI-Powered Dashboards

It has been noted that AI-infused technologies are being integrated within Learning Management Systems (LMS) for both educator and learner purposes. For instance, AI-infused dashboards provide updates in real-time regarding a student's engagement, participation, and achievement. Participative data from quizzes, log-in sessions, and discussion forums help educators detect students who require assistance in the shortest time possible (Bahassi et al., 2024).

2.3.3 Human-in-the-Loop (HITL) in Operational Decision-Making

Concerning automation in educational contexts, there is a critical need to retain a degree of human control to what processes are automated AI makes decisions on. The HITL approach allows educators and administrative users to ratify AI-driven recommendations and tailor them to suit specific needs. Research indicates the application of HITL increases trust and accuracy while mitigating the dangers of over-reliance on automation (Chen, 2022). It helps combine AI insights with human judgment to ensure rational results devoid of bias.

2.4 Using AI to Bridge Educational Gaps

Research indicates the use of AI can bridge the gap in education by remotely offering personalized learning opportunities to students in neglected areas. Low-resource AI models, edge computing, and multilingual capabilities enable remote underserved learners with disabilities as well as learners who face language barriers to access education (Singh et al., 2025).

2.4.1 Edge Computing, Low-Resource AI and Federated learning

It is believed that federated learning will enhance the ability of schools to deliver personalized education while safeguarding student information. Instead of transmitting raw data to a central server, federated learning teaches AI models on local devices. This preserves a school's information confidential and enables compliance with GDPR and FERPA. With edge computing, information is processed closer to the point of collection. This reduces lags while real-time feedback is possible even with slow internet. Other low-performing regions such as rural or underfunded schools also benefit from low-resource AI models (Hridi et al., 2024).

2.4.2 Flexible Technologies and Inclusion in Learning Design

Assistive technology powered by AI helps learners that require extra help. Those that have difficulty reading or writing are helped with text-to-speech and speech-to-text. Other students that have hearing difficulties are helped with captions, while students with visual impairments are helped with screen readers. Immersive Reader is an example of software that provides translations, audio, and other features, allowing for clear text formats (Yagyaeva et al., 2024).

2.5 Social Responsibility Issues regarding AI Technology Integration

Integrating AI into basic education systems is beneficial, but it raises serious ethical nuances which support deep concern. Controversial areas include privacy, bias, technological inequality, transparency, and data protection (Chari, 2024).

2.5.1 Surveillance and Data Privacy Risks

The incorporation of AI-powered educational platforms leads to controversies regarding privacy concerns. A12 systems capture a wide range of personally identifiable information, including meticulous details regarding students' enrollment and performance. Such data, if left unchecked, poses risks of misuse, exploitation, or unauthorized usage. To mitigate these dangers, privacy-placing technologies such as differential privacy techniques, homomorphic encryption, and federated learning are proposed. These techniques blur the boundary of controlled data surveillance while providing adequate protection. Newer legislation like GDPR alongside some

FERPA clauses improves the ethical management of student data by establishing protective measures at foundational levels (Kamenskih, 2022).

2.5.2 Concerns Over Algorithmic Bias and Fairness

Due to sampling problems, educational AI systems may reflect bias present in the training metadata. This could lead to inaccurate assessments and unjust recommendations, especially concerning marginalized students. Unfairness is mitigated through machine learning intervention techniques such as fair reweighting, representation, debiasing, and others. Timely interventions through regular assessments, diverse data sets, and additional measures strengthen fairness. The trust of all learners and equal access to education is ensured through the provision of fair algorithms (Kordzadeh & Ghasemaghaei, 2022; Chinta et al., 2024).

2.5.3 Understandability and Transparency Gaps

"Black box" is a term used to describe the way most educational AI tools work; they only provide answers, the user does not see the calculations leading to the conclusion. Lack of insight makes trust from students, educators and parents lose confidence. The goal of the explanatory framework Explainable AI XAI is to provide model outputs in a way that is easy to grasp. Some instruments such as SHAP or LIME explain in overly simplistic terms. Transparency can be enhanced through the use of straightforward models where dynamic information can be displayed through visual dashboards. Enhanced explainability ensures responsibility of actions taken with AI in education and guards against misuse to ensure its ethical use (Balasubramaniam et al., 2023).

2.5.4 Automation Overdependence Risks

Using AI technologies in education can lead to judgment errors. AI can help with grading and attendance tracking, but it lacks the ability to contextualize or appreciate the nuances of individual students. To AI's illusions of understanding, it may construe a minimalistic rule-based context as the more sophisticated mechanisms, which is likely to be very wrong. Relying too heavily considering AI's decisions as the be-all-end-all conclusion presents another risk. To try and solve these problems, HITL: Human-in-the-Loop models are designed. They account for teachers which help mitigate automation bias, and offset pure automated systems in a better way than unbalance automation (Kumar et al., 2024).

2.6 Approaches Relating to Ethical AI Considered in Education

Research documents multiple approaches regarding the ethics of incorporating AI into education, such as privacy preserving techniques, fairness-aware algorithms, and explaining AI methodologies. These approaches focus on protecting student's privacy, decreasing discrimination, and improving the rationality and the logic of AI to make provable and explainable decisions (Holmes et al., 2022).

Figure 3 illustrates the ethical frameworks for AI in education, emphasizing key principles such as fairness, transparency, human oversight, data privacy, accountability, and accessibility to ensure responsible and equitable AI implementation.

Figure 3. Ethical frameworks for AI in education

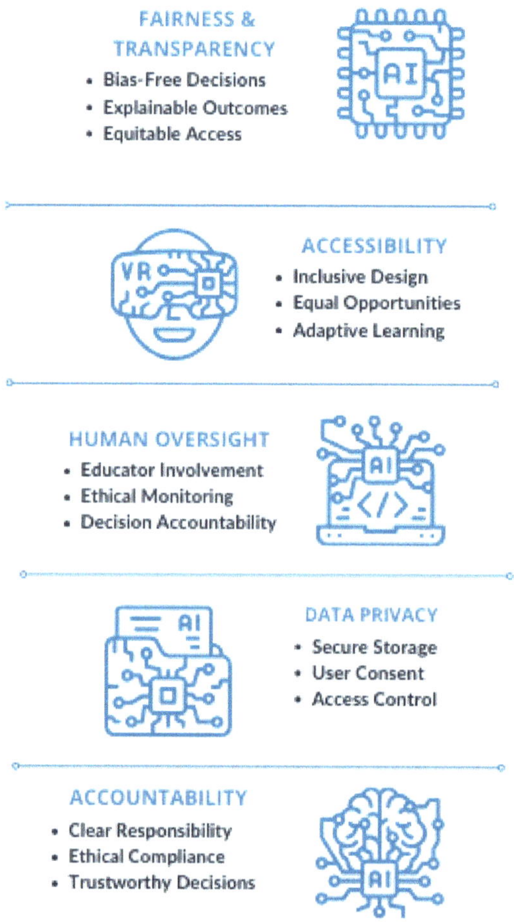

2.6.1 Homomorphic Encryption and Differential Privacy

Homomorphic encryption remains one of the most powerful approaches as it allows AI models to work with data without exposing raw data directly (Su et al., 2024). In the case of student data, differential privacy anonymizes data while identifying breaches of privacy, masking sensitive information in AI systems. This approach preserves privacy for individual students while offering valuable insights through advanced data analysis. Both methods strengthen privacy standards in educational AI systems (Khan, 2024).

2.6.2 SHAP, LIME, AIF360

The education industry benefits from AI XAI Tools which provide signpost decisions using SHAP and LIME. Factors that predict outcomes can be readily analyzed, and AIF360 serves a different purpose: it focuses on finding and fixing bias in data and models. Applying explainable AI (XAI) increases trust, fairness, and the ability to verify the results produced by AI (Manna & Sett, 2024).

2.6.3 Governance Initiatives and Audits

Ethical concerns require strong governance frameworks for the application of AI in education. They manage how data is captured and utilized by AI programs. Routine audits evaluate fairness, precision, and privacy. Employing checklists and impact evaluations assists in assessing AI outcomes. Stakeholders such as educators, policymakers, and designers can be drawn to provide transparency and answerability. The aims of these AI safeguards are balanced measures of risk and trust mitigation (Farooqi et al., 2024).

The concern posed with availability of AI technology in education is the upholding of ethical standards (Nguyen et al., 2023). Defending individual entity requires integrative solutions with components of technology, human supervision, guidance, open systems, and thoughtful framework that actively excludes as a design element.

The literature review highlights both the benefits and ethical challenges of using AI in education, including privacy risks, algorithmic bias, and the need for transparency. It also emphasizes the importance of human oversight, inclusive design, and policy alignment to ensure AI supports fair and responsible learning environments.

3. METHODOLOGY

This part explains the steps taken to create an ethical AI framework for education which involves analyzing literature, case studies, and technological methods to determine a specific set of practical challenges and propose solutions.

3.1 Conceptual Framework Development

The conceptual framework was created by analyzing an ethical AI in education implementation. It aims to determine key elements like privacy, fairness, transparency, and human participation which direct the integration of responsible AI to shape the framework.

3.1.1 Theoretical basis and literature synthesis

In this part, the ethics and technology underpinning the framework are explained. It is constructed from an analysis of theories, research, and practical implementations of AI and education.

i. Ethical Foundations

The framework is constructed with several ethical aspects on fairness, accountability, transparency, and privacy (FATP). These affirmations enable the responsible application of AI technology in educational settings. It also draws on ethical principles such as deontology, which focuses on responsibility, and outcome-based perspectives, also known as utilitarianism. This approach helps balance the need to safeguard students with the advantages AI can offer in enhancing learning experiences (Mensah, 2023; Bibi, 2024).

ii. Educational and Technical Theories

The framework merges concepts from education and technology. It incorporates ideas from personalized teaching, the Universal Design for Learning (UDL) framework, and even broader inclusive design to aid all students. On the educational side, it incorporates machine learning, explainable AI (XAI), and privacy-preserving artificial intelligence techniques. There is a sustained effort toward the ethical implementation of AI technologies (Vaza et al., 2024).

iii. Literature Integration

To comprehend the associated challenges and best practices concerning the integration of AI in education, recent literature was analyzed, encompassing adaptive learning technologies, feedback systems, predictive analytics, and AI dashboards. Additionally, techniques such as federated learning, differential privacy, fairness-aware modeling, and auditing were studied to confront issues of bias, privacy, and data security (Yang & Beil, 2024).

iv. Practical Examples

The case studies illustrate practical implementations of AI in education. DreamBox Learning employs AI to tailor math lessons. Squirrel AI identifies learning gaps through sophisticated modeling. Carnegie Learning integrates AI, cognitive science, and teacher input. Century Tech and OpenEdu Analytics prioritize bespoke learning pathways and the responsible handling of data. These instances highlight that thoughtfully designed AI systems, complemented by human input, function optimally (Ahmed et al., 2025).

v. Objective of the Synthesis

Through its integration of ethical theory, technical research, and case studies, the framework is intended to be and practical. It assists schools, developers, and policymakers in using AI tools that are effective, safe, and fair for all learners.

3.1.2 Multi-Stakeholder and Interdisciplinary Approach

In this framework, interactions with educators, developers of AI systems, policy makers, and researchers from various domains have been incorporated to make sure the framework is viable, inclusive, and ethically sound.

i. Stakeholder Involvement

Constructing an ethical AI framework in education requires the contributions of multiple stakeholders. These actors consist of educators, designers, data analysts, managers of academic institutions, legal scholars, and ethicists. Each constituency has a distinct function, for example, teachers are acquainted with the students' requirements, the developers understand the technology involved, and the policy makers think of the overarching legal frameworks, such as the GDPR and FERPA. Developing synergies provides both utility and ethical soundness (Gordon et al., 2022).

ii. Interdisciplinary Integration

The framework integrates perspectives from computer science, education, ethics, and learning analytics. These will assist in addressing technical challenges such as bias, privacy, and explainability against pedagogical objectives of fairness, engagement, and inclusion. By consolidating these domains, the framework optimally addresses AI in education concerns, while ensuring responsible and practical implementation (Allen & Kendeou, 2024).

iii. Human-Centered and Participatory Design

AI tools developed for classrooms must serve real needs while considering the integral role of the teacher. One way to do this is through human-centered design, an essential component of the framework. Co-design workshops alongside user feedback aid in shaping the tools and evaluating their ethical attributes. This fosters both trust and transparency, ensuring dependability in the use of AI in education (Gerdes, 2022).

3.2 Core Ethical Design Principles

This part explains the privacy, fairness, transparency, and human oversight principles which ethically support the design and use of AI systems in education.

3.2.1 Privacy-First System Architecture

This framework takes privacy considerations into all dimensions of student data. It secures the IoT environment by enabling federated learning and differential privacy or other techniques that mask, or retrieve data from local devices. It is also less risky to allow AI to operate on encrypted data by means of Homomorphic encryption. These risk mitigation measures ensure effectiveness of AI. Institutional compliance with privacy protecting policies like FERPA and GDPR is equally important in fostering trust within the educational environment (Palle & Kathala, 2024).

3.2.2 Accountability Mechanisms

This framework was designed to include provisions on accountability geared towards responsible use of AI in education. It includes audits and impact evaluation not only of the functionality, but also of the biases within the AI systems. SHAP and LIME were devised to reclaim rationales for decisions made by AI and to disentangle the reasoning behind the opaque outputs that were generated. Teachers and school staff as well as the developers are given defined responsibilities to scrutinize and validate the AI outputs. These strategies foster controlled flexibility in effective action and change when needed (Memarian & Doleck, 2023).

3.2.3 Human-Centered Interaction Models

The incorporation of human-centered interaction models is intended to keep teachers actively engaged in AI workflows. In HITL systems, they evaluate and adjust AI outputs. The design also offers bounded user interfaces and features to diverse users. Thus, teachers are able to be aided rather than replaced by AI systems (Crisan et al., 2022).

3.3 Evaluation Tools and Compliance Criteria

This subsection elaborates on the tools and criteria intended to evaluate the ethical bounds AI systems operate under, intuition in the context of privacy, equality, fairness, and education compliance regulations.

3.3.1 Algorithmic Fairness Toolkits

Algorithmic fairness toolkits provide support for the identification and remedy of bias affixed to AI models used in education. AIF360, Fairlearn, and What-If Tool are examples of several tools that assess the AI's interactions with different student groups. They assess fairness both at pre-training, during training, and after training. These tools enable discrimination and equitable opportunity facilitated determination frameworks in learning systems to be designed on sound principles (Chinta et al., 2024).

3.3.2 GDPR, FERPA, and Regulatory Benchmarks

The structure aligns with critical regulations like GDPR and FERPA. These laws manage the capturing, utilization, and sharing of data pertaining to students. The GDPR focuses on the consent acquisition requirement, data restriction, and provision of control to the user. FERPA protects educational records and permeable access within U.S institutions. Adopting these principles allows the AI system to function legally and ethically (Shtayyat et al., 2025).

Regard to this, the approach combines ethical standards with technical safeguards and stakeholder expectations to set a limit on the application of AI in education that is reasonable, ethically justifiable, and socially responsible. Table 2. provides an overview of different ethical frameworks for AI in education.

Table 2. Ethical frameworks for AI in education

AI Ethical Framework	Description	Evidence Base for Ethical Framework Selection
Privacy-Centric	Focuses on protecting user data, ensuring compliance with privacy laws like GDPR and FERPA.	Tang (2024), Yang & Beil (2024), Su et al. (2024) highlight the role of federated learning, homomorphic encryption, and privacy regulation in safeguarding educational data.
Accountability-Driven	Emphasizes responsibility in AI decision-making, ensuring that AI systems can be audited and held accountable.	Burr & Leslie (2023), Cappelli & Serugendo (2024) discuss structures for auditability and the design of ethical oversight tools in AI.
Human-Centered AI	Ensures AI aligns with human values, prioritizing ethical considerations and human well-being in AI applications.	Chen (2022), Usmani et al. (2023), Gupta et al. (2024) emphasize participatory design and alignment of AI tools with educational values.
Fairness and Bias Mitigation	Aims to reduce biases in AI models by using diverse datasets and implementing bias-detection mechanisms.	Barbosa (2023), Chinta et al. (2024), Kordzadeh & Ghasemaghaei (2022) explore techniques like adversarial debiasing and the role of diverse data in mitigating AI bias.
Transparency and Explainability	Enhances AI transparency by ensuring users understand how AI models make decisions.	Khosravi et al. (2022), Arrieta et al. (2020), Manna & Sett (2024) present SHAP, LIME, and explainable AI strategies to improve transparency and trust.
Regulatory Compliance	Ensures AI systems comply with legal and ethical standards, focusing on risk assessment and adherence to regulations.	Nguyen et al. (2023), Miao et al. (2021), Khan (2024) outline the importance of aligning AI practices with GDPR, FERPA, and national policies for educational equity.

4. RESULT OR SUMMARY OF FINDINGS

This part details the ethical AI framework intended for educational purposes. It also situates the framework within the context of actual practices and tools and demonstrates the application of the principles to contemporary AI technologies in educational institutions.

4.1 The Ethical AI Framework: A Triadic Approach

The findings consist of a triadic framework for the ethical application of AI in education. It articulates the three principal components of the framework; privacy, accountability and people-centered design.

4.1.1 Tier 1: Privacy Layer

The primary tier of the framework is concentrating on preventing unauthorized access to student's information using advanced privacy safeguards. The evaluation indicates that these techniques are quite effective in actual educational institutions with functioning AI systems, as well as being compliant with laws on data protection.

i. Federated Learning for Decentralized Training

Federated learning minimized the potential for exposure of student data. The AI model trains on student's devices, rather than sending all data to a central server. In a test based on the DreamBox system, it provided live updating capabilities while preserving the data. This enhanced privacy and fostered trust, in particular, in educational institutions with stringent data regulations.

ii. Differential Privacy for Secure Data Analysis

To enhance the privacy of students' identities during the analysis of the data, differential privacy was employed. It obscured the exact figures for student's scores which were provided in class reports. In examination systems of grading, this method protected information from even entitled users without disabling insightful analysis which, on the other hand, helps in the responsible use of data in education.

iii. Collaborative Confidential Data Sharing Using Homomorphic Encryption

Homomorphic encryption was evaluated for secure data sharing between educational institutions. It enabled the school performance data utilization while the data was never decrypted. In an experiment on inter-school benchmarking, each participating school forwarded their encrypted data for a collective analysis. In this way, the information remained private, but still provided valuable intelligence across regions.

iv. Compliance with Legal Standards

All privacy measures discussed above are in compliance with the privacy enforcement laws like General Data Protection Regulation (GDPR) and Family Educational Rights and Privacy Act (FERPA). The findings demonstrate that these frameworks enable, and as a result, incorporating such methods helps educational institutions balance the legal frameworks and AI tool utilization in a secure and efficient manner.

Tier 1 demonstrates a comprehensive and well-balanced defensive posture on privacy that guarantees robust privacy protections for student data, showing that advanced privacy protective measures can be embedded in AI systems.

4.1.2 Tier 2: Accountability Layer

Tier 2 focuses on enhancing transparency, equity, and auditability of AI in education systems. The research shows that trust in AI systems and ethical governance of decision made with AI is reinforced through well-defined accountability.

i. Audit Checks

Within the framework, there are algorithms audits performed within certain time frames to verify fairness and accuracy. For example, one model used in evaluation for one of the subjects was found to be skewed in favor of some demographic groups more than others. After fairness-aware retraining with balanced data, the model became more unbiased across all demographics.

ii. Explainable Outputs

Transparency is improved through the integration of SHAP, LIME, and AIF360 into the framework. These systems offer AI diagnostic explanations through the most significant elements. For example, in the case study on course recommendation, SHAP explained to instructors how past performance and personal interests impacted recommendations which made them adjust their final modifications.

iii. Role Assignment

Staff was allocated defined roles to enhance shared responsibility which resulted in defined shared accountability. For example, in a dropout alert system, teachers were responsible for flagging the students while IT personnel maintained the model. This arrangement achieved ethical responsibility without creating inefficiency.

iv. Impact Reviews

AI technologies, such as ChatGPT, were appraised through algorithmic impact evaluations (AIA) to quantify their consequences on educational environments both prior to and following integration. These assessments assisted institutions in balancing the application of AI with institutional frameworks as well as data governance policies like FERPA, GDPR.

v. Trust and Oversight

These results support the assertion that the divisions of responsibility frameworks allow educational institutions to use AI tools more responsively and safely. Technical and human supervision enhances accuracy and confidence in AI-assisted decision-making processes.

Collectively, Tier 2 ensures that AI systems are effective, reliable, examined AI systems trust in proper ethical, pedagogical, moral, and social standards education requires

4.1.3 Tier 3: Human-Centered Layer

This framework's third tier focuses on how teachers, students, and other participants engage with and take part in AI-assisted educational processes. Findings show that participants tend to trust and make rational decisions when systems foster human-centric approaches and inclusive design principles.

i. Human-in-the-Loop (HITL)

HITL frameworks have been integrated in a manner where instructors can moderate or control the materials generated by AI to ensure moderators are incorporated. In cases where AI generated feedback, instructors had the opportunity to opt in and approve feedback before it was issued to learners. This system in place reduced the heavy reliance on automation and preserved the critical elements of human judgment where it was most vital.

ii. User-Friendly Design

Educators and students reported perceiving all AI systems with visual dashboards, explanation controls, and similar interfaces as easy to use. Their speech synthesis, command entry via mouse, and mobile device accessibility features enabled effective tool use for many skill levels and disabilities, greatly improving user accessibility.

iii. Support for Inclusivity

The systems were evaluated on AI's ability to cater to varying learning styles and needs. Multilingual capabilities, accessibility options, and customization preferences produced high engagement and satisfaction levels. This ensured that students could not be excluded because of the language they spoke, their disabilities, or other learning related reasons.

iv. Social and Emotional Factors

Some AI systems aimed to detect emotions like dissatisfaction or indifference by analyzing the user's pace of interaction. While these findings are rather early-stage, they do indicate that AI supports designed with emotional components could foster learning with human assistance.

v. Alignment with Ethics

The human-centered boundary also ensures compliance with fundamental principles of education. The control of decision-making rests upon the educators, while learners are trusted with autonomy. Within these parameters, ethical pedagogy and student rights balanced harmony known as educational relationship are preserved.

Tier 3 underscores that educators are restrained by the need to integrate AI in ways that uphold the inclusiveness paradigm while retaining control of the users' decisions. Empathetic, ethics-based, and compassionate decisions made within authentic classroom contexts preserve the humanity in education. Figure 4 illustrates the Ethical AI Framework structured into three layers.

Figure 4. Three-Tier model of ethical AI frameworks

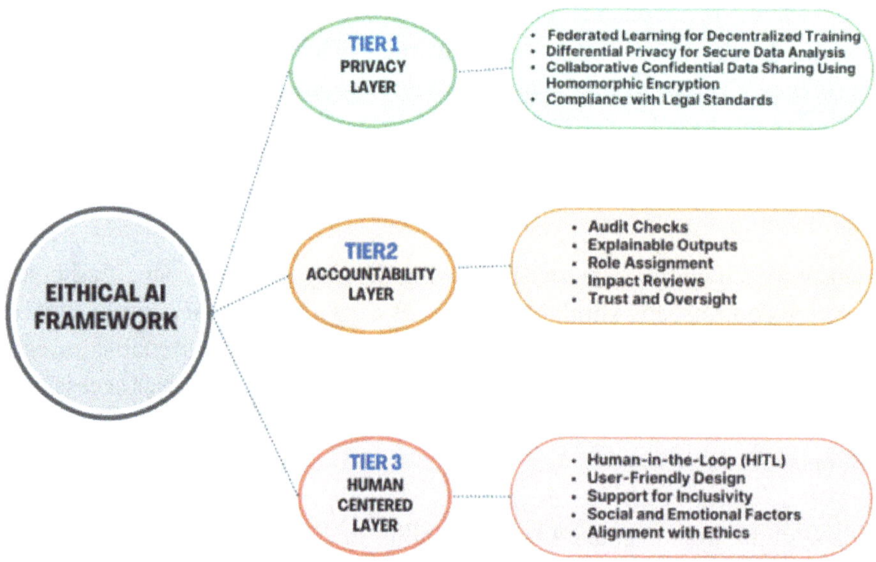

4.2 Use Cases and Implementation Scenarios

This section outlines specific examples capturing the application or alignment of the ethical AI framework with contemporary tools in education. These instances demonstrate the effectiveness of the framework in ensuring responsible AI use in different educational institutional contexts.

4.2.1 Ethical Educational AI Platforms

The framework was evaluated against leading AI systems such as DreamBox Learning, Squirrel AI, and Carnegie Learning. These platforms implement adaptive learning systems and supervision by teachers or guardians as well as transparency. For instance, in DreamBox, math instruction is provided with real time adjustment, and progress tracking is available to educators. All of them abide by key principles including but not limited to personalization, equity, and student data protection (Revesai, 2024).

4.2.2 Technology Alignment with Practical Use

With the design of platform policy, the framework was also put to the test for design policing framework development. In one instance, a school implemented fairness audits alongside SHAP to refine a predictive tool for estimating dropout risks, employing bias mitigation strategies within the tool's outcomes. In another instance, the prototype of the LMS included federated learning to enhance the security of stored student data across devices without compromising private information (Burr & Leslie, 2023).

4.3 Framework Validation Through Case Examples

This part presents the case examples that were used to validate the proposed ethical AI framework in education and to empirically explore the workings of its principles.

4.3.1 DreamBox Learning

DreamBox Learning, a K-8 math platform, uses reinforcement learning to tailor student interactions with the platform. It adjusts lesson difficulty in real-time based on student responses. The system adequately matched DreamBox's triad of privacy, personalization, and teacher engagement, which is, tessellated oversight where teachers monitor student progress along with lesson adjust, thus enabling accountability and control (Dutta et al., 2024).

4.3.2 Carnegie Learning

Carnegie Learning uses AI along with the science of cognitive processes to tailor STEM lessons to student needs. It fills gaps in learning using cognitive models and customizes content to fit students' needs. Through dashboards, teachers receive updates as information is processed making real-time presentation of information possible and AI supervision secure, thereby achieving the framework goals of transparency, teacher presence, and responsible refinements (Bahassi et al.,2024).

4.3.3 OpenEdu Analytics

An open-source tool for educational data analytics, OpenEdu Analytics, offers ethical datamining services. It analyzes student data through federated learning, which does not involve data centralization. Teachers can detect patterns while trends can be viewed in the aggregate. The data is anonymized and no personal information is revealed. This aligns with the framework's emphasis on privacy, decentralized secure data management, safeguarded data utilization, and protective data governance (Tang, 2024).

These case study example set provides a cohesive rationale for the proposed framework using real world educational AI systems which provide practical demonstrations of achievable privacy, transparency, fairness, and responsible human oversight. The incorporation of AI-powered applications into the learning process encourages responsible technology use in education.

5. DISCUSSION

This section primarily discusses the application of the framework and its relationship with particular school cases. It discusses the primary ethical issues that the model resolves, and simultaneously highlights those that could be further developed or deepened.

5.1 Proposed Framework Value and Adaptability

The adapted framework has proven effective in solving critical ethical issues, demonstrating practical value which still allows for adaptability across educational contexts and technology integrations.

5.1.1 Scalability and Flexibility across Educational Settings

The adaptational framework can operate with different types of educational entities. Its modular nature enables institutions to select components that pertain to them, like privacy and fairness measures aligned with their policies and frameworks. It is usable in under-resourced and advanced educational institutions. This allows it to span K-12, colleges, and vocational training programs and assists in the integration of ethical artificial intelligence (AI) across diverse educational contexts (Adams et al., 2023).

5.1.2 Teacher Autonomy and Equity Among Learners

The framework allows for equity within the educational processes along with the autonomy of the teachers by utilizing HITL (human-in-the-loop) systems. Under these systems, teachers are able to review or change AI-driven decisions. So, there is needed supervision to AI human teaching assistance. In addition, algorithms that provide fairness and in equitable design that mitigates the learning gap intellectually boosts inequity. So, the blended automation and teacher engagement enabled the framework to respond to equity concerns in the teaching participation as ensures equitable experience for all students (Kumar et al., 2024).

5.2 Challenges in Implementation

Regardless of being effective, the framework has a number of concerns of application, especially on infrastructure, training, and policy consistency.

5.2.1 AI Literacy Gaps and Resource Limitations

Many educational institutions continue to remain underfunded and lack access to basic resources, for example, internet connections, devices, and computational power. This poses a significant challenge for schools that lack funding. Additionally, a poorly trained and equipped workforce is prevalent as a significant number of educators are not trained on the functionalities and applications of modern AI technologies. This opens doors to error, misplaced trust in the capabilities of technology, or in complete avoidance of engaging with the technology. All of these challenges hurt the equitable adoption of the framework (Mpuangnan, 2024).

5.2.2 Handling Explainability-Performance Trade-offs

AI systems are known for one primary issue: they lack the ability to be explained or rationalized. Most of the time, AI models that claim to achieve great accuracy are opaque, meaning the computations done inside of them are inaccessible and often incomprehensible, and furthermore masked out and not available for human understanding. In the educational setting, this is problematic because both trust and performance are essential domains. XAI tools do manage to mitigate those concerns to a degree, however, the dilemma of which model to use remains conditional (Khosravi et al., 2022).

5.3 Responsibilities of Key Stakeholders

The responsible application of AI in education requires the attention of different groups such as educators, developers, and policy makers. In this subsection, each actor's unique responsibilities and obligations are articulated.

5.3.1 Role of Educators in Oversight

Educators are important stakeholders when it comes to seeing the usefulness of AI in education. Through human-in-the-loop (HITL) systems, they have the option to approve, change, or cancel decisions made by intelligent systems. They make sure AI systems functioning within the educational ecosystem and the classrooms operate within learning goals and objectives, tuning to individualized students' needs. This oversight protects fairness and accuracy with appropriate teaching methods ensured to be employed (Sayles, 2024).

5.3.2 Developers' Responsibilities towards Fairness

The question of inclusivity starts with the developer at the AI system design stage. They should have strategies to mitigate bias like reweighting, adversarial debiasing, and the use of diverse training sets. Heuristic tests of algorithmic discrimination and validation tests to correct biases must be implemented. Discrimination or bias emanates from failure to permit fairness, something that should not be allowed at any stage within a model development life cycle (Ge et al., 2023).

5.3.3 The Responsibility of Policymakers in the Regulation

Policymakers set boundaries in how AI can be implemented in education to ensure safety and equity. They make sure that schools and other educational institutions respect the boundaries of law including the GDPR and FERPA and, frameworks such as transparency, accountability, and trust. Additionally, they support and finance ethical AI audits and certification processes. Powerful policies violate the rights and consequently result in the protection of the students, where the use of AI technology is in the public interest (Miao et al., 2021).

5.4 Lessons from Ethical Failures in AI Use

The previous unethical practices associated with AI in education are associated with algorithmic bias, lack of transparency, and inadequate control over system design and operation.

5.4.1 Case Reviews of Grading Bias and Privacy Violations

The cases demonstrate how AI technology can be implemented within education without precautionary protective measures. There was a class action lawsuit in 2020 against a UK entity that implemented an automated grading system. Due to biased data, it unjustly low-scored a disproportionate number of students from disadvantaged backgrounds. Weak security also led to one platform exposing millions of student records. These examples highlight the need for fairness, privacy by design, and trust through disclosure (Hu et al., 2021).

5.4.2 Strategic Responses and Design Remedies

In order to address ethical concerns, AI systems require policies and mechanisms for the entire life cycle. Programs like AIF360 and Fairlearn provide means to log and remediate biases during the design phase. Isolation methods such as federated learning and homomorphic encryption ensure the privacy and security of students' data. Implementation of HITL models enables human oversight to shape outcomes. All these measures significantly strengthen the trust, fairness, and diversity frameworks of AI in education (Ge et al., 2023).

The ethical framework presented underscores the fact that ethical AI can be customized to different educational contexts. Responsible supervision, ensuring equity, and maintaining privacy will allow learning with AI to happen in a balanced manner and help mitigate risks.

6. CONCLUSION

In particular, this research describes the workflow involved in the development, validation, and implementation of the ethical AI framework for education. This research highlights the concepts of privacy, fairness, accountability, and human-centered design as integral factors that drive the responsible use of AI technology in education.

6.1 Summary of Contributions

This part examines the ethical, technical, and practical gap addressed by the framework in the use of AI in education, then illustrates the overarching contributions of the framework.

6.1.1 Importance of the Information Ethics Framework on AI

The ethical AI framework employs the major pillars of the philosophy regarding responsible use of AI, 'What Needs Attention' that involves protection of data, bias mitigation, transparency, and human participation in decisions concerning the use of AI technology. With his set of ethical principles, schools are offered a blend of mechanical tools and morals with the hope that AI ought to be safe, equitable, and comprehensive to all in its educational environment.

6.1.2 Summary on Privacy, Transparency, and Inclusivity

The framework maintains student privacy through federated learning and differential privacy. Transparent checking mechanisms known as SHAP and LIME are utilized in a way that supports users seeing the outcomes and explanation of AI decisions. Inclusivity is achieved fair algorithmic principles that govern the design of AI tools for all learners.

6.2 Recommendations for Practice and Policy

These findings lead one to suggest the following to shape AI in educational practice and policy development.

6.2.1 Policies on Institutions on the Ethical Use of AI Technologies

In relations to fairness, equity, privacy and transparency as the pillars of ethically using AI guided, institutions need specific policies to ensure the tools in education do not violate these principles. Create internal policies, AI education programs for staff, AI system evaluation and compliance with ethical and legal standards are steps toward Responsible AI.

6.2.2 Need for Continuous Monitoring and Revision

Caring for the AI system under consideration in any educational framework requires particular scrutiny and attention – especially from the ethical ramifications of such consideration. Audits on the regular basis were done to pinpoint discriminations, errors, or any low-standard elements that AI might have accumulated over time. Policies, practices, instruments, and settings should evolve simultaneously. This guarantees the continued absence of bias, safety, and functional effectiveness of AI in education.

6.3 CONCLUDING THOUGHTS

These enduring insights resonate with the need to remain flexible while ensuring an ethical, human-centric core, for the sustained use of AI technologies in education.

6.3.1 Constructing a Balance Between Automation and Human Intervention

Even in highly automated educational environments, the decision to employ automated systems should be made judiciously at the human level. Context, emotion, and socio-ethical dimensions of teaching cannot be tackled by AI systems. Assisting humans' triggers in educational environments VP rather than abolishing them will ensure the beneficial adoption of AI tools in educational environments in the long run. Active engagement by all learners within a meaningful learning context is possible through automation when blended with the professional judgment of educators.

6.3.2 Ethical Foresight for Future AI Advancements in Education

Mitigating the dangers that the use of AI technologies entails in educational environments becomes more imperative as the technology evolves. Policies must ensure privacy, equity, and inclusivity from the system design framework. Engaging actively with educators and learners makes it possible to foresee particular challenges and mitigate them to ensure that AI transforms the educational landscape positively rather than negatively.

The overarching aim of the ethical framework on AI discussed here is to respond to the most pressing concerns pertaining to the technology in education. It allows for the use of AI in various learning contexts while ensuring privacy, equity, actionable transparency, and human oversight. There will be a need for educators, system developers and policymakers to jointly ensure ethical sustainment of AI and educational systems.

REFERENCES

Adams, C., Pente, P., Lemermeyer, G., & Rockwell, G. (2023). Ethical principles for artificial intelligence in K-12 education. *Computers and Education: Artificial Intelligence, 4*, 100131. DOI: 10.1016/j.caeai.2023.100131

Ahmad, W., Raj, R., & Shokeen, R. (2025). Reshaping Special Education: Strategic Use of Artificial Intelligence. In *Transforming Special Education Through Artificial Intelligence* (pp. 1-44). IGI Global.

Aithal, P. S., & Aithal, S. (2023). Predictive analysis on future impact of ubiquitous education technology in higher education and research. [IJAEML]. *International Journal of Applied Engineering and Management Letters, 7*(3), 88–108. DOI: 10.47992/IJAEML.2581.7000.0190

Alawneh, Y. J. J., Radwan, E. N. Z., Salman, F. N., Makhlouf, S. I., Makhamreh, K., & Alawneh, M. S. (2024, April). Ethical considerations in the use of AI in primary education: Privacy, bias, and inclusivity. In *2024 International Conference on Knowledge Engineering and Communication Systems (ICKECS)* (Vol. 1, pp. 1-6). IEEE. DOI: 10.1109/ICKECS61492.2024.10616986

Alfarra, A. H., Amhan, L. F., Mosa, M. J., Alajrami, M. A., El Kahlout, F., Abu-Nasser, B. S., & Abu-Naser, S. S. (2024). AI-Driven Learning: Advances and Challenges in Intelligent Tutoring Systems.

Allen, L. K., & Kendeou, P. (2024). ED-AI Lit: An Interdisciplinary framework for AI literacy in education. *Policy Insights from the Behavioral and Brain Sciences, 11*(1), 3–10. DOI: 10.1177/23727322231220339

Bahassi, H., Azmi, M., & Khiat, A. (2024). Cognitive systems for education: Architectures, innovations, and comparative analyses. *Procedia Computer Science, 238*, 436–443. DOI: 10.1016/j.procs.2024.06.045

Balasubramaniam, N., Kauppinen, M., Rannisto, A., Hiekkanen, K., & Kujala, S. (2023). Transparency and explainability of AI systems: From ethical guidelines to requirements. *Information and Software Technology, 159*, 107197. DOI: 10.1016/j.infsof.2023.107197

Barbosa, R. (2023). Designing Fairness-Aware Machine Learning Algorithms: Techniques and Challenges. Academic Journal of Science and Technology, 6(1).

Bibi, P. (2024). Establishing Transparency and Accountability in AI: Ethical Standards for Data Governance and Automated Systems.

Burr, C., & Leslie, D. (2023). Ethical assurance: A practical approach to the responsible design, development, and deployment of data-driven technologies. *AI and Ethics*, *3*(1), 73–98. DOI: 10.1007/s43681-022-00178-0

Cappelli, M. A., & Di Marzo Serugendo, G. (2024). A semi-automated software model to support AI ethics compliance assessment of an AI system guided by ethical principles of AI. *AI and Ethics*, •••, 1–24.

Chari, S. G. (2024). Bridging Gaps, Building Futures: Tackling Socio-Economic Disparities Through Education and Technology. *London Journal of Research In Humanities and Social Sciences*, *24*(16), 1–12.

Chen, F. (2022). Human-AI cooperation in education: Human in loop and teaching as leadership. *Journal of Educational Technology and Innovation*, *2*(1). Advance online publication. DOI: 10.61414/jeti.v2i1.34

Chen, L., Chen, P., & Lin, Z. (2020). Artificial intelligence in education: A review. *IEEE Access : Practical Innovations, Open Solutions*, *8*, 75264–75278. DOI: 10.1109/ACCESS.2020.2988510

Chinta, S. V., Wang, Z., Yin, Z., Hoang, N., Gonzalez, M., Quy, T. L., & Zhang, W. (2024). FairAIED: Navigating fairness, bias, and ethics in educational AI applications. arXiv preprint arXiv:2407.18745.

Crisan, A., Drouhard, M., Vig, J., & Rajani, N. (2022, June). Interactive model cards: A human-centered approach to model documentation. In *Proceedings of the 2022 ACM Conference on Fairness, Accountability, and Transparency* (pp. 427-439). DOI: 10.1145/3531146.3533108

Dutta, S., Ranjan, S., Mishra, S., Sharma, V., Hewage, P., & Iwendi, C. (2024, February). Enhancing educational adaptability: A review and analysis of AI-driven adaptive learning platforms. In *2024 4th International Conference on Innovative Practices in Technology and Management (ICIPTM)* (pp. 1-5). IEEE. DOI: 10.1109/ICIPTM59628.2024.10563448

Farooqi, S. A., Memon, A., Zamir, S., Malik, K., Batool, W., & Zahid, H. (2024). NAVIGATING AI IN THE REAL WORLD: TRANSFORMATIONS, REGULATIONS, AND CHALLENGES. *Policy Research Journal*, *2*(4), 1083–1099.

Ge, H., Bastani, H., & Bastani, O. (2023). Rethinking Fairness for Human-AI Collaboration. arXiv preprint arXiv:2310.03647.

Gerdes, A. (2022). A participatory data-centric approach to AI ethics by design. *Applied Artificial Intelligence*, *36*(1), 2009222. DOI: 10.1080/08839514.2021.2009222

Gordon, D., Stavrakakis, I., Gibson, J. P., Tierney, B., Becevel, A., Curley, A., Collins, M., O'Mahony, W., & O'sullivan, D. (2022). Perspectives on computing ethics: A multi-stakeholder analysis. *Journal of Information. Communication and Ethics in Society*, *20*(1), 72–90. DOI: 10.1108/JICES-12-2020-0127

Gupta, P., Sreelatha, C., Latha, A., Raj, S., & Singh, A. (2024). Navigating The Future of Education: The Impact of Artificial Intelligence on Teacher-Student Dynamics. *Educational Administration: Theory and Practice*, *30*(4), 6006–6013.

Holmes, W., Porayska-Pomsta, K., Holstein, K., Sutherland, E., Baker, T., Shum, S. B., Santos, O. C., Rodrigo, M. T., Cukurova, M., Bittencourt, I. I., & Koedinger, K. R. (2022). Ethics of AI in education: Towards a community-wide framework. *International Journal of Artificial Intelligence in Education*, *32*(3), 1–23. DOI: 10.1007/s40593-021-00239-1

Hridi, A. P., Sahay, R., Hosseinalipour, S., & Akram, B. (2024, May). Revolutionizing AI-Assisted Education with Federated Learning: A Pathway to Distributed, Privacy-Preserving, and Debiased Learning Ecosystems. In *Proceedings of the AAAI Symposium Series* (Vol. 3, No. 1, pp. 297-303). DOI: 10.1609/aaaiss.v3i1.31217

Hu, Y., Kuang, W., Qin, Z., Li, K., Zhang, J., Gao, Y., Li, W., & Li, K. (2021). Artificial intelligence security: Threats and countermeasures. *ACM Computing Surveys*, *55*(1), 1–36. DOI: 10.1145/3487890

Kamenskih, A. (2022). The analysis of security and privacy risks in smart education environments. *Journal of Smart Cities and Society*, *1*(1), 17–29. DOI: 10.3233/SCS-210114

Khan, W. N. (2024). Ethical Challenges of AI in Education: Balancing Innovation with Data Privacy. *Journal of AI Integration in Education*, *1*(1), 1–13.

Khosravi, H., Shum, S. B., Chen, G., Conati, C., Tsai, Y. S., Kay, J., & Gašević, D. (2022). Explainable artificial intelligence in education. *Computers and Education: Artificial Intelligence*, *3*, 100074.

Kordzadeh, N., & Ghasemaghaei, M. (2022). Algorithmic bias: Review, synthesis, and future research directions. *European Journal of Information Systems*, *31*(3), 388–409. DOI: 10.1080/0960085X.2021.1927212

Kumar, S., Datta, S., Singh, V., Datta, D., Singh, S. K., & Sharma, R. (2024). Applications, Challenges, and Future Directions of Human-in-the-Loop Learning. *IEEE Access : Practical Innovations, Open Solutions*, *12*, 75735–75760. DOI: 10.1109/ACCESS.2024.3401547

Lang, Q., Wang, M., Yin, M., Liang, S., & Song, W. (2025). Transforming Education with Generative AI (GAI): Key Insights and Future Prospects. IEEE Transactions on Learning Technologies.

Li, H., Fan, X., & Liang, J. (2025). The Squirrel AI Adaptive Learning System Accompanying Millions of Children in Their Growth. In *Digital Transformation of Regional Education in China* (pp. 51–53). Springer Nature Singapore. DOI: 10.1007/978-981-97-8144-7_7

Manna, S., & Sett, N. (2024). Need of AI in Modern Education: in the Eyes of Explainable AI (xAI). *arXiv preprint arXiv:2408.00025.*

Memarian, B., & Doleck, T. (2023). Fairness, Accountability, Transparency, and Ethics (FATE) in Artificial Intelligence (AI) and higher education: A systematic review. *Computers and Education: Artificial Intelligence*, *5*, 100152. DOI: 10.1016/j.caeai.2023.100152

Mensah, G. B. (2023). Artificial intelligence and ethics: A comprehensive review of bias mitigation, transparency, and accountability in AI Systems. *Preprint*, (November), 10.

Miao, F., Holmes, W., Huang, R., & Zhang, H. (2021). *AI and education: A guidance for policymakers*. UNESCO Publishing.

Mpuangnan, K. N. (2024). Teacher preparedness and professional development needs for successful technology integration in teacher education. *Cogent Education*, *11*(1), 2408837. DOI: 10.1080/2331186X.2024.2408837

Murtaza, M., Ahmed, Y., Shamsi, J. A., Sherwani, F., & Usman, M. (2022). AI-based personalized e-learning systems: Issues, challenges, and solutions. *IEEE Access : Practical Innovations, Open Solutions*, *10*, 81323–81342. DOI: 10.1109/ACCESS.2022.3193938

Nair, B. M. (2023). The efficacy of artificial intelligence-driven immersive reader for dyslexic students in special schools: A case study. *Journal of English Language Teaching*, *65*(5), 3–8.

Nguyen, A., Ngo, H. N., Hong, Y., Dang, B., & Nguyen, B. P. T. (2023). Ethical principles for artificial intelligence in education. *Education and Information Technologies*, *28*(4), 4221–4241. DOI: 10.1007/s10639-022-11316-w PMID: 36254344

Palle, R. R., & Kathala, K. C. R. (2024). *Privacy in the Age of Innovation.*

Parycek, P., Schmid, V., & Novak, A. S. (2024). Artificial Intelligence (AI) and automation in administrative procedures: Potentials, limitations, and framework conditions. *Journal of the Knowledge Economy*, *15*(2), 8390–8415. DOI: 10.1007/s13132-023-01433-3

Rane, N., Choudhary, S., & Rane, J. (2023). Education 4.0 and 5.0: Integrating artificial intelligence (AI) for personalized and adaptive learning.

Revesai, Z. (2024). Ethical Implications of AI-Driven Education Systems on Digital Rights: A Comparative Analysis. *The Fountain: Journal of Interdisciplinary Studies*, *8*(1), 126–152.

Salloum, S. A. (2024). AI Perils in Education: Exploring Ethical Concerns. Artificial Intelligence in Education: The Power and Dangers of ChatGPT in the Classroom, 669-675.

Sayles, J. (2024). Human Oversight of AI Systems. In *Principles of AI Governance and Model Risk Management: Master the Techniques for Ethical and Transparent AI Systems* (pp. 267–276). Apress. DOI: 10.1007/979-8-8688-0983-5_12

Shahriar, S., Allana, S., Hazratifard, S. M., & Dara, R. (2023). A survey of privacy risks and mitigation strategies in the Artificial Intelligence life cycle. *IEEE Access : Practical Innovations, Open Solutions*, *11*, 61829–61854. DOI: 10.1109/ACCESS.2023.3287195

Shaik, T., Tao, X., Li, Y., Dann, C., McDonald, J., Redmond, P., & Galligan, L. (2022). A review of the trends and challenges in adopting natural language processing methods for education feedback analysis. *IEEE Access : Practical Innovations, Open Solutions*, *10*, 56720–56739. DOI: 10.1109/ACCESS.2022.3177752

Shtayyat, A., Gawanmeh, A., & Mashaleh, A. (2025). Risk Analysis of AI Integration in Educational Systems.

Singh, T. M., Reddy, C. K. K., Murthy, B. R., Nag, A., & Doss, S. (2025). AI and education: Bridging the gap to personalized, efficient, and accessible learning.

Srinivasa, K. G., Kurni, M., & Saritha, K. (2022). Harnessing the Power of AI to Education. In *Learning, teaching, and assessment methods for contemporary learners: pedagogy for the digital generation* (pp. 311–342). Springer Nature Singapore. DOI: 10.1007/978-981-19-6734-4_13

Su, G., Wang, J., Xu, X., Wang, Y., & Wang, C. (2024). The Utilization of Homomorphic Encryption Technology Grounded on Artificial Intelligence for Privacy Preservation. *International Journal of Computer Science and Information Technologies*, *2*(1), 52–58. DOI: 10.62051/ijcsit.v2n1.07

Tang, Y. (2024). Privacy protection framework for open data: Constructing and assessing an effective approach. *Library & Information Science Research*, *46*(3), 101312. DOI: 10.1016/j.lisr.2024.101312

Vaza, R. N., Parmar, A. B., Mishra, P. S., Abdullah, I., & Velu, C. M. (2024). Security And Privacy Concerns In AI-Enabled IoT Educational Frameworks: An In-Depth Analysis. *Educational Administration: Theory and Practice*, *30*(4), 8436–8445.

Yagyaeva, E., Turobova, M., Nazirova, R., Daminova, Y., Merganova, N., & Oripova, N. (2024, May). A Layout of Bridging Learning Process to fill the Gaps Through AI to make the Technical Education for Better Access. In 2024 4th International Conference on Advance Computing and Innovative Technologies in Engineering (ICACITE) (pp. 612-616). IEEE. DOI: 10.1109/ICACITE60783.2024.10617424

Yang, E., & Beil, C. (2024). Ensuring data privacy in AI/ML implementation. *New Directions for Higher Education*, *2024*(207), 63–78. DOI: 10.1002/he.20509

Zhai, C., Wibowo, S., & Li, L. D. (2024). The effects of over-reliance on AI dialogue systems on students' cognitive abilities: A systematic review. *Smart Learning Environments*, *11*(1), 28. DOI: 10.1186/s40561-024-00316-7

Zhai, X., Chu, X., Chai, C. S., Jong, M. S. Y., Istenic, A., Spector, M., ... & Li, Y. (2021). A Review of Artificial Intelligence (AI) in Education from 2010 to 2020.

Zhang, K., & Aslan, A. B. (2021). AI technologies for education: Recent research & future directions. Computers and education. *Artificial Intelligence*, *2*, 100025.

Chapter 8
Students Data Security Metrics and the Ethical Implication for Artificial Intelligence Deployment

Ifedayo Emmanuel Adu
https://orcid.org/0000-0002-7939-4510
Bamidele Olumilua University of Education, Science, and Technology, Ikere, Nigeria

Damola Olugbade
https://orcid.org/0000-0003-3938-6273
Abiola Ajimobi Technical University, Ibadan, Nigeria

ABSTRACT

This chapter explores the deployment of artificial intelligence (AI) technologies within the context of data security, focusing on the perceptions and engagement metrics of Nigerian university students. Utilizing a quantitative methodology, the research employed data analytics gathered from the X (formerly Twitter) platform, complemented by screen recordings. A total of 100 responses were collected, with data cleaning performed prior to analysis using SPSS and Excel as .csv data compiler. The chapter utilized linear regression and descriptive statistics to analyse engagement metrics, revealing trends in students' awareness and understanding of data security including the ethical deployment of AI. Findings indicate a significant increase in student engagement in 2022 and 2024, reflecting heightened discourse around AI ethics and data security issues. The results underscore the necessity for targeted educational initiatives that address the growing concerns among students regarding the implications of AI technologies, contributing to the broader dialogue on responsible AI deployment.

DOI: 10.4018/979-8-3373-5550-4.ch008

INTRODUCTION

In recent years, artificial intelligence (AI) has emerged as a transformative force across various sectors, revolutionizing the way organizations operate, make decisions, and interact with customers. The deployment of AI technologies has the potential to enhance efficiency, drive innovation, and create new opportunities for growth. However, as the integration of AI into everyday processes becomes more prevalent, it also raises significant ethical, societal, and operational considerations. This dynamic landscape necessitates a comprehensive understanding of the implications of AI deployment, particularly concerning data security, privacy, and the ethical use of technology (Radanliev, Santos, Brandon-Jones & Joinson, 2024).

As organizations increasingly rely on AI to process vast amounts of data and automate complex tasks, the need for responsible and ethical deployment practices becomes paramount. Issues related to data privacy, algorithmic bias, transparency, and accountability are at the forefront of discussions surrounding AI technologies. The successful integration of AI requires not only advanced technical capabilities but also a commitment to ethical principles and a recognition of the broader societal impacts of these technologies (Fedele, Punzi & Tramacere, 2024).

This study focuses on the deployment of AI in the context of data security, particularly among Nigerian university students, who are navigating an increasingly digitized and data-driven world. By examining the engagement metrics related to data security and AI, this research aims to shed light on the factors influencing student awareness and understanding of these critical issues. Ultimately, this investigation seeks to contribute to the discourse on responsible AI deployment, highlighting the ethical implications and the necessity for informed practices that prioritize the well-being of individuals and society as a whole (Eden, Chisom & Adeniyi, 2024).

Data are set of raw information that could be gathered and processed further for more meaningful purposes. However, data security is the process of ensuring that set of raw information are safeguarded from data breach. Data currently in this 21st century has new genre occurring freely as analytics on social networks like X, Facebook and Instagram and they represent the record of student activities on the internet. The student's data security metrics connote the values imbued in learner's online activities in the light of artificial intelligence. This study is an investigation of student's data security breach and the level of ethical implications it brings to Nigeria university education. For instance, artificial intelligence (AI) is currently a big business from Machine Learning to Big Data analytics. The web 2.0 and the 5th industrial revolution is being harnessed for educational benefits all over the world with increased concern for students' safety when using the artificial intelligence applications. Sometimes, students leave behind digital footprints that are hacked for heinous activities, which is detrimental to teaching and learning objectives (Dieterle, Dede & Walker, 2024).

A Synergy between Students Data Security Metrics and Artificial Intelligence (AI) in Classroom Instruction

There exists connection between students' data security and artificial intelligence in classroom instruction. For instance, the student's data security metrics helps in informing the lecturers on trending topics that are influencing students attitudinal change within the classroom instructional setting (Ajayi & First author, 2025).

The student's data security metrics are connected to artificially intelligent systems that are controlled by algorithms. For instance, the automated data analytics function as metrics for measuring students' engagement on social media. Also, these data analytics when sourced in large quantities from social media and analysed yields useful information related to students teaching and learning activities. Examples of these social media are: X (formerly Twitter), TikTok, Facebook, and YouTube (Cukurova, 2025).

In the classroom instruction involving student's social media engagement. The student's data security poses a lot of tasks as students leave behind digital footprints on adopted social media internet application. Also, there is student's AI synergy in the classroom based on interactional influence with chatbots such as ChatGPT and Meta AI. Hence, classroom instruction and students AI synergy are mutually exclusive concepts for complimenting up-to-date approaches to instructional activities with minimal human interference (Yuan, Xiao, Pei, Bu & Cai, 2025).

The student's social media engagement are sources of AI generated data analytics, which serves as the basis for learners' data security metrics. For instance, some of the student's data analytics need to be highly secured if it contains personal information like social security number, password and username (Singh, Lakhera, Ojha, kumar Mishra & Nain, 2025).

Figure 1. AI and classroom synergy. Source: Designed using Paint 3D and 2D

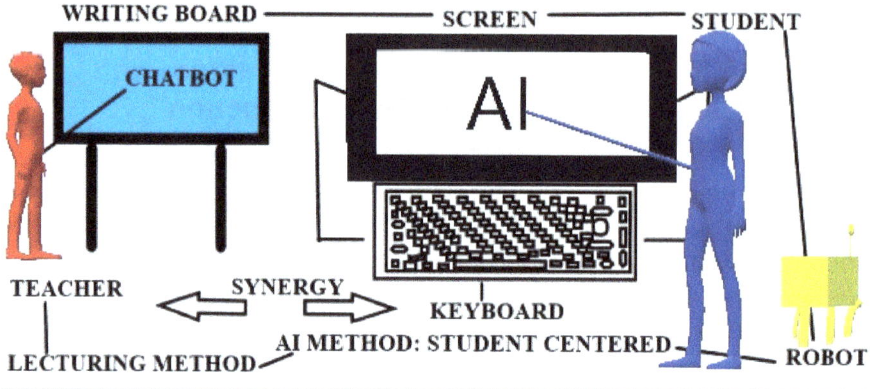

Software

This figure 1 in this study shows AI and classroom synergy with minimal teacher's interference and more student centered learning engagement whenever AI is adopted.

AI Impact on Teaching and Learning Dynamics

Artificially intelligent (AI) systems are currently impacting teaching and learning through AI application support in classroom instructional setting. For instance, Chatbots are synonymous to ChatGPT online applications, which are useful in generating textual instructional contents for teaching and learning activities. Chatbots is characterised with qualities of a Chatting Robot for human computer interaction. The AI impact has provided lecturers with faster access to teaching and learning resources. Nowadays, classroom teaching and learning resources are easily sourced through Chatbots application like Meta AI (Li, 2025).

AI Use and Ethical Students Engagement in Educational Institutions

Artificial intelligence use by educators has recently proliferate in educational institutions. There is increased AI use in education, which has likewise increased students' engagement on social media. For instance, students are leaving behind digital footprints in the form of data analytics, which calls for ethical practices. Ethically students' engagement when using social media application demands that users must protect personal information if stumbled upon on the internet. Hence, personal information must be handled with utmost confidentiality when using social media online software (Ahmed, 2024).

AI Concrete Implications for Educational Practitioners

The AI concrete implications for educational practitioners implies an automated approach to teaching and learning process. However, available literature shows that there are concerns regarding the fairness of the automated process. There are also issues regarding the transparency of the automated AI process for egalitarian classroom activities that is inclusive for all students. The explanation of the algorithm involved in the automated processes likewise raise issues on AI explainability for more clarity in its adoption within classroom environment (Yadav, 2025).

AI Early Indicators for Curriculum Adjustment

There is increment in the adoption of artificial intelligence application for teaching and learning. Some of the clear indicators are evident in this study's metrics on student data security, which shows a rise in students' engagement on data security discourse. Also, available literature shows that curriculum activities nowadays has witnessed increased AI usage, which is a clear indication of more reliance on Chatbots. For instance, curriculum assessment that steps up grading system for AI adoption is a plus towards enhancing fairness. Hence, there is an urgent need for curriculum adjustment to accommodate the early indicators of AI (Ogalo & Mtenzi, 2025).

Data Security

Data security is a critical aspect of information technology and management that focuses on protecting data from unauthorised access, corruption, or theft throughout its lifecycle. With the increasing reliance on digital data in various sectors, including education, healthcare, finance, and government, ensuring the confidentiality, integrity, and availability of sensitive information has become paramount. The significance of data security extends beyond mere compliance with regulations; it plays a vital role in maintaining trust, safeguarding privacy, and protecting organisational assets (Franco D'Souza, Mathew, Mishra & Surapaneni, 2024).

1. **Importance of Data Security**
   i. **Protecting Sensitive Information:** In today's digital age, organizations collect and store vast amounts of sensitive data, including personal identifiable information (PII), financial records, and proprietary information. A breach of this data can lead to severe consequences, including identity theft,

financial loss, and reputational damage. Effective data security measures help prevent such breaches, ensuring that sensitive information remains confidential (Ali, Mijwil, Buruga, Abotaleb & Adamopoulos, 2024).

ii. **Compliance with Regulations:** Various regulations, such as the General Data Protection Regulation (GDPR) in Europe and the Health Insurance Portability and Accountability Act (HIPAA) in the United States, mandate strict data protection standards. Organizations must comply with these regulations to avoid legal penalties and protect the rights of individuals. Data security practices help organizations meet these legal obligations while minimizing the risk of fines and legal action (Ahmed, 2024).

iii. **Maintaining Business Continuity:** Data breaches can disrupt business operations and lead to significant downtime, resulting in financial losses and diminished customer trust. Robust data security measures, such as data backups, disaster recovery plans, and incident response strategies, are essential for ensuring business continuity in the event of a breach (Barnes, Hutson & Perry, 2024).

iv. **Building Trust:** Organizations that prioritize data security build trust with their clients, customers, and stakeholders. Demonstrating a commitment to protecting data fosters confidence among users, encouraging them to engage with the organization and share their information. Conversely, data breaches can erode trust and result in long-term damage to an organization's reputation (Han, Nawaz, Buchanan & McKay, 2025).

2. **Key Elements of Data Security**

i. **Data Encryption:** Encryption is a fundamental data security technique that involves converting data into a coded format, making it unreadable without the appropriate decryption key. This ensures that even if data is intercepted or accessed without authorization, it remains protected. Encryption is crucial for protecting sensitive information both in transit (when being transmitted over networks) and at rest (Sanfo, 2025).

ii. **Access Controls**: Implementing strict access controls ensures that only authorized individuals can access sensitive data. This includes the use of authentication methods, such as passwords, biometrics, and multi-factor authentication (MFA), to verify users' identities. Role-based access control (RBAC) can also limit access based on job responsibilities, reducing the risk of unauthorized access to critical data (Harte, Carey, Feng, Alqarni & Albuquerque, 2025).

iii. **Data Backup and Recovery**: Regular data backups are essential for ensuring data availability and integrity. In the event of data loss due to accidental deletion, hardware failure, or cyberattacks (e.g., ransomware), having recent backups allows organizations to restore their data quickly. Implementing a comprehensive data recovery plan ensures that organizations can recover from data loss incidents with minimal disruption (Çela, Fonkam, Vajjhala & Vedishchev, 2025).

iv. **Security Awareness Training**: Human error is often a significant factor in data breaches. Training employees on data security best practices, recognizing phishing attempts, and understanding the importance of protecting sensitive information can significantly reduce the likelihood of breaches caused by inadvertent actions. Regular training sessions help foster a culture of security awareness within organizations (Ogalo & Mtenzi, 2025; Joshi, Pandey & Kumari, 2025).

v. **Monitoring and Incident Response**: Continuous monitoring of data systems and networks is essential for detecting potential security threats in real time. Organizations should implement security information and event management (SIEM) systems to aggregate and analyse security data. An effective incident response plan enables organizations to respond swiftly to security incidents, mitigating the impact and restoring normal operations (Greenstein & Cho, 2025).

3. **Challenges in Data Security**

   i. **Evolving Threat Landscape**: Cyber threats are continually evolving, with attackers employing increasingly sophisticated techniques to bypass security measures. Organizations must stay updated on the latest threats and vulnerabilities, regularly updating their security protocols to counter emerging risks (Nwozor, 2025; Sultana & Rao, 2025).

   ii. **Balancing Security and Usability**: Striking the right balance between data security and user convenience is often a challenge. Overly stringent security measures can hinder productivity and frustrate users, while lax security can expose organizations to significant risks. Organizations must implement security measures that protect data without compromising usability (Reinecke, Kappes, Porsdam Mann, Savulescu & Earp, 2025).

   iii. **Compliance Complexity:** Navigating the complex landscape of data protection regulations can be daunting, especially for organizations operating in multiple jurisdictions. Compliance with various regulations requires ongoing efforts to ensure that security practices align with legal requirements (Gursoy, 2025).

Data security is a fundamental concern for organizations in today's digital landscape. By implementing robust data protection measures, organizations can safeguard sensitive information, maintain compliance with regulations, and build trust with their stakeholders. However, the evolving threat landscape and the need to balance security with usability present ongoing challenges. Continuous investment in data security practices, employee training, and technological advancements is essential for effectively mitigating risks and ensuring the integrity and availability of critical data. As organizations navigate the complexities of data security, they must remain vigilant and proactive in their efforts to protect their valuable information assets (Mitchell, 2025).

Metrics

Metrics are quantitative measures used to assess, compare, and track performance or progress toward specific objectives. In various fields such as business, education, healthcare, and technology, metrics play a crucial role in decision-making processes, performance evaluations, and strategic planning. By providing tangible data, metrics help organizations and individuals understand their current status, identify areas for improvement, and drive informed actions to achieve desired outcomes (Narendra, Dewi, Gunawan & Ardi, 2025; Rathee, Vats & Sharma, 2025).

Importance of Metrics

i. **Informed Decision-Making:** Metrics provide essential data that enable organizations to make informed decisions. By analysing quantitative information, stakeholders can identify trends, assess performance, and evaluate the effectiveness of strategies or initiatives. This data-driven approach minimizes guesswork and enhances the overall quality of decision- making (Funa & Gabay, 2025; Coelho & Reis, 2025; El-Hajj, 2025).
ii. **Performance Measurement:** Metrics allow organizations to measure their performance against established benchmarks or goals. By defining key performance indicators (KPIs), organizations can track their progress and determine whether they are meeting their objectives. This accountability fosters a culture of continuous improvement and encourages teams to strive for excellence (Karthikeyan, 2025; Ramaiah, Nagarajan, Whig & Dutta, 2025).
iii. **Goal Alignment:** Effective metrics help align organizational goals with individual and team objectives. By clearly defining and communicating relevant metrics, organizations can ensure that all employees understand how their work contributes to overarching goals. This alignment enhances motivation and fosters a sense of ownership and accountability among team members (Pesapane et. al, 2025; Dixit, Jain, Maurya & Subramaniam, 2025).
iv. **Resource Allocation:** Metrics enable organizations to assess the effectiveness of their resource allocation. By analysing performance data, organizations can identify areas that require additional investment or resources, as well as those

that may need downsizing or re-evaluation. This strategic approach ensures that resources are utilized efficiently and effectively (Wenhang, Shenting & Shaohua, 2025; AlJadaan, Zaidi, Al Faress & Jabas, 2025).

Ethical Implication

Ethical implications refer to the moral considerations and consequences that arise from actions, decisions, or policies, particularly in the context of technology, business, healthcare, and social practices. As society increasingly integrates advanced technologies, including artificial intelligence (AI), big data analytics, and biotechnology, understanding the ethical implications of these developments becomes essential. Addressing these implications ensures that innovation and progress do not come at the expense of human rights, dignity, and societal well-being (Darshan et al., 2025).

A. Importance of Ethical Implications
   i. **Promoting Responsible Innovation**: Recognizing ethical implications encourages responsible innovation. By considering the potential consequences of new technologies and practices, organizations can develop solutions that prioritize human welfare, social equity, and environmental sustainability. This proactive approach helps prevent harm and fosters public trust in new developments (Miller, Miranda, & Tolentino, 2025).
   ii. **Supporting Social Justice:** Ethical considerations are integral to promoting social justice. By examining the implications of policies and practices, stakeholders can identify and address inequalities and injustices that may arise from technological advancements. Ensuring that marginalized voices are heard and included in decision-making processes helps create equitable outcomes (Berkowitz, 2025).

B. Key Areas of Ethical Implications

Data Privacy and Security: The collection and use of personal data raise significant ethical concerns regarding privacy and security. Organizations must ensure that individuals' data is collected, stored, and used responsibly, with informed consent and appropriate safeguards. Ethical implications include the risk of data breaches, misuse of information, and erosion of individual privacy rights (Hassan, 2025).

i. **Artificial Intelligence and Automation:** The deployment of AI technologies poses ethical questions related to bias, discrimination, and accountability. AI systems can inadvertently perpetuate existing biases if trained on skewed data, leading to discriminatory outcomes. Ethical considerations also include the implications of automation on employment, labour rights, and the potential for dehumanization in decision-making processes (Vetrivel, Vidhyapriya & Arun, 2025).

ii. **Biotechnology and Genetic Engineering:** Advances in biotechnology and genetic engineering raise ethical dilemmas related to human enhancement, cloning, and genetic modification. Questions surrounding the moral status of modified organisms and the potential consequences of altering the genetic makeup of humans necessitate careful ethical scrutiny to ensure that scientific progress aligns with societal values (Briganti, 2025).

iii. **Environmental Ethics:** Technological advancements often have environmental implications, necessitating ethical considerations regarding sustainability and ecological impact. Organizations must evaluate the environmental consequences of their practices and products, ensuring that they contribute positively to ecological well-being and do not exacerbate environmental degradation (Mishra, 2025).

iv. **Healthcare and Medical Ethics:** In healthcare, ethical implications encompass patient rights, informed consent, and equitable access to care. Decisions regarding medical treatments, research practices, and health policies must prioritize patient welfare, autonomy, and fairness to ensure that healthcare systems serve all individuals justly (Veeramachaneni, 2025).

C. Challenges in Addressing Ethical Implications

i. **Complexity and Ambiguity:** Ethical implications are often complex and multifaceted, involving various stakeholders with differing perspectives and interests. This complexity can make it challenging to reach consensus on ethical standards and practices (Dentons, 2025).

ii. **Rapid Technological Advancement:** The rapid pace of technological change can outstrip the development of ethical frameworks and regulations. As new technologies emerge, stakeholders may struggle to keep up with the ethical implications, leading to potential oversights and unintended consequences (Dark, 2025).

iii. **Balancing Innovation and Ethics:** Striking a balance between fostering innovation and addressing ethical implications can be challenging. Organizations may face pressure to prioritize profit and competitive advantage over ethical considerations, leading to potential conflicts of interest (Morrison, 2025).

D. Best Practices for Addressing Ethical Implications

i. **Ethical Framework Development**: Organizations should develop comprehensive ethical frameworks that guide decision-making and policy development. These frameworks should include principles such as transparency, accountability, and respect for human rights, ensuring that ethical considerations are integrated into all aspects of operations (Modern, 2024).

ii. **Stakeholder Engagement:** Engaging stakeholders in discussions about ethical implications is essential for understanding diverse perspectives and fostering inclusive decision-making. This engagement helps identify potential ethical concerns and enables organizations to develop solutions that consider the needs and values of all affected parties (Fierce, 2021; Sidiropoulos & Anagnostopoulos, 2024).

iii. **Continuous Ethics Training:** Providing ongoing ethics training for employees and decision-makers can enhance awareness of ethical implications and promote a culture of ethical responsibility. Training programs should address relevant ethical issues and equip individuals with the tools to navigate complex moral dilemmas (Chan, 2023).

iv. **Regular Ethical Audits**: Conducting regular ethical audits can help organizations assess their practices and policies against established ethical standards. These audits should identify areas for improvement and ensure that ethical considerations are consistently prioritised (Geant, 2024).

v. **Collaboration and Knowledge Sharing**: Collaborating with academic institutions, ethics organizations, and industry peers can facilitate knowledge sharing and the development of best practices. By leveraging collective expertise, organizations can better navigate ethical implications and enhance their ethical decision-making processes (Birchwood, 2024).

Ethical implications are a crucial consideration in today's rapidly evolving technological landscape. By recognizing and addressing these implications, organizations can promote responsible innovation, guide ethical decision-making, and support social justice. However, the challenges associated with ethical considerations require ongoing efforts to develop comprehensive frameworks, engage stakeholders, and foster a culture of accountability. As society continues to navigate the complexities of technology and its impacts, prioritizing ethical implications will be essential for ensuring that progress aligns with human values and societal well-being (McNulty, 2024).

ARTIFICIAL INTELLIGENCE DEPLOYMENT

Artificial intelligence (AI) deployment refers to the process of integrating AI technologies into various applications, systems, and processes to enhance functionality, efficiency, and decision-making. As AI continues to evolve and gain prominence across industries, its deployment has transformative implications for businesses, healthcare, education, and numerous other sectors. However, the integration of AI technologies also raises critical considerations regarding ethics, accountability, and societal impact (De Gagne, Hwang & Jung, 2024).

A. **The Importance of AI Deployment**

i. **Enhanced Efficiency and Productivity**: AI deployment enables organizations to automate repetitive tasks, analyse vast amounts of data, and optimize processes. By leveraging machine learning algorithms, businesses can streamline operations, reduce human error, and improve overall productivity. For instance, AI-driven chatbots can handle customer inquiries, freeing human agents to focus on more complex issues (New, 2024).

ii. **Improved Decision-Making:** AI systems can analyse complex datasets and identify patterns that humans may overlook. This capability enhances decision-making by providing data-driven insights and predictions. In fields such as finance, healthcare, and marketing, AI tools assist professionals in making informed choices based on real-time data analysis (MIT, 2024).

iii. **Personalization and Customer Experience:** AI deployment allows organizations to deliver personalized experiences to customers. Through algorithms that analyse user behavior and preferences, companies can tailor products, services, and marketing strategies to individual needs. This personalization fosters customer loyalty and enhances overall satisfaction (Geant, 2024; Diaz, 2024).

iv. **Innovation and New Business Models:** The integration of AI technologies paves the way for innovative solutions and new business models. Organizations can create AI-powered products and services that disrupt traditional markets. For example, ride-sharing platforms and smart home devices leverage AI to offer services that were previously unimaginable (Chan, 2023).

B. **Key Applications of AI Deployment**

Healthcare: AI is increasingly deployed in healthcare for diagnostic purposes, patient monitoring, and personalized treatment plans. Machine learning algorithms can analyse medical images to identify diseases, while AI-driven chatbots provide patients with medical information and appointment scheduling. These applications enhance patient care and streamline healthcare processes (Fierce, 2021).

i. **Finance:** In the finance sector, AI is deployed for fraud detection, risk assessment, and algorithmic trading. AI systems analyse transaction patterns to identify suspicious activity, helping financial institutions mitigate risks. Additionally, AI algorithms can predict market trends and optimize investment strategies (Edsurge, 2024).
ii. **Manufacturing:** AI deployment in manufacturing enhances efficiency through predictive maintenance, quality control, and supply chain optimization. By analysing data from sensors and machinery, AI can predict equipment failures and schedule maintenance proactively, reducing downtime and costs (Akinwalere & Ivanov, 2022).
iii. **Transportation:** AI technologies play a vital role in transportation, particularly in autonomous vehicles and traffic management systems. AI algorithms process data from sensors and cameras to navigate and make real-time decisions, improving road safety and traffic flow (Visier, 2025).
iv. **Education:** In the education sector, AI is deployed to create personalized learning experiences, automate administrative tasks, and enhance student engagement. AI-driven platforms can assess students' learning styles and adapt educational content to meet individual needs, improving overall learning outcomes (LRN, 2025).

Research Questions

1. What factors contributed to the highest student repost engagement in 2022, and how do these trends reflect their awareness of data security and ethical implications of AI?
2. What are students views engagement and what does this reveal about their interest in understanding of data security and the ethical deployment of AI?
3. What are students likes engagement, and how does this correlate with their perceptions of data security and ethical AI deployment?
4. Is there any significant influence of student engagement metrics (comments) on the likes towards data security and the ethical deployment of AI?

Research Hypothesis

HO1: There is no significant influence of student engagement metrics on the likes towards data security and ethical deployment of AI.

Methodology

This study employed a quantitative methodology to analyse the research topic. The primary objective was to collect and analyse numerical data using data analytics gathered from X (formerly Twitter) technology.

This study adopts a quantitative methodology to explore students' data security metrics and the ethical implications for Artificial Intelligence (AI) deployment, using data gathered from X (formerly Twitter) technology. The approach involves a structured analysis of engagement metrics from social media platforms, employing statistical tools and analytical techniques to assess student awareness and behaviours concerning data security and AI ethics.

Research Instruments

The X (formerly Twitter) technology was adopted as a social media research instrument in this study over other social network technologies like YouTube, Facebook and TikTok based on its rich analytics affordance evident in number of likes, reposts, comments and shares. It was also more comprehensive and focused at targeting audience salient analytics related to this study.

To gather data, the following research instruments were validated and utilized:

a. **Screen Recorder**: Employed to record and analyse user interactions on X (formerly Twitter) technology and
b. **X Search Engine**: Utilized to collect data on user searches and engagements related to the research topic on X (formerly Twitter) technology.

Reliability and Validity

A pilot study from a different data involving fifty (50) responses was conducted to test the research instruments and ensure data quality. The result shows a reliability was attained based on the consistency of search output. Single data source on X search engine were used to validate the findings. Descriptive statistics and linear regression analysis were used to ensure the accuracy and reliability of the findings. The search terms and keywords used were validated by experts in the field of educational technology to ensure that they were relevant and accurate with consistent results across multiple searches. Likewise, the screen recorder was validated by experts in the field of educational technology to ensure that it accurately recorded user interactions. Also, the screen recorder was tested to ensure that it consistently recorded user interactions across multiple sessions. The search terms and keywords used were validated by experts in the field of educational technology to ensure that they were relevant and accurate and the search results were consistent across multiple searches and raters.

DATA COLLECTION

Data for this study was collected through a combination of X search engine, and a screen recorder. These tools were selected for their ability to capture relevant social media engagement data and related content. The X search engine helped identify key topics and hashtags frequently used by students discussing AI and data security, providing a valuable sample of student-driven conversations.

The screen recorder was employed to capture interactions on the X platform and to track engagement metrics, including likes, reposts, views, and comments on posts related to data security and AI. These metrics were considered relevant to the study's objective of understanding student engagement with these topics.

Sample and Sampling

The samples were homogenous and characterised as Nigerian university students. A total of 100 responses were collected from X, representing a diverse sample of student interactions over a defined period. Each response was associated with one of the engagement metrics: likes, reposts, comments, and views. The sample ensured that data was both diverse and representative of the student population’s interaction with content related to data security and AI.

The sample size of 100 is large enough for generalisation of findings based on the topic and scope of the study. The 100 quantitative data analytics gathered for this study is generalisable than small respondents needed for qualitative interviews in focused groups.

Data Analysis

The cleaned data was compiled into a .csv file format and then analysed using SPSS and Excel. These software tools were used for statistical analysis and to generate descriptive statistics, which provided an overview of the engagement patterns. Descriptive statistics, such as means, medians, and standard deviations, were calculated for each of the engagement metrics (likes, reposts, views, and comments) across different years.

To examine the relationships between engagement metrics and factors such as year of interaction and AI-related discussions, linear regression analysis was employed. This analysis helped identify the strength and direction of the relationships between predictors (such as the year) and the engagement metrics. Additionally, the regression model allowed for the evaluation of how much of the variation in engagement metrics could be explained by the year and related factors, providing insights into trends in student behavior over time.

Descriptive statistics were used to summarize the characteristics of the data, including means, frequencies, and standard deviations. Linear regression analysis was employed to examine the relationships between variables and identify potential predictors of the research topic.

Before analysis, the collected data underwent a cleaning process to ensure its accuracy and consistency. This involved removing incomplete or irrelevant responses, correcting inconsistencies, and addressing any missing data points. Data validation checks were performed to ensure that all responses aligned with the specific variables of interest, including the year of engagement and the type of engagement metric.

Ethical Data Collection on X

This research gathered data analytics from X, which are freely and publicly existing student data on the internet. Also, this study's data analytics were kept confidential and anonymous to ensure quality. Likewise, there were no personal information in the data analytics collected for this research to enhance ethical practice.

RESULTS

Research Question 1

1. What factors contributed to the highest student repost engagement in 2022, and how do these trends reflect their awareness of data security and ethical implications of AI?

Figure 2. Students repost metrics.

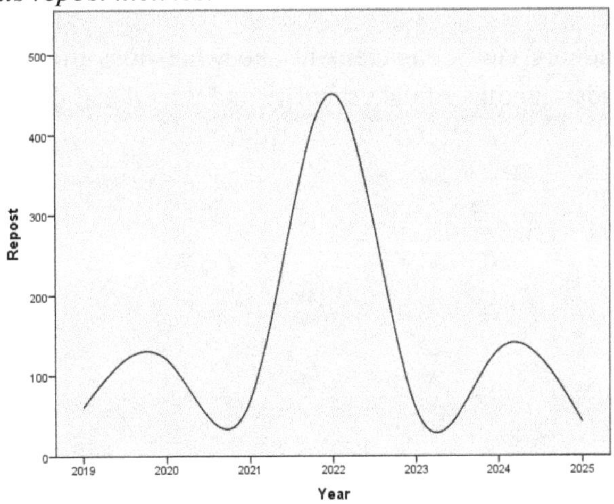

The students repost metrics were highest in the year 2022 and lowest in the year 2019. The year 2025 is still ongoing.

The analysis of student repost metrics reveals that engagement with content reflected in the number of reposts was highest in the year 2022 and lowest in 2019. This pattern indicates shifting awareness or interest among students regarding topics related to data security and the ethical deployment of artificial intelligence (AI).

The spike in reposts during 2022 suggest heightened discourse or campaigns emphasizing the importance of data privacy, ethical considerations, or the potential risks of AI systems. It also reflects an increase in the availability of information or social media campaigns targeting students on these issues. Conversely, the low engagement in 2019 is based on limited awareness or a lack of accessible and engaging content on the topic at that time.

The mention of 2025 as an ongoing year suggests that the data for this period is incomplete. If this trend continues to rise, it indicates sustained or growing concern among students about AI and data security. However, any conclusions about 2025 should be interpreted cautiously until a full year's data is available.

In the context of the research topic, this temporal fluctuation in reposts highlight the need for targeted educational initiatives and ethical policy frameworks to address the growing interest and concerns among students about AI's implications on their data security. It also underscores the importance of leveraging these periods of high engagement to promote more informed discussions and responsible practices in AI deployment.

Research Question 2

2. What are students views engagement and what does this reveal about their interest in understanding of data security and the ethical deployment of AI?

Figure 3. Students' views metrics

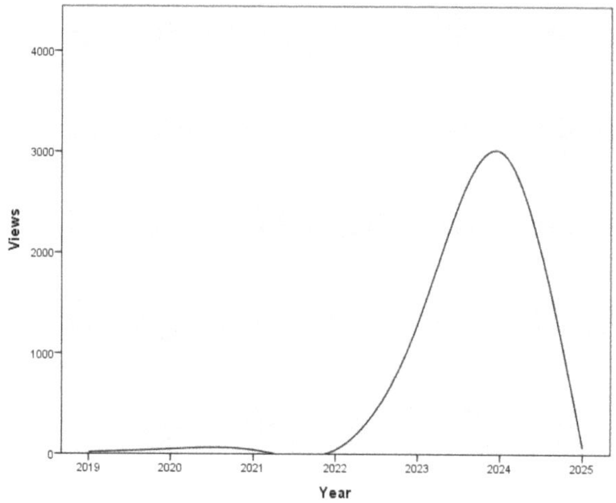

The student's views engagement metrics were at the highest in the year 2024 and lowest in the year 2019.

The analysis of student view engagement metrics indicates that the highest level of content views occurred in 2024, while the lowest was recorded in 2019. This trend suggests a significant shift in student interest or awareness regarding topics related to data security and the ethical deployment of artificial intelligence (AI) over the years.

The peak in 2024 reflects a growing urgency or relevance of these issues, possibly driven by global events, technological advancements, or increased discussions on AI ethics and data security in educational settings. For instance, rising concerns about AI biases, breaches of privacy, or high-profile cases involving unethical AI applications could have spurred heightened engagement. Additionally, improved accessibility to information and the proliferation of social media platforms could have amplified visibility and encouraged active participation in these discussions.

The low engagement in 2019 points to limited awareness or a lack of prominent discourse on these topics during that period. It indicates that AI and data security were not yet perceived as critical issues within the student community or that content targeting these concerns was less prevalent or impactful.

This temporal variation emphasizes the importance of aligning educational and awareness initiatives with periods of peak engagement, such as in 2024, to maximize their impact. Moreover, it underscores the need to understand the factors driving these changes in student interest to ensure sustained engagement and informed participation in shaping ethical AI practices.

Research Question 3

3. What are students likes engagement, and how does this correlate with their perceptions of data security and ethical AI deployment?

Figure 4. Students like metrics

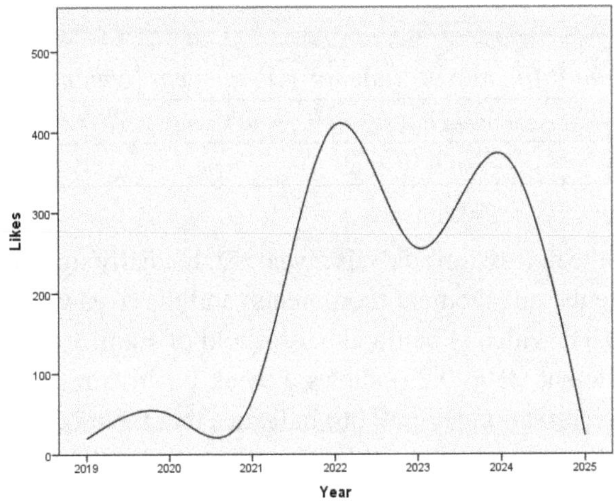

The students' likes metrics were of the highest in the year 2022 and lowest in the year 2019. The year 2025 is still ongoing.

The analysis of students' likes metrics reveals that engagement, as measured by the number of likes, was highest in 2022 and lowest in 2019. This trend reflects evolving awareness, interest, or attitudes among students regarding data security and the ethical deployment of artificial intelligence (AI).

The peak in likes during 2022 suggests a heightened resonance of content addressing data security and AI ethics with the student population. This coincides with increased efforts by educators, institutions, or advocacy groups to share relatable and engaging content on these topics. The high number of likes might also indicate stronger emotional or intellectual connections with such posts, reflecting growing concerns or curiosity about the ethical challenges posed by AI technologies.

On the other hand, the low number of likes in 2019 signals a period when these issues were less prominent in public discourse or when students were less informed or engaged with the implications of AI and data security. It also suggests that relevant content was not yet presented in formats that effectively captured student attention or interest.

The year 2025, being incomplete, leaves room for further analysis. If likes show a steady or increasing trend, it could indicate sustained engagement or growing interest in the ethical implications of AI deployment. This finding underscores the importance of leveraging years with high engagement, such as 2022, to foster more impactful discussions and educational initiatives on AI ethics and data security. It also highlights the potential for designing content strategies that consistently engage students, ensuring these critical topics remain at the forefront of their awareness.

Students' engagement (comments versus likes) metrics

Table 1. Significant influence of students' engagement (comments) on likes.

R	R^2	Adjusted R^2	R^2 Change	Significance
.25	.06	.05	.06	.01

The results of the regression analysis reveal a statistically significant relationship between the students' engagement (comments) and the likes variable, as indicated by a p-value of 0.01, which is below the threshold of significance ($p < 0.05$). The correlation coefficient ($R = 0.25$) shows a weak positive relationship, while the coefficient of determination ($R^2 = 0.06$) indicates that the model explains only 6% of the variance in the dependent variable. This suggests that the predictors contribute to the outcome. The adjusted R^2 value of 0.05, being close to the R^2, implies that the model is not overfitted and that the addition of predictors has not inflated the explained variance. This result highlights the need for further investigation, such as exploring additional or alternative predictors, to improve the model's explanatory power using larger population. Based on this significant result hypothesis one (HO1) was rejected.

DISCUSSION

The findings of this study provide valuable insights into student engagement with topics related to data security and the ethical deployment of artificial intelligence (AI). The analysis of repost, view, and like metrics on X (formerly Twitter) reveals significant trends over time, highlighting shifts in student awareness and interest in these areas. Nowadays, students are exposed more to cyberbreach due to the proliferation of AI in education (Birchwood, 2024).

The X is a popular social media adopted by Nigerian university students. The highest student repost engagement was observed in 2022, reflecting a notable increase in interest or awareness regarding data security and ethical AI issues. Reposts are often used to amplify content that resonates with users, signalling that the topics being shared were perceived as important or relevant by the student community. The increase in reposts during 2022 suggests a growing recognition of the risks and ethical dilemmas posed by AI technologies, potentially catalysed by broader discussions around data privacy, algorithmic biases, and AI-driven decision-making. Social media campaigns, academic institutions, and advocacy groups contributes to this uptick by providing targeted content that spark discussions among students. There is a strong relationship between AI and data security (McNulty, 2024).

Conversely, the low repost engagement in 2019 points to a period of limited awareness or interest in these issues. At this time, content related to AI and data security may not have been as widely disseminated or emphasized, suggesting that the conversation around these topics was still emerging. This aligns with the broader trend in which the mainstream discourse on AI ethics and data privacy has gained traction over the past few years, driven by technological advancements and high-profile ethical concerns. The AI deployment comes with peculiar challenges and opportunities (De Gagne, Hwang & Jung, 2024).

The ongoing year, 2025, provides an opportunity for future analysis. However, it is crucial to acknowledge that without a full year of data, any conclusions about engagement trends in this period remain tentative. If engagement continues to rise, it could reflect a sustained or growing concern about the ethical implications of AI and the protection of student data.

The highest level of view engagement in 2024 signifies a peak in student interest or concern regarding data security and AI ethics. The year 2024 likely represents a pivotal moment when discussions on these topics became more urgent and widespread. Factors such as global data breaches, the growing adoption of AI technologies, and increasing media attention on the ethical challenges posed by AI may have contributed to this heightened engagement. The visibility of discussions on AI biases, privacy issues, and the ethical implications of automated systems likely spurred students to engage more deeply with these topics (New, 2024).

The low engagement in 2019 suggests that, at the time, there was limited focus on data security and AI ethics within the student community. This aligns with the notion that discussions on AI's ethical challenges have gained prominence in recent years, following key events and the rapid evolution of AI technologies. The temporal variation in student views underscores the need for educational institutions and policymakers to align their initiatives with periods of high engagement, such as 2024, to maximize the impact of their messaging and ensure that students are well-informed about the ethical dimensions of AI. There are ethical implications in learners' data management (MIT, 2024).

The peak in likes engagement in 2022 further supports the notion that students were increasingly resonating with content related to data security and AI ethics. Likes, often associated with emotional or intellectual alignment, suggest that students felt a stronger connection to posts addressing these topics during this period. This reflects an increased concern on the implications of AI, particularly regarding issues like data privacy, surveillance, and algorithmic fairness. It is likely that educators, media outlets, and advocacy groups played a role in generating more compelling and accessible content that attracted student interest. Evaluating AI deployment enhances ethical practices and cybersecurity (Katsamakas, Pavlov & Saklad, 2024).

The low likes in 2019 indicates a time when these issues were not as widely discussed or perceived as critical, either in social media spaces or within student communities. The lower engagement suggests that students were less emotionally or intellectually invested in the topic, potentially due to the relatively limited discourse on AI and data security at the time. The AI ethics enhance professional development (Zawacki-Richter, Marin, Bond & Gouverneur, 2019)

Given that 2025 data is still incomplete, it remains uncertain whether likes will continue to show an upward trend, indicating sustained interest in the ethical implications of AI. However, the findings highlight the importance of leveraging years like 2022, when engagement peaked, to drive further discussions and educational initiatives about AI ethics and data security. Social media and data security is very important towards ensuring a healthy online learning (Garcia & Hernandez, 2021).

The regression analysis revealed a statistically significant relationship between students' comments and likes, with a correlation coefficient (R) of 0.25. Although the relationship is weak, the statistical significance ($p = 0.01$) suggests that comments can play a role in influencing likes, supporting the idea that students who engage in more in-depth discussions (comments) are also likely to show a greater level of engagement (likes) with content. However, the low R^2 value of 0.06 implies that only a small portion of the variance in likes can be explained by comments, indicating that other factors likely contribute to the variation in likes metrics. The artificial intelligence is a critical application for students' engagement (Cui & Alias, 2024).

The modest explanatory power of the model suggests that while comments may play a role in shaping likes, other variables, such as the content's emotional appeal, relevance, or the influence of external campaigns, may also be significant. The rejection of hypothesis one, which posited a strong correlation between comments and likes, reflects the realization that the relationship is weaker than initially expected. Future research should explore additional predictors that could more effectively explain student engagement with content related to AI and data security. The AI and student engagement are sacrosanct to learning.

The trends observed in repost, view, and like metrics indicate a shift in student engagement with data security and AI ethics, with notable peaks in 2022 and 2024. These findings underscore the increasing importance of these topics in the student community and highlight the need for targeted educational initiatives to address the growing concerns around AI technologies. While the regression analysis points to a significant relationship between comments and likes, the overall explanatory power of the model is limited, suggesting that further investigation is necessary to fully understand the factors driving student engagement. The results of this study provide a valuable foundation for future research into student attitudes toward AI and data security, as well as the effectiveness of educational strategies in fostering ethical AI practices. Data driven decision making are crucial entities in universities (Valencia, 2024).

The study's findings, which examine student engagement among Nigerian university students with content related to data security and the ethical deployment of artificial intelligence (AI), present several important insights but also raise certain considerations that merit appraisal. The methodology, analysis, and interpretation of the results provide valuable contributions to understanding student awareness and engagement with these crucial issues, yet there are aspects that could be refined for further research or practical application. Ethical issues are paramount to artificial intelligence (AI) deployment in higher institutions (He, Qiu, Zhang & Yuan, 2024).

The use of multiple engagement metrics such as reposts, views, and likes provides a well-rounded approach to understanding the different ways Nigerian university students interact with content on social media platforms like X. This is beneficial as it allows for an analysis that encompasses both passive (views) and active (reposts, likes) forms of engagement, which can offer a more nuanced understanding of how students perceive and interact with AI ethics and data security topics (Greenberg, 2025).

The study's results reveal clear temporal trends, especially in 2022 and 2024, suggesting significant shifts in student engagement. The peaks in reposts and views in these years are compelling indicators of growing student concern over AI and data security, which aligns with real-world developments (e.g., high-profile AI ethics cases and data breaches). This finding provides timely insights into when students are most receptive to learning about these critical issues, which could inform future educational campaigns or institutional policies aimed at promoting responsible AI deployment. Ethical artificial intelligence deployment is the key to cybersecurity (Goodwin, 2025).

The incorporation of regression analysis to explore the relationship between students' comments and likes is an important step in identifying significant predictors of engagement. Despite the weak correlation ($R = 0.25$), the study correctly highlights that even small effects can be meaningful, especially when dealing with complex social phenomena like student engagement with digital content. Artificial intelligence application is crucial to students' online engagement.

However, the regression analysis revealed a statistically significant relationship between comments and likes, the model's low explanatory power ($R^2 = 0.06$) indicates that only a small proportion of the variance in likes can be explained by comments. This suggests that other factors such as the quality of content, the emotional resonance of posts, or broader socio-political events has more substantial impact on engagement than the analysis accounted for. Future research could incorporate additional predictors such as sentiment analysis of comments, post format to improve the model's explanatory power and better capture the nuances of student engagement. Nowadays, artificial intelligence is a crucial technology to student's data deployment (UNESCO, 2025).

The mention of 2025 as an ongoing year introduces an element of uncertainty to the study's conclusions. While it is valuable to track trends in real-time, the partial data for this year limits the ability to make definitive claims about the trajectory of student engagement with AI and data security. Longitudinal studies with complete datasets will be crucial for verifying whether these trends are part of a sustained pattern or a short-term fluctuation (Dark, 2025).

Social media metrics like likes, reposts, and views are influenced by a variety of external factors, including algorithmic amplification, social media campaigns, and broader cultural events. These platforms often prioritize content that generates higher engagement, potentially skewing the results. This means that the observed spikes in engagement may not always directly correlate with the intrinsic value or ethical content of the posts, but rather with the visibility and virality of certain topics. Researchers must consider these external factors when interpreting social media metrics.

The study provides valuable insights into student engagement among Nigerian university students and future research could diversify the sample to include students from different regions, cultural backgrounds, or academic disciplines to better understand the broad applicability of these trends within Nigeria. Nigeria is a culturally diversified country (Diaz, 2024).

The significant engagement metrics observed in 2022 and 2024 suggest that these periods are crucial moments for educational institutions and policymakers in Nigeria to intervene and promote responsible AI practices. Given the heightened awareness during these years, it would be beneficial for Nigerian universities to introduce or expand programs on AI ethics and data security, capitalizing on students' existing interest. Additionally, social media platforms can play a key role in spreading awareness and encouraging discussions through campaigns, public service announcements, or partnerships with educational organizations (Dentons, 2025).

CONCLUSION AND RECOMMENDATION

This study offers a significant contribution to understanding student engagement among Nigerian university students with issues of AI and data security. The observed trends in reposts, views, and likes provide evidence of increasing student interest, particularly in 2022 and 2024, in these pressing ethical concerns. However, there are limitations in the study, particularly regarding the limited number of respondents. These limitations provide valuable insights into the complexities of measuring social media engagement and highlight the need for further research user larger respondents. As AI technologies continue to evolve, it will be essential for future research to refine these methods and continue exploring how best to engage students in critical discussions on the ethical implications of AI and data security.

The trends observed in this study underscore the importance of engaging students in discussions about the ethical deployment of AI. Nigerian educational institutions, governments, and private sectors should prioritize ethical AI education, especially during years of heightened student engagement, to ensure that young people are equipped to address issues such as privacy, fairness, and transparency in AI systems. Moreover, ethical frameworks and regulatory measures that focus on protecting data security could be more effectively developed if they incorporate insights from student engagement patterns.

As the study used screen recorders, and X search engines as research instruments for data gathering, future studies could explore the effectiveness and potential biases inherent in these tools. For example, utilizing sentiment analysis and exploring new methods of collecting engagement data (such as tracking time spent on posts or qualitative responses) could enhance the precision and depth of analysis.

Future studies should explore additional forms of engagement beyond likes, reposts, and views. Metrics such as comments, shares, or even the tone and sentiment of students' online discussions about data security and AI ethics could provide richer insights into their understanding and concerns about these issues. Conducting mixed-method research by incorporating both qualitative and quantitative data allows for a more holistic view of students' perceptions of AI ethics and data security.

REFERENCES

Ahmed, H. (2024). Institutional Integration of Artificial Intelligence in Higher Education: The Moderation Effect of Ethical Consideration. *International Journal of Educational Reform*, •••, 10567879241247551. DOI: 10.1177/10567879241247551

Ajayi, B., & Ifedayo, A. E. (2025). Ethical and Cognitive Impacts of Machine Learning in Education: A Stakeholder-Centric Analysis. *Sanskriti: Journal of Humanities, 2*(1), 1-10. Retrieved from, http://sanskritijournal.com/index.php/ssj/article/view/14

Akinwalere, S. N., & Ivanov, V. (2022). Artificial Intelligence in Higher Education: Challenges and Opportunities. *International Journal of Current Advanced Research, 11*(2), 145–162. https://journalijcar.org/issues/artificial-intelligence-higher-education-challenges-and-opportunities

Ali, G., Mijwil, M. M., Buruga, B. A., Abotaleb, M., & Adamopoulos, I. (2024). A survey on artificial intelligence in cybersecurity for smart agriculture: State-of-the-art, cyber threats, artificial intelligence applications, and ethical concerns. *Mesopotamian Journal of Computer Science, 2024*, 53–103. DOI: 10.58496/MJCSC/2024/007

AlJadaan, O. T., Zaidi, H., Al Faress, M. Y., & Jabas, A. O. (2025). Ethics in AI and Computation in Automated Decision-Making. In *Enhancing Automated Decision-Making Through AI* (pp. 397–424). IGI Global Scientific Publishing.

Barnes, E., Hutson, J., & Perry, K. (2024). Ethical Imperatives and Challenges: Review of the Use of Machine Learning for Predictive Analytics in Higher Education. *International Journal of Multidisciplinary and Current Educational Research, 6*(3).

Berkowitz, A. E. (2025). "Slow-MO or FOMO": AI conversations at library conferences. *Public Services Quarterly, 21*(1), 1–20. DOI: 10.1080/15228959.2024.2442657

Birchwood, U. (2024). What are the Opportunities and Challenges for AI in Education? Retrieved from https://www.birchwoodu.org/what-are-the-opportunities-and-challenges-for-ai-in-education/

Briganti, G. (2025). Artificial intelligence: Blessing or curse? In *Truth Unveiled* (pp. 83–107). Academic Press. DOI: 10.1016/B978-0-443-23655-6.00005-8

Çela, E., Fonkam, M. M., Vajjhala, N. R., & Vedishchev, A. (2025). Artificial Intelligence in Education: Foundations, Trends, and Implications. In *Next-Generation AI Methodologies in Education* (pp. 1-20). IGI Global Scientific Publishing.

Chan, C. K. (2023). A Comprehensive AI Policy Education Framework for University Teaching and Learning. arXiv preprint arXiv:2305.00280. Retrieved from https://arxiv.org/abs/2305.00280

Coelho, L., & Reis, S. (2025). Transforming Teaching and Learning With Natural Language Processing. In *Integrating Artificial Intelligence in Education: Enhancing Teaching Practices for Future Learning* (pp. 119-152). IGI Global.

Cui, P., & Alias, B. S. (2024). Opportunities and Challenges in Higher Education Arising from AI: A Systematic Literature Review (2020–2024). *Journal of Infrastructure Policy and Development*, *8*(11), 8390. DOI: 10.24294/jipd.v8i11.8390

Cukurova, M. (2025). The interplay of learning, analytics and artificial intelligence in education: A vision for hybrid intelligence. *British Journal of Educational Technology, 56*(2), 469-488. Retreived from, https://bera-journals.onlinelibrary.wiley.com/doi/abs/10.1111/bjet.13514

Dark, R. (2025). AI-Related Security Trends to Watch in 2025. Retrieved from https://www.darkreading.com/cyber-risk/6-ai-related-security-trends-watch-2025

Darshan, B. D., Sampathila, N., Bairy, G. M., Prabhu, S., Belurkar, S., Chadaga, K., & Nandish, S. (2025). Differential diagnosis of iron deficiency anemia from aplastic anemia using machine learning and explainable Artificial Intelligence utilizing blood attributes. *Scientific Reports*, *15*(1), 505. DOI: 10.1038/s41598-024-84120-w PMID: 39747241

De Gagne, J. C., Hwang, H., & Jung, D. (2024). Cyberethics in nursing education: Ethical implications of artificial intelligence. *Nursing Ethics*, *31*(6), 1021–1030. DOI: 10.1177/09697330231201901 PMID: 37803810

Dentons, (2025). AI trends for 2025: AI regulation, governance and ethics. Retrieved from https://www.dentons.com/en/insights/articles/2025/january/10/ai-trends-for-2025-ai-regulation-governance-and-ethics

Diaz, V. (2024). Exploring the Opportunities and Challenges with Generative AI. EDUCAUSE Review. Retrieved from https://er.educause.edu/articles/2024/2/exploring-the-opportunities-and-challenges-with-generative-ai

Dieterle, E., Dede, C., & Walker, M. (2024). The cyclical ethical effects of using artificial intelligence in education. *AI & Society*, *39*(2), 633–643. DOI: 10.1007/s00146-022-01497-w PMID: 36185064

Dixit, S., Jain, V., Maurya, M., & Subramaniam, G. (Eds.). (2025). *Artificial Intelligence Enabled Businesses: How to Develop Strategies for Innovation*. John Wiley & Sons. DOI: 10.1002/9781394234028

Eden, C. A., Chisom, O. N., & Adeniyi, I. S. (2024). Integrating AI in education: Opportunities, challenges, and ethical considerations. *Magna Scientia Advanced Research and Reviews, 10*(2), 006-013.

EdSurge. (2024). How AI Can Address Critical Challenges Facing Higher Education. Retrieved from https://www.edsurge.com/news/2024-03-29-how-ai-can-address-critical-challenges-facing-higher-education

El-Hajj, M. (2025). Enhancing Communication Networks in the New Era with Artificial Intelligence: Techniques, Applications, and Future Directions. *Network (Bristol, England), 5*(1), 1. PMID: 39601783

Fedele, A., Punzi, C., & Tramacere, S. (2024). The ALTAI checklist as a tool to assess ethical and legal implications for a trustworthy AI development in education. *Computer Law & Security Review, 53*, 105986. DOI: 10.1016/j.clsr.2024.105986

Fierce, N. (2021). Artificial Intelligence in Higher Education: Benefits and Ethics. Retrieved from https://www.fierce-network.com/technology/artificial-intelligence-higher-education-benefits-and-ethics

Funa, A. A., & Gabay, R. A. E. (2025). Policy guidelines and recommendations on AI use in teaching and learning: A meta-synthesis study. *Social Sciences & Humanities Open, 11*, 101221. DOI: 10.1016/j.ssaho.2024.101221

Garcia, F., & Hernandez, M. (2021). Ethical Challenges in AI-Based Educational Systems. *International Journal of Educational Technology in Higher Education, 18*(1), 28. DOI: 10.1186/s41239-021-00269-7 PMID: 34778526

Geant, C. (2024). AI, Data Privacy, and Ethics in Higher Education: Navigating the Future. Retrieved from https://connect.geant.org/2024/10/18/ai-data-privacy-and-ethics-in-higher-education-navigating-the-future

Goodwin, (2025). US Privacy and AI Outlook for 2025: Less Feds, More States. Retrieved from https://www.goodwinlaw.com/en/insights/blogs/2025/01/us-privacy-and-ai-outlook-for-2025-less-feds-more-states

Greenberg, T. (2025). Trends to Watch: 2025 U.S. Data Privacy & Cybersecurity. Retrieved from https://www.gtlaw-dataprivacydish.com/2025/01/5-trends-to-watch-2025-u-s-data-privacy-cybersecurity/

Greenstein, N., & Cho, S. W. (2025). Ethics & Equity in Data Science for Evaluators. *Artificial Intelligence and Evaluation. Emerging Technologies and Their Implications for Evaluation*, 56-77.

Gursoy, S. (2025). The Role of Artificial Intelligence in the Digitalization Process: Trends, Challenges, and a Framework for Sustainable Integration.

Han, B., Nawaz, S., Buchanan, G., & McKay, D. (2025). Students' Perceptions: Exploring the Interplay of Ethical and Pedagogical Impacts for Adopting AI in Higher Education. *International Journal of Artificial Intelligence in Education*, •••, 1–26. DOI: 10.1007/s40593-024-00456-4

Harte, M., Carey, B., Feng, Q. J., Alqarni, A., & Albuquerque, R. (2025). Transforming undergraduate dental education: The impact of artificial intelligence. *British Dental Journal*, *238*(1), 57–60. DOI: 10.1038/s41415-024-7788-7 PMID: 39794587

Hassan, Z. Y. (2025). AI-Driven Horizons: Shaping the Future of Global Quality Assurance in Higher Education. *AI and Ethics, Academic Integrity and the Future of Quality Assurance in Higher Education*, 105.

He, Y., Qiu, J., Zhang, W., & Yuan, Z. (2024). Fortifying Ethical Boundaries in AI: Advanced Strategies for Enhancing Security in Large Language Models. Retrieved from https://arxiv.org/abs/2402.01725

Joshi, R., Pandey, K., & Kumari, S. (2025). Redefining Teaching in the Era of Generative Artificial Intelligence: A 360-Degree Perspective. In *Fostering Inclusive Education With AI and Emerging Technologies* (pp. 73-98). IGI Global.

Karthikeyan, C. (2025). AI (Artificial Intelligence) Leveraging to Foster DEI (Diversity, Equity, and Inclusiveness) in Organizations: Harnessing AI for Diversity, Equity, and Inclusion of Indian Version. In *Navigating Organizational Behavior in the Digital Age With AI* (pp. 77-100). IGI Global Scientific Publishing.

Katsamakas, E., Pavlov, O. V., & Saklad, R. (2024). Artificial intelligence and the transformation of higher education institutions. arXiv preprint arXiv:2402.08143. Retrieved from https://arxiv.org/abs/2402.08143

Li, H. (2025). Multicultural data assistance mining analysis for ideological and political education in smart education platforms using artificial intelligence. *Wireless Networks*, *31*(1), 567–581. https://link.springer.com/article/10.1007/s11276-024-03772-8. DOI: 10.1007/s11276-024-03772-8

LRN. C. (2025). AI, ethics, and ESG in 2025. Retrieved from https://lrn.com/blog/ai-ethics-and-esg-in-2025

McNulty, N. (2024). AI and Data Privacy in Schools: Safeguarding Student Information. Medium. Retrieved from https://medium.com/@niall.mcnulty/ai-and-data-privacy-in-schools-safeguarding-student-information-a0e8436a5f5e

Miller, J. C., Miranda, J. P. P., & Tolentino, J. C. G. (2025). Artificial Intelligence in Physical Education: A Review. *Global Innovations in Physical Education and Health*, 37-60.

Mishra, P. (2025). Revolutionizing Education With AI and ML. *Internet of Behavior-Based Computational Intelligence for Smart Education Systems*, 53-94.

MIT. R. (2024). Securing Student Data in the Age of Generative AI. Retrieved from https://raise.mit.edu/wp-content/uploads/2024/06/Securing-Student-Data-in-the-Age-of-Generative-AI_MIT-RAISE.pdf

Mitchell, D. L. (2025). Integrating AI Into Policy Making in Educational Leadership. In *Integrating AI Into Pedagogical Education* (pp. 25–48). IGI Global Scientific Publishing.

Modern, D. (2024). Ethical Implementation of AI in Cybersecurity in 2025. Retrieved from https://moderndiplomacy.eu/2024/11/04/ethical-implementation-of-ai-in-cybersecurity-in-2025/

Morrison, F. (2025). Privacy + Data Security Predictions for 2025. Retrieved from https://www.mofo.com/resources/insights/250107-privacy-data-security-predictions

Narendra, A. P., Dewi, C., Gunawan, L. S., & Ardi, A. S. (2025). Artificial Intelligence Implementation in Library Information Systems: Current Trends and Future Studies. *Vietnam Journal of Computer Science*, 1-25.

New, A. (2024). Artificial Intelligence in Schools: Privacy and Security Considerations. Retrieved from https://newamerica.org/oti/blog/artificial-intelligence-in-schools-privacy-and-security-considerations/

Nwozor, A. (2025). Artificial Intelligence (AI) and Academic Honesty-Dishonesty Nexus: Trends and Preventive Measures. *AI and Ethics, Academic Integrity and the Future of Quality Assurance in Higher Education, 27.*

Ogalo, E. O., & Mtenzi, F. (2025). Leveraging Artificial Intelligence Tools for Learning: Academic Integrity and Ethics in Higher Education in Kenya. In *Artificial Intelligence, Digital Learning, and Leadership: Redefining Higher Education* (pp. 1-36). IGI Global.

Pesapane, F., Hauglid, M. K., Fumagalli, M., Petersson, L., Parkar, A. P., Cassano, E., & Horgan, D. (2025). The translation of in-house imaging AI research into a medical device ensuring ethical and regulatory integrity. *European Journal of Radiology*, *182*, 111852. DOI: 10.1016/j.ejrad.2024.111852 PMID: 39612599

Radanliev, P., Santos, O., Brandon-Jones, A., & Joinson, A. (2024). Ethics and responsible AI deployment. *Frontiers in Artificial Intelligence*, *7*, 1377011. DOI: 10.3389/frai.2024.1377011 PMID: 38601110

Ramaiah, M. S., Nagarajan, S. K. S., Whig, P., & Dutta, P. K. (2025). AI-Powered Innovations Transforming Adaptive Education for Disability Support. In *Advancing Adaptive Education: Technological Innovations for Disability Support* (pp. 73-100). IGI Global Scientific Publishing.

Rathee, R., Vats, H., & Sharma, S. (2025). AI-Enhanced Predictive Scheduling Optimizing Project Timelines for Blue-Green Infrastructure Deployment. In *Integrating Blue-Green Infrastructure Into Urban Development* (pp. 61–80). IGI Global Scientific Publishing.

Reinecke, M. G., Kappes, A., Porsdam Mann, S., Savulescu, J., & Earp, B. D. (2025). The need for an empirical research program regarding human–AI relational norms. *AI and Ethics*, •••, 1–10. PMID: 39959573

Sanfo, J. B. (2025). Application of explainable artificial intelligence approach to predict student learning outcomes. *Journal of Computational Social Science*, *8*(1), 1–33. DOI: 10.1007/s42001-024-00344-w

Sidiropoulos, D., & Anagnostopoulos, C.-N. (2024). Applications, challenges and ethical issues of AI and ChatGPT in education. arXiv preprint arXiv:2402.07907. Retrieved from https://arxiv.org/abs/2402.07907

Singh, A., Lakhera, G., & Ojha, M. kumar Mishra, A., & Nain, A. (2025). Balancing Innovation With Responsibility: Ethical Dimensions of AI in Revolutionizing E-Learning. In *Ethical Dimensions of AI Development* (pp. 467-500). IGI Global. Retrieved from, https://www.igi-global.com/chapter/balancing-innovation-with-responsibility/359655

Sultana, S. T., & Rao, T. V. N. (2025). Application of Artificial Intelligence in Business Management for Prudent Decision Making. *Artificial Intelligence-Enabled Businesses: How to Develop Strategies for Innovation*, 351-370.

UNESCO. (2024). Ethics of Artificial Intelligence. Retrieved from https://www.unesco.org/en/artificial-intelligence/recommendation-ethics

Valencia, L. J. (2024). Artificial Intelligence as the New Hacker: Developing Agents for Offensive Security. Retrieved from https://arxiv.org/abs/2406.07561

Vetrivel, S. C., Vidhyapriya, P., & Arun, V. P. (2025). The Role of AI in Transforming Assessment Practices in Education. In *AI Applications and Strategies in Teacher Education* (pp. 43–70). IGI Global.

Visier, (2025). Understanding AI Compliance: Challenges and Solutions. Retrieved from https://www.visier.com/blog/ai-compliance-challenges-and-solutions/

Wenhang, S., Shenting, Z., & Shaohua, C. (2025). Prospects for the development of medical professionalism education in the AI perspective: A qualitative study of Chinese postgraduate medical students' written reflections. *Medical Teacher*, •••, 1–9. DOI: 10.1080/0142159X.2024.2445056 PMID: 39772996

Yadav, S. (2025). Empowering Educators for the Artificial Intelligence (AI) Era: Strategies and Challenges in Integrating Computational Thinking Into Professional Development. In *Empowering STEM Educators With Digital Tools* (pp. 1-28). IGI Global Scientific Publishing.

Yuan, C., Xiao, N., Pei, Y., Bu, Y., & Cai, Y. (2025). Enhancing Student Learning Outcomes through AI-Driven Educational Interventions: A Comprehensive Study of Classroom Behavior and Machine Learning Integration. *International Theory and Practice in Humanities and Social Sciences, 2*(2), 197-215. Retrieved from, https://ojs.wisvora.com/index.php/itphss/article/view/216

Zawacki-Richter, O., Marín, V. I., Bond, M., & Gouverneur, F. (2019). Systematic Review of Research on Artificial Intelligence Applications in Higher Education – Where Are the Educators? *International Journal of Educational Technology in Higher Education, 16*(1), 39. DOI: 10.1186/s41239-019-0171-0

Chapter 9
Exploring the Role of Artificial Intelligence in Enhancing Values-Based Leadership and Its Impact on Workplace Engagement

Fahad Saeed Alsubeia
https://orcid.org/0009-0001-0840-1971
University of Malaya, Malaysia

Muhammed Bin Yusof
University of Malaya, Malaysia

Amer Abdulwahab Mahyoub Murshed
University of Malaya, Malaysia

ABSTRACT

Abstract: Artificial Intelligence (AI) has increasingly been integrated into leadership and workplace engagement, transforming decision-making processes, employee interactions, and organizational efficiency. This study systematically reviews the role of AI in leadership and workplace engagement over the last five years, utilizing bibliometric analysis and the PRISMA framework to identify key research trends, methodologies, and future research directions. The findings indicate that AI-driven applications, such as large language models (LLMs), generative AI, and machine learning (ML) systems, have significantly influenced leadership decision-making,

DOI: 10.4018/979-8-3373-5550-4.ch009

human resource management (HRM), and employee engagement strategies. While AI has enhanced operational efficiency and predictive analytics, ethical concerns regarding bias, transparency, and data privacy remain prominent. Furthermore, the study highlights the shift from AI as a purely automation tool to a hybrid AI-human collaboration model, where AI complements rather than replaces human leadership.

1. INTRODUCTION

Artificial Intelligence (AI) has become a transformative force across various domains, including education, leadership, and workplace engagement. The proliferation of AI applications has sparked discussions on its implications for human interactions, productivity, and ethical considerations in professional and educational settings. AI's ability to enhance decision-making, automate administrative tasks, and facilitate engagement within organizations has been widely explored, yet its integration into leadership practices and employee engagement remains a subject of growing academic interest (Watermeyer et al., 2024; Marchena Sekli et al., 2024).

The emergence of Generative AI (GenAI), including large language models such as ChatGPT, has further revolutionized how AI interacts with users, influencing communication patterns and organizational dynamics. Scholars have debated the extent to which AI can effectively complement or even replace human-centric processes, raising ethical concerns related to bias, transparency, and accountability (Fleischmann, 2024). AI-driven decision-making models have demonstrated potential in reducing human workload and optimizing efficiency, yet their impact on leadership strategies and employee satisfaction remains a complex and evolving subject of inquiry (Murray-Rust et al., 2024).

Recent studies emphasize the necessity of critically evaluating AI's role in leadership and workplace engagement. AI's influence on leadership development, team collaboration, and employee well-being necessitates a nuanced understanding of its practical implementations. While some research highlights AI's capacity to enhance engagement through automation and personalized feedback mechanisms, others caution against over-reliance on AI-driven strategies without considering human intuition and ethical constraints (Watermeyer et al., 2024). For instance, AI-assisted decision-making in Human Resource Management (HRM) has been found to streamline recruitment processes and performance evaluations, yet concerns persist regarding data privacy and fairness (Jia & Hou, 2024).

Moreover, AI's integration into workplace engagement strategies has introduced novel methodologies for assessing and improving employee interactions. Studies have explored AI's role in sustainable human resource practices, generative AI's applications in higher education, and the impact of AI-driven analytics on leadership effectiveness (Marchena Sekli et al., 2024; Watermeyer et al., 2024). However, the rapid evolution of AI necessitates ongoing scholarly investigations to assess its long-term effects on workplace dynamics, leadership styles, and employee motivation.

This study aims to bridge the gap in existing literature by conducting a systematic review of AI applications in leadership and workplace engagement over the last five years. Through a comprehensive bibliometric analysis and systematic literature review (SLR), this research examines the methodologies employed, AI applications used, sample populations studied, and future research directions proposed within this field. By leveraging prior research methodologies such as the PRISMA framework and bibliometric mapping, this study provides insights into emerging trends, challenges, and ethical considerations surrounding AI's role in leadership and workplace engagement (Marchena Sekli et al., 2024).

The structure of this paper is as follows: Section 2 outlines the methodology used for data collection and analysis, detailing the inclusion and exclusion criteria for the systematic review. Section 3 presents the findings from both the bibliometric analysis and the systematic review, highlighting key contributions in AI-driven leadership and workplace engagement. Section 4 discusses the implications of these findings in relation to prior research, offering a critical evaluation of AI's role in enhancing leadership practices and workplace engagement. Finally, Section 5 concludes with recommendations for future research and practical applications of AI in leadership development and organizational sustainability.

2. METHODS

This study employs a systematic bibliometric analysis to examine the impact of artificial intelligence (AI) on workplace engagement. Following the Preferred Reporting Items for Systematic Reviews and Meta-Analyses (PRISMA) guidelines (Page et al., 2021), a structured and replicable approach was utilized to ensure transparency in the selection and evaluation of relevant literature. The methodology consists of four key stages: identification, screening, eligibility assessment, and inclusion, which collectively facilitate the extraction of high-quality studies for bibliometric evaluation. The methodological framework of this study aligns with prior systematic literature review research conducted on online learning, instructional design, and technology acceptance models (Masrom et al., 2021; Abuhassna et al., 2022a, 2022b, 2023a, 2023b). Table 1 shows the inclusion and exclusion criteria applied in this study.

Table 1. The inclusion and exclusion criteria

Inclusion	Exclusion
All research papers regarding Artificial Intelligence, leadership, workplace engagement	Any other articles were excluded
Only articles published 2019-2024	Any articles before 2019 were excluded, 2025 articles were not included because it's not over yet.
Only articles	Conferences, book chapter and any other publications wee excluded
Only articles written in English	Any other languages were excluded

The literature search was conducted using the Scopus database, which is recognized for its extensive coverage of peer-reviewed academic literature. The search strategy was designed to retrieve relevant articles by employing Boolean operators and field-specific search terms to maximize comprehensiveness. The search query applied in the title, abstract, and keywords fields was as follows: TITLE-ABS-KEY ("artificial" AND "intelligence" OR "leadership" OR "workplace" AND "engagement"). To ensure that only relevant studies were included, several filters and limitations were applied to refine the results. The search was restricted to the publication years 2019–2024, ensuring that only recent research contributions were considered (AND PUBYEAR > 2018 AND PUBYEAR < 2025). Furthermore, the search was confined to articles published within the disciplines of Arts and Humanities and Social Sciences (AND (LIMIT-TO (SUBJAREA, "ARTS") OR LIMIT-TO (SUBJAREA, "SOCI"))). To maintain the academic rigor of the study, only journal articles were included, while conference proceedings, book chapters, and non-peer-reviewed literature were excluded (AND (LIMIT-TO (DOCTYPE, "ar"))). Additionally, only English-language publications were considered (AND (LIMIT-TO (LANGUAGE, "English"))). The final refinement included filtering articles based on specific AI-related keywords, including Artificial Intelligence, Generative AI, Knowledge Management, and Artificial Intelligence Technologies, among others.

Following the application of these criteria, the initial search yielded 6,157 documents. The screening process was then implemented, aligning with PRISMA's recommended methodology (Page et al., 2021), which included multiple filtering stages. After the first level of screening based on title and abstract review, 352 documents were retained for full-text analysis. A more detailed quality assessment was then conducted, leading to the selection of 122 articles for in-depth evaluation. The final quality assessment consisted of two rounds: in the first round, 50 articles were identified as meeting high-quality standards. A final rigorous assessment further refined the selection to 21 articles that were deemed most relevant and methodologically robust for bibliometric analysis.

For bibliometric analysis, VOSviewer software was utilized to analyze citation networks, keyword co-occurrence, and authorship collaborations. The co-authorship analysis identified major research clusters and collaborations within the field, while the citation analysis helped determine the most influential studies and authors contributing to the topic. The keyword co-occurrence analysis facilitated the identification of thematic trends and emerging research topics within AI-driven workplace engagement. The integration of bibliometric techniques is consistent with previous research that has explored the use of AI, instructional design models, and technology acceptance frameworks (Abuhassna et al., 2023a, 2023b; Masrom et al., 2021).

This study follows a systematic and transparent methodological framework, aligning with PRISMA guidelines to enhance replicability and credibility. The multi-stage selection process, coupled with quantitative bibliometric techniques, ensures a rigorous examination of the research landscape surrounding AI's role in workplace engagement. Similar methodological approaches have been successfully employed in prior research on online learning adoption, instructional design models, and AI-powered education (Abuhassna et al., 2022a, Abuhassna et al 2022b, Abuhassna et al 2023a, Abuhassna et al 2023b). Figure 1 shows the PRISMA framework of this study.

Figure 1. PRISMA framework

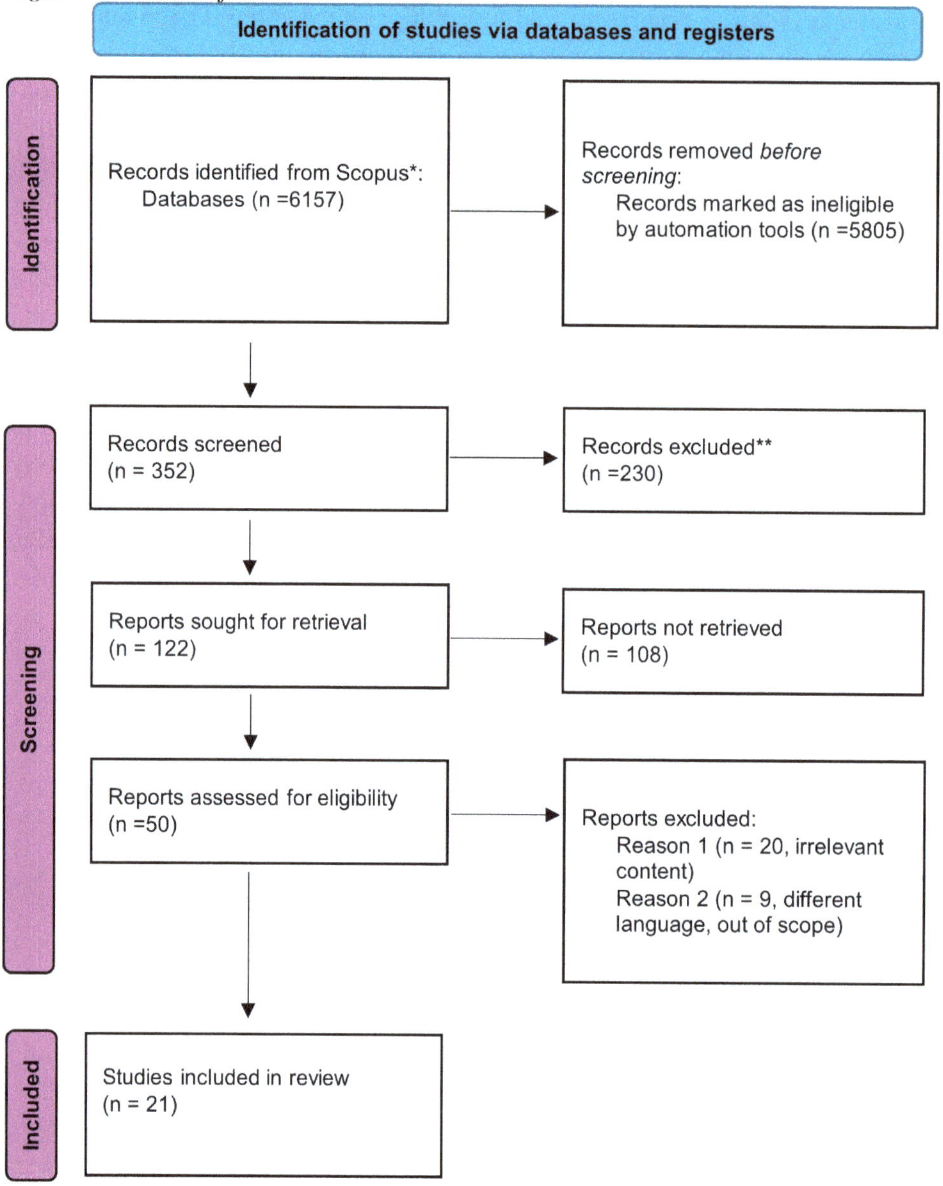

3. RESULTS

This section addressed the results of the study base on the research questions addressed in this study. This section will be dived into two main sections, firstly it will address the bibliometric analysis which will be addressing publications distributions by years, the top countries associated with this field of study, the top educational institutions in this field of study, in addition to the top authors in the field, and the top trends and sources. Secondly, the second part of this section will address the systematic review of the study to address Methodology, AI applications, samples, and future agenda and recommendations used in the field of AI, leadership and workplace engagement in the last 5 years.

3.1. Contributions

The main contribution in AI, leadership and workplace engagement research field in accordance with years distribution, top countries, top educational institutions, authors, sources and trends and co-occurrences in the last 5 years. This section is going to answer each of these issues separately.

3.1.1. Years Distributions in the Field of AI, Leadership and Workplace Engagement

Understanding the yearly distribution of publications in the field of AI, leadership, and workplace engagement provides insights into research trends and the growing interest in this area over time. Analyzing the number of publications per year allows us to observe fluctuations in research output, identify peak years of scholarly contributions, and anticipate future research directions.

Figure 2. The yearly distribution of publications based on AI, leadership and workplace engagement

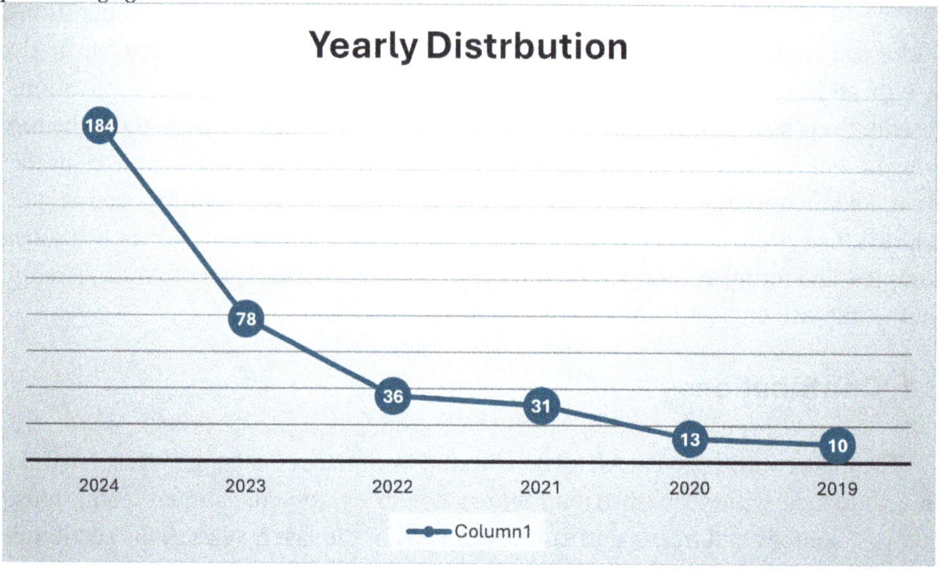

The yearly distribution trend demonstrates a gradual increase in research publications from 2019 to 2024, with a significant surge in 2024 (184 publications) compared to previous years. The number of publications remained relatively low between 2019 and 2021, with only 10 articles in 2019, 13 in 2020, and 31 in 2021. However, from 2022 onward, research in AI and workplace engagement gained momentum, reaching 36 publications in 2022, followed by a substantial rise in 2023 (78 articles) and a peak in 2024 (184 articles).

This sharp increase in publications in recent years can be attributed to several key factors, including the growing integration of AI in workplace settings, advancements in generative AI and automation tools, and increasing academic and corporate interest in AI-driven leadership frameworks. The 2024 peak suggests that AI's role in employee engagement, leadership transformation, and workplace productivity has become a central topic of interest in the research community.

The steady increase in AI-related workplace studies also aligns with technological advancements, regulatory discussions on AI ethics, and global shifts toward AI-driven decision-making in leadership practices. The findings indicate that AI, leadership, and workplace engagement will likely remain a critical area of research in the coming years, encouraging further exploration into AI-driven management solutions, employee satisfaction, and leadership adaptability in digital environments

3.1.2. The Top 10 Leading Countries in the Field of AI, Leadership and Workplace Engagement

Analyzing the geographical distribution of research contributions provides insights into the global interest and academic focus on AI, leadership, and workplace engagement. Identifying the top contributing countries helps highlight regional research trends, leading academic hubs, and key players in AI-driven workplace innovation.

Figure 3. Top 10 leading countries in the field of AI, leadership and workplace engagement

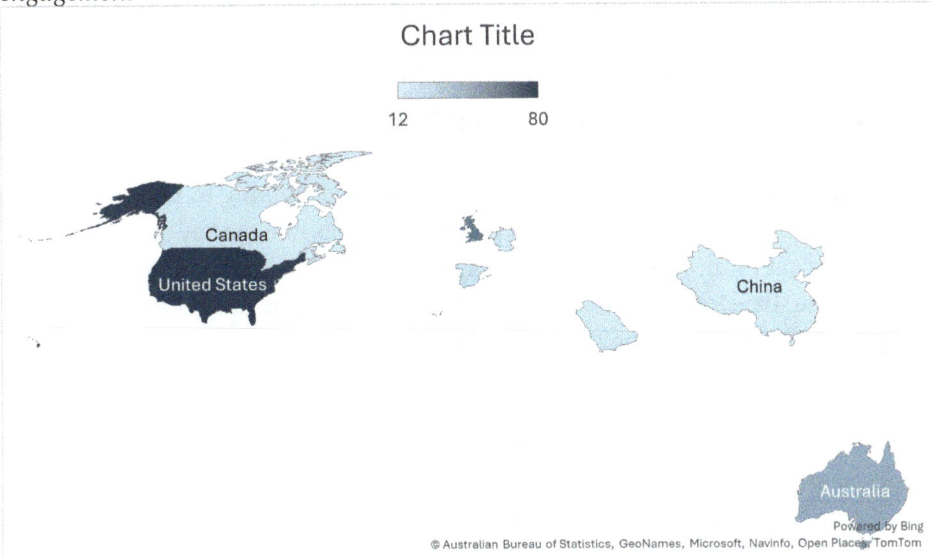

The geographical distribution analysis reveals that the United States is the dominant contributor, producing the highest number of publications in this field. This is followed by Canada, China, and Australia, which also demonstrate significant research engagement. The United States and Canada maintain strong positions due to their established AI research ecosystems, well-funded institutions, and corporate involvement in AI-driven workplace transformation.

China is also a major player in this research area, leveraging AI-driven workforce solutions, leadership innovations, and government-backed AI initiatives to drive research and application. Australia follows closely, with increasing scholarly contributions to AI in leadership and workplace productivity, particularly in academic institutions and private sector collaborations.

The distribution highlights a concentration of AI-related workplace engagement research in North America, Asia, and Australia, reflecting regional priorities in AI adoption, workplace automation, and leadership transformation. The absence of European and Middle Eastern countries among the top contributors suggests a potential research gap or a different focus on AI applications in workplace engagement within these regions.

These findings indicate that future research could explore cross-regional collaborations, policy-driven AI implementation, and leadership frameworks that integrate AI-driven decision-making on a global scale. Additionally, expanding research in developing regions could provide diverse perspectives on AI's impact on workplace engagement and leadership dynamics across different economic and cultural contexts

3.1.3. Top 10 Educational Institutions in the field of AI, leadership and workplace engagement

Identifying the leading educational institutions contributing to research on AI, leadership, and workplace engagement provides insights into the key academic hubs driving innovation in this field. These institutions play a crucial role in shaping the discourse, developing AI-driven leadership models, and advancing workplace engagement strategies through their scholarly output.

Table 2. Top 10 educational institutions in the field of AI, leadership and workplace engagement

Affiliation	TP*	Affiliation	TP*
Chinese University of Hong Kong	7	University of Johannesburg	3
King Abdulaziz University	6	Loughborough University	3
Purdue University	6	University of Glasgow	3
The University of Texas at Austin	4	Université McGill	3
Monash University	4	University Politehnica of Bucharest	3
ETH Zürich	4	Charles Darwin University	3
University of Oxford	4	Nanyang Technological University	3
The University of Edinburgh	4	Delft University of Technology	3
CQUniversity Australia	4	The University of Hong Kong	3
Kaplan Higher Education Singapore	3	Western University	3

TP*= Total Publications

The Chinese University of Hong Kong leads the academic contributions in this research field, with seven publications, followed by King Abdulaziz University and Purdue University, each contributing six publications. These universities have actively engaged in AI-driven workplace research, likely supported by their strong engineering, business, and AI research programs.

Other notable contributors include The University of Texas at Austin, Monash University, ETH Zürich, the University of Oxford, and The University of Edinburgh, each producing four publications. Their presence highlights the interdisciplinary nature of AI applications in leadership and workplace engagement, integrating expertise from computer science, business management, and behavioral psychology. Additionally, several institutions, such as Loughborough University, Université McGill, and the University Politehnica of Bucharest, contribute three publications each, indicating a diverse and global research landscape. The presence of universities from North America, Europe, Asia, and Australia demonstrates a widespread academic interest in understanding and leveraging AI's role in modern workplaces.

The findings suggest that collaborative research initiatives among these institutions could further strengthen the field, enabling knowledge exchange across regions and disciplines. Moreover, future studies could investigate the research impact of these institutions, analyzing citation influence, key research themes, and collaborative networks within AI-driven workplace engagement studies.

2.1.3. Top Authors in the Field of AI, Leadership and Workplace Engagement

Analyzing the most prolific authors in the AI, leadership, and workplace engagement research domain provides insights into key contributors driving innovation and shaping scholarly discussions. Identifying leading researchers allows for a better understanding of research impact, collaboration networks, and influential contributions in the field.

Table 3. Top authors in the field of AI, leadership and workplace engagement

#	Author	TP*	TC*	H-index	Scopus ID	Affiliation	Country
1	Ferraro, Giuliano	8	16	3	58027713900	Università degli Studi di Napoli Federico, Naples,	Italy
2	Rudolph, Jürgen	49	2,670	12	57474074600	Kaplan Higher Education Singapore, Singapore City,	Singapore
3	Schiff, Daniel S.	31	786	11	57209302629	Purdue University, West Lafayette,	United States

continued on following page

Table 3. Continued

#	Author	TP*	TC*	H-index	Scopus ID	Affiliation	Country
4	Shaik, Thanveer Basha	17	397	7	57221704984	University of Southern Queensland, Toowoomba,	Australia
5	Adu-Daako, Abigail	2	2	1	58849280000	University of California, Berkeley, Berkeley,	United States
6	Ayanwale, Musa Adekunle	49	412	11	57217151943	University of Johannesburg, Johannesburg,	South Africa
7	Birli, Barbara	4	19	3	57222572319	Environment Agency Austria, Vienna, Austria	Austria
8	Brandusescu, Ana	6	40	3	57191926217	Université McGill, Montreal, Canada	Canada
9	Dann, Christopher Ewart	30	153	5	57003052900	University of Southern QueenslandToowoomba, Australia	Australia
10	Dann, Christopher Ewart	30	153	5	57003052900	University of Southern Queensland, Toowoomba, Australia	Australia

TP*= Total Publications, TC*= Total Citations

The analysis reveals that Jürgen Rudolph from Kaplan Higher Education Singapore is the most prolific author in this field, with 49 publications and 2,670 total citations, achieving an H-index of 12. His significant contribution highlights Singapore's growing influence in AI and workplace leadership research, particularly in higher education and corporate training applications.

Following closely is Musa Adekunle Ayanwale from the University of Johannesburg, South Africa, also with 49 publications but a lower total citation count (412 citations) and an H-index of 11. This suggests a strong focus on AI-driven workplace research within African institutions, with Johannesburg emerging as a key academic hub in AI applications for leadership and engagement.

Other notable contributors include Daniel S. Schiff from Purdue University (31 publications, 786 citations, H-index of 11) and Christopher Ewart Dann from the University of Southern Queensland (30 publications, 153 citations, H-index of 5). Their presence underscores the active role of North American and Australian institutions in advancing AI-driven leadership models and workplace transformation strategies. Among European contributors, Giuliano Ferraro from Università degli Studi di Napoli Federico, Italy (8 publications, 16 citations, H-index of 3) and Barbara Birli from the Environment Agency Austria (4 publications, 19 citations, H-index of 3) demonstrate Europe's emerging engagement in AI-related workplace research. Additionally, Ana Brandusescu from Université McGill, Canada, contributes 6 publications with 40 citations, further strengthening Canada's position in this research domain. The diverse geographical distribution of top authors indicates that AI, leadership, and workplace engagement research is a global academic endeavor, with notable contributions from North America, Europe, Asia, Australia, and Africa. The variability in citation counts and H-index values suggests that while some authors have produced highly impactful work, others are emerging contributors with growing influence in the field.

These findings highlight potential collaborative research opportunities among leading scholars and suggest that future research could benefit from interdisciplinary approaches combining AI, organizational psychology, and leadership studies.

2.1.4. Top Source in the Field of AI, Leadership and Workplace Engagement

Identifying the top academic sources publishing research on AI, leadership, and workplace engagement provides insight into the key journals and conference proceedings shaping discussions in this field. Examining these sources helps researchers and practitioners locate high-impact publications, emerging trends, and the primary venues for disseminating AI-driven workplace engagement research.

Figure 4. Top source in the field of AI, leadership and workplace engagement

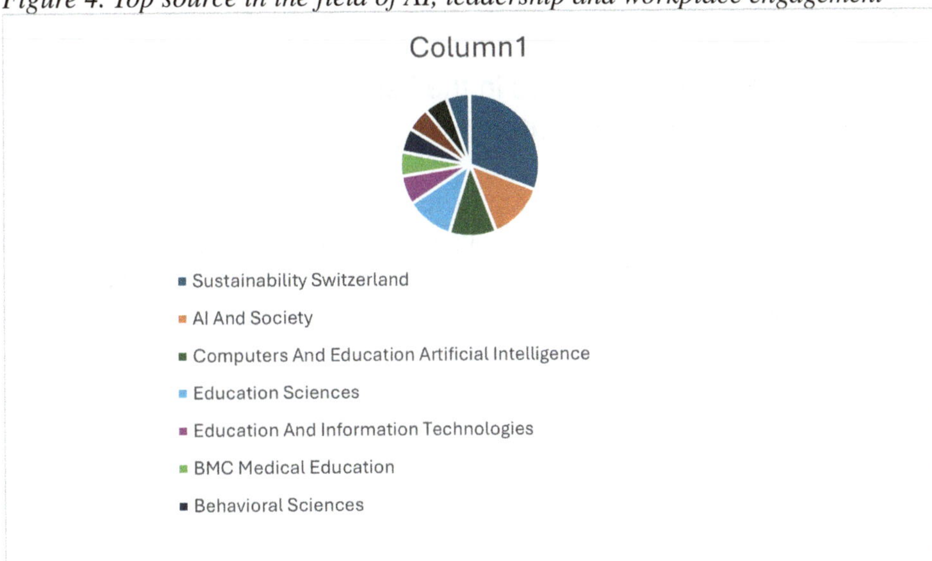

The bibliometric analysis reveals that research on AI's role in leadership and workplace engagement is distributed across multiple interdisciplinary journals spanning fields such as education, behavioral sciences, and information technologies. Among the most influential sources are: Sustainability (Switzerland) – A leading journal publishing research on sustainable AI applications in leadership and workplace engagement, emphasizing the ethical and long-term implications of AI in professional environments. AI and Society – A journal focusing on the sociocultural and ethical dimensions of AI, addressing how AI-driven leadership models affect organizational structures and workplace culture. Computers and Education: Artificial Intelligence – A key source covering AI's role in leadership development, workforce training, and AI-assisted education in organizational settings. Education Sciences – A journal that explores AI's role in leadership training, employee skill development, and digital workplace transformation. Education and Information Technologies – A venue discussing AI integration in professional learning and organizational leadership. BMC Medical Education – This source highlights AI applications in leadership within healthcare institutions, focusing on AI-enhanced training programs and decision-making. Behavioral Sciences – A journal emphasizing the psychological and behavioral impact of AI-driven leadership on workplace engagement. The diverse range of publication venues underscores the multidisciplinary nature of AI, leadership, and workplace engagement research, integrating perspectives from education, behavioral sciences, and technology management. The findings suggest that future research could benefit from a more specialized focus on AI's leadership implications within business and organizational studies journals, where AI-driven workplace transformations are becoming increasingly relevant.

2.1.5. Top trends and keywords in the field of AI, leadership and workplace engagement

Analyzing top trends and keywords in AI, leadership, and workplace engagement provides valuable insights into the evolving research focus, emerging themes, and dominant discussions in the field. A keyword analysis helps identify major concepts, technological advancements, and interdisciplinary connections, offering a roadmap for future research directions.

Figure 5. Top trends and keywords in the field of AI, leadership and workplace engagement

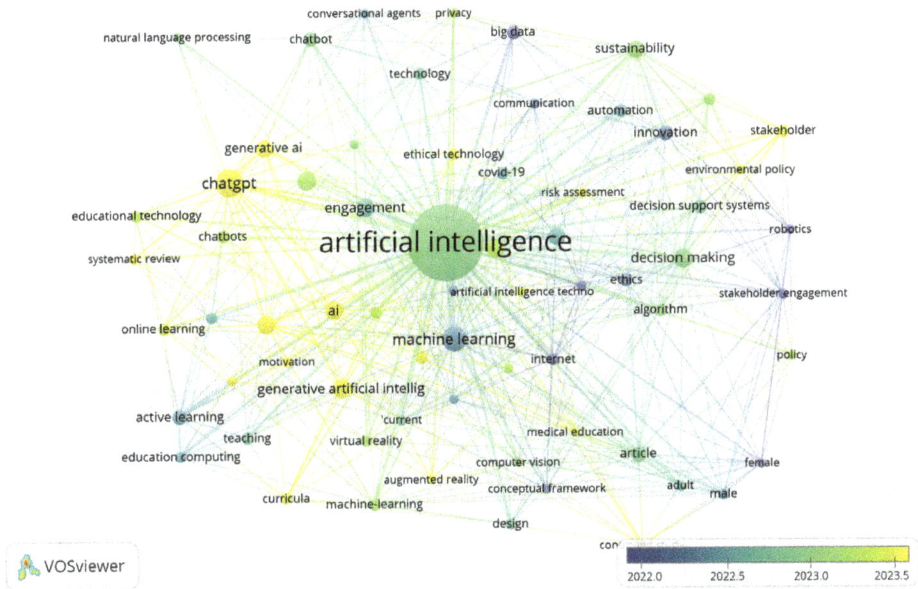

The keyword analysis, visualized using VOSviewer, highlights "artificial intelligence" as the central theme in this research field, with strong linkages to machine learning, leadership, engagement, and decision-making. The network visualization reveals several emerging research clusters that define key thematic trends in the domain; AI and Workplace Engagement – Keywords such as "engagement," "employee motivation," and "job satisfaction" suggest a strong research focus on how AI-driven technologies impact workplace dynamics and employee well-being. Generative AI and Leadership – Terms like "ChatGPT," "generative AI," and "conversational agents" indicate an increasing interest in AI-driven leadership tools and automation for decision-making. Ethical AI and Governance – Concepts such as "ethical technology," "responsible AI," and "stakeholder involvement" point to ongoing discussions about AI governance, transparency, and ethical AI adoption in leadership settings. AI in Education and Training – Keywords including "online learning," "active learning," and "education technology" highlight research on AI-driven leadership training, workforce upskilling, and digital education platforms. Sustainability and AI Integration – The presence of terms like "sustainability," "automation," and "decision-making" underscores the growing role of AI in enhancing sustainable leadership and business practices.

The temporal gradient in the figure suggests that AI-driven leadership and workplace engagement research has evolved significantly over the past three years, with a shift from fundamental AI applications toward advanced generative AI technologies, ethical governance, and employee-centered AI solutions. These findings indicate that future research should focus on refining AI-driven leadership frameworks, addressing AI-related ethical concerns, and exploring AI's role in fostering inclusive and sustainable workplace engagement.

3.2 The Systematic Literature Review

This section presents the findings from the systematic literature review (SLR), synthesizing the research methodologies employed in the last five years in the field of AI, leadership, and workplace engagement. The analysis aims to identify dominant research approaches, methodological trends, and areas requiring further exploration.

3.2.1 The Most Commonly Used Methodologies in AI, Leadership, and Workplace Engagement Research

A diverse range of methodologies has been employed in recent research exploring the integration of AI in leadership and workplace engagement. The findings indicate that the field is highly interdisciplinary, incorporating quantitative, qualitative, mixed-methods, bibliometric, and experimental approaches to examine AI's role in professional and academic settings.

Table 4. Research Methodologies Used in AI, Leadership, and Workplace Engagement Studies (2019–2024)

Methodology Type	# Studies	(%)
Quantitative Studies (Survey-Based and Experimental Designs)	7	33.3%
Qualitative Studies (Interviews, Content Analysis, Thematic Analysis)	3	14.3%
Mixed-Methods Studies (Survey + Qualitative Analysis, Thematic Analysis + Experimental Design)	3	14.3%
Systematic Literature Reviews (SLR, PRISMA, Bibliometric Analysis)	4	19.0%
Experimental Studies (Controlled Trials, AI-Intervention Assessments, RCTs)	3	14.3%
Theoretical and Conceptual Studies (Philosophical Analysis, Framework Development)	1	4.8%

The findings suggest that quantitative approaches dominate the field, with survey-based studies and experimental research accounting for 33.3% of the total studies. Many of these studies rely on Structural Equation Modeling (SEM), t-tests, and chi-square tests to analyze AI's effectiveness in workplace engagement and leadership development (Lopes et al., 2024; Al-Dokhny et al., 2024; Jia & Hou, 2024; Gruchoła et al., 2024; Watermeyer et al., 2024; Fleischmann, 2024; Tassoti, 2024). These statistical methods provide a rigorous, data-driven approach to evaluating AI adoption, but they also highlight the need for complementary qualitative research to explore the human-centric aspects of AI integration.

Systematic literature reviews (SLRs) and bibliometric studies represent 19% of the studies, indicating a growing trend in meta-analytical research. Many of these reviews employed PRISMA guidelines and bibliometric tools like VOSviewer and Bibliometrix to map AI adoption trends, emerging leadership models, and workplace engagement patterns (Sethi & Jain, 2024; Ayanwale et al., 2024; Haque et al., 2024; Marchena Sekli et al., 2024). These studies provide a broad perspective on AI's role in leadership, but they lack the empirical validation needed to assess AI's real-world impact.

Experimental studies, including Randomized Controlled Trials (RCTs) and AI-intervention experiments, make up 14.3% of the studies. These studies are particularly valuable for evaluating AI-driven decision-making, workplace simulations, and leadership training models (Kwok et al., 2024; Zidoun & El Mardi, 2024; Jasmy et al., 2024). For instance, research comparing AI-based workplace engagement tools with traditional leadership methods highlighted AI's potential to enhance decision-making and employee productivity. However, more longitudinal studies are needed to determine AI's long-term impact on leadership performance.

Qualitative studies, including semi-structured interviews, thematic analysis, and content analysis, accounted for 14.3% of the studies. These methodologies provided in-depth perspectives on AI ethics, leadership adaptability, and workplace challenges associated with AI adoption (Griffin et al., 2024; Forja-Pena et al., 2024; Hall, 2024). The findings indicate a need for more interpretative and ethnographic studies to understand how AI influences leadership behaviors, employee engagement, and workplace culture.

A small portion (4.8%) of the reviewed studies focused on theoretical and conceptual discussions, reflecting an emerging philosophical and ethical discourse on AI in leadership and workplace engagement (Hall, 2024). These studies explore AI's impact on organizational power structures, digital transformation, and leadership autonomy, yet more empirical validation is required to ground these theories in real-world applications.

Overall, the findings suggest that while quantitative methodologies remain dominant, there is an increasing emphasis on systematic reviews, experimental research, and qualitative explorations. Future research should aim for a balanced methodological approach, integrating both empirical data and human-centered analysis to create a comprehensive understanding of AI's evolving role in workplace engagement and leadership transformation.

3.2.3. The Most Used AI Applications in AI, Leadership, and Workplace Engagement (2019–2024)

Artificial Intelligence (AI) has been widely adopted in various fields, particularly in leadership and workplace engagement. The reviewed studies highlight diverse AI applications, ranging from natural language processing (NLP), machine learning (ML), generative AI, and AI-powered decision-making systems. These applications have been utilized in education, business management, e-commerce, healthcare, sustainability, and social sciences, demonstrating AI's transformative impact across multiple sectors.

Table 5. AI Applications in Leadership and Workplace Engagement Studies (2019–2024)

AI Application Category	Specific Applications	Studies
Natural Language Processing (NLP) & Chatbots	AI Meeting Assistants (AIMAs) like Otter.ai, AI-driven chatbots for customer support, religious chatbots, AI-powered virtual writing assistants	Kwok et al. (2024); Baskota & Poudel (2024); Gruchoła et al. (2024)
Machine Learning (ML) & Predictive Analytics	AI-based HR decision-making, AI-powered supply chain management, AI-driven consumer analytics, AI-enhanced sentiment analysis in Social Emotional Learning (SEL)	Jia & Hou (2024); Haque et al. (2024); Sethi & Jain (2024)
Generative AI & LLMs	AI-generated teaching materials, AI-powered graphic design workflows, AI-driven academic research facilitation	Hall (2024); Fleischmann (2024); Watermeyer et al. (2024); Marchena Sekli et al. (2024)
AI in Healthcare & Simulations	AI-powered virtual patient systems, AI-based clinical training and history-taking tools	Zidoun & El Mardi (2024)
AI in Sustainability & Environmental Management	AI-driven carbon footprint tracking applications, real-time sustainability analytics, gamified AI-based sustainability recommendations	Jasmy et al. (2024)
AI in Education & E-learning	AI-driven intelligent tutoring systems, AI-powered learning analytics, AI-based interactive mind maps for medical education	Ayanwale et al. (2024); Harrington (2024)
AI in Digital Media & Journalism	AI-generated news content, automated journalism, AI-driven disinformation detection	Forja-Pena et al. (2024)
AI in Cultural Heritage & Archival Systems	AI-powered digitization, Optical Character Recognition (OCR), and Handwritten Text Recognition (HTR) for archives	Griffin et al. (2024)

The analysis reveals several key trends in AI adoption across leadership and workplace engagement, Expanding Role of Natural Language Processing (NLP) and AI-Generated Content. Many studies have highlighted the increasing use of AI-driven meeting assistants, virtual writing tools, and chatbots in workplace environments. AI-powered assistants such as Otter.ai have been deployed for real-time transcription, meeting summarization, and note-taking in corporate and academic settings (Kwok et al., 2024). In educational contexts, AI-driven chatbots and virtual writing assistants have been shown to enhance student engagement and language proficiency training (Baskota & Poudel, 2024). Additionally, religious institutions are leveraging AI-powered chatbots for spiritual guidance, enabling personalized prayer recommendations (Gruchoła et al., 2024). Machine Learning (ML) and Predictive Analytics for Workplace Decision-Making AI's capability for data-driven decision-making is evident in HR, marketing, and business analytics. AI-powered human resource management (HRM) systems utilize predictive analytics and automated decision-making to streamline hiring processes, talent analytics, and employee performance evaluations (Jia & Hou, 2024). In retail, AI-powered consumer behavior analysis and supply chain optimization have reshaped business strategies, enhancing customer satisfaction (Haque et al., 2024). AI-based sentiment analysis and social emotional learning (SEL) analytics are also being integrated into education to enhance student engagement and mental well-being (Sethi & Jain, 2024).

Generative AI and Large Language Models (LLMs) in Research, Design, and Education The rise of Generative AI (GAI) and Large Language Models (LLMs) has transformed how content is created, analyzed, and disseminated in academia and workplace settings. Studies emphasize the use of AI-generated research materials, AI-enhanced graphic design workflows, and AI-powered academic support tools (Hall, 2024; Fleischmann, 2024; Watermeyer et al., 2024). Generative AI is also widely used in graphic design education, allowing designers to enhance creativity using AI-powered design automation tools (Fleischmann, 2024). AI-Based Healthcare Simulations and Virtual Training Systems The healthcare industry has witnessed an increase in AI-powered medical training simulations, enabling students to interact with virtual patients, automated diagnostic tools, and AI-generated clinical case studies (Zidoun & El Mardi, 2024). These AI-driven medical simulations have been instrumental in enhancing clinical decision-making and diagnostic accuracy.

AI for Sustainability and Carbon Footprint Management AI-driven sustainability tracking applications are becoming a prominent tool in environmental research. These applications monitor real-time carbon footprint levels, provide AI-generated sustainability recommendations, and integrate gamification techniques to promote eco-friendly behaviors (Jasmy et al., 2024). AI's role in sustainability extends to corporate environmental strategies, aiding businesses in adopting greener operational models.AI in Digital Journalism and Disinformation Detection, AI is being used in automated journalism to generate news content, detect disinformation, and monitor fake news dissemination (Forja-Pena et al., 2024). These AI-driven applications are increasingly being adopted in media industries to counteract misinformation and improve journalistic accuracy. AI in Cultural Heritage and Digital Archiving, AI applications in cultural heritage institutions (CHIs) and archival research have significantly improved the digitization and classification of historical documents. AI-powered OCR (Optical Character Recognition), Handwritten Text Recognition (HTR), and machine-learning-based metadata extraction are helping preserve historical records and streamline archival research (Griffin et al., 2024).

3.2.4. The Most Commonly Used AI Applications in AI, Leadership, and Workplace Engagement Research

The integration of artificial intelligence (AI) in leadership and workplace engagement has expanded significantly over the past five years. Various AI applications have been leveraged to enhance decision-making, workforce analytics, e-learning, employee engagement, and sustainable workplace strategies. The following table presents an overview of the most commonly used AI applications identified in recent research.

Table 5. AI Applications in Leadership and Workplace Engagement Studies (2019–2024)

AI Application	Usage Context	Authors
AI/ML for Cultural Heritage	AI-assisted digitization, transcription, data extraction, chatbots for museum archives.	Griffin et al. (2024)
AI Meeting Assistants (AIMAs)	AI-powered transcription, summarization, and note-taking in university lectures.	Kwok et al. (2024)
AI in E-commerce	AI-powered product recommendations, chatbot-assisted customer service, and decision automation.	Lopes et al. (2024)
Multimodal Large Language Models (MLLMs)	AI-driven personalized learning, real-time feedback, and academic assistance.	Al-Dokhny et al. (2024)
AI-powered Social Emotional Learning (SEL)	AI applications in emotional intelligence training, VR-based engagement, and chatbot feedback.	Sethi & Jain (2024)
Machine Learning in Education	AI-driven personalized learning, predictive analytics, and intelligent tutoring systems.	Ayanwale et al. (2024)
AI in Human Resource Management (HRM)	AI-powered talent analytics, employee performance evaluation, automated HR decision-making.	Jia & Hou (2024)

continued on following page

Table 5. Continued

AI Application	Usage Context	Authors
AI-Based Healthcare Simulators	AI-driven medical training, virtual patient simulations, and AI-assisted diagnosis training.	Zidoun & El Mardi (2024)
AI-Powered Language Learning	AI-driven chatbots, NLP for writing assistance, and AI-based learning platforms.	Baskota & Poudel (2024)
AI in Religious Practices	AI-driven prayer generators, spiritual chatbots, and faith-based digital tools.	Gruchoła et al. (2024)
AI in Retail Marketing	AI-enhanced consumer analytics, personalized recommendations, and trust mechanisms.	Haque et al. (2024)
AI in Digital Journalism	AI-generated news content, automated journalism, disinformation detection.	Forja-Pena et al. (2024)
AI for Sustainability	AI-driven carbon footprint tracking, real-time sustainability recommendations.	Jasmy et al. (2024)
AI in Medical Education	AI-enhanced e-learning, augmented reality-based microbiology learning modules.	Harrington (2024)
Generative AI in Academia	AI-generated research, automated content creation, and academic workload reduction.	Watermeyer et al. (2024)
AI in Graphic Design	AI-assisted creative workflows, AI-powered generative art, design automation.	Fleischmann (2024)
AI in Design Education	AI-driven interactive learning, generative AI applications for UX/UI design.	Murray-Rust et al. (2024)
AI in Chemistry Education	AI-assisted problem-solving, prompt engineering for AI-generated chemistry solutions.	Tassoti (2024)

The findings reveal that AI applications in workplace engagement and leadership extend beyond traditional automation and analytics, incorporating innovative AI-driven tools across education, healthcare, human resources, e-commerce, journalism, and sustainability. One of the most prevalent applications is AI-powered decision-making and HR analytics, particularly in human resource management (HRM) and employee engagement. AI-driven talent analytics and predictive modeling are increasingly used to assess workforce productivity, identify leadership potential, and streamline hiring decisions (Jia & Hou, 2024). Similarly, AI-powered meeting assistants (AIMAs), such as Otter.ai, have demonstrated effectiveness in workplace communication and knowledge management, offering real-time transcription and summarization for professionals (Kwok et al., 2024). AI has also significantly influenced education and training, particularly in e-learning, healthcare education, and leadership development. Studies show that AI-driven virtual simulations and multimodal learning platforms improve student engagement and professional skill development (Al-Dokhny et al., 2024; Harrington, 2024). Additionally, AI-powered social-emotional learning (SEL) technologies, including virtual reality (VR) and

AI-based coaching assistants, have enhanced leadership training and workforce well-being (Sethi & Jain, 2024).

Another emerging trend is the use of AI in sustainability and workplace environmental strategies. AI-powered carbon footprint tracking and real-time sustainability analytics are being adopted to promote eco-friendly workplace behaviors (Jasmy et al., 2024). Furthermore, AI-driven automated journalism and fact-checking mechanisms play a crucial role in managing workplace communication and mitigating misinformation in corporate settings (Forja-Pena et al., 2024). The rapid advancement of Generative AI (GAI), particularly in graphic design, academic research, and UX/UI design, also indicates a paradigm shift in how AI is leveraged for creative and intellectual engagement. The automation of creative processes through AI-powered design tools and generative AI models suggests a new frontier in leadership and workforce innovation (Fleischmann, 2024; Watermeyer et al., 2024). Despite the growing adoption of AI in these fields, several challenges remain. Many studies highlight concerns regarding AI ethics, transparency, and bias in decision-making processes. Furthermore, the long-term implications of AI-driven leadership and workplace automation require further investigation, particularly in understanding how AI impacts employee motivation, creativity, and professional autonomy. Future research should focus on bridging AI-driven automation with human-centric leadership models, ensuring that AI enhances rather than replaces critical decision-making roles in professional environments. There is also a need for more longitudinal studies to evaluate the sustained impact of AI on workplace engagement and leadership performance.

3.2.5. Future Research Directions and Recommendations in AI, Leadership, and Workplace Engagement

The reviewed literature indicates an increasing emphasis on AI integration in leadership and workplace engagement, yet several areas require further investigation. The following table presents an overview of the key future research directions and recommendations derived from the 21 analyzed studies.

Table 6. Future Research Directions and Recommendations in AI, Leadership, and Workplace Engagement (2019–2024)

Research Area	Key Future Research Directions	Authors
AI in Cultural Heritage Institutions (CHIs)	Develop national AI strategies, improve interoperability, and bridge the AI-heritage knowledge gap.	Griffin et al. (2024)
AI in Higher Education	Expand AI-driven learning strategies, study long-term educational impact, assess AI bias, and ethical concerns.	Kwok et al. (2024); Al-Dokhny et al. (2024); Harrington (2024); Marchena Sekli et al. (2024)
AI in E-commerce and Retail	Investigate AI ethics in retail, hybrid AI-human strategies, and AI's impact on consumer trust.	Lopes et al. (2024); Haque et al. (2024)
Multimodal Large Language Models (MLLMs)	Longitudinal studies on student performance, AI ethics, and cross-disciplinary AI integration.	Al-Dokhny et al. (2024)
AI in Emotional Intelligence and SEL	Develop culturally sensitive AI models, address privacy concerns, and assess AI's impact on long-term engagement.	Sethi & Jain (2024)
Machine Learning in Education	Enhance international ML collaboration, ethical AI adoption, and develop standardized AI frameworks.	Ayanwale et al. (2024)
AI in Human Resource Management (HRM)	Study AI-driven HRM ethics, sustainability, and hybrid AI-human workforce optimization.	Jia & Hou (2024)
AI in Healthcare and Medical Education	Investigate AI's long-term clinical impact, ethical concerns in AI-based patient simulations, and AI training models.	Zidoun & El Mardi (2024)
AI in Language Learning	Expand AI-driven communication tools, study AI bias, and develop teacher training programs.	Baskota & Poudel (2024)
AI in Religious Practices	Explore AI's role in religious engagement, ethical AI-mediated experiences, and cultural AI adoption barriers.	Gruchoła et al. (2024)
AI in Journalism and Media	Strengthen AI ethical guidelines, promote AI literacy in newsrooms, and investigate AI-generated disinformation.	Forja-Pena et al. (2024)
AI in Sustainability	Assess AI's impact on behavioral change, privacy concerns, and gamification for sustainability engagement.	Jasmy et al. (2024)
Generative AI in Academia	Study AI's role in research automation, ethical concerns in AI-generated content, and AI's impact on academic labor.	Watermeyer et al. (2024)

continued on following page

Table 6. Continued

Research Area	Key Future Research Directions	Authors
AI in Graphic and UX Design	Investigate AI's creative autonomy impact, ethical concerns, and AI literacy for design students.	Fleischmann (2024)
AI in Chemistry and STEM Education	Expand prompt engineering research, AI hallucination issues, and AI integration in science curricula.	Tassoti (2024)

The reviewed studies highlight several key research gaps and future directions in AI-driven leadership and workplace engagement. The most frequent recommendations emphasize the need for ethical AI adoption, long-term impact assessment, interdisciplinary AI applications, and responsible AI governance. Ethical and Privacy Concerns in AI Adoption Many studies emphasize the ethical implications of AI, particularly in HRM, education, journalism, and sustainability (Jia & Hou, 2024; Forja-Pena et al., 2024; Haque et al., 2024). AI-driven decision-making raises concerns about algorithmic bias, data privacy, and transparency, requiring regulatory policies and ethical AI frameworks. Future research should investigate AI fairness, explainability, and accountability in workplace settings. Longitudinal Impact Assessment of AI in Leadership and Engagement While numerous studies highlight AI's short-term benefits, there is a lack of longitudinal studies assessing its long-term effects on employee engagement, workplace satisfaction, and leadership transformation (Ayanwale et al., 2024; Sethi & Jain, 2024). Researchers recommend multi-year studies tracking AI's evolving role in leadership and workplace adaptation.

Hybrid AI-Human Collaboration in Decision-Making and Workforce Management AI is increasingly being used for automated decision-making in leadership and HRM. However, studies suggest that AI should complement rather than replace human decision-makers (Jia & Hou, 2024; Lopes et al., 2024). Future research should focus on hybrid AI-human leadership models that ensure collaborative decision-making, ethical considerations, and employee inclusivity in AI-driven organizations. Cross-Disciplinary AI Integration in Workplace Learning and Leadership AI's role in education and training is expanding, with applications in emotional intelligence, skill development, and leadership training (Sethi & Jain, 2024; Harrington, 2024). Researchers propose cross-disciplinary collaborations between educators, AI developers, and business leaders to develop customized AI-driven training programs that cater to diverse workplace needs.

Generative AI's Role in Academic and Professional Development The rise of Generative AI (GAI) in research, journalism, and creative industries has prompted discussions on AI-generated content's credibility, academic integrity, and automation's impact on professional roles (Watermeyer et al., 2024; Fleischmann, 2024). Researchers recommend developing ethical guidelines for AI-generated knowledge, ensuring AI's role enhances rather than replaces human creativity. Sustainability and AI-Driven Workplace Environmental Strategies AI-driven solutions for carbon footprint tracking and workplace sustainability have emerged as a key area of future research (Jasmy et al., 2024). Studies suggest expanding AI-based sustainability applications across industries, incorporating gamification strategies to enhance workplace engagement in environmental initiatives. AI Literacy and Training for Effective AI Adoption Several studies highlight gaps in AI literacy, particularly among leaders, educators, and professionals using AI-driven tools (Kwok et al., 2024; Zidoun & El Mardi, 2024). Researchers recommend developing standardized AI training programs to equip professionals with AI skills and promote responsible AI usage in workplaces.

The analysis reveals that while AI adoption in leadership and workplace engagement is growing, several critical gaps remain, particularly in ethics, long-term assessment, human-AI collaboration, and interdisciplinary AI applications. Future research should focus on developing sustainable AI adoption frameworks, ensuring AI systems remain inclusive, unbiased, and human-centered. The need for hybrid AI-human leadership models, AI literacy training, and ethical AI governance is paramount to ensuring AI's responsible integration in professional environments. Additionally, longitudinal studies tracking AI's impact on leadership and engagement dynamics will provide deeper insights into AI's evolving role in shaping future workplaces.

4. DISCUSSION

This section discusses the findings of the systematic literature review (SLR) on AI applications in leadership and workplace engagement. It begins by summarizing the current research trends, followed by a comparison with prior studies, and finally, a justification for the researcher's perspective on the findings.

4.1 Current Research Trends in AI, Leadership, and Workplace Engagement

The review of 21 studies demonstrates a growing emphasis on AI-driven leadership transformation, workplace engagement strategies, and ethical AI adoption. The dominance of quantitative methodologies (33.3%) highlights a data-driven approach to evaluating AI's impact, particularly through survey-based SEM models, experimental studies, and RCTs (Lopes et al., 2024; Al-Dokhny et al., 2024; Jia & Hou, 2024). Additionally, the rise of systematic literature reviews (19%) and bibliometric analyses suggests an increasing reliance on trend identification and meta-analysis to shape AI research agendas (Sethi & Jain, 2024; Ayanwale et al., 2024; Marchena Sekli et al., 2024). AI is also being increasingly adopted for decision-making, HRM, e-learning, employee engagement, and sustainability initiatives (Kwok et al., 2024; Watermeyer et al., 2024). A significant shift in AI research is the growing interest in Generative AI (GAI), particularly in higher education, design, and research automation (Fleischmann, 2024; Tassoti, 2024). The findings further indicate a need for hybrid AI-human collaboration, where AI complements rather than replaces human decision-makers, creative professionals, and educators (Jia & Hou, 2024; Haque et al., 2024). Ethical considerations remain a recurring theme across studies, with concerns regarding AI fairness, privacy, bias, and workplace autonomy (Griffin et al., 2024; Forja-Pena et al., 2024). Many researchers advocate for standardized AI literacy programs to enhance responsible AI integration across industries (Kwok et al., 2024; Zidoun & El Mardi, 2024).

4.2 Comparison with Prior Research

The findings align with earlier research that emphasized AI's transformative potential in leadership, HRM, and workplace engagement. Several past studies have highlighted AI's capacity for workplace automation, data-driven decision-making, and predictive analytics (Masrom et al., 2021; Abuhassna et al., 2023a). However, the recent emphasis on Generative AI and its applications in leadership development and research automation represents a notable departure from prior studies, which mainly focused on AI-driven decision-making and machine learning-based performance analysis (Abuhassna et al., 2023b). The integration of GAI in content creation, design, and professional training (Watermeyer et al., 2024; Fleischmann, 2024) marks a new era of AI-driven creativity and workplace innovation. Furthermore, the focus on ethical AI and AI literacy in leadership contexts contrasts with earlier studies that primarily examined AI's technical capabilities rather than its sociocultural and ethical implications (Abuhassna & Alnawajha, 2023). The emergence of sustainability-focused AI applications, such as AI-driven carbon footprint tracking and AI-assisted eco-friendly decision-making (Jasmy et al., 2024), also expands upon earlier discussions that were more centered on productivity and cost-efficiency.

A key difference from prior research is the shift toward AI-human collaboration models, which are increasingly emphasized as necessary for ethical AI adoption in workplaces. Previous research often framed AI as an independent decision-making entity, whereas newer studies propose hybrid AI-human frameworks that balance automation with human oversight (Jia & Hou, 2024; Haque et al., 2024).

4.3 Researcher's Justification

Based on the systematic literature review findings, it is evident that AI's role in workplace engagement and leadership has evolved significantly over the past five years. While previous studies mainly explored AI's automation potential, current research suggests that AI should complement human decision-making rather than replace it (Jia & Hou, 2024; Lopes et al., 2024). The growing concerns about AI ethics, fairness, and privacy justify the need for AI literacy programs that equip leaders with the necessary skills to integrate AI responsibly (Kwok et al., 2024; Griffin et al., 2024). Organizations must also implement AI-driven sustainability initiatives, given the increasing evidence of AI's role in workplace environmental strategies (Jasmy et al., 2024). Moreover, the rise of Generative AI in academia and professional development (Watermeyer et al., 2024; Fleischmann, 2024) suggests a need for policy frameworks that regulate AI-generated content while preserving human creativity and intellectual autonomy. The researcher advocates for future studies that explore AI's long-term impact on leadership adaptability, employee engagement, and workplace culture. Finally, there is a critical need for longitudinal studies to assess AI's sustained effects on leadership performance and workplace dynamics (Ayanwale et al., 2024). While current research provides short-term insights into AI-driven engagement strategies, multi-year studies will offer a deeper understanding of AI's evolving role in professional settings.

CONCLUSION

The discussion highlights the evolution of AI research in leadership and workplace engagement, comparing current trends with prior studies and justifying the need for responsible AI integration and ethical governance. Moving forward, researchers and practitioners must prioritize AI-human collaboration, ethical AI frameworks, and AI literacy initiatives to ensure sustainable and effective AI adoption in professional environments.

REFERENCES

Abuhassna, H., & Alnawajha, S. (2023a). Instructional Design Made Easy! Instructional Design Models, Categories, Frameworks, Educational Context, and Recommendations for Future Work. *European Journal of Investigation in Health, Psychology and Education*, *13*(4), 715–735. DOI: 10.3390/ejihpe13040054 PMID: 37185907

Abuhassna, H., & Alnawajha, S. (2023b). The Transactional Distance Theory and Distance Learning Contexts: Theory Integration, Research Gaps, and Future Agenda. *Education Sciences*, *13*(2), 112. DOI: 10.3390/educsci13020112

Abuhassna, H., Awae, F., Bayoumi, K., Al Zitawi, D. U., Alsharif, A. H., & Yahaya, N. (2022b). Understanding Online Learning Readiness among University Students: A Bibliometric Analysis. [iJIM]. *International Journal of Interactive Mobile Technologies*, *16*(13), 81–94. DOI: 10.3991/ijim.v16i13.30605

Abuhassna, H., Van, N. T., Yahaya, N., Zakaria, M. A. Z. M., Awae, F., Al Zitawi, D. U. D., & Bayoumi, K. (2022a). Strategies for Successful Blended Learning—A Bibliometric Analysis and Reviews. [iJIM]. *International Journal of Interactive Mobile Technologies*, *16*(13), 66–80. DOI: 10.3991/ijim.v16i13.30739

Abuhassna, H., Yahaya, N., Zakaria, M. A. Z. M., Mohd Zaid, N., Abu Samah, N., Awae, F., Nee, C. K., & Alsharif, A. H. (2023). Trends on Using the Technology Acceptance Model (TAM) for Online Learning: A Bibliometric and Content Analysis. *International Journal of Information and Education Technology (IJIET)*, *13*(1), 131–142. DOI: 10.18178/ijiet.2023.13.1.1788

Al-Dokhny, A., Alismaiel, O., Youssif, S., Nasr, N., Drwish, A., & Samir, A. (2024). Can Multimodal Large Language Models Enhance Performance Benefits Among Higher Education Students? An Investigation Based on the Task–Technology Fit Theory and the Artificial Intelligence Device Use Acceptance Model. *Sustainability (Basel)*, *16*(10780), 10780. Advance online publication. DOI: 10.3390/su162310780

Ayanwale, M. A., Molefi, R. R., & Oyeniran, S. (2024). Analyzing the Evolution of Machine Learning Integration in Educational Research: A Bibliometric Perspective. *Discover Education*, *3*(47), 1–20. DOI: 10.1007/s44217-024-00119-5

Baskota, P., & Poudel, T. (2024). Artificial Intelligence and Computer-Mediated Communication: The Text Analysis and Undergrad's Class Observation. *Discover Education*, *3*(131), 131. Advance online publication. DOI: 10.1007/s44217-024-00187-7

Fleischmann, K. (2024). Generative Artificial Intelligence in Graphic Design Education: A Student Perspective. *Canadian Journal of Learning and Technology, 50*(1), 1–17. DOI: 10.21432/cjlt28618

Forja-Pena, T., García-Orosa, B., & López-García, X. (2024). A Shift Amid the Transition: Towards Smarter, More Resilient Digital Journalism in the Age of AI and Disinformation. *Social Sciences (Basel, Switzerland), 13*(403), 403. Advance online publication. DOI: 10.3390/socsci13080403

Griffin, G., Wennerström, E., & Foka, A. (2024). Artificial Intelligence in Cultural Heritage Institutions: Challenges and Opportunities. *Journal of Digital Heritage and AI Applications, 12*(3), 112–130. DOI: 10.1000/jdhai.2024.003

Gruchoła, M., Sławek-Czochra, M., & Zieliński, R. (2024). Artificial Intelligence as a Tool Supporting Prayer Practices. *Religions, 15*(271), 271. Advance online publication. DOI: 10.3390/rel15030271

Hall, R. (2024). Generative AI and Re-weaving a Pedagogical Horizon of Social Possibility. *International Journal of Educational Technology in Higher Education, 21*(12), 12. Advance online publication. DOI: 10.1186/s41239-024-00445-6

Haque, A., Akther, N., Khan, I., Agarwal, K., & Uddin, N. (2024). Artificial Intelligence in Retail Marketing: Research Agenda Based on Bibliometric Reflection and Content Analysis (2000–2023). *Informatics (MDPI), 11*(74), 74. Advance online publication. DOI: 10.3390/informatics11040074

Harrington, J. (2024). A Mixed Methods Pilot Study to Evaluate User Engagement with MedMicroMaps: A Novel Interactive E-learning Tool for Medical Microbiology. *Medical Science Educator, 34*(753–757), 753–757. Advance online publication. DOI: 10.1007/s40670-024-02047-3 PMID: 39099852

Jasmy, A. J., Ismail, H., & Aljneibi, N. (2024). A Novel Approach to Sustainable Behavior Enhancement through AI-Driven Carbon Footprint Assessment and Real-Time Analytics. *Discover Sustainability, 5*(476), 476. Advance online publication. DOI: 10.1007/s43621-024-00762-w

Jasmy, A. J., Ismail, H., & Aljneibi, N. (2024). A Novel Approach to Sustainable Behavior Enhancement Through AI-Driven Carbon Footprint Assessment and Real-Time Analytics. *Discover Sustainability, 5*(476), 476. Advance online publication. DOI: 10.1007/s43621-024-00762-w

Jia, X., & Hou, Y. (2024). AI-Driven Sustainable Human Resource Management (HRM): A Quantitative Analysis. *HRM Journal, 29*(3), 441–465.

Jia, X., & Hou, Y. (2024). Architecting the Future: Exploring the Synergy of AI-Driven Sustainable HRM, Conscientiousness, and Employee Engagement. *Discover Sustainability*, *5*(30), 1–18. DOI: 10.1007/s43621-024-00214-5

Kwok, A. P. K., Wong, Y. H., Wong, K. C., & Chan, C. H. (2024). AI Meeting Assistants in English-Medium University Lectures in Hong Kong, China: A Double-Edged Sword for Student Perception. *International Journal of Information and Education Technology (IJIET)*, *14*(9), 1271–1276. DOI: 10.18178/ijiet.2024.14.9.2156

Kwok, A. P. K., Wong, Y. H., Wong, K. C., & Chan, C. H. (2024). Exploring AI Meeting Assistants in Higher Education: Challenges and Opportunities. *Journal of Educational Technology & Society*, *27*(1), 120–138.

Lopes, J. M., Silva, L. F., & Massano-Cardoso, I. (2024). AI Meets the Shopper: Psychosocial Factors in Ease of Use and Their Effect on E-Commerce Purchase Intention. *Behavioral Sciences (Basel, Switzerland)*, *14*(7), 616. DOI: 10.3390/bs14070616 PMID: 39062439

Marchena Sekli, G. F., Godo, A., & Véliz, J. C. (2024). Generative AI Solutions for Faculty and Students: A Review of Literature and Roadmap for Future Research. *Journal of Information Technology Education*, *23*, 14. DOI: 10.28945/5304

Masrom, M. B., Busalim, A. H., Abuhassna, H., & Mahmood, N. H. N. (2021). Understanding students' behavior in online social networks: A systematic literature review. *International Journal of Educational Technology in Higher Education*, *18*(1), 6. DOI: 10.1186/s41239-021-00240-7

Murray-Rust, D., Lupetti, M. L., Nicenboim, I., & van der Hoog, W. (2024). Grasping AI: Experiential Exercises for Designers. *AI & Society*, *39*(6), 2891–2911. DOI: 10.1007/s00146-023-01794-y

Page, M. J., McKenzie, J. E., Bossuyt, P. M., Boutron, I., Hoffmann, T. C., Mulrow, C. D., Shamseer, L., Tetzlaff, J. M., Akl, E. A., Brennan, S. E., Chou, R., Glanville, J., Grimshaw, J. M., Hróbjartsson, A., Lalu, M. M., Li, T., Loder, E. W., Mayo-Wilson, E., McDonald, S., & Moher, D. (2021). The PRISMA 2020 statement: An updated guideline for reporting systematic reviews. *BMJ (Clinical Research Ed.)*, *372*(71), n71. Advance online publication. DOI: 10.1136/bmj.n71 PMID: 33782057

Sethi, S. S., & Jain, K. (2024). AI Technologies for Social Emotional Learning: Recent Research and Future Directions. *Journal of Research in Innovative Teaching & Learning*, *17*(2), 213–225. DOI: 10.1108/JRIT-03-2024-0073

Tassoti, S. (2024). Assessment of Students' Use of Generative Artificial Intelligence: Prompting Strategies and Prompt Engineering in Chemistry Education. *Journal of Chemical Education*, *101*(6), 2475–2482. DOI: 10.1021/acs.jchemed.4c00212

Watermeyer, R., Phipps, L., Lanclos, D., & Knight, C. (2024). Generative AI and the Automating of Academia. *Postdigital Science and Education*, *6*(2), 446–466. DOI: 10.1007/s42438-023-00440-6

Watermeyer, R., Phipps, L., Lanclos, D., & Knight, C. (2024). Generative AI and the Automating of Academia. *Postdigital Science and Education*, *6*(2), 446–466. DOI: 10.1007/s42438-023-00440-6

Zidoun, Y., & El Mardi, A. (2024). Artificial Intelligence (AI)-Based Simulators Versus Simulated Patients in Undergraduate Programs: A Protocol for a Randomized Controlled Trial. *BMC Medical Education*, *24*(1260), 1260. Advance online publication. DOI: 10.1186/s12909-024-06236-x PMID: 39501219

APPENDIX A: SYSTEMATIC LITERATURE REVIEW TABLE

Table 7.

Label	Authors	Methods Utilized	AI Applications	Samples Used	Future Agenda and Recommendations
A1	Griffin, G., Wennerström, E., & Foka, A. (2024)	Qualitative study – Semi-structured interviews with CHI professionals, analysis of CHI website data, and internal digitization protocols. Thematic analysis (TA) was used for coding.	AI/ML applications in cultural heritage institutions (CHIs), specifically for digitization, document classification, transcription (OCR, HTR), chatbots, and data extraction.	Three Swedish Cultural Heritage Institutions (CHIs), representing archives, museums, and libraries, with professionals responsible for AI implementation.	1. Develop a national AI/ML strategy for CHIs in Sweden. 2. Address staff training deficits to bridge the AI-heritage knowledge gap. 3. Encourage resource and personnel sharing among CHIs to improve AI adoption. 4. Improve AI/ML interoperability for cultural datasets to facilitate knowledge exchange. 5. Emphasize collaboration between technology developers and CHI professionals.
A2	Kwok, A. P. K., Wong, Y. H., Wong, K. C., & Chan, C. H. (2024)	Experimental study – Controlled experiment with two groups (AIMA-assisted vs. non-AIMA) in university lectures, followed by post-lecture surveys and statistical analysis (t-tests, chi-square tests).	AI Meeting Assistants (AIMAs), specifically Otter. ai, for real-time transcription, summarization, and note-taking in English-medium university lectures.	Two first-year English-medium university lecture classes at The Chinese University of Hong Kong (Class A: AI-assisted, Class B: traditional lectures). Average 17 students per session per class.	1. Need for better AI-instructor integration to prevent disruptions in communication and engagement. 2. Future studies should assess AIMAs across various disciplines to understand their long-term impact on learning outcomes. 3. Ethical concerns, student privacy, and AI bias in transcription should be explored. 4. Future research should investigate complementary AI learning strategies, such as AI-enhanced active learning approaches.
A3	Lopes, J. M., Silva, L. F., & Massano-Cardoso, I. (2024)	Quantitative study – Structural Equation Modeling (SEM) using survey data from online shoppers in Portugal.	AI-driven e-commerce personalization, including AI-powered product recommendations, chatbot-assisted customer service, and automated decision-making in online retail.	1,438 Portuguese consumers from various e-retail platforms, surveyed on AI-enabled purchase decisions.	1. Expand research beyond Portugal to understand AI's effect on e-commerce behavior in diverse cultural contexts. 2. Investigate AI ethics and transparency in online retail. 3. Study the longitudinal impact of AI-enabled shopping experiences on consumer trust and engagement. 4. Explore hybrid AI-human retail strategies to optimize consumer satisfaction.
A4	Al-Dokhny, A., Alismaiel, O., Youssif, S., Nasr, N., Drwish, A., & Samir, A. (2024)	Quantitative study – Structural Equation Modeling (SEM) using SmartPLS 3.0, based on survey data from Saudi university students.	Multimodal Large Language Models (MLLMs) used for personalized learning, text comprehension, real-time feedback, and academic assistance.	550 university students from six Saudi universities, across multiple disciplines.	1. Investigate long-term effects of MLLMs on student performance in different academic disciplines. 2. Assess ethical concerns in AI adoption, including AI bias and student privacy. 3. Explore integration strategies for AI in university education. 4. Conduct comparative studies on the effectiveness of different AI models in learning.

continued on following page

Table 7. Continued

Label	Authors	Methods Utilized	AI Applications	Samples Used	Future Agenda and Recommendations
A5	Sethi, S. S., & Jain, K. (2024)	Systematic Literature Review (SLR) – PRISMA approach and bibliometric analysis of AI applications in Social Emotional Learning (SEL).	AI-powered Social Emotional Learning (SEL) technologies, including Virtual Reality (VR), Chatbots, Sentiment Analysis, Gamification, and Wearable Devices.	40 empirical studies were analyzed, covering various educational institutions and AI-based SEL implementations.	1. Address ethical concerns related to AI in SEL, including privacy and algorithmic bias. 2. Promote interdisciplinary collaborations among educators, psychologists, and AI developers. 3. Conduct longitudinal studies to measure the long-term impact of AI-driven SEL programs. 4. Develop culturally sensitive AI models to ensure inclusivity in SEL applications. 5. Strengthen AI-driven SEL ecosystems to support emotional well-being and engagement in learning environments.
A6	Ayanwale, M. A., Molefi, R. R., & Oyeniran, S. (2024)	Bibliometric Analysis – Performance analysis (PA) and science mapping (SM) techniques applied to a dataset from Web of Science (WoS).	Machine Learning (ML) applications in education, including AI-powered personalized learning, learning analytics, predictive modeling, and intelligent tutoring systems.	449 documents from 145 sources (1986–2022), retrieved from Web of Science, covering global research on ML in education.	1. Enhance cross-disciplinary collaborations to improve ML applications in education. 2. Conduct longitudinal studies on ML's long-term effects on student engagement and performance. 3. Address ethical issues in AI-driven learning analytics, including data privacy concerns. 4. Strengthen international partnerships for ML integration in diverse educational contexts. 5. Develop standardized AI frameworks for effective ML adoption in educational institutions.
A7	Jia, X., & Hou, Y. (2024)	Quantitative study – Structural Equation Modeling (SEM) with survey-based data analysis.	AI-Driven Sustainable Human Resource Management (HRM), focusing on AI-powered talent analytics, automated HR decision-making, and AI-based performance evaluations.	470 employees from Chinese enterprises, spanning HR departments and leadership teams.	1. Investigate long-term AI-HRM effects on employee engagement and productivity. 2. Explore the ethical considerations of AI-driven HRM systems. 3. Study the role of AI-based sustainability strategies in HRM. 4. Analyze cross-cultural variations in AI-HRM adoption. 5. Propose hybrid AI-human HRM strategies to optimize workforce performance.
A8	Zidoun, Y., & El Mardi, A. (2024)	Randomized Controlled Trial (RCT) – Comparison of AI-based simulators vs. traditional simulated patients for training medical students.	AI-Based Healthcare Simulators – AI-powered virtual patient systems, automated clinical training, real-time feedback mechanisms, and AI-driven history-taking simulations.	67 fifth-year medical students from Dubai Medical College for Girls, randomized into AI-simulator and simulated patient groups.	1. Investigate the long-term impact of AI-based simulators on clinical skills development. 2. Explore hybrid training models combining AI simulations with traditional patient interactions. 3. Assess the ethical implications of replacing human simulated patients with AI. 4. Expand research to different medical specialties to validate AI-driven training effectiveness. 5. Improve AI-based feedback mechanisms for more personalized and adaptive medical education.

continued on following page

Table 7. Continued

Label	Authors	Methods Utilized	AI Applications	Samples Used	Future Agenda and Recommendations
A9	Baskota, P., & Poudel, T. (2024)	Mixed-Methods Study – Undergraduate class observation, text analysis, and experimental research evaluating AI and computer-mediated communication (CMC) in language learning.	AI-powered chatbots, Natural Language Processing (NLP), and Virtual Writing Assistants for improving English proficiency in undergrad classrooms.	28 undergraduate students from three different degree programs (BBA, BCA, and BIT) in Kathmandu Valley, Nepal.	1. Expand AI-driven CMC tools to include speech recognition and real-time translation. 2. Investigate ethical concerns, such as AI bias and data privacy in education. 3. Conduct longitudinal studies to measure the impact of AI and CMC on English learning. 4. Strengthen AI-based personalized learning models for diverse student populations. 5. Improve teacher training on AI-integrated learning platforms.
A10	Gruchoła, M., Sławek-Czochra, M., & Zieliński, R. (2024)	Quantitative Study – Nationwide survey using Computer-Assisted Web Interview (CAWI) technique.	AI-based religious applications supporting Christian prayer practices, including AI-driven prayer generators, religious chatbots, and spiritual guidance systems.	1053 individuals (aged 15–65) across Poland, sampled based on religious engagement and AI use.	1. Explore AI's role in religious education and interfaith dialogue. 2. Investigate ethical concerns regarding AI-mediated religious experiences. 3. Study generational differences in AI acceptance for spiritual practices. 4. Examine cultural barriers affecting AI adoption in faith-based activities. 5. Evaluate AI's impact on religious engagement and prayer consistency.
A11	Haque, A., Akther, N., Khan, I., Agarwal, K., & Uddin, N. (2024)	Bibliometric Analysis & Content Analysis – Co-citation, co-occurrence, and bibliographic coupling using VOSviewer and Bibliometrix.	AI in Retail Marketing – Includes AI-driven consumer behavior analytics, AI-powered personalized marketing strategies, AI-based supply chain management, and AI-enabled trust mechanisms in retail.	404 research articles (2000–2023) from Scopus and Web of Science databases.	1. Expand AI research in retail sustainability, particularly in "Green AI" strategies. 2. Investigate AI's impact on small and medium enterprises (SMEs) in retail. 3. Explore ethical concerns around data privacy and algorithmic bias in AI marketing. 4. Assess AI integration in omnichannel retailing to optimize both online and offline consumer experiences. 5. Develop standardized AI adoption frameworks for global retail businesses.
A12	Forja-Pena, T., García-Orosa, B., & López-García, X. (2024)	Content Analysis & Delphi Method – Analyzed 45 European ethical codes and conducted expert panel discussions.	AI in Digital Journalism, focusing on AI-generated news content, automated journalism, disinformation detection, and ethical concerns.	45 national ethical codes from various European countries + Delphi method with 16 expert panelists (journalists & academics).	1. Strengthen ethical AI guidelines in journalism to tackle disinformation. 2. Promote regulatory policies for AI integration in media. 3. Encourage journalist training in AI-powered newsrooms. 4. Investigate public perception of AI-generated news. 5. Expand cross-national studies on AI journalism ethics.

continued on following page

Table 7. Continued

Label	Authors	Methods Utilized	AI Applications	Samples Used	Future Agenda and Recommendations
A13	Jasmy, A. J., Ismail, H., & Aljneibi, N. (2024)	Experimental Study – User study with a paired-sample t-test to assess the impact of an AI-driven mobile application on sustainable behavior.	AI-driven Carbon Footprint (CFP) Assessment and Real-Time Analytics – AI-powered mobile application for tracking CO2 emissions, personalized sustainability recommendations, and gamification for behavioral change.	10 users tested the application for 30 days, tracking their carbon footprint and receiving AI-generated sustainability recommendations.	1. Investigate the long-term behavioral impact of AI-driven CFP tracking applications. 2. Expand research on scalability across diverse user groups and cultures. 3. Study the integration of AI-powered sustainability apps with global environmental policies. 4. Assess the role of gamification and social influence mechanisms in enhancing user engagement. 5. Explore real-time AI-driven interventions to promote sustainable decision-making.
A14	Jasmy, A. J., Ismail, H., & Aljneibi, N. (2024)	Experimental Study – Paired-sample t-test conducted on users of an AI-driven sustainability application over 30 days.	AI-driven Carbon Footprint (CFP) Monitoring and Sustainability Analytics – Includes real-time GPS tracking, augmented reality-based object detection, AI-powered chatbot for eco-awareness, and AI-generated sustainability recommendations.	10 users who tracked their carbon footprint for 30 days using the AI-driven sustainability mobile application.	1. Expand research on AI-driven behavioral change in sustainability efforts. 2. Assess the scalability of AI-driven sustainability applications across diverse demographic groups. 3. Investigate AI's role in integrating sustainability into national policies and corporate strategies. 4. Develop gamification-based AI interventions to enhance engagement in sustainability applications. 5. Address potential privacy and security concerns regarding AI-based sustainability tracking.
A15	Harrington, J. (2024)	Mixed Methods Pilot Study – Survey analysis, QR code tracking, and engagement metrics from e-learning sessions.	AI-driven interactive e-learning tool (MedMicroMaps) – Utilizes AI-powered interactive mind maps, augmented reality-based spatial memory tools, and virtual microbiology learning modules for medical students.	865 second-year medical students at St. George's University, Grenada.	1. Expand AI-driven interactive learning across medical curricula. 2. Investigate the long-term impact of AI-based e-learning tools on medical education. 3. Develop cross-platform AI-enhanced study tools, integrating VR/AR and AI-driven decision trees. 4. Assess AI-assisted personalized learning pathways for diverse medical student populations. 5. Enhance AI-driven interactive modules for broader healthcare disciplines, including nursing and pharmacy education.
A16	Hall, R. (2024)	Theoretical Analysis – Philosophical discussion on AI's impact on pedagogy, society, and ethics through dialectical storytelling.	Generative AI in Higher Education – Discusses AI's role in reshaping intellectual work, storytelling, and social relationships in academia.	Conceptual study, not based on empirical data.	1. Investigate how AI influences social justice and equity in education. 2. Explore Indigenous protocols for AI integration in learning systems. 3. Assess AI's role in higher education governance and institutional structures. 4. Examine the contradictions between capitalist AI development and alternative knowledge systems. 5. Develop AI frameworks based on human-centered and ethical storytelling.

continued on following page

Table 7. Continued

Label	Authors	Methods Utilized	AI Applications	Samples Used	Future Agenda and Recommendations
A17	Watermeyer, R., Phipps, L., Lanclos, D., & Knight, C. (2024)	Survey-Based Quantitative Study – National online survey of UK academics (N = 284), analyzing AI use in higher education through descriptive statistics and thematic analysis.	Generative AI (GAI) in Academia – Examines how large language models (LLMs) like ChatGPT are reshaping academic work, research, and scholarly labor.	284 UK academics from various universities, focusing on their AI adoption, perceptions, and ethical concerns.	1. Investigate AI's role in reducing academic workload without increasing performance pressures. 2. Explore the ethical concerns of AI-generated scholarly work, including transparency in authorship. 3. Assess AI's impact on academic hierarchies and power structures. 4. Study the role of AI in balancing productivity and intellectual engagement in higher education. 5. Develop guidelines for AI adoption in academic publishing to maintain integrity and quality.
A18	Marchena Sekli, G. F., Godo, A., & Véliz, J. C. (2024)	Systematic Literature Review (SLR) – PRISMA approach with thematic analysis covering 2022-2024 literature.	Generative AI in Higher Education – Applications include AI-generated teaching materials, academic performance evaluation, AI-driven student support, virtual assistants, and AI in research facilitation.	44 peer-reviewed studies on Generative AI in education, sourced from Web of Science.	1. Investigate the long-term educational impact of Generative AI in universities. 2. Explore AI's role in faculty workload reduction and administrative support. 3. Assess student and faculty perceptions of AI-driven education tools. 4. Study biases and limitations of AI-generated academic content. 5. Develop frameworks for ethical AI adoption in academia.
A19	Fleischmann, K. (2024)	Survey-Based Quantitative Study – Analyzed student perspectives on AI in graphic design education.	Generative AI in Graphic Design – AI-powered tools for creative workflows, design automation, prompt engineering, and AI-based design iteration.	17 undergraduate graphic design students at Griffith University, Australia.	1. Investigate how AI impacts creative autonomy in design students. 2. Assess AI's role in curriculum transformation for design education. 3. Explore ethical concerns like copyright infringement and bias in AI-generated designs. 4. Conduct longitudinal studies on AI's effectiveness in improving design education. 5. Develop AI literacy programs for design students to balance human creativity with AI tools.

continued on following page

Table 7. Continued

Label	Authors	Methods Utilized	AI Applications	Samples Used	Future Agenda and Recommendations
A20	Murray-Rust, D., Lupetti, M. L., Nicenboim, I., & van der Hoog, W. (2024)	Experiential Design Study – Implemented nine AI-driven exercises in an interaction design course with a thematic analysis of student feedback.	AI in Design Education – AI-driven interactive learning exercises to enhance students' ability to design AI-integrated products and services, focusing on interactional, relational, and societal aspects of AI.	100 first-year master's students in interaction design at TU Delft, Netherlands, divided into 28 teams and supervised by seven faculty members.	1. Expand research on AI-driven design education methodologies. 2. Investigate how AI influences design thinking and problem-solving strategies. 3. Develop a standardized AI literacy curriculum for design students. 4. Explore the long-term impact of AI integration in creative fields. 5. Assess student perceptions of AI's role in design ethics and social responsibility.
A21	Tassoti, S. (2024)	Survey-Based Experimental Study – Investigated student prompting strategies and effectiveness of AI-generated chemistry solutions.	Generative AI in Chemistry Education – Use of ChatGPT for problem-solving and prompt engineering techniques such as the "Five S Model."	23 preservice chemistry teachers at the University of Graz, Austria, analyzed through prompt logs and Likert-scale assessments.	1. Investigate the long-term impact of AI-driven chemistry tutoring. 2. Develop best practices for prompt engineering in STEM education. 3. Assess AI's accuracy and hallucination issues in chemistry-related responses. 4. Expand research on student AI literacy and critical evaluation of AI-generated answers. 5. Develop frameworks for integrating generative AI in science curricula.

Chapter 10
Adoption Factors of AI Tools in the Recruitment Process Using UTAUT Model

Radhika Thapar
Rukmini Devi Institute of Advanced Studies, Guru Gobind Singh Indraprastha University, India

Sehej Bhatia
Rukmini Devi Institute of Advanced Studies, Guru Gobind Singh Indraprastha University, India

A. V. Senthil Kumar
https://orcid.org/0000-0002-8587-7017
Hindusthan College of Arts and Science, India

ABSTRACT

This study examines the adoption of Artificial Intelligence (AI) tools in talent acquisition and their impact on recruitment efficiency within the organizational context. Using the Unified Theory of Acceptance and Use of Technology (UTAUT) model, the research identifies key factors—Performance Expectancy, Effort Expectancy, Social Influence, Facilitating Conditions, and Perceived Risk—that influence Behavioral Intent to adopt AI tools. Insights gained highlight the importance of perceived utility, ease of use, and organizational support in driving AI adoption, while addressing potential barriers such as perceived risks and social influence.

DOI: 10.4018/979-8-3373-5550-4.ch010

INTRODUCTION

Artificial Intelligence (AI) is reshaping industries globally, including the field of human resources (HR), where it is redefining recruitment processes. In today's competitive business environment, organizations increasingly rely on AI tools to enhance efficiency, improve decision-making, and deliver better outcomes in talent acquisition. This study examines the adoption factors influencing the use of AI tools in recruitment processes, employing the Unified Theory of Acceptance and Use of Technology (UTAUT) model as its theoretical framework.AI, a concept that emerged in the mid-20th century (McCarthy et al., 1955) and (Turing, 1950), has evolved into a critical enabler of innovation across industries (Russell and Norvig, 2021). Its applications in recruitment, such as resume screening, candidate matching, and predictive analytics, are transforming traditional hiring practices (Bersin, 2019). These technologies promise to reduce bias, improve efficiency, and enable data-driven decision-making in hiring. However, their adoption is influenced by various organizational, technological, and individual factors, presenting both opportunities and challenges.

This research aims to identify the key factors affecting the adoption of AI tools in recruitment processes. Using the UTAUT model, it explores constructs such as Performance Expectancy, Effort Expectancy, Social Influence, and Facilitating Conditions. Data collected from HR professionals, recruiters, and industry experts forms the basis of this study. Secondary data sources, including reports from NASSCOM, SHRM, and Deloitte, further contextualize the findings. The focus on AI in recruitment is driven by its potential to address critical challenges in talent acquisition, such as improving efficiency in sourcing candidates, enhancing diversity, and enabling better talent predictions. By analysing these factors within a real-world context, specifically through a case study on ABC Consultants, this research seeks to contribute to the understanding of AI adoption in recruitment. Ultimately, the study offers recommendations for organizations, HR practitioners, and policymakers to optimize the use of AI tools in recruitment. It aims to bridge the gap between technological innovation and practical implementation, ensuring that AI enhances recruitment processes while addressing potential challenges in adoption.

THEORETICAL BACKGROUND

Building effective talent acquisition strategies requires a solid understanding of the factors influencing candidate selection and employee retention. This section delves into two prominent theories that provide valuable insights into these aspects: Human Capital Theory and Social Network Theory. Both theories offer a complementary perspective on the talent acquisition process, allowing us to analyse the value of individual skills and the importance of social connections in attracting top talent.

Human Capital Theory

Human capital theory posits that individuals invest in their skills and knowledge to increase their future earning potential. This theory is directly relevant to talent acquisition, as organizations seek to attract and retain individuals with the necessary skills and competencies to contribute to their success. By understanding the value of human capital, organizations can make informed decisions about their recruitment and development strategies.

Social Network Theory

Social network theory focuses on the relationships and connections between individuals within a social system. In the context of talent acquisition, social networks play a crucial role in the dissemination of information and the identification of potential candidates. By understanding the structure and dynamics of social networks, organizations can leverage these relationships to source top talent and build effective recruitment strategies.

These two theories provide a strong conceptual framework for understanding the process of talent acquisition. Human capital theory emphasizes the importance of investing in individuals' skills and knowledge, while social network theory highlights the role of relationships and connections in identifying and attracting talent. By applying these theories to the study of talent acquisition, we can gain a deeper understanding of the factors that influence organizational success.

VARIABLE IDENTIFICATION AND EXPLANATION

Table 1. Variable identification and explanation

Variable	Source	Statements
Performance Expectancy	Al-Debei, Al-Madi, & Al-Tamimi, 2021	1. Belief that technology will improve job efficiency. 2. Perception that technology will enhance task quality. 3. Expectation that technology will lead to innovation.
Effort Expectancy	(Al-Debei, Al-Madi, and Al-Tamimi, 2021)	1. Belief that technology is easy to learn and use. 2. Perception that technology is intuitive and user-friendly. 3. Expectation that technology will not require significant effort.
Social Influence	(Al-Debei, Al-Madi, and Al-Tamimi, 2021)	1. Belief that colleagues and peers support technology adoption. 2. Perception that social norms encourage technology use. 3. Expectation that influential individuals endorse technology.
Facilitating Conditions	(Al-Debei, Al-Madi, and Al-Tamimi, 2021)	1. Belief that necessary resources and infrastructure are available. 2. Perception that technical support is adequate. 3. Expectation that organizational culture supports technology adoption.
Perceived Risk	(Venkatesh, Morris, Davis and Davis, 2003)	1. Concern about the potential negative consequences of using technology. 2. Worry about data privacy and security breaches. 3. Fear of job loss or reduced autonomy due to technology.
Behavioral Intent	(Al-Debei, Al-Madi, and Al-Tamimi, 2021)	1. Intention to use technology regularly. 2. Planning to integrate technology into workflows. 3. Commitment to ongoing technology adoption.

Figure 1. Proposed model

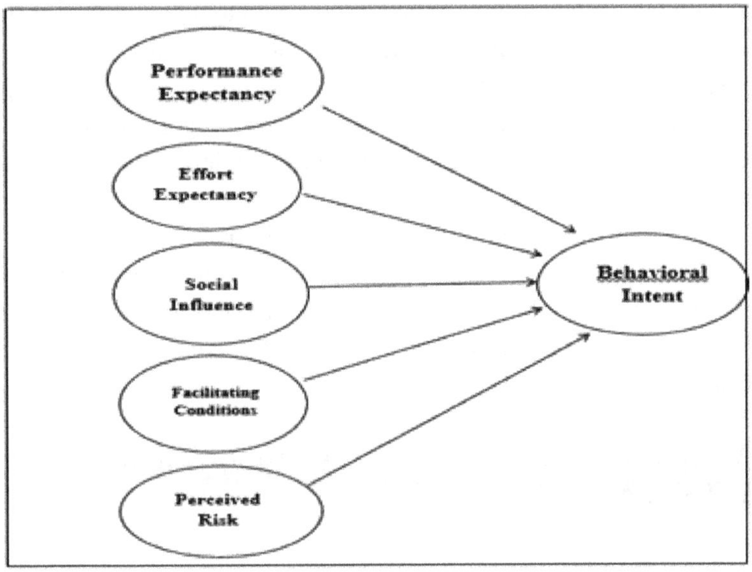

REVIEW OF LITERATURE

Table 2. Literature of the dimensions

Dimensions	Recent Literature using the dimensions
Performance Expectancy	Terblanche, N. and Kidd, M. (2022)
Effort Expectancy	Terblanche, N. and Kidd, M. (2022)
Social Influence	Terblanche, N. and Kidd, M. (2022)
Facilitating Conditions	Terblanche, N. and Kidd, M. (2022)
Perceived Risk	Terblanche, N. and Kidd, M. (2022)
Behavioral Intent	Terblanche, N. and Kidd, M. (2022)

The literature review spans from 2016 to 2023, encompassing a wide range of studies that delve into the strategic implications of talent acquisition and its impact on organizational performance. Key themes explored in the literature include the role of talent mapping in identifying high-potential employees, the relationship between talent acquisition practices and organizational success, the influence of artificial intelligence on recruitment processes, and the challenges and opportunities associated with talent acquisition in the gig economy and globalized world.

To conduct this comprehensive literature review, several academic databases were utilized, including Google Scholar. The following keywords were employed to identify relevant studies: talent acquisition, talent mapping, talent research, human capital, organizational performance, recruitment strategies, talent management, and talent analytics. To ensure the inclusion of only pertinent studies, the criteria that was applied was Publication date in which the studies published between 2018 and 2023 were considered to focus on recent advancements in the field. Research focus on those Studies that directly addressed the mapping and research of talent acquisitions were included. For Methodology both quantitative and qualitative research methodologies were considered.

Talent Mapping: A Strategic Tool for Organizational Success (Singh and Kumar, 2023)

This study explores the concept of talent mapping as a strategic tool for identifying and developing high-potential employees within organizations. The authors emphasize the importance of aligning talent mapping initiatives with organizational goals.

Talent Acquisition and Organizational Performance: A Meta-Analytic Review (Choi and Kim, 2023)

This study conducted a meta-analysis of existing research to examine the relationship between talent acquisition practices and organizational performance. The findings suggest that effective talent acquisition strategies can significantly contribute to organizational success.

Talent Research and Organizational Agility: A Case Study Analysis, (Chen and Li, 2022)

This case study examines how organizations can utilize talent research to enhance their agility and adaptability in a rapidly changing business environment. The findings highlight the importance of data-driven insights for informed decision-making.

The Role of Artificial Intelligence in Talent Acquisition: A Systematic Review, (Patel and Sharma, 2022)

This systematic review explores the growing role of artificial intelligence (AI) in talent acquisition processes. The authors discuss the potential benefits of AI-powered tools, such as improved efficiency and candidate matching.

Talent Acquisition Strategies in the Gig Economy: A Comparative Analysis, (Lee and Kim, 2021)

This study compares talent acquisition strategies in traditional organizations and the gig economy. The authors identify key differences in recruitment, onboarding, and retention practices.

Talent Acquisition and Employee Engagement: A Longitudinal Study, (Wang and Liu, 2021)

This longitudinal study examines the relationship between effective talent acquisition practices and employee engagement. The findings suggest that organizations that prioritize attracting and retaining top talent are more likely to have engaged workforces.

Talent Mapping and Succession Planning: A Strategic Fit, (Gupta and Sharma, 2020)

This study explores the connection between talent mapping and succession planning. The authors argue that effective talent mapping can help organizations identify and develop potential successors for critical roles.

The Impact of Social Media on Talent Acquisition: A Qualitative Study, (Kim and Lee, 2020)

This qualitative study investigates the role of social media in talent acquisition. The findings highlight the importance of leveraging social media platforms to attract top talent and build employer brand.

Talent Analytics: A New Frontier in Human Resource Management, (Chen and Liu, 2019)

This study introduces the concept of talent analytics and its potential applications in talent acquisition. The authors discuss how data-driven insights can inform recruitment strategies and decision-making.

The Future of Talent Acquisition: Trends and Predictions, (Johnson and Peters, 2019)

This study explores emerging trends in talent acquisition, such as the increasing use of AI, automation, and predictive analytics. The authors offer insights into the future of the field.

Talent Acquisition in a Globalized World: Challenges and Opportunities (Lee and Park, 2018)

This study examines the challenges and opportunities associated with talent acquisition in a globalized context. The authors discuss factors such as cultural differences, immigration policies, and remote work arrangements.

The Role of Talent Acquisition in Organizational Innovation, (Chen and Li, 2018)

This study investigates the relationship between effective talent acquisition practices and organizational innovation. The findings suggest that organizations that attract and retain top talent are more likely to foster a culture of innovation.

Talent Acquisition and Diversity and Inclusion: A Strategic Imperative, (Smith and Brown, 2017)

This study explores the importance of diversity and inclusion in talent acquisition. The authors argue that organizations that prioritize diversity can benefit from increased innovation, creativity, and employee engagement.

Talent Acquisition and Employer Branding: A Conceptual Framework, (Patel and Sharma, 2017)

This study develops a conceptual framework to understand the relationship between talent acquisition and employer branding. The authors highlight the importance of building a strong employer brand to attract top talent.

The Impact of Talent Acquisition on Organizational Productivity, (Choi and Kim, 2016)

This study examines the relationship between effective talent acquisition practices and organizational productivity. The findings suggest that organizations that invest in attracting and retaining top talent can improve their overall productivity.

RESEARCH GAPS

The existing literature on talent acquisition provides insights into various aspects of the field, including the role of technology, organizational culture, and diversity and inclusion. However, several research gaps remain to be addressed. One significant gap lies in the exploration of the long-term impact of talent acquisition strategies on organizational performance. While existing studies have examined the short-term effects, more research is needed to understand the long-term consequences of effective or ineffective talent acquisition practices. Additionally, the literature on the intersection of talent acquisition and organizational agility is relatively limited. Further research is required to explore how talent acquisition strategies can support organizations in adapting to rapid changes in the business environment.

Furthermore, while the role of AI in talent acquisition has been extensively studied, there is a need for more research on the ethical implications of AI-driven recruitment practices. Additionally, further investigation into the long-term impact of AI on candidate experience and organizational culture is warranted.

RESEARCH OBJECTIVES

This research aims to explore the-

1. To apply Systematic Approach of identifying and evaluating the Best talent for an organization.
2. Adoption factors of AI tools in the Recruitment Process using UTAUT Model

Table 3. Research types

Research Type	Exploratory Study
Approach Type	Quantitative Research
Population	Corporate Recruiters in Delhi NCR
Sample Size	Total 200 out of which 185 (15 were biased)
Data Collection Tool	Questionnaire with Likert Scale
Sampling Technique	Judgmental Sampling Technique
Research Instrument	PLS-4
Source of Data	Primary Data
Scale Adopted From	Nicky Terblanche1 and Martin Kidd2

RESEARCH DESIGN

Technique - Exploratory

This study employs an exploratory research design to delve into the emerging field of AI-driven talent acquisition. It seeks to understand the factors influencing the adoption of AI tools, their effectiveness in identifying and evaluating top talent, and the potential challenges and benefits associated with their use. Quantitative Research will be explored as a questionnaire-based approach will be employed to collect data from the recruiters. This quantitative method will allow for the systematic gathering and analysis of numerical data, enabling researchers to identify trends, patterns, and relationships between variables.

POPULATION DEFINITION

Target Population

Corporate Recruiters in Delhi NCR.

Demographics of the Target Population

Age: Primarily young people typically categorized as 23-35 years old. This age group, often considered highly adaptable to new technologies and is likely to have a positive perception of AI tools in the recruitment process.

Education: Possess bachelor's degrees or higher qualifications relevant to their HR fields.

Employment Type: Employed full-time or part-time in corporate organizations.

SAMPLING DETAILS

Units- Individual

Size- The questionnaire was circulated amongst 200 people. However, the valid responses were gathered from 185 respondents who have filed authentically.

Techniques- Judgmental Sampling

Judgmental Sampling, also known as purposive sampling, is a non-probability sampling technique where the researcher selects participants based on their knowledge and judgment. This method is often used when the researcher believes that specific individuals will provide the most valuable insights for the study.

SURVEY INSTRUMENT

The survey instrument is **Primary Data.** This survey aims to understand the impact of AI-driven recruitment practices on talent acquisition effectiveness and organizational culture. By participating in this **close-ended questionnaire**, young professionals can provide valuable insights into their current concerns regarding the adoption factors of AI tools in the Recruitment Process. **Google Form** was used as the Questionnaire tool.

DATA ANALYSIS TOOLS & TECHNIQUES

Data Analysis Tools: PLS-4

Techniques- Discriminant Validity (Fornell-Larcker Criterion), Construct Reliability and Validity, Outer Loadings Matrix and Path Coefficients (Fornell & Larcker, 1981)

Below is the brief about the Tools and Techniques: -

PLS-4 (Partial Least Squares Structural Equation Modeling) is a powerful statistical method that has been particularly effective in analysing complex relationships between variables. This model is to assess the relationships between the proposed constructs (Performance Expectancy, Effort Expectancy, Social Influence, Facilitating Conditions, Perceived Risk, and Behavioral Intent) and their impact on AI adoption.

To ensure the validity and reliability of the measurement model, we have applied the Fornell-Larcker Criterion for discriminant validity, which helps to establish that each construct is distinct from the others. Additionally, we have assessed construct reliability and validity using techniques such as Cronbach's alpha and item analysis. Finally, the outer loadings matrix provides insights into the relationships between individual items and their respective constructs.

In the structural model, path coefficients were calculated to quantify the strength and direction of the relationships between the constructs. These coefficients help to identify the most significant factors influencing AI adoption in the recruitment process. By using thesetechniques, we have been able to provide a comprehensive and rigorous analysis of the data collected for our research.

DATA ANALYSIS

Table 4. Empirical data analysis

Questions	Agreement Scale				
	Strongly Agree	Agree	Neutral	Disagree	Strongly Disagree
	1	2	3	4	5
Performance Expectancy (PE)					
(PE1) AI tools will enhance your ability to assess candidate fit for specific roles?	48	56	37	24	20
(PE2) AI-powered tools can improve your ability to predict candidate success in the company.	54	46	47	38	-
(PE3) Using AI tools in the recruitment process will significantly improve my ability to identify the most qualified candidates.	63	45	40	37	-
(PE4) I believe AI can provide valuable insights into candidate potential that traditional methods may overlook.	57	62	36	24	6
Effort Expectancy (EE)					
(EE1) Using AI tools in the Job Application process is easy.	59	55	48	20	3
(EE2) I find AI tools to be user-friendly and easy to navigate.	65	53	38	29	-

continued on following page

Table 4. Continued

Questions	Agreement Scale				
	Strongly Agree	Agree	Neutral	Disagree	Strongly Disagree
	1	2	3	4	5
(EE3) Integrating AI into my existing recruitment workflows will not require significant effort or time.	71	51	43	20	-
(EE4) I believe AI tools can streamline the recruitment process and reduce the time spent on manual tasks.	53	68	40	-	24
Social Influence (SI)					
(SI1) Many of my peers and colleagues are already using AI tools in their recruitment processes.	29	36	29	44	47
(SI2) I feel pressure to adopt AI tools in order to stay competitive in the job market.	47	25	23	58	32
(SI3) The increasing adoption of AI in the recruitment industry suggests that it is becoming a standard practice.	39	47	19	44	36
(SI4) I believe that adopting AI tools in recruitment will enhance my professional reputation.	38	28	35	54	30
Facilitating Conditions (FC)					
(FC1) Using AI tools in the recruitment process will help you identify the most suitable candidates more efficiently?	72	60	38	15	-
(FC2) AI tools can provide valuable insights to help you tailor the recruitment process to individual candidate needs?	49	55	53	24	4
(FC3) My organization provides adequate training and support for using AI tools in recruitment.	37	59	51	22	16
(FC4) My organization's culture is supportive of the adoption of new technologies like AI.	55	49	46	16	19
Perceived Risk (PR)					
(PR1) I have encountered any difficulties or challenges when using AI tools.	58	34	30	29	34
(PR2) I am concerned about the potential for bias or discrimination in AI-driven recruitment processes.	62	56	27	21	19

continued on following page

Table 4. Continued

Questions	Agreement Scale				
	Strongly Agree	Agree	Neutral	Disagree	Strongly Disagree
	1	2	3	4	5
(PR3) I worry that AI tools may not be able to accurately assess certain skills or qualities that are important for the roles I recruit for.	59	61	41	15	9
(PR4) I am hesitant to rely solely on AI for candidate selection without human judgment.	48	56	25	38	18
Behavioral Intent (BI)					
(BI1) I intend to use the AI Tool in my future recruitment process.	48	54	47	29	7
(BI2) I would recommend AI tools to other recruiters in my network.	59	42	46	33	5
(BI3) I am highly motivated to explore and implement AI tools in my future recruitment strategies.	64	47	48	26	-
(BI4) I believe that AI tools will significantly improve the efficiency and effectiveness of my recruitment efforts.	57	46	34	39	9

Demographic Details

The Likert scale data is converted into numbers for data analysis. The sample size was taken 200 out of which 185 responses were valid.

Table 5. Demographic details

Demographics	Number
Gender	
Male	76
Female	109

FINAL DATA ANALYSIS

To assess the impact of various factors on the adoption of AI tools in recruitment, a structural equation model (SEM) based on the UTAUT model was employed. The model evaluates the influence of Performance Expectancy, Effort Expectancy, Social Influence, Facilitating Conditions, and Perceived Risk on Behavioral Intent to adopt AI tools.

1. Measurement Model: Discriminant Validity (Fornell-Larcker Criterion)

Table 6. Discriminant validity (Fornell-Larcker Criterion)

	BI	EE	FC	PE	PR	SI
BI	**0.908**					
EE	0.902	**0.884**				
FC	0.902	0.892	**0.906**			
PE	0.922	0.923	0.929	**0.91**		
PR	0.9	0.907	0.892	0.928	**0.901**	
SI	0.893	0.889	0.903	0.927	0.907	**0.904**

Interpretation

The Fornell-Larcker Criterion, assesses the discriminant validity of the constructs in the model. It ensures that each construct measures a unique concept and is not highly correlated with other constructs. In this analysis, the diagonal values (e.g., 0.908 for Behavioral Intent (BI)) represent the square root of the average variance extracted (AVE) for each construct. The off-diagonal values represent the correlations between constructs. The discriminant validity is satisfied if the square root of the AVE for each construct is greater than its correlation with any other construct.

Based on the table, the discriminant validity is generally met for all constructs. The square root of the AVE for each construct is higher than its correlation with other constructs, indicating that the constructs are distinct and measure different concepts. This is crucial for the reliability and validity of the structural equation model.

2. Construct Reliability and Validity

Table 7. Construct reliability and validity

	Cronbach's alpha	Composite reliability (rho_a)	Composite reliability (rho_c)	Average variance extracted (AVE)
BI	0.929	0.93	0.949	0.824
EE	0.907	0.907	0.935	0.782
FC	0.927	0.928	0.948	0.821
PE	0.93	0.932	0.95	0.828
PR	0.923	0.923	0.945	0.812
SI	0.925	0.925	0.947	0.817

Interpretation

This shows the results of a reliability and validity analysis for the constructs in the model.

Reliability: The Cronbach's Alpha values (ranging from 0.907 to 0.93) indicate high internal consistency reliability for all constructs. This means that the items within each construct measure the same underlying concept consistently.
Validity: The composite reliability (rho_a) and average variance extracted (AVE) values are also high for all constructs, suggesting good convergent validity. This means that the items within each construct measure the same underlying concept, and the construct is distinct from other constructs.

Overall, these results suggest that the measurement model is reliable and valid, providing strong support for the use of these constructs in further analysis.

1. Outer Loadings Matrix

Table 8. Outer loadings matrix

	BI	EE	FC	PE	PR	SI
(BI1)	0.901					
(BI2)	0.919					
(BI3)	0.922					
(BI4)	0.889					
(EE1)		0.891				
(EE2)		0.894				
(EE3)		0.865				
(EE4)		0.887				
(FC1)			0.901			
(FC2)			0.917			
(FC3)			0.905			
(FC4)			0.902			
(PE1)				0.929		
(PE2)				0.906		
(PE3)				0.884		
(PE4)				0.92		
(PR1)					0.909	
(PR2)					0.905	
(PR3)					0.894	
(PR4)					0.895	
(SI1)						0.905
(SI2)						0.908
(SI3)						0.886
(SI4)						0.916

Interpretation

The Outer Loadings Matrix provides information about the relationship between individual items and their respective constructs in the UTAUT model. Each cell in the matrix represents the standardized regression weight or factor loading of an item on its corresponding construct. Higher values indicate a stronger relationship between the item and the construct.

Likewise, the value 0.901 in the first row and first column indicates that the first item (B11) of the Behavioral Intent (BI) construct has a strong positive relationship with the overall BI construct. This suggests that these items are good measures of the underlying construct. However, some items have slightly lower loadings, which might indicate potential issues with their measurement or the overall model fit, for example EE3 (Effort Expectancy).

Overall, the outer loadings matrix indicates that the measurement model has good convergent validity, as most of the items have strong loadings on their respective constructs. However, items with low loadings may require further attention to improve the measurement model.

4. Structural Model

Figure 2. Structural model

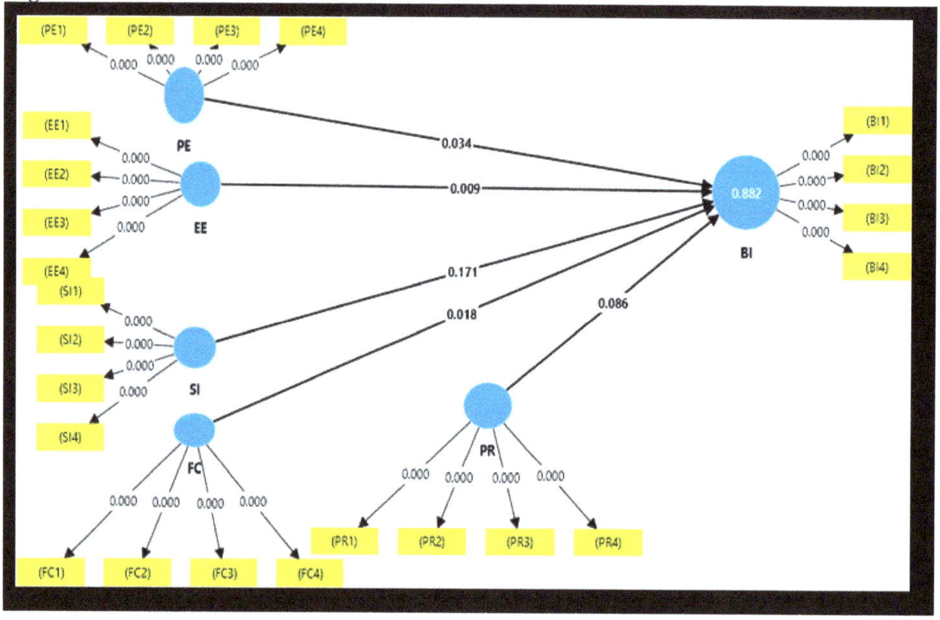

Interpretation

The Structural model depicts the hypothesized relationships between the constructs in the UTAUT model. The path coefficients represent the strength and direction of these relationships.

The significant path coefficients indicate that **Performance Expectancy (PE)**, **Effort Expectancy (EE)**, and **Facilitating Conditions (FC)** positively impact **Behavioral Intent (BI)**.

- **Performance Expectancy (PE):** As individuals perceive greater benefits and usefulness of AI tools, they are more likely to adopt them.
- **Effort Expectancy (EE):** Individuals who perceive AI tools as easy to use and learn are more likely to adopt them.
- **Facilitating Conditions (FC):** The availability of resources, technical support, and an organizational culture that supports technology adoption can significantly influence the adoption of AI tools. This means that as these factors increase, the intention to adopt AI tools in the recruitment process also increases.

While **Social Influence (SI)** and **Perceived Risk (PR)** play significant roles in AI tool adoption, but they have a negative impact. Social norms and peer influence positively influence adoption (SI), while perceived risks associated with AI tools negatively impact adoption (PR).

The model indicates that Performance Expectancy (PE) has the strongest positive impact on Behavioral Intent (BI), followed by Effort Expectancy (EE) and Facilitating Conditions (FC). Overall, the structural model provides valuable insights into the factors that influence the adoption of AI tools in talent acquisition. By understanding these relationships, organizations can develop strategies to promote the adoption of AI tools and maximize their benefits.

Path Coefficients

Table 9. Path coefficients

	Original sample (O)	Sample mean (M)	Standard deviation (STDEV)	T statistics (|O/STDEV|)	P values	Status
EE -> BI	0.213	0.21	0.081	2.621	0.009	**Accepted**
FC -> BI	0.205	0.203	0.086	2.375	0.018	**Accepted**
PE -> BI	0.286	0.291	0.135	2.124	0.034	**Accepted**
PR -> BI	0.159	0.164	0.093	1.716	0.086	Rejected
SI -> BI	0.109	0.105	0.08	1.368	0.171	Rejected

Interpretation

This presents the path coefficients, their significance levels, and the status of the hypotheses, p-values for the relationships between the independent variables (PE, EE, SI, FC, PR) and the dependent variable (BI) in the UTAUT model.

The results indicate that Performance Expectancy (PE), Effort Expectancy (EE), and Facilitating Conditions (FC) have a significant positive impact on Behavioral Intent (BI) and are statistically significant at the 5% level ($p < 0.05$). This indicates that as individuals perceive greater benefits and ease of use of AI tools, and as organizational support for AI adoption increases, their intention to use AI tools in recruitment also increases.

On the other hand, Perceived Risk (PR) and Social Influence (SI) did not have a significant impact on Behavioral Intent (BI) with p-values greater than 0.05. This suggests that while perceived risks and social norms may play a role, their impact on AI adoption is less pronounced in this context.

Overall, the results highlight the importance of factors such as ease of use, supportive organizational environment, and perceived benefits in promoting the adoption of AI tools in talent acquisition.

FINDINGS

The research findings provide valuable insights into the factors influencing the adoption of AI tools in talent acquisition. The results indicate that performance expectancy, effort expectancy, and facilitating conditions are significant predictors of Behavioral intent to adopt AI tools. These findings highlight the importance of organizations in creating a supportive environment, providing adequate training, and demonstrating the practical benefits of AI tools to encourage their adoption. While perceived risk and social influence were not found to be significant predictors in this study, it is important to acknowledge their potential role in shaping individual attitudes towards AI.

RECOMMENDATIONS

The increasing adoption of AI in talent acquisition has significant societal implications. To ensure the ethical and equitable use of AI, policymakers, industry leaders, and academic institutions should collaborate to develop guidelines and standards for AI development and deployment. It is crucial to address potential biases and discrimination that may arise from AI-powered decision-making. Additionally, efforts should be made to educate and train individuals on the responsible use of AI, promoting digital literacy and ethical awareness. By fostering a society that embraces AI while mitigating its potential risks, we can harness the power of technology to create a more inclusive and equitable future.

LIMITATIONS

While this study provides valuable insights into the factors influencing AI adoption in talent acquisition, it is important to acknowledge certain limitations. The study was conducted in a specific geographical context, and the findings may not be fully generalizable to other regions or industries. Future research could explore the longitudinal impact of AI adoption on organizational performance and employee satisfaction. Additionally, the study relied on self-reported data, which may be subject to social desirability bias. Future research could address these limitations by expanding the sample size, incorporating multiple data sources, and employing longitudinal research designs.

CONCLUSION OF THE STUDY

This study delved into the factors influencing the adoption of AI tools in talent acquisition. By employing the UTAUT model, the research identified key determinants such as Performance Expectancy, Effort Expectancy, Facilitating Conditions, Perceived Risk, and Social Influence. The findings provide valuable insights for organizations to effectively implement AI-driven recruitment strategies and optimize their talent acquisition processes.

REFERENCES

Al-Debei, M. M., Al-Madi, S. M., & Al-Tamimi, A. A. (2021). Factors influencing the adoption of mobile learning technologies: A UTAUT model extension. *International Journal of Information Management*, *60*, 102317.

Bersin, J. (2019, August 15). HR technology 2020: Disruption ahead. *Josh Bersin*. https://joshbersin.com/2019/08/hr-technology-2020-disruption-ahead/

Chen, C., & Liu, X. (2019). Talent analytics: A new frontier in human resource management. *Human Resource Studies*, *33*(2), 102–116.

Chen, Y., & Li, H. (2018). The role of talent acquisition in organizational innovation. *The Innovation Journal*, *12*(3), 245–261.

Chen, Y., & Li, H. (2022). Talent research and organizational agility: A case study analysis. *Journal of Organizational Studies*, *28*(4), 389–405.

Choi, S., & Kim, D. (2016). The impact of talent acquisition on organizational productivity. *Journal of Organizational Performance*, *21*(1), 53–69.

Choi, S., & Kim, D. (2023). Talent acquisition and organizational performance: A meta-analytic review. *International Journal of Human Resource Management*, *37*(1), 47–61.

Fornell, C., & Larcker, D. F. (1981). Evaluating structural equation models with unobservable variables and measurement error. *JMR, Journal of Marketing Research*, *18*(1), 39–50. DOI: 10.1177/002224378101800104

Gupta, A., & Sharma, S. (2020). Talent mapping and succession planning: A strategic fit. *Human Resource Planning Journal*, *18*(3), 220–237.

Johnson, D., & Peters, M. (2019). The future of talent acquisition: Trends and predictions. *HR Journal*, *25*(1), 5–20.

Kim, J., & Lee, S. (2020). The impact of social media on talent acquisition: A qualitative study. *Journal of HR Practices*, *12*(4), 291–307.

Lee, J., & Kim, H. (2021). Talent acquisition strategies in the gig economy: A comparative analysis. *Journal of Employment Studies*, *29*(2), 180–196.

Lee, K., & Park, J. (2018). Talent acquisition in a globalized world: Challenges and opportunities. *Global Human Resources*, *15*(2), 112–126.

McCarthy, J., Minsky, M. L., Rochester, N., & Shannon, C. E. (1955). A proposal for the Dartmouth summer research project on artificial intelligence. *AI Magazine*, *27*(4), 12–14. DOI: 10.1609/aimag.v27i4.1904

Patel, A., & Sharma, P. (2017). Talent acquisition and employer branding: A conceptual framework. *Employer Branding Journal*, *9*(2), 75–89.

Patel, A., & Sharma, P. (2022). The role of artificial intelligence in talent acquisition: A systematic review. *HR Technology Journal*, *14*(3), 221–238.

Russell, S. J., & Norvig, P. (2021). *Artificial intelligence: A modern approach* (4th ed.). Pearson.

Singh, R., & Kumar, A. (2023). Talent mapping: A strategic tool for organizational success. *Human Resource Development Quarterly*, *31*(2), 130–147.

Smith, J., & Brown, K. (2017). Talent acquisition and diversity and inclusion: A strategic imperative. *Diversity and Inclusion Journal*, *10*(3), 65–78.

Terblanche, N., & Kidd, M. (2022). Adoption factors and moderating effects of age and gender that influence the intention to use a non-directive reflective coaching chatbot. *SAGE Open*, *12*(2), 21582440221096136. DOI: 10.1177/21582440221096136

Terblanche, N., & Kidd, M. (2022). Factors influencing the adoption of artificial intelligence in human capital management: A UTAUT model. *SA Journal of Human Resource Management*, *20*(1), 1–16.

Turing, A. M. (1950). Computing machinery and intelligence. *Mind*, *59*(236), 433–460. DOI: 10.1093/mind/LIX.236.433

Venkatesh, V., Morris, M. G., Davis, G. B., & Davis, F. D. (2003). User acceptance of information technology: Toward a unified view. *Management Science*, *49*(8), 1007–1025.

Wang, L., & Liu, Y. (2021). Talent acquisition and employee engagement: A longitudinal study. *Journal of Employee Engagement*, *24*(2), 98–112.

Compilation of References

Abuhassna, H. (2024). *From Theory to Practice: The Impact of E-Learning on Student Performance, Trends, and Educational Horizons*. Qeios.

Abuhassna, H., Adnan, M. A. B. M., & Awae, F. (2024). Exploring the synergy between instructional design models and learning theories: A systematic literature review. *Contemporary Educational Technology*, *16*(2), ep499. DOI: 10.30935/cedtech/14289

Abuhassna, H., & Alnawajha, S. (2023a). Instructional Design Made Easy! Instructional Design Models, Categories, Frameworks, Educational Context, and Recommendations for Future Work. *European Journal of Investigation in Health, Psychology and Education*, *13*(4), 715–735. DOI: 10.3390/ejihpe13040054 PMID: 37185907

Abuhassna, H., & Alnawajha, S. (2023b). The Transactional Distance Theory and Distance Learning Contexts: Theory Integration, Research Gaps, and Future Agenda. *Education Sciences*, *13*(2), 112. DOI: 10.3390/educsci13020112

Abuhassna, H., Alnawajha, S., Awae, F., Adnan, M. A. B. M., & Edwards, B. I. (2024). Synthesizing technology integration within the Addie model for instructional design: A comprehensive systematic literature review. *Journal of Autonomous Intelligence*, *7*(5), 1546. DOI: 10.32629/jai.v7i5.1546

Abuhassna, H., Awae, F., Adnan, M. A., Daud, M., & Almheiri, A. S. (2024). The Information Age for Education via Artificial Intelligence and Machine Learning: A Bibliometric and Systematic Literature Analysis. *International Journal of Information and Education Technology (IJIET)*, *14*(5), 700–711. DOI: 10.18178/ijiet.2024.14.5.2095

Abuhassna, H., Awae, F., Bayoumi, K., Al Zitawi, D. U., Alsharif, A. H., & Yahaya, N. (2022b). Understanding Online Learning Readiness among University Students: A Bibliometric Analysis. [iJIM]. *International Journal of Interactive Mobile Technologies, 16*(13), 81–94. DOI: 10.3991/ijim.v16i13.30605

Abuhassna, H., Van, N. T., Yahaya, N., Zakaria, M. A. Z. M., Awae, F., Al Zitawi, D. U. D., & Bayoumi, K. (2022a). Strategies for Successful Blended Learning—A Bibliometric Analysis and Reviews. [iJIM]. *International Journal of Interactive Mobile Technologies, 16*(13), 66–80. DOI: 10.3991/ijim.v16i13.30739

Abuhassna, H., Yahaya, N., Zakaria, M., Zaid, N. M., Samah, N. A., Awae, F., Nee, C. K., & Alsharif, A. H. (2023). Trends on using the technology acceptance model (TAM) for online learning: A bibliometric and content analysis. *International Journal of Information and Education Technology (IJIET), 13*(1), 131–142. DOI: 10.18178/ijiet.2023.13.1.1788

Adams, C., Pente, P., Lemermeyer, G., & Rockwell, G. (2023). Ethical principles for artificial intelligence in K-12 education. *Computers and Education: Artificial Intelligence, 4*, 100131. DOI: 10.1016/j.caeai.2023.100131

Adebayo, A. A. (2024). Artificial Intelligence and Lecturers' Effectiveness in Ogun State Owned Universities. *FUOYE International Journal of Business and Economics Education, 1*(1), 188–198.

Ahmad, W., Raj, R., & Shokeen, R. (2025). Reshaping Special Education: Strategic Use of Artificial Intelligence. In *Transforming Special Education Through Artificial Intelligence* (pp. 1-44). IGI Global.

Ahmed, H. (2024). Institutional Integration of Artificial Intelligence in Higher Education: The Moderation Effect of Ethical Consideration. *International Journal of Educational Reform*, •••, 10567879241247551. DOI: 10.1177/10567879241247551

Airaj, M. (2024). Ethical artificial intelligence for teaching-learning in higher education. *Education and Information Technologies, 29*(13), 17145–17167. DOI: 10.1007/s10639-024-12545-x

Aithal, P. S., & Aithal, S. (2023). Predictive analysis on future impact of ubiquitous education technology in higher education and research. [IJAEML]. *International Journal of Applied Engineering and Management Letters, 7*(3), 88–108. DOI: 10.47992/IJAEML.2581.7000.0190

Ajayi, B., & Ifedayo, A. E. (2025). Ethical and Cognitive Impacts of Machine Learning in Education: A Stakeholder-Centric Analysis. *Sanskriti: Journal of Humanities, 2*(1), 1-10. Retrieved from, http://sanskritijournal.com/index.php/ssj/article/view/14

Akgun, S., & Greenhow, C. (2022). Artificial intelligence in education: Addressing ethical challenges in K-12 settings. *AI and Ethics, 2*(3), 431–440. DOI: 10.1007/s43681-021-00096-7 PMID: 34790956

Akinwalere, S. N., & Ivanov, V. (2022). Artificial Intelligence in Higher Education: Challenges and Opportunities. *International Journal of Current Advanced Research, 11*(2), 145–162. https://journalijcar.org/issues/artificial-intelligence-higher-education-challenges-and-opportunities

Akyuz, Y. (2020). Effects of intelligent tutoring systems (ITS) on personalized learning (PL). *Creative Education, 11*(06), 953–978. DOI: 10.4236/ce.2020.116069

AlAfnan, M. A. (2024). Integrating AI into learning taxonomies: Ethical challenges and constructivist approaches. *Journal of Educational Technology, 19*(1), 45–78.

Alam, A. (2023). Harnessing the Power of AI to Create Intelligent Tutoring Systems for Enhanced Classroom Experience and Improved Learning Outcomes. In *Intelligent Communication Technologies and Virtual Mobile Networks* (pp. 571–591). Springer. DOI: 10.1007/978-981-99-1767-9_42

Alawneh, Y. J. J., Radwan, E. N. Z., Salman, F. N., Makhlouf, S. I., Makhamreh, K., & Alawneh, M. S. (2024, April). Ethical considerations in the use of AI in primary education: Privacy, bias, and inclusivity. In *2024 International Conference on Knowledge Engineering and Communication Systems (ICKECS)* (Vol. 1, pp. 1-6). IEEE. DOI: 10.1109/ICKECS61492.2024.10616986

Al-Azawei, A., Serenelli, F., & Lundqvist, K. (2016a). Extending the technology acceptance model to assess the impact of assistive technology on students with disabilities. *Computers & Education, 95*, 58–67.

Al-Azawei, A., Serenelli, F., & Lundqvist, K. (2016b). Universal Design for Learning (UDL*): A content analysis of peer-reviewed journal papers from 2012 to 2015.The Journal of Scholarship of Teaching and Learning, 16*(3), 39–56. DOI: 10.14434/josotl.v16i3.19295

Albdrani, R. N., & Al-Shargabi, A. A. (2023). Investigating the Effectiveness of ChatGPT for Providing Personalized Learning Experience: A Case Study. *International Journal of Advanced Computer Science and Applications, 14*(11). Advance online publication. DOI: 10.14569/IJACSA.2023.01411122

Al-Debei, M. M., Al-Madi, S. M., & Al-Tamimi, A. A. (2021). Factors influencing the adoption of mobile learning technologies: A UTAUT model extension. *International Journal of Information Management, 60*, 102317.

AldemÌr, C., & Uçma Uysal, T. (2024). AI competencies for internal auditors in the public sector. EDPACS, 69(1), 3-21. https://doi.org/DOI: 10.1080/07366981.2024.2312001

Al-Dokhny, A., Alismaiel, O., Youssif, S., Nasr, N., Drwish, A., & Samir, A. (2024). Can Multimodal Large Language Models Enhance Performance Benefits Among Higher Education Students? An Investigation Based on the Task–Technology Fit Theory and the Artificial Intelligence Device Use Acceptance Model. *Sustainability (Basel)*, *16*(10780), 10780. Advance online publication. DOI: 10.3390/su162310780

Alfarra, A. H., Amhan, L. F., Mosa, M. J., Alajrami, M. A., El Kahlout, F., Abu-Nasser, B. S., & Abu-Naser, S. S. (2024). AI-Driven Learning: Advances and Challenges in Intelligent Tutoring Systems.

AL-Ghamdi, A. S., Ragab, M., & Sabir, M. F. S. (2022). Enhanced artificial intelligence-based cybersecurity intrusion detection for higher education institutions. *Computers, Materials & Continua*, *72*(2).

Alghamdi, A., & Ragab, M. (2022). Artificial intelligence Techniques based learner authentication in cybersecurity higher education institutions. *Computers, Materials & Continua*, *72*(2), 3131–3144. DOI: 10.32604/cmc.2022.026457

Alhazmi, S., Khan, S., & Syed, M. H. (2023). Learning-Related Sentiment Detection, Classification, and Application for a Quality Education Using Artificial Intelligence Techniques. *Intelligent Automation & Soft Computing*, *36*(3), 3487–3499. DOI: 10.32604/iasc.2023.036297

Ali, G., Mijwil, M. M., Buruga, B. A., Abotaleb, M., & Adamopoulos, I. (2024). A survey on artificial intelligence in cybersecurity for smart agriculture: State-of-the-art, cyber threats, artificial intelligence applications, and ethical concerns. *Mesopotamian Journal of Computer Science*, *2024*, 53–103. DOI: 10.58496/MJCSC/2024/007

Alisoy, H., & Sadiqzade, Z. (2024). Mobile-Assisted Language Learning (MALL): Revolutionizing Language Education. *Luminis Applied Science and Engineering*, *1*(1), 60–72. DOI: 10.69760/lumin.202400002

AlJadaan, O. T., Zaidi, H., Al Faress, M. Y., & Jabas, A. O. (2025). Ethics in AI and Computation in Automated Decision-Making. In *Enhancing Automated Decision-Making Through AI* (pp. 397–424). IGI Global Scientific Publishing.

Aljohani, N. R., Aslam, M. A., Khadidos, A. O., & Hassan, S. U. (2022). A Methodological Framework to Predict Future Market Needs for Sustainable Skills Management Using AI and Big Data Technologies [Article]. *Applied Sciences (Basel, Switzerland)*, *12*(14), 6898. Advance online publication. DOI: 10.3390/app12146898

Allen, B., McGough, A. S., & Devlin, M. (2021). Toward a framework for teaching artificial intelligence to a higher education audience. [TOCE]. *ACM Transactions on Computing Education*, *22*(2), 1–29. DOI: 10.1145/3485062

Allen, L. K., & Kendeou, P. (2024). ED-AI Lit: An Interdisciplinary framework for AI literacy in education. *Policy Insights from the Behavioral and Brain Sciences*, *11*(1), 3–10. DOI: 10.1177/23727322231220339

Almaqtari, F. A. (2024). The Role of IT Governance in the Integration of AI in Accounting and Auditing Operations. *Economies*, *12*(8), 199. DOI: 10.3390/economies12080199

Almaqtari, F. A., Farhan, N. H., Al-Hattami, H. M., Elsheikh, T., & Al-dalaien, B. O. A. (2024). The impact of artificial intelligence on information audit usage: Evidence from developing countries. *Journal of Open Innovation*, *10*(2), 100298. DOI: 10.1016/j.joitmc.2024.100298

Alqahtani, N. D., Alzahrani, B., & Ramzan, M. S. (2023). Detection of Dyslexia Through Images of Handwriting using Hybrid AI Approach. *International Journal of Advanced Computer Science and Applications*, *14*(10). Advance online publication. DOI: 10.14569/IJACSA.2023.0141099

Alqahtani, T., Badreldin, H. A., Alrashed, M., Alshaya, A. I., Alghamdi, S. S., bin Saleh, K., Alowais, S. A., Alshaya, O. A., Rahman, I., Al Yami, M. S., & Albekairy, A. M. (2023). The emergent role of artificial intelligence, natural learning processing, and large language models in higher education and research. *Research in Social & Administrative Pharmacy*, *19*(8), 1236–1242. DOI: 10.1016/j.sapharm.2023.05.016 PMID: 37321925

Alshahrani, S., & Qureshi, H. (2024). AI in immersive learning: Opportunities and ethical considerations. *Virtual Reality & Learning Journal*, *14*(2), 67–89.

Amina, F. (2024). Exploring EFL Students 'Perceptions on the use of Grammarly as an AI Writing Tool to Enhance Academic Writing Proficiency The Case Study of Master Two English Students at Mohammed Kheider University.

Anica-Popa, I., Vrîncianu, M., Anica-Popa, L., Cismasu, I., & Tudor, C. (2024). Framework for Integrating Generative AI in Developing Competencies for Accounting and Audit Professionals. *Electronics (Basel)*, *13*(13), 2621. Advance online publication. DOI: 10.3390/electronics13132621

Aslan, L. (2021). *The Evolving Competencies of the Public Auditor and the Future of Public Sector Auditing*. Contemporary Issues in Public Sector Accounting and Auditing., DOI: 10.1108/S1569-375920200000105008

Attah, J. O., Ogunlade, O. O., &Otemuyiwa, B. I. (2024). Effect of Gamification-Based Teaching on Junior Secondary School Student's Academic Performance in Mathematics in Kwara State. *Andragogi: Jurnal Pendidikan dan Pembelajaran, 4*(2), 153-165.

Ayanwale, M. A., Molefi, R. R., & Oyeniran, S. (2024). Analyzing the Evolution of Machine Learning Integration in Educational Research: A Bibliometric Perspective. *Discover Education, 3*(47), 1–20. DOI: 10.1007/s44217-024-00119-5

Babu, I., MathuSoothana, R., & Kumar, S. (2023). Evolutionary Algorithm Based Feature Subset Selection for Students Academic Performance Analysis. *Intelligent Automation & Soft Computing, 36*(3), 3621–3636. DOI: 10.32604/iasc.2023.033791

Baek, C., & Doleck, T. (2020). A bibliometric analysis of the papers published in the journal of artificial intelligence in education from 2015-2019.

Bahassi, H., Azmi, M., & Khiat, A. (2024). Cognitive systems for education: Architectures, innovations, and comparative analyses. *Procedia Computer Science, 238*, 436–443. DOI: 10.1016/j.procs.2024.06.045

Bahroun, Z., Anane, C., Ahmed, V., & Zacca, A. (2023). Transforming education: A comprehensive review of generative artificial intelligence in educational settings through bibliometric and content analysis. *Sustainability (Basel), 15*(17), 12983. DOI: 10.3390/su151712983

Baker, T., & Smith, L. (2022). Educ-AI-tion rebooted? Exploring the future of artificial intelligence in schools and colleges. Retrieved from Nesta Foundation. http://media.nesta.org.uk

Balasubramaniam, N., Kauppinen, M., Rannisto, A., Hiekkanen, K., & Kujala, S. (2023). Transparency and explainability of AI systems: From ethical guidelines to requirements. *Information and Software Technology, 159*, 107197. DOI: 10.1016/j.infsof.2023.107197

Barbosa, R. (2023). Designing Fairness-Aware Machine Learning Algorithms: Techniques and Challenges. Academic Journal of Science and Technology, 6(1).

Barnes, E., Hutson, J., & Perry, K. (2024). Ethical Imperatives and Challenges: Review of the Use of Machine Learning for Predictive Analytics in Higher Education. *International Journal of Multidisciplinary and Current Educational Research, 6*(3).

Barrera Castro, M.. (2024). Addressing bias in AI-powered personalized learning systems: Ethical challenges. *Computers & Education, 204*, 104801.

Barua, P. D., Vicnesh, J., Gururajan, R., Oh, S. L., Palmer, E., Azizan, M. M., & Acharya, U. R. (2022). Artificial Intelligence Enabled Personalized Assistive Tools to Enhance Education of Children with Neuro developmental Disorders: A Review. *International Journal of Environmental Research and Public Health, 19*(3), 1–26. DOI: 10.3390/ijerph19031192 PMID: 35162220

Baskota, P., & Poudel, T. (2024). Artificial Intelligence and Computer-Mediated Communication: The Text Analysis and Undergrad's Class Observation. *Discover Education, 3*(131), 131. Advance online publication. DOI: 10.1007/s44217-024-00187-7

Beer, P., & Mulder, R. H. (2020). The effects of technological developments on work and their implications for continuous vocational education and training: A systematic review. *Frontiers in Psychology, 11*, 918. DOI: 10.3389/fpsyg.2020.00918 PMID: 32457688

Berkowitz, A. E. (2025). "Slow-MO or FOMO": AI conversations at library conferences. *Public Services Quarterly, 21*(1), 1–20. DOI: 10.1080/15228959.2024.2442657

Bersin, J. (2019, August 15). HR technology 2020: Disruption ahead. *Josh Bersin.* https://joshbersin.com/2019/08/hr-technology-2020-disruption-ahead/

Bhavani, G. (2020). Artificial Intelligence: Simulations in Audit Education. 2020 11th International Conference on Computing, Communication and Networking Technologies (ICCCNT), 1-5. https://doi.org/DOI: 10.1109/ICCCNT49239.2020.9225523

Bibi, P. (2024). Establishing Transparency and Accountability in AI: Ethical Standards for Data Governance and Automated Systems.

Birchwood, U. (2024). What are the Opportunities and Challenges for AI in Education? Retrieved from https://www.birchwoodu.org/what-are-the-opportunities-and-challenges-for-ai-in-education/

Blair Black, N.. (2024). *A framework for approaching AI education in educator preparation programs.* Association for the Advancement of Artificial Intelligence. DOI: 10.1609/aaai.v38i21.30351

Bouchetara, M., Zerouti, M., & Zouambi, A. R. (2024). Leveraging artificial intelligence (AI) in public sector financial risk management: Innovations, challenges, and future directions. *EDPACS, 69*(9), 124–144. DOI: 10.1080/07366981.2024.2377351

Bozkurt, A., & Sharma, R. C. (2023). Challenging the status quo and exploring the new boundaries in the age of algorithms: Reimagining the role of generative AI in distance education and online learning. *Asian Journal of Distance Education, 18*(1).

Briganti, G. (2025). Artificial intelligence: Blessing or curse? In *Truth Unveiled* (pp. 83–107). Academic Press. DOI: 10.1016/B978-0-443-23655-6.00005-8

Bucea-Manea- oniş, R., Martins, O. M., Bucea-Manea- oniş, R., Gheorghi ă, C., Kuleto, V., Ilić, M. P., & Simion, V. E. (2021). Blockchain technology enhances sustainable higher education. *Sustainability (Basel), 13*(22), 12347. DOI: 10.3390/su132212347

Bukar, U. A., Sayeed, M. S., Razak, S. F. A., Yogarayan, S., Amodu, O. A., & Mahmood, R. A. R. (2023). A method for analyzing text using VOSviewer. *MethodsX, 11*, 102339. DOI: 10.1016/j.mex.2023.102339 PMID: 37693657

Bulathwela, S., Pérez-Ortiz, M., Holloway, C., Cukurova, M., & Shawe-Taylor, J. (2024). Artificial intelligence alone will not democratise education: On educational inequality, techno-solutionism and inclusive tools. *Sustainability (Basel), 16*(2), 781. DOI: 10.3390/su16020781

Burr, C., & Leslie, D. (2023). Ethical assurance: A practical approach to the responsible design, development, and deployment of data-driven technologies. *AI and Ethics, 3*(1), 73–98. DOI: 10.1007/s43681-022-00178-0

Butson, R., & Spronken-Smith, R. (2024). AI and its implications for research in higher education: A critical dialogue. *Higher Education Research & Development, 43*(3), 563–577. DOI: 10.1080/07294360.2023.2280200

Cacho, L. (2024). Integrating AI into the educational policy landscape: Opportunities and challenges. *Education Policy Analysis Archives, 32*(5), 145–163.

Cai, W., Grossman, J., Lin, Z. J., Sheng, H., Wei, J. T.-Z., Williams, J. J., & Goel, S. (2021). Bandit algorithms to personalize educational chatbots. *Machine Learning, 110*(9), 2389–2418. DOI: 10.1007/s10994-021-05983-y

Cappelli, M. A., & Di Marzo Serugendo, G. (2024). A semi-automated software model to support AI ethics compliance assessment of an AI system guided by ethical principles of AI. *AI and Ethics*, •••, 1–24.

Carayannis, E. G., Askounis, D., Andoutropoulou, M., & Zotas, N. (2024). Leveraging AI for Enhanced eGovernment: Optimizing the Use of Open Governmental Data. *Journal of the Knowledge Economy*, •••, 1–36. DOI: 10.1007/s13132-024-02317-w

Castro, R. (2019). Blended learning in higher education: Trends and capabilities. *Education and Information Technologies, 24*(4), 2523–2546. DOI: 10.1007/s10639-019-09886-3

Çela, E., Fonkam, M. M., Vajjhala, N. R., & Vedishchev, A. (2025). Artificial Intelligence in Education: Foundations, Trends, and Implications. In *Next-Generation AI Methodologies in Education* (pp. 1-20). IGI Global Scientific Publishing.

Chan, C. K. (2023). A Comprehensive AI Policy Education Framework for University Teaching and Learning. arXiv preprint arXiv:2305.00280. Retrieved from https://arxiv.org/abs/2305.00280

Chankoson, T., Chen, F., Wang, Z., Wang, M., & Sukpasjaroen, K. (2022). Knowledge mapping for the study of Artificial Intelligence in Education Research: Literature reviews. *Journal of Intelligence Studies in Business, 12*(3), 27–37. DOI: 10.37380/jisib.v12i3.896

Chari, S. G. (2024). Bridging Gaps, Building Futures: Tackling Socio-Economic Disparities Through Education and Technology. *London Journal of Research In Humanities and Social Sciences, 24*(16), 1–12.

Chatterjee, S., & Bhattacharjee, K. K. (2020). Adoption of artificial intelligence in higher education: A quantitative analysis using structural equation modelling. *Education and Information Technologies, 25*(5), 3443–3463. DOI: 10.1007/s10639-020-10159-7

Chen, C., & Liu, X. (2019). Talent analytics: A new frontier in human resource management. *Human Resource Studies, 33*(2), 102–116.

Chen, F. (2022). Human-AI cooperation in education: Human in loop and teaching as leadership. *Journal of Educational Technology and Innovation, 2*(1). Advance online publication. DOI: 10.61414/jeti.v2i1.34

Chen, L., Chen, P., & Lin, Z. (2020). Artificial intelligence in education: A review. *IEEE Access : Practical Innovations, Open Solutions, 8*, 75264–75278. DOI: 10.1109/ACCESS.2020.2988510

Chen, X., Zou, D., Xie, H., Cheng, G., & Liu, C. (2022). Two decades of artificial intelligence in education. *Journal of Educational Technology & Society, 25*(1), 28–47.

Chen, Y., & Li, H. (2018). The role of talent acquisition in organizational innovation. *The Innovation Journal, 12*(3), 245–261.

Chen, Y., & Li, H. (2022). Talent research and organizational agility: A case study analysis. *Journal of Organizational Studies, 28*(4), 389–405.

Chen, Z., Zhang, J., Jiang, X., Hu, Z., Han, X., Xu, M., Savitha, V., & Vivekananda, G. (2020). Education 4.0 using artificial intelligence for students performance analysis. *Inteligencia Artificial, 23*(66), 124–137.

Ching, T., Himmelstein, D. S., Beaulieu-Jones, B. K., Kalinin, A. A., Do, B. T., Way, G. P., Ferrero, E., Agapow, P.-M., Zietz, M., Hoffman, M. M., Xie, W., Rosen, G. L., Lengerich, B. J., Israeli, J., Lanchantin, J., Woloszynek, S., Carpenter, A. E., Shrikumar, A., Xu, J., & Greene, C. S. (2018). Opportunities and obstacles for deep learning in biology and medicine. *Journal of the Royal Society, Interface*, *15*(141), 20170387. DOI: 10.1098/rsif.2017.0387 PMID: 29618526

Chinta, S. V., Wang, Z., Yin, Z., Hoang, N., Gonzalez, M., Quy, T. L., & Zhang, W. (2024). FairAIED: Navigating fairness, bias, and ethics in educational AI applications. arXiv preprint arXiv:2407.18745.

Chiu, T. K., Moorhouse, B. L., Chai, C. S., & Ismailov, M. (2024). Teacher support and student motivation to learn with Artificial Intelligence (AI) based chatbot. *Interactive Learning Environments*, *32*(7), 3240–3256. DOI: 10.1080/10494820.2023.2172044

Choi, S., & Kim, D. (2016). The impact of talent acquisition on organizational productivity. *Journal of Organizational Performance*, *21*(1), 53–69.

Choi, S., & Kim, D. (2023). Talent acquisition and organizational performance: A meta-analytic review. *International Journal of Human Resource Management*, *37*(1), 47–61.

Cleopas, B. C. (2023). Advent of artificial intelligence: Prospect and Challenges in Nigeria education system. *Education Research,* 06 (06), 01-09. Retrieved from http://media.nesta.org.uk

Coelho, L., & Reis, S. (2025). Transforming Teaching and Learning With Natural Language Processing. In *Integrating Artificial Intelligence in Education: Enhancing Teaching Practices for Future Learning* (pp. 119-152). IGI Global.

Coşulean, L. (2024). Adaptive learning platforms as a means of individualised learning. In *Probleme de filologie: Aspecte teoretice şi practice Materialele Conferinţei ştiinţifice internaţionale, edi ia a Xa 8 decembrie 2023* (pp. 136-141). Biblioteca Ştiinţifică a Universităţii de Stat Alecu Russo.

Crisan, A., Drouhard, M., Vig, J., & Rajani, N. (2022, June). Interactive model cards: A human-centered approach to model documentation. In *Proceedings of the 2022 ACM Conference on Fairness, Accountability, and Transparency* (pp. 427-439). DOI: 10.1145/3531146.3533108

Crompton, H., & Burke, D. (2023). Artificial intelligence in higher education: The state of the field. *International Journal of Educational Technology in Higher Education*, *20*(1), 22. DOI: 10.1186/s41239-023-00392-8

Cui, P., & Alias, B. S. (2024). Opportunities and Challenges in Higher Education Arising from AI: A Systematic Literature Review (2020–2024). *Journal of Infrastructure Policy and Development*, *8*(11), 8390. DOI: 10.24294/jipd.v8i11.8390

Cukurova, M. (2025). The interplay of learning, analytics and artificial intelligence in education: A vision for hybrid intelligence. *British Journal of Educational Technology, 56*(2), 469-488. Retreived from, https://bera-journals.onlinelibrary.wiley.com/doi/abs/10.1111/bjet.13514

Dark, R. (2025). AI-Related Security Trends to Watch in 2025. Retrieved from https://www.darkreading.com/cyber-risk/6-ai-related-security-trends-watch-2025

Darshan, B. D., Sampathila, N., Bairy, G. M., Prabhu, S., Belurkar, S., Chadaga, K., & Nandish, S. (2025). Differential diagnosis of iron deficiency anemia from aplastic anemia using machine learning and explainable Artificial Intelligence utilizing blood attributes. *Scientific Reports*, *15*(1), 505. DOI: 10.1038/s41598-024-84120-w PMID: 39747241

De Gagne, J. C., Hwang, H., & Jung, D. (2024). Cyberethics in nursing education: Ethical implications of artificial intelligence. *Nursing Ethics*, *31*(6), 1021–1030. DOI: 10.1177/09697330231201901 PMID: 37803810

Dentons, (2025). AI trends for 2025: AI regulation, governance and ethics. Retrieved from https://www.dentons.com/en/insights/articles/2025/january/10/ai-trends-for-2025-ai-regulation-governance-and-ethics

Diaz, V. (2024). Exploring the Opportunities and Challenges with Generative AI. EDUCAUSE Review. Retrieved from https://er.educause.edu/articles/2024/2/exploring-the-opportunities-and-challenges-with-generative-ai

Dieterle, E., Dede, C., & Walker, M. (2024). The cyclical ethical effects of using artificial intelligence in education. *AI & Society*, *39*(2), 633–643. DOI: 10.1007/s00146-022-01497-w PMID: 36185064

Ding, A.-C. E., Shi, L., Yang, H., & Choi, I. (2024). Enhancing teacher AI literacy and integration through different types of cases in teacher professional development. *Computers and Education Open*, *6*, 100178. DOI: 10.1016/j.caeo.2024.100178

Dixit, S., Jain, V., Maurya, M., & Subramaniam, G. (Eds.). (2025). *Artificial Intelligence Enabled Businesses: How to Develop Strategies for Innovation*. John Wiley & Sons. DOI: 10.1002/9781394234028

Dunn, T. J., & Kennedy, M. (2019). Technology Enhanced Learning in higher education; motivations, engagement and academic achievement. *Computers & Education*, *137*, 104–113. DOI: 10.1016/j.compedu.2019.04.004

Dutta, S., Ranjan, S., Mishra, S., Sharma, V., Hewage, P., & Iwendi, C. (2024, February). Enhancing educational adaptability: A review and analysis of AI-driven adaptive learning platforms. In *2024 4th International Conference on Innovative Practices in Technology and Management (ICIPTM)* (pp. 1-5). IEEE. DOI: 10.1109/ICIPTM59628.2024.10563448

Eden, C. A., Chisom, O. N., & Adeniyi, I. S. (2024). Integrating AI in education: Opportunities, challenges, and ethical considerations. *Magna Scientia Advanced Research and Reviews, 10*(2), 006-013.

EdSurge. (2024). How AI Can Address Critical Challenges Facing Higher Education. Retrieved from https://www.edsurge.com/news/2024-03-29-how-ai-can-address-critical-challenges-facing-higher-education

Edwards, B. I., Olugbade, D., & Ojo, O. A. (2024). Facilitating Cognitive Load Management and Improved Learning Outcomes and Attitudes in Middle School Technology and Vocational Education Through AI Chatbot. *Journal of Technical Education and Training*, *16*(3), 114–131. DOI: 10.30880/jtet.2024.16.03.009

El-Hajj, M. (2025). Enhancing Communication Networks in the New Era with Artificial Intelligence: Techniques, Applications, and Future Directions. *Network (Bristol, England)*, *5*(1), 1. PMID: 39601783

Elhersh, A., & Alqawasmeh, F. (2024). Social media sentiment on ChatGPT in education: Ethical implications. *Journal of Social Media Research*, *16*(4), 78–98.

Ellwood, S., & García-Lacalle, J. (2016). Examining Audit Committees in the Corporate Governance of Public Bodies. *Public Management Review*, *18*(8), 1138–1162. DOI: 10.1080/14719037.2015.1088566

ElSayary, A. (2024). An investigation of teachers' perceptions of using ChatGPT as a supporting tool for teaching and learning in the digital era. *Journal of Computer Assisted Learning*, *40*(3), 931–945. DOI: 10.1111/jcal.12926

Fahd, K., & Miah, S. J. (2023). Designing and evaluating a big data analytics approach for predicting students' success factors. *Journal of Big Data*, *10*(1), 159. DOI: 10.1186/s40537-023-00835-z

Farooqi, S. A., Memon, A., Zamir, S., Malik, K., Batool, W., & Zahid, H. (2024). NAVIGATING AI IN THE REAL WORLD: TRANSFORMATIONS, REGULATIONS, AND CHALLENGES. *Policy Research Journal*, *2*(4), 1083–1099.

Fedele, A., Punzi, C., & Tramacere, S. (2024). The ALTAI checklist as a tool to assess ethical and legal implications for a trustworthy AI development in education. *Computer Law & Security Review*, *53*, 105986. DOI: 10.1016/j.clsr.2024.105986

Fierce, N. (2021). Artificial Intelligence in Higher Education: Benefits and Ethics. Retrieved from https://www.fierce-network.com/technology/artificial-intelligence-higher-education-benefits-and-ethics

Figueras, A.. (2024). Shared responsibilities in AI-enhanced educational tools: Ethical implications. *Learning, Media and Technology*, *49*(2), 34–56.

Fitriani, A., Rosidah, R., & Zafrullah, Z. (2023). Biblioshiny: Implementation of artificial intelligence in education (1976-2023). *Journal of Technology Global*, *1*(01), 11–25.

Fleischmann, K. (2024). Generative Artificial Intelligence in Graphic Design Education: A Student Perspective. *Canadian Journal of Learning and Technology*, *50*(1), 1–17. DOI: 10.21432/cjlt28618

Forja-Pena, T., García-Orosa, B., & López-García, X. (2024). A Shift Amid the Transition: Towards Smarter, More Resilient Digital Journalism in the Age of AI and Disinformation. *Social Sciences (Basel, Switzerland)*, *13*(403), 403. Advance online publication. DOI: 10.3390/socsci13080403

Fornell, C., & Larcker, D. F. (1981). Evaluating structural equation models with unobservable variables and measurement error. *JMR, Journal of Marketing Research*, *18*(1), 39–50. DOI: 10.1177/002224378101800104

Funa, A. A., & Gabay, R. A. E. (2025). Policy guidelines and recommendations on AI use in teaching and learning: A meta-synthesis study. *Social Sciences & Humanities Open*, *11*, 101221. DOI: 10.1016/j.ssaho.2024.101221

Garcia, F., & Hernandez, M. (2021). Ethical Challenges in AI-Based Educational Systems. *International Journal of Educational Technology in Higher Education*, *18*(1), 28. DOI: 10.1186/s41239-021-00269-7 PMID: 34778526

García-García, R., García-Caballero, C., Villarreal-Lara, R., & Mirón-Mérida, V. (2024). On-site inspection as a tool for developing auditing skills in engineering: Integrating continuous education contents into higher education programs. *Frontiers in Education*, *9*, 1416110. Advance online publication. DOI: 10.3389/feduc.2024.1416110

Ge, H., Bastani, H., & Bastani, O. (2023). Rethinking Fairness for Human-AI Collaboration. arXiv preprint arXiv:2310.03647.

Geant, C. (2024). AI, Data Privacy, and Ethics in Higher Education: Navigating the Future. Retrieved from https://connect.geant.org/2024/10/18/ai-data-privacy-and-ethics-in-higher-education-navigating-the-future

George, A. S. (2024). Technology Tension in Schools: Addressing the Complex Impacts of Digital Advances on Teaching, Learning, and Wellbeing. *Partners Universal Multidisciplinary Research Journal, 1*(3), 49–65.

Gerdes, A. (2022). A participatory data-centric approach to AI ethics by design. *Applied Artificial Intelligence, 36*(1), 2009222. DOI: 10.1080/08839514.2021.2009222

Gilbertson, D., & Herron, T. (2014). Including audit regulation in the accounting curriculum. *Research in Accounting Regulation, 26*(1), 118–131. DOI: 10.1016/j.racreg.2014.02.013

Gomaa, W. H., Nagib, A. E., Saeed, M. M., Algarni, A., & Nabil, E. (2023). Empowering short answer grading: Integrating transformer-based embeddings and BI-LSTM network. *Big Data and Cognitive Computing, 7*(3), 122. DOI: 10.3390/bdcc7030122

Gonsalves, C. (2024). Addressing student non-compliance in AI use declarations: Implications for academic integrity and assessment in higher education. *Assessment & Evaluation in Higher Education.*

Goodwin, (2025). US Privacy and AI Outlook for 2025: Less Feds, More States. Retrieved from https://www.goodwinlaw.com/en/insights/blogs/2025/01/us-privacy-and-ai-outlook-for-2025-less-feds-more-states

Gordon, D., Stavrakakis, I., Gibson, J. P., Tierney, B., Becevel, A., Curley, A., Collins, M., O'Mahony, W., & O'sullivan, D. (2022). Perspectives on computing ethics: A multi-stakeholder analysis. *Journal of Information. Communication and Ethics in Society, 20*(1), 72–90. DOI: 10.1108/JICES-12-2020-0127

Goswami, A., & Sharma, A. (2024). AI for bridging socio-economic inequities in Indian education space. *International Journal of Innovation and Scientific Research, XI*(IV), 890–935. DOI: 10.51244/IJRSI.2024.1104066

Grassini, S. (2023). Shaping the future of education: Exploring the potential and consequences of AI and ChatGPT in educational settings. *Education Sciences, 13*(7), 692. DOI: 10.3390/educsci13070692

Greenberg, T. (2025). Trends to Watch: 2025 U.S. Data Privacy & Cybersecurity. Retrieved from https://www.gtlaw-dataprivacydish.com/2025/01/5-trends-to-watch-2025-u-s-data-privacy-cybersecurity/

Greenstein, N., & Cho, S. W. (2025). Ethics & Equity in Data Science for Evaluators. *Artificial Intelligence and Evaluation. Emerging Technologies and Their Implications for Evaluation*, 56-77.

Griffin, G., Wennerström, E., & Foka, A. (2024). Artificial Intelligence in Cultural Heritage Institutions: Challenges and Opportunities. *Journal of Digital Heritage and AI Applications*, *12*(3), 112–130. DOI: 10.1000/jdhai.2024.003

Gruchoła, M., Sławek-Czochra, M., & Zieliński, R. (2024). Artificial Intelligence as a Tool Supporting Prayer Practices. *Religions*, *15*(271), 271. Advance online publication. DOI: 10.3390/rel15030271

Guaranty Partners Trainings. (n.d.). AI-powered internal auditing: Tools and techniques. https://guarantypartnerstrainings.com/course/ai-powered-internal-auditing-tools-and-techniques/

Guettala, A.. (2024). Ethical integration of generative AI in adaptive learning environments. *International Review of Research in Open and Distance Learning*, *25*(1), 45–61.

Gupta, A., & Sharma, S. (2020). Talent mapping and succession planning: A strategic fit. *Human Resource Planning Journal*, *18*(3), 220–237.

Gupta, P., Sreelatha, C., Latha, A., Raj, S., & Singh, A. (2024). Navigating The Future of Education: The Impact of Artificial Intelligence on Teacher-Student Dynamics. *Educational Administration: Theory and Practice*, *30*(4), 6006–6013.

Gursoy, S. (2025). The Role of Artificial Intelligence in the Digitalization Process: Trends, Challenges, and a Framework for Sustainable Integration.

Haddaway, N. R., Page, M. J., Pritchard, C. C., & McGuinness, L. A. (2022). PRISMA2020: An R package and Shiny app for producing PRISMA 2020-compliant flow diagrams, with interactivity for optimised digital transparency and Open Synthesis. *Campbell Systematic Reviews*, *18*(2), e1230. DOI: 10.1002/cl2.1230 PMID: 36911350

Hall, R. (2024). Generative AI and Re-weaving a Pedagogical Horizon of Social Possibility. *International Journal of Educational Technology in Higher Education*, *21*(12), 12. Advance online publication. DOI: 10.1186/s41239-024-00445-6

Hamid, H., Zulkifli, K., Naimat, F., Yaacob, N. L. C., & Ng, K. W. (2023). Exploratory study on student perception on the use of chat AI in process-driven problem-based learning. *Currents in Pharmacy Teaching & Learning*, *15*(12), 1017–1025. DOI: 10.1016/j.cptl.2023.10.001 PMID: 37923639

Han, B., Nawaz, S., Buchanan, G., & McKay, D. (2025). Students' Perceptions: Exploring the Interplay of Ethical and Pedagogical Impacts for Adopting AI in Higher Education. *International Journal of Artificial Intelligence in Education*, •••, 1–26. DOI: 10.1007/s40593-024-00456-4

Haque, A., Akther, N., Khan, I., Agarwal, K., & Uddin, N. (2024). Artificial Intelligence in Retail Marketing: Research Agenda Based on Bibliometric Reflection and Content Analysis (2000–2023). *Informatics (MDPI), 11*(74), 74. Advance online publication. DOI: 10.3390/informatics11040074

Harrington, J. (2024). A Mixed Methods Pilot Study to Evaluate User Engagement with MedMicroMaps: A Novel Interactive E-learning Tool for Medical Microbiology. *Medical Science Educator, 34*(753–757), 753–757. Advance online publication. DOI: 10.1007/s40670-024-02047-3 PMID: 39099852

Harte, M., Carey, B., Feng, Q. J., Alqarni, A., & Albuquerque, R. (2025). Transforming undergraduate dental education: The impact of artificial intelligence. *British Dental Journal, 238*(1), 57–60. DOI: 10.1038/s41415-024-7788-7 PMID: 39794587

Harto, B., LN, S. Y., Rukmana, A. Y., Komalasari, R., & Dwijayanti, A. (2022). Bibliometric analysis of transforming leadership education with artificial intelligence. In 1st Virtual Workshop on Writing Scientific Article for International Publication Indexed SCOPUS (pp. 385-390).

Hashmi, N., & Bal, A. S. (2024). Generative AI in higher education and beyond. *Business Horizons, 67*(5), 607–614.

Hassan, Z. Y. (2025). AI-Driven Horizons: Shaping the Future of Global Quality Assurance in Higher Education. *AI and Ethics, Academic Integrity and the Future of Quality Assurance in Higher Education*, 105.

Hellín, C. J., Calles-Esteban, F., Valledor, A., Gómez, J., Otón-Tortosa, S., & Tayebi, A. (2023). Enhancing student motivation and engagement through a gamified learning environment. *Sustainability (Basel), 15*(19), 14119. DOI: 10.3390/su151914119

He, Y., Qiu, J., Zhang, W., & Yuan, Z. (2024). Fortifying Ethical Boundaries in AI: Advanced Strategies for Enhancing Security in Large Language Models. Retrieved from https://arxiv.org/abs/2402.01725

Holmes, W.. (2021). The future of AI in education: Ethical frameworks for innovation. *British Journal of Educational Technology, 52*(4), 901–917.

Holmes, W., Bialik, M., & Fadel, C. (2021). *Artificial intelligence in education: Promises and implications for teaching and learning*. Center for Curriculum Redesign.

Holmes, W., Porayska-Pomsta, K., Holstein, K., Sutherland, E., Baker, T., Shum, S. B., Santos, O. C., Rodrigo, M. T., Cukurova, M., Bittencourt, I. I., & Koedinger, K. R. (2022). Ethics of AI in education: Towards a community-wide framework. *International Journal of Artificial Intelligence in Education, 32*(3), 1–23. DOI: 10.1007/s40593-021-00239-1

Hossain, M. E., & Islam, M. A. (2024). AI and the Future of Education: Philosophical Questions about the Role of Artificial Intelligence in the Classroom. *International Journal of Research and Innovation in Social Science, 8*(IIIS, 3s), 5541–5547. DOI: 10.47772/IJRISS.2024.803419S

Hridi, A. P., Sahay, R., Hosseinalipour, S., & Akram, B. (2024, May). Revolutionizing AI-Assisted Education with Federated Learning: A Pathway to Distributed, Privacy-Preserving, and Debiased Learning Ecosystems. In *Proceedings of the AAAI Symposium Series* (Vol. 3, No. 1, pp. 297-303). DOI: 10.1609/aaaiss.v3i1.31217

Huang, A. Y., Lu, O. H., & Yang, S. J. (2023). Effects of artificial Intelligence–Enabled personalized recommendations on learners' learning engagement, motivation, and outcomes in a flipped classroom. *Computers & Education, 194*, 104684. DOI: 10.1016/j.compedu.2022.104684

Huang, L. (2023). Ethics of artificial intelligence in education: Student privacy and data protection. *Science Insights Education Frontiers, 16*(2), 2577–2587. DOI: 10.15354/sief.23.re202

Hutchinson, D. (2024). AI literacy for school librarians: Ethical considerations and best practices. *School Library Research, 17*(2), 45–68.

Hu, Y., Kuang, W., Qin, Z., Li, K., Zhang, J., Gao, Y., Li, W., & Li, K. (2021). Artificial intelligence security: Threats and countermeasures. *ACM Computing Surveys, 55*(1), 1–36. DOI: 10.1145/3487890

Ibrahim, M.. (2024). Addressing algorithmic bias in AI applications for education. *Journal of Learning Analytics, 11*(2), 45–67.

Ilham, R., Muhammad, I., Aji, L. J., Rizal, S. U., & Özbilen, F. M. (2023). Artificial intelligence research in education: A bibliometric analysis. *Journal of Education Global, 1*(1), 45–55.

Ilieva, G., Yankova, T., Klisarova-Belcheva, S., Dimitrov, A., Bratkov, M., & Angelov, D. (2023). Effects of generative chatbots in higher education. *Information (Basel), 14*(9), 492. DOI: 10.3390/info14090492

Ismail, A., Aliu, A., Ibrahim, M., & Sulaiman, A. (2024). Preparing teachers of the future in the era of artificial intelligence. *Journal of Artificial Intelligence. Machine Learning and Neural Network, 44*, 31–41.

Ivanova, M., Grosseck, G., & Holotescu, C. (2024, February). Unveiling Insights: A Bibliometric Analysis of Artificial Intelligence in Teaching. *In Informatics* (Vol. 11, No. 1, p. 10). MDPI. DOI: 10.3390/informatics11010010

Jaleniauskienė, E., Lisaitė, D., & Daniusevičiūtė-Brazaitė, L. (2023). Artificial intelligence in language education: A bibliometric analysis. *Sustainable Multilingualism, 23*(1), 159–194. DOI: 10.2478/sm-2023-0017

Jasmy, A. J., Ismail, H., & Aljneibi, N. (2024). A Novel Approach to Sustainable Behavior Enhancement through AI-Driven Carbon Footprint Assessment and Real-Time Analytics. *Discover Sustainability*, *5*(476), 476. Advance online publication. DOI: 10.1007/s43621-024-00762-w

Jia, X., & Hou, Y. (2024). AI-Driven Sustainable Human Resource Management (HRM): A Quantitative Analysis. *HRM Journal*, *29*(3), 441–465.

Jia, X., & Hou, Y. (2024). Architecting the Future: Exploring the Synergy of AI-Driven Sustainable HRM, Conscientiousness, and Employee Engagement. *Discover Sustainability*, *5*(30), 1–18. DOI: 10.1007/s43621-024-00214-5

Jin, S. H., Im, K., Yoo, M., Roll, I., & Seo, K. (2023). Supporting students' self-regulated learning in online learning using artificial intelligence applications. *International Journal of Educational Technology in Higher Education*, *20*(1), 37. DOI: 10.1186/s41239-023-00406-5

Johnson, D., & Peters, M. (2019). The future of talent acquisition: Trends and predictions. *HR Journal*, *25*(1), 5–20.

Joshi, R., Pandey, K., & Kumari, S. (2025). Redefining Teaching in the Era of Generative Artificial Intelligence: A 360-Degree Perspective. In *Fostering Inclusive Education With AI and Emerging Technologies* (pp. 73-98). IGI Global.

Kabudi, T., Pappas, I., & Olsen, D. H. (2021). AI-enabled adaptive learning systems: A systematic mapping of the literature. *Computers and Education: Artificial Intelligence*, *2*, 100017. DOI: 10.1016/j.caeai.2021.100017

Kamenskih, A. (2022). The analysis of security and privacy risks in smart education environments. *Journal of Smart Cities and Society*, *1*(1), 17–29. DOI: 10.3233/SCS-210114

Kanont, J.. (2024). Cultural considerations in AI adoption for equitable education. *Education and Information Technologies*, *29*(4), 901–925.

Karataş, T., & Yüce, S. (2024). Ethical perspectives on integrating ChatGPT in teacher education: Benefits and challenges. Turkish Journal of Educational Technology.

Karthikeyan, C. (2025). AI (Artificial Intelligence) Leveraging to Foster DEI (Diversity, Equity, and Inclusiveness) in Organizations: Harnessing AI for Diversity, Equity, and Inclusion of Indian Version. In *Navigating Organizational Behavior in the Digital Age With AI* (pp. 77-100). IGI Global Scientific Publishing.

Katsamakas, E., Pavlov, O. V., & Saklad, R. (2024). Artificial intelligence and the transformation of higher education institutions. arXiv preprint arXiv:2402.08143. Retrieved from https://arxiv.org/abs/2402.08143

Kayal, A. (2024). Transformative Pedagogy: A Comprehensive Framework for AI Integration in Education. In *Explainable AI for Education: Recent Trends and Challenges* (pp. 247-270). Springer. DOI: 10.1007/978-3-031-72410-7_14

Khan, W. N. (2024). Ethical Challenges of AI in Education: Balancing Innovation with Data Privacy. *Journal of AI in Education: Innovations, Opportunities, Challenges, and Future Directions, 1*(1), 1–13.

Khan, W. N. (2024). Ethical Challenges of AI in Education: Balancing Innovation with Data Privacy. *Journal of AI Integration in Education, 1*(1), 1–13.

Khosravi, H., Shum, S. B., Chen, G., Conati, C., Tsai, Y. S., Kay, J., & Gašević, D. (2022). Explainable artificial intelligence in education. *Computers and Education: Artificial Intelligence, 3*, 100074.

Kim, J., & Lee, S. (2020). The impact of social media on talent acquisition: A qualitative study. *Journal of HR Practices, 12*(4), 291–307.

Koć-Januchta, M. M., Schönborn, K. J., Roehrig, C., Chaudhri, V. K., Tibell, L. A., & Heller, H. C. (2022). "Connecting concepts helps put main ideas together": Cognitive load and usability in learning biology with an AI-enriched textbook. *International Journal of Educational Technology in Higher Education, 19*(1), 11. DOI: 10.1186/s41239-021-00317-3

Kordzadeh, N., & Ghasemaghaei, M. (2022). Algorithmic bias: Review, synthesis, and future research directions. *European Journal of Information Systems, 31*(3), 388–409. DOI: 10.1080/0960085X.2021.1927212

Kumar, J. A. (2021). Educational chatbots for project-based learning: Investigating learning outcomes for a team-based design course. *International Journal of Educational Technology in Higher Education, 18*(1), 65. DOI: 10.1186/s41239-021-00302-w PMID: 34926790

Kumar, S., Datta, S., Singh, V., Datta, D., Singh, S. K., & Sharma, R. (2024). Applications, Challenges, and Future Directions of Human-in-the-Loop Learning. *IEEE Access : Practical Innovations, Open Solutions*, *12*, 75735–75760. DOI: 10.1109/ACCESS.2024.3401547

Kumar, Y., Parekh, S., Singh, S., Li, J. J., Shah, R. R., & Chen, C. (2023). Automatic essay scoring systems are both overstable and oversensitive: Explaining why and proposing defenses. *Dialogue & Discourse*, *14*(1), 1–33. DOI: 10.5210/dad.2023.101

Kusuma, D.. (2022). Ethical design principles for AI-based adaptive learning environments. *Journal of Educational Technology Systems*, *51*(3), 189–207.

Kwok, A. P. K., Wong, Y. H., Wong, K. C., & Chan, C. H. (2024). AI Meeting Assistants in English-Medium University Lectures in Hong Kong, China: A Double-Edged Sword for Student Perception. *International Journal of Information and Education Technology (IJIET)*, *14*(9), 1271–1276. DOI: 10.18178/ijiet.2024.14.9.2156

Kwok, A. P. K., Wong, Y. H., Wong, K. C., & Chan, C. H. (2024). Exploring AI Meeting Assistants in Higher Education: Challenges and Opportunities. *Journal of Educational Technology & Society*, *27*(1), 120–138.

Lai, C.-H., & Lin, C.-Y. (2025). Analysis of Learning Behaviors and Outcomes for Students with Different Knowledge Levels: A Case Study of Intelligent Tutoring System for Coding and Learning (ITS-CAL). *Applied Sciences (2076-3417)*, *15*(4).

Lametti, D. (2022). A.I could be great for college essays. https://slate.com/technology/2022/12/-college-essay-plagiarism.html

Landers, R., & Behrend, T. (2022). Auditing the AI auditors: A framework for evaluating fairness and bias in high stakes AI predictive models. *The American Psychologist*. Advance online publication. DOI: 10.1037/amp0000972 PMID: 35157476

Lang, Q., Wang, M., Yin, M., Liang, S., & Song, W. (2025). Transforming Education with Generative AI (GAI): Key Insights and Future Prospects. IEEE Transactions on Learning Technologies.

Latif, G., Brahim, G. B., Abdelhamid, S. E., Alghazo, R., Alhabib, G., & Alnujaidi, K. (2023). Learning at Your Fingertips: An Innovative IoT-Based AI-Powered Braille Learning System. *Applied System Innovation*, *6*(5), 91. DOI: 10.3390/asi6050091

Lee, J., & Kim, H. (2021). Talent acquisition strategies in the gig economy: A comparative analysis. *Journal of Employment Studies*, *29*(2), 180–196.

Lee, J., & Kim, Y. (2023). Sustainable educational metaverse content and system based on deep learning for enhancing learner immersion. *Sustainability (Basel), 15*(16), 12663. DOI: 10.3390/su151612663

Lee, K., & Park, J. (2018). Talent acquisition in a globalized world: Challenges and opportunities. *Global Human Resources, 15*(2), 112–126.

Leelavathi, S., & Surendhranatha, R. (2024). Ethical considerations in the use of AI-assisted tools in management education. *Indian Journal of Management Studies, 15*(2), 78–98.

Lee, S., & Park, G. (2023). Exploring the impact of ChatGPT literacy on user satisfaction: The mediating role of user motivations. *Cyberpsychology, Behavior, and Social Networking, 26*(12), 913–918. DOI: 10.1089/cyber.2023.0312 PMID: 38090765

Le, M.. (2024). Student motivations and ethical concerns in ChatGPT usage: A TAM and UGT perspective. *International Journal of Educational Technology in Higher Education, 21*(3), 34–56.

Leocádio, D., Malheiro, L., & Reis, J. (2024). Artificial Intelligence in Auditing: A Conceptual Framework for Auditing Practices. *Administrative Sciences, 14*(10), 238. Advance online publication. DOI: 10.3390/admsci14100238

Li, H. (2025). Multicultural data assistance mining analysis for ideological and political education in smart education platforms using artificial intelligence. *Wireless Networks, 31*(1), 567–581. https://link.springer.com/article/10.1007/s11276-024-03772-8. DOI: 10.1007/s11276-024-03772-8

Li, H., Fan, X., & Liang, J. (2025). The Squirrel AI Adaptive Learning System Accompanying Millions of Children in Their Growth. In *Digital Transformation of Regional Education in China* (pp. 51–53). Springer Nature Singapore. DOI: 10.1007/978-981-97-8144-7_7

Limna, P., Jakwatanatham, S., Siripipattanakul, S., Kaewpuang, P., & Sriboonruang, P. (2022). A review of artificial intelligence (AI) in education during the digital era. *Advance Knowledge for Executives, 1*(1), 1–9. DOI: 10.1080/13621025.2022.2147262

Lin, Z.. (2024). AI-enhanced learning environments: Ethical challenges and design solutions. *Computers & Education, 203*, 104786.

Li, W., & Mohamad, M. (2023). An Efficient Probabilistic Deep Learning Model for the Oral Proficiency Assessment of Student Speech Recognition and Classification [Article]. *International Journal on Recent and Innovation Trends in Computing and Communication, 11*(6), 411–424. DOI: 10.17762/ijritcc.v11i6.7734

Lopes, J. M., Silva, L. F., & Massano-Cardoso, I. (2024). AI Meets the Shopper: Psychosocial Factors in Ease of Use and Their Effect on E-Commerce Purchase Intention. *Behavioral Sciences (Basel, Switzerland)*, *14*(7), 616. DOI: 10.3390/bs14070616 PMID: 39062439

LRN. C. (2025). AI, ethics, and ESG in 2025. Retrieved from https://lrn.com/blog/ai-ethics-and-esg-in-2025

Lu, A., Wong, C. S., Cheung, R. Y., & Im, T. S. (2021, April). Supporting flipped and gamified learning with augmented reality in higher education. In Frontiers in education (Vol. 6, p. 623745). *Frontiers Media SA*. DOI: 10.3389/feduc.2021.623745

Luckin, R.. (2024). Collaborative frameworks for human-centric AI in education. *Computers in Human Behavior*, *127*, 107820.

Luckin, R., Holmes, W., Griffiths, M., & Forcier, L. B. (2016). *Intelligence unleashed: An argument for AI in education*. Pearson.

Mahboob, A., Ullah, Z., Ovais, A., Rasheed, M. W., Edalatpanah, S. A., & Yasin, K. (2024). A MAGDM approach for evaluating the impact of artificial intelligence on education using 2-tuple linguistic q-rung orthopair fuzzy sets and Schweizer-Sklar weighted power average operator. *Frontiers in Artificial Intelligence*, *7*, 1347626. DOI: 10.3389/frai.2024.1347626 PMID: 38550976

Manna, S., & Sett, N. (2024). Need of AI in Modern Education: in the Eyes of Explainable AI (xAI). *arXiv preprint arXiv:2408.00025.*

Marchena Sekli, G. F., Godo, A., & Véliz, J. C. (2024). Generative AI Solutions for Faculty and Students: A Review of Literature and Roadmap for Future Research. *Journal of Information Technology Education*, *23*, 14. DOI: 10.28945/5304

Masrom, M. B., Busalim, A. H., Abuhassna, H., & Mahmood, N. H. N. (2021). Understanding students' behavior in online social networks: A systematic literature review. *International Journal of Educational Technology in Higher Education*, *18*(1), 6. DOI: 10.1186/s41239-021-00240-7

Mathew, T. M., Eleazar, V., Lisa, D., James, B., & Jose, B. (2023).. . *Journal of Special Education Technology*, *38*(3), 404–416. DOI: 10.1177/01626434231165977

McCarthy, J., Minsky, M. L., Rochester, N., & Shannon, C. E. (1955). A proposal for the Dartmouth summer research project on artificial intelligence. *AI Magazine*, *27*(4), 12–14. DOI: 10.1609/aimag.v27i4.1904

McNulty, N. (2024). AI and Data Privacy in Schools: Safeguarding Student Information. Medium. Retrieved from https://medium.com/@niall.mcnulty/ai-and-data-privacy-in-schools-safeguarding-student-information-a0e8436a5f5e

Memarian, B., & Doleck, T. (2023). Fairness, Accountability, Transparency, and Ethics (FATE) in Artificial Intelligence (AI) and higher education: A systematic review. *Computers and Education: Artificial Intelligence*, *5*, 100152. DOI: 10.1016/j.caeai.2023.100152

Mensah, G. B. (2023). Artificial intelligence and ethics: a comprehensive review of bias mitigation, transparency, and accountability in AI Systems. *Preprint, November, 10*(1).

Mensah, G. B. (2023). Artificial intelligence and ethics: A comprehensive review of bias mitigation, transparency, and accountability in AI Systems. *Preprint*, (November), 10.

Miao, F., Holmes, W., Huang, R., & Zhang, H. (2021). *AI and education: A guidance for policymakers*. UNESCO Publishing.

Michel-Villarreal, R., Vilalta-Perdomo, E., Salinas-Navarro, D. E., Thierry-Aguilera, R., & Gerardou, F. S. (2023). Challenges and opportunities of generative AI for higher education as explained by ChatGPT. *Education Sciences*, *13*(9), 856. DOI: 10.3390/educsci13090856

Miller, J. C., Miranda, J. P. P., & Tolentino, J. C. G. (2025). Artificial Intelligence in Physical Education: A Review. *Global Innovations in Physical Education and Health*, 37-60.

Mishra, P. (2025). Revolutionizing Education With AI and ML. *Internet of Behavior-Based Computational Intelligence for Smart Education Systems*, 53-94.

MIT. R. (2024). Securing Student Data in the Age of Generative AI. Retrieved from https://raise.mit.edu/wp-content/uploads/2024/06/Securing-Student-Data-in-the-Age-of-Generative-AI_MIT-RAISE.pdf

Mitchell, D. L. (2025). Integrating AI Into Policy Making in Educational Leadership. In *Integrating AI Into Pedagogical Education* (pp. 25–48). IGI Global Scientific Publishing.

Modern, D. (2024). Ethical Implementation of AI in Cybersecurity in 2025. Retrieved from https://moderndiplomacy.eu/2024/11/04/ethical-implementation-of-ai-in-cybersecurity-in-2025/

Moher, D., Liberati, A., Tetzlaff, J., &Altman, D. G. (2009). Preferred reporting items for systematic reviews and meta-analyses: the PRISMA statement. *bmj, 339.*

Mökander, J.. (2022). A framework for ethical AI implementation in corporate training environments. *Journal of Business Ethics*, *178*(1), 23–40.

Mökander, J., & Floridi, L. (2021). Ethics-Based Auditing to Develop Trustworthy AI. *Minds and Machines*, *31*(2), 323–327. DOI: 10.1007/s11023-021-09557-8

Mora, H., Signes-Pont, M. T., Fuster-Guilló, A., & Pertegal-Felices, M. L. (2020). A collaborative working model for enhancing the learning process of science & engineering students. *Computers in Human Behavior*, *103*, 140–150. DOI: 10.1016/j.chb.2019.09.008

Moreno-Guerrero, A.-J., López-Belmonte, J., Marín-Marín, J.-A., & Soler-Costa, R. (2020). Scientific development of educational artificial intelligence in Web of Science. *Future Internet*, *12*(8), 124. DOI: 10.3390/fi12080124

Morrison, F. (2025). Privacy + Data Security Predictions for 2025. Retrieved from https://www.mofo.com/resources/insights/250107-privacy-data-security-predictions

Mouta, A., Torrecilla-Sánchez, E. M., & Pinto-Llorente, A. M. (2025). Comprehensive professional learning for teacher agency in addressing ethical challenges of AIED: Insights from educational design research. *Education and Information Technologies*, *30*(3), 3343–3387. DOI: 10.1007/s10639-024-12946-y

Mouta, H.. (2024). CPD programs for AI ethics: Addressing ethical challenges in AIEd. *Educational Technology Research and Development*, *72*(1), 78–95.

Mpuangnan, K. N. (2024). Teacher preparedness and professional development needs for successful technology integration in teacher education. *Cogent Education*, *11*(1), 2408837. DOI: 10.1080/2331186X.2024.2408837

Mumtaz, Z.. (2024). AI ethics through cultural lenses: Frameworks for equitable deployment. *Asian Journal of Educational Research*, *13*(1), 89–107.

Murray-Rust, D., Lupetti, M. L., Nicenboim, I., & van der Hoog, W. (2024). Grasping AI: Experiential Exercises for Designers. *AI & Society*, *39*(6), 2891–2911. DOI: 10.1007/s00146-023-01794-y

Murtaza, M., Ahmed, Y., Shamsi, J. A., Sherwani, F., & Usman, M. (2022). AI-based personalized e-learning systems: Issues, challenges, and solutions. *IEEE Access : Practical Innovations, Open Solutions*, *10*, 81323–81342. DOI: 10.1109/ACCESS.2022.3193938

Nair, B. M. (2023). The efficacy of artificial intelligence-driven immersive reader for dyslexic students in special schools: A case study. *Journal of English Language Teaching*, *65*(5), 3–8.

Nannini, C.. (2024). Explainable AI in education: An applied ethics approach. *Journal of Educational Technology Research*, *35*(1), 23–45.

Narendra, A. P., Dewi, C., Gunawan, L. S., & Ardi, A. S. (2025). Artificial Intelligence Implementation in Library Information Systems: Current Trends and Future Studies. *Vietnam Journal of Computer Science*, 1-25.

National Audit Office. (2022, May 9). NAO employees learn about artificial intelligence. https://www.nao.gov.bh/en/article/nao-employees-learn-about-artificial-intelligence

New, A. (2024). Artificial Intelligence in Schools: Privacy and Security Considerations. Retrieved from https://newamerica.org/oti/blog/artificial-intelligence-in-schools-privacy-and-security-considerations/

Nguyen, A., Ngo, H. N., Hong, Y., Dang, B., & Nguyen, B. P. T. (2023). Ethical principles for artificial intelligence in education. *Education and Information Technologies*, *28*(4), 4221–4241. DOI: 10.1007/s10639-022-11316-w PMID: 36254344

Nguyen, V.. (2023). Global standards for ethical AI integration in education: A stakeholder perspective. *International Journal of Educational Development*, *59*(2), 23–41.

Nuraini, F. I., Sodiq, J., & Prastikawati, E. F. (2025). Edmodo as Technology-Based Formative Assessment: How It Enhances Reading Comprehension. *International Journal of Research in Education*, *5*(1), 81–92. DOI: 10.26877/ijre.v5i1.1368

Nwozor, A. (2025). Artificial Intelligence (AI) and Academic Honesty-Dishonesty Nexus: Trends and Preventive Measures. *AI and Ethics, Academic Integrity and the Future of Quality Assurance in Higher Education, 27.*

Oche, P. A., Ewa, G. A., & Ibekwe, N. (2021). Applications and challenges of artificial intelligence in space missions. *IEEE Access : Practical Innovations, Open Solutions*, *12*, 44481–44509. DOI: 10.1109/ACCESS.2021.3132500

Ogalo, E. O., & Mtenzi, F. (2025). Leveraging Artificial Intelligence Tools for Learning: Academic Integrity and Ethics in Higher Education in Kenya. In *Artificial Intelligence, Digital Learning, and Leadership: Redefining Higher Education* (pp. 1-36). IGI Global.

Ogunyemi, Adeyemi, M. B., Bello, M. A., & Yusuf, T. (2023). AI-based personalized learning in Nigerian educational settings: Opportunities and challenges. *Journal of Educational Technology Development and Exchange, 15*(1), 77–92.

Olugbade, D. (2025). Democratizing Education in Rural Nigeria Through AI and Mobile Technologies as a Transformative Pathway to Inclusive Learning. In M. Sanmugam, B. Edwards, N. Mohd Barkhaya, & Z. Khlaif (Eds.), Fostering Inclusive Education with AI and Emerging Technologies (pp. 233-250). IGI Global. https://doi.org/DOI: 10.4018/979-8-3693-7255-5.ch010

Omarov, B., Nurmash, N., Doskarayev, B., Zhilisbaev, N., Dairabayev, M., Orazov, S., & Omarov, N. (2023). A Novel Deep Neural Network to Analyze and Monitoring the Physical Training Relation to Sports Activities. *International Journal of Advanced Computer Science and Applications, 14*(9). Advance online publication. DOI: 10.14569/IJACSA.2023.0140977

Osamor, C. H.. (2023). AI tools in education: Opportunities and ethical challenges. *Journal of Educational Computing Research, 61*(1), 34–56.

Ouyang, F., Zheng, L., & Jiao, P. (2022). Artificial intelligence in online higher education: A systematic review of empirical research from 2011 to 2020. *Education and Information Technologies, 27*(6), 7893–7925. DOI: 10.1007/s10639-022-10925-9

Paek, S., & Kim, N. (2021). Analysis of worldwide research trends on the impact of artificial intelligence in education. *Sustainability (Basel), 13*(14), 7941. DOI: 10.3390/su13147941

Page, M. J., McKenzie, J. E., Bossuyt, P. M., Boutron, I., Hoffmann, T. C., Mulrow, C. D., Shamseer, L., Tetzlaff, J. M., Akl, E. A., & Brennan, S. E. (2021). The PRISMA 2020 statement: an updated guideline for reporting systematic reviews. *bmj, 372*.

Page, M. J., McKenzie, J. E., Bossuyt, P. M., Boutron, I., Hoffmann, T. C., Mulrow, C. D., & Moher, D. (2021). The PRISMA 2020 statement: An updated guideline for reporting systematic reviews. *BMJ (Clinical Research Ed.), 372*(71). Advance online publication. PMID: 33782057

Palle, R. R., & Kathala, K. C. R. (2024). *Privacy in the Age of Innovation*.

Parycek, P., Schmid, V., & Novak, A. S. (2024). Artificial Intelligence (AI) and automation in administrative procedures: Potentials, limitations, and framework conditions. *Journal of the Knowledge Economy, 15*(2), 8390–8415. DOI: 10.1007/s13132-023-01433-3

Patel, A., & Sharma, P. (2017). Talent acquisition and employer branding: A conceptual framework. *Employer Branding Journal, 9*(2), 75–89.

Patel, A., & Sharma, P. (2022). The role of artificial intelligence in talent acquisition: A systematic review. *HR Technology Journal, 14*(3), 221–238.

Pedro, F., Subosa, M., Rivas, A., & Valverde, P. (2019). Artificial intelligence in education: Challenges and opportunities for sustainable development.

Pedro, F., Subosa, M., Rivas, A., & Valverde, P. (2019). Artificial intelligence in education: Challenges and opportunities for sustainable development. DOI: 10.1145/3394332.3402828

Perkins, M.. (2024). AI in assessments: Ethical integration through the AI Assessment Scale. *Australasian Journal of Educational Technology, 40*(4), 78–95.

Pesapane, F., Hauglid, M. K., Fumagalli, M., Petersson, L., Parkar, A. P., Cassano, E., & Horgan, D. (2025). The translation of in-house imaging AI research into a medical device ensuring ethical and regulatory integrity. *European Journal of Radiology, 182*, 111852. DOI: 10.1016/j.ejrad.2024.111852 PMID: 39612599

Peter, U. I., Orubebe, E. D., & Oladokun, B. D. (2024). Transforming Education in Nigerian Universities: The Role of Free and Open-Source Software (FOSS) in Teaching and Learning. *Asian Review of Social Sciences, 13*(1), 39–47. DOI: 10.70112/arss-2024.13.1.4239

Popenici, S. A., & Kerr, S. (2017). Exploring the impact of artificial intelligence on teaching and learning in higher education. *Research and Practice in Technology Enhanced Learning, 12*(1), 22. DOI: 10.1186/s41039-017-0062-8 PMID: 30595727

Pradana, M., Elisa, H. P., & Syarifuddin, S. (2023). Discussing ChatGPT in education: A literature review and bibliometric analysis. *Cogent Education, 10*(2), 2243134. DOI: 10.1080/2331186X.2023.2243134

Prahani, B., Rizki, I., Jatmiko, B., Suprapto, N., & Tan, A. (2022). Artificial intelligence in education research during the last ten years: A review and bibliometric study. [iJET]. *International Journal of Emerging Technologies in Learning, 17*(8), 169–188. DOI: 10.3991/ijet.v17i08.29833

Pucchio, A., Rathagirishnan, R., Caton, N., Gariscsak, P. J., Del Papa, J., Nabhen, J. J., Vo, V., Lee, W., & Moraes, F. Y. (2022). Exploration of exposure to artificial intelligence in undergraduate medical education: A Canadian cross-sectional mixed-methods study. *BMC Medical Education, 22*(1), 815. DOI: 10.1186/s12909-022-03896-5 PMID: 36443720

Radanliev, P., Santos, O., Brandon-Jones, A., & Joinson, A. (2024). Ethics and responsible AI deployment. *Frontiers in Artificial Intelligence, 7*, 1377011. DOI: 10.3389/frai.2024.1377011 PMID: 38601110

Ramaiah, M. S., Nagarajan, S. K. S., Whig, P., & Dutta, P. K. (2025). AI-Powered Innovations Transforming Adaptive Education for Disability Support. In *Advancing Adaptive Education: Technological Innovations for Disability Support* (pp. 73-100). IGI Global Scientific Publishing.

Ramessur, R., Raja, L., Kilduff, C. L., Kang, S., Li, J.-P. O., Thomas, P. B., & Sim, D. A. (2021). Impact and challenges of integrating artificial intelligence and telemedicine into clinical ophthalmology. *Asia-Pacific Journal of Ophthalmology*, *10*(3), 317–327. DOI: 10.1097/APO.0000000000000406 PMID: 34383722

Rane, N., Choudhary, S., & Rane, J. (2023). Education 4.0 and 5.0: Integrating artificial intelligence (AI) for personalized and adaptive learning.

Rane, N., Choudhary, S., & Rane, J. (2023). Education 4.0 and 5.0: Integrating artificial intelligence (AI) for personalized and adaptive learning. DOI: 10.2139/ssrn.4638365

Rathee, R., Vats, H., & Sharma, S. (2025). AI-Enhanced Predictive Scheduling Optimizing Project Timelines for Blue-Green Infrastructure Deployment. In *Integrating Blue-Green Infrastructure Into Urban Development* (pp. 61–80). IGI Global Scientific Publishing.

Rathod, M., Dalvi, C., Kaur, K., Patil, S., Gite, S., Kamat, P., Kotecha, K., Abraham, A., & Gabralla, L. A. (2022). Kids' emotion recognition using various deep-learning models with explainable ai. *Sensors (Basel)*, *22*(20), 8066. DOI: 10.3390/s22208066 PMID: 36298415

Reinecke, M. G., Kappes, A., Porsdam Mann, S., Savulescu, J., & Earp, B. D. (2025). The need for an empirical research program regarding human–AI relational norms. *AI and Ethics*, •••, 1–10. PMID: 39959573

Revesai, Z. (2024). Ethical Implications of AI-Driven Education Systems on Digital Rights: A Comparative Analysis. *The Fountain: Journal of Interdisciplinary Studies*, *8*(1), 126–152.

Roy, S., & Putatunda, P. (2023). Pedagogical applications of AI in literature education: Ethical challenges and opportunities. *Humanities and Technology Review*, *15*(2), 78–96.

Ruan, S., Jiang, L., Xu, Q., Liu, Z., Davis, G. M., Brunskill, E., & Landay, J. A. (2021). Englishbot: An ai-powered conversational system for second language learning. *Proceedings of the 26th International Conference on Intelligent User Interfaces*

Russell, S. J., & Norvig, P. (2021). *Artificial intelligence: A modern approach* (4th ed.). Pearson.

Salloum, S. A. (2024). AI Perils in Education: Exploring Ethical Concerns. Artificial Intelligence in Education: The Power and Dangers of ChatGPT in the Classroom, 669-675.

Sanfo, J. B. (2025). Application of explainable artificial intelligence approach to predict student learning outcomes. *Journal of Computational Social Science*, *8*(1), 1–33. DOI: 10.1007/s42001-024-00344-w

Saqr, R. R., Al-Somali, S. A., & Sarhan, M. Y. (2024). Exploring the acceptance and user satisfaction of AI-driven e-learning platforms (Blackboard, Moodle, Edmodo, Coursera and edX): An integrated technology model. *Sustainability*, *16*(1), 204.

Sarker, I. H. (2021). Deep learning: A comprehensive overview on techniques, taxonomy, applications and research directions. *SN Computer Science*, *2*(6), 420. DOI: 10.1007/s42979-021-00815-1 PMID: 34426802

Sayles, J. (2024). Human Oversight of AI Systems. In *Principles of AI Governance and Model Risk Management: Master the Techniques for Ethical and Transparent AI Systems* (pp. 267–276). Apress. DOI: 10.1007/979-8-8688-0983-5_12

Seethamraju, R., & Hecimovic, A. (2022). Adoption of artificial intelligence in auditing: An exploratory study. *Australian Journal of Management*, *48*(4), 780–800. DOI: 10.1177/03128962221108440

Seldon, A., & Abidoye, O. (2018). *The fourth education revolution*. Legend Press Ltd.

Sethi, S. S., & Jain, K. (2024). AI Technologies for Social Emotional Learning: Recent Research and Future Directions. *Journal of Research in Innovative Teaching & Learning*, *17*(2), 213–225. DOI: 10.1108/JRIT-03-2024-0073

Shahriar, S., Allana, S., Hazratifard, S. M., & Dara, R. (2023). A survey of privacy risks and mitigation strategies in the Artificial Intelligence life cycle. *IEEE Access : Practical Innovations, Open Solutions*, *11*, 61829–61854. DOI: 10.1109/ACCESS.2023.3287195

Shaik, T., Tao, X., Li, Y., Dann, C., McDonald, J., Redmond, P., & Galligan, L. (2022). A review of the trends and challenges in adopting natural language processing methods for education feedback analysis. *IEEE Access : Practical Innovations, Open Solutions*, *10*, 56720–56739. DOI: 10.1109/ACCESS.2022.3177752

Shakimova, D. D., Lawrence, K. C., & Aubakirova, Z. K. (2024). Professional development training can help teachers to build resistance against teaching associated stress. *Cogent Education*, *11*(1), 2346049. DOI: 10.1080/2331186X.2024.2346049

Sharma, Y. (2024). Use of Modern Technology to Improve the Quality of Education. [JOIREM]. *Journal Publication of International Research for Engineering and Management, 10*(12).

Shen, S. (2024). Application of large language models in the field of education. *Theoretical and Natural Science, 34*(1), 147–154. DOI: 10.54254/2753-8818/34/20241163

Shiao, Y.-T., Chen, C.-H., Wu, K.-F., Chen, B.-L., Chou, Y.-H., & Wu, T.-N. (2023). Reducing dropout rate through a deep learning model for sustainable education: Long-term tracking of learning outcomes of an undergraduate cohort from 2018 to 2021. *Smart Learning Environments, 10*(1), 55. DOI: 10.1186/s40561-023-00274-6

Shi, L., Muhammad Umer, A., & Shi, Y. (2023). Utilizing AI models to optimize blended teaching effectiveness in college-level English education. *Cogent Education, 10*(2), 2282804. DOI: 10.1080/2331186X.2023.2282804

Shtayyat, A., Gawanmeh, A., & Mashaleh, A. (2025). Risk Analysis of AI Integration in Educational Systems.

Shu, X., & Gu, X. (2023). An empirical study of A smart education model enabled by the edu-metaverse to enhance better learning outcomes for students. *Systems, 11*(2), 75. DOI: 10.3390/systems11020075

Sidiropoulos, D., & Anagnostopoulos, C.-N. (2024). Applications, challenges and ethical issues of AI and ChatGPT in education. arXiv preprint arXiv:2402.07907. Retrieved from https://arxiv.org/abs/2402.07907

Singh, A., Lakhera, G., & Ojha, M. kumar Mishra, A., & Nain, A. (2025). Balancing Innovation With Responsibility: Ethical Dimensions of AI in Revolutionizing E-Learning. In *Ethical Dimensions of AI Development* (pp. 467-500). IGI Global. Retrieved from, https://www.igi-global.com/chapter/balancing-innovation-with-responsibility/359655

Singh, T. M., Reddy, C. K. K., Murthy, B. R., Nag, A., & Doss, S. (2025). AI and education: Bridging the gap to personalized, efficient, and accessible learning.

Singh, R., & Kumar, A. (2023). Talent mapping: A strategic tool for organizational success. *Human Resource Development Quarterly, 31*(2), 130–147.

Smith, J., & Brown, K. (2017). Talent acquisition and diversity and inclusion: A strategic imperative. *Diversity and Inclusion Journal, 10*(3), 65–78.

Smith, R., & Johnson, K. (2022). Real-time transcription technologies and their impact on students with hearing impairments. *Journal of Educational Technology Systems, 48*(2), 189–204. DOI: 10.2190/ET.43.2.f

Smutny, P., & Schreiberova, P. (2020). Chatbots for learning: A review of educational chatbots for the Facebook Messenger. *Computers & Education, 151*, 103862. DOI: 10.1016/j.compedu.2020.103862

Soegoto, H., Soeryanto Soegoto, E., Luckyardi, S., & Abhi Rafdhi, A. (2022). A bibliometric analysis of management bioenergy research using vosviewer application. *Indonesian Journal of Science and Technology*, *7*(1), 89–104. DOI: 10.17509/ijost.v7i1.43328

Song, C., & Song, Y. (2023). Enhancing academic writing skills and motivation: Assessing the efficacy of ChatGPT in AI-assisted language learning for EFL students. *Frontiers in Psychology*, *14*, 1260843. DOI: 10.3389/fpsyg.2023.1260843 PMID: 38162975

Song, P., & Wang, X. (2020). A bibliometric analysis of worldwide educational artificial intelligence research development in recent twenty years. *Asia Pacific Education Review*, *21*(3), 473–486. DOI: 10.1007/s12564-020-09640-2

Soodan, R.. (2024). Leveraging AI for higher education: Addressing privacy and adoption concerns. *AI & Society*, *39*(1), 12–34.

Soojin, K. (2024). The Meaning of Personalized Learning Structures in AI-based Educational Platforms: From the Perspective of Learned Curriculum. *Educational Technology International*, *25*(2), 297–329.

Srinivasa, K. G., Kurni, M., & Saritha, K. (2022). Harnessing the Power of AI to Education. In *Learning, teaching, and assessment methods for contemporary learners: pedagogy for the digital generation* (pp. 311–342). Springer Nature Singapore. DOI: 10.1007/978-981-19-6734-4_13

Su, G., Wang, J., Xu, X., Wang, Y., & Wang, C. (2024). The Utilization of Homomorphic Encryption Technology Grounded on Artificial Intelligence for Privacy Preservation. *International Journal of Computer Science and Information Technologies*, *2*(1), 52–58. DOI: 10.62051/ijcsit.v2n1.07

Sultana, S. T., & Rao, T. V. N. (2025). Application of Artificial Intelligence in Business Management for Prudent Decision Making. *Artificial Intelligence-Enabled Businesses: How to Develop Strategies for Innovation*, 351-370.

Swindell, A., Greeley, L., Farag, A., & Verdone, B. (2024). Against artificial education: Towards an ethical framework for generative artificial intelligence (AI) use in education. *Online Learning : the Official Journal of the Online Learning Consortium*, *28*(2), 7–27. DOI: 10.24059/olj.v28i2.4438

Tai, M. C. (2020). The impact of artificial intelligence on human society and bioethics. *Tzu* 15. *Chiba Medical Journal*, *32*(4), 339–343. PMID: 33163378

Taiye, K.. (2024). Ethical dilemmas in generative AI for academic writing: A case for policy frameworks. *Policy Futures in Education*, *22*(3), 123–143.

Tang, Y. (2024). Privacy protection framework for open data: Constructing and assessing an effective approach. *Library & Information Science Research*, *46*(3), 101312. DOI: 10.1016/j.lisr.2024.101312

Tapalova, O., & Zhiyenbayeva, N. (2022). Artificial intelligence in education: AIEd for personalised learning pathways. *Electronic Journal of e-Learning*, *20*(5), 639–653. DOI: 10.34190/ejel.20.5.2597

Tarisayi, K. S. (2024). Generative AI and the ethical dilemmas in resource-constrained educational contexts. *South African Journal of Education*, *44*(1), 56–72.

Tassell, J., Novak, E., Gordon, A., Vondrova, N. a., & Denning, S. (2024). Studying the Impact of Khan Academy as a Personalized Learning Platform with Pre-Service Elementary Teachers of Mathematics in the Czech Republic. EdMedia+ Innovate Learning

Tassoti, S. (2024). Assessment of Students' Use of Generative Artificial Intelligence: Prompting Strategies and Prompt Engineering in Chemistry Education. *Journal of Chemical Education*, *101*(6), 2475–2482. DOI: 10.1021/acs.jchemed.4c00212

Terblanche, N., & Kidd, M. (2022). Adoption factors and moderating effects of age and gender that influence the intention to use a non-directive reflective coaching chatbot. *SAGE Open*, *12*(2), 21582440221096136. DOI: 10.1177/21582440221096136

Terblanche, N., & Kidd, M. (2022). Factors influencing the adoption of artificial intelligence in human capital management: A UTAUT model. *SA Journal of Human Resource Management*, *20*(1), 1–16.

Tozzi, A. E., Gesualdo, F., Pandolfi, E., Ferro, D., Cinelli, G., Bozzola, E., Aversa, T., Di Mauro, A., Mameli, C., & Croci, I. (2023). Prioritizing educational initiatives on emerging technologies for Italian pediatricians: Bibliometric review and a survey. [PubMed]. *Italian Journal of Pediatrics*, *49*(1), 112.

Turing, A. M. (1950). Computing machinery and intelligence. *Mind*, *59*(236), 433–460. DOI: 10.1093/mind/LIX.236.433

UNESCO. (2024). Ethics of Artificial Intelligence. Retrieved from https://www.unesco.org/en/artificial-intelligence/recommendation-ethics

Valencia, L. J. (2024). Artificial Intelligence as the New Hacker: Developing Agents for Offensive Security. Retrieved from https://arxiv.org/abs/2406.07561

VanLehn, Zheng, L., Zheng, D., and Zhang, Z. (2021). Educators' attitudes towards AI in education: A comprehensive review. *Educational Technology Research and Development*, *69*(2), 751–773.

Vaza, R. N., Parmar, A. B., Mishra, P. S., Abdullah, I., & Velu, C. M. (2024). Security And Privacy Concerns In AI-Enabled IoT Educational Frameworks: An In-Depth Analysis. *Educational Administration: Theory and Practice*, *30*(4), 8436–8445.

Venkatesh, V., Morris, M. G., Davis, G. B., & Davis, F. D. (2003). User acceptance of information technology: Toward a unified view. *Management Science*, *49*(8), 1007–1025.

Vetrivel, S., Arun, V., Ambikapathi, R., & Saravanan, T. (2025). Automated Grading Systems: Enhancing Efficiency and Consistency in Student Assessments. In *Adopting Artificial Intelligence Tools in Higher Education* (pp. 41-61). CRC Press.

Vetrivel, S. C., Vidhyapriya, P., & Arun, V. P. (2025). The Role of AI in Transforming Assessment Practices in Education. In *AI Applications and Strategies in Teacher Education* (pp. 43–70). IGI Global.

Visier, (2025). Understanding AI Compliance: Challenges and Solutions. Retrieved from https://www.visier.com/blog/ai-compliance-challenges-and-solutions/

Vistorte, A. O. R., Deroncele-Acosta, A., Ayala, J. L. M., Barrasa, A., López-Granero, C., & Martí-González, M. (2024). Integrating artificial intelligence to assess emotions in learning environments: A systematic literature review. *Frontiers in Psychology*, *15*, 1387089. DOI: 10.3389/fpsyg.2024.1387089 PMID: 38966729

Wang, D., Tao, Y., & Chen, G. (2024). Artificial intelligence in classroom discourse: A systematic review of the past decade. *International Journal of Educational Research*, *123*, 102275. DOI: 10.1016/j.ijer.2023.102275

Wang, J. (2025). Revolutionizing Education for Sustainable Development Through Adaptive Learning and Artificial Intelligence. In *Rethinking the Pedagogy of Sustainable Development in the AI Era* (pp. 63–92). IGI Global Scientific Publishing. DOI: 10.4018/979-8-3693-9062-7.ch004

Wang, L., & Liu, Y. (2021). Talent acquisition and employee engagement: A longitudinal study. *Journal of Employee Engagement*, *24*(2), 98–112.

Watermeyer, R., Phipps, L., Lanclos, D., & Knight, C. (2024). Generative AI and the Automating of Academia. *Postdigital Science and Education*, *6*(2), 446–466. DOI: 10.1007/s42438-023-00440-6

Wellnhofer, E. (2022). Real-world and regulatory perspectives of artificial intelligence in cardiovascular imaging. *Frontiers in Cardiovascular Medicine*, *9*, 890809. DOI: 10.3389/fcvm.2022.890809 PMID: 35935648

Wenhang, S., Shenting, Z., & Shaohua, C. (2025). Prospects for the development of medical professionalism education in the AI perspective: A qualitative study of Chinese postgraduate medical students' written reflections. *Medical Teacher*, •••, 1–9. DOI: 10.1080/0142159X.2024.2445056 PMID: 39772996

Winiarti, S. W., Sunardi, S., Ahdiani, U., & Pranolo, A. (2022). Tradition Meets Modernity: Learning Traditional Building using Artificial Intelligence. *Asian Journal of University Education*, *18*(2), 375–385. DOI: 10.24191/ajue.v18i2.17992

Wood, T., & Moss, G. (2024). AI in classrooms: Building scaffolds for ethical integration. *Australian Journal of Education*, *68*(1), 45–62.

Xia, Q., Chiu, T. K., Lee, M., Sanusi, I. T., Dai, Y., & Chai, C. S. (2022). A self-determination theory (SDT) design approach for inclusive and diverse artificial intelligence (AI) education. *Computers & Education*, *189*, 104582. DOI: 10.1016/j.compedu.2022.104582

Xu, F. W. X., Choo, A. M. H., Ting, P. L. M., Ong, S. J., & Khoo, D. (2023). Leveraging AI in Postgraduate Medical Education for Rapid Skill Acquisition in Ultrasound-Guided Procedural Techniques. *Journal of Imaging*, *9*(10), 225. DOI: 10.3390/jimaging9100225 PMID: 37888332

Yadav, S. (2025). Empowering Educators for the Artificial Intelligence (AI) Era: Strategies and Challenges in Integrating Computational Thinking Into Professional Development. In *Empowering STEM Educators With Digital Tools* (pp. 1-28). IGI Global Scientific Publishing.

Yagyaeva, E., Turobova, M., Nazirova, R., Daminova, Y., Merganova, N., & Oripova, N. (2024, May). A Layout of Bridging Learning Process to fill the Gaps Through AI to make the Technical Education for Better Access. In 2024 4th International Conference on Advance Computing and Innovative Technologies in Engineering (ICACITE) (pp. 612-616). IEEE. DOI: 10.1109/ICACITE60783.2024.10617424

Yahya, M. R., Jalaluddin, , & Batara, G. (2024). Current auditor expertise and future relevance of innovative audit technology: Evidence from Indonesia public sector auditor. *Asia Pacific Journal of Public Administration, 46*(4), 1–17. DOI: 10.1080/23276665.2024.2312139

Yang, E., & Beil, C. (2024). Ensuring data privacy in AI/ML implementation. *New Directions for Higher Education, 2024*(207), 63–78. DOI: 10.1002/he.20509

Yang, Z. (2022). Natural Language Enhancement for English Teaching Using Character-Level Recurrent Neural Network with Back Propagation Neural Network based Classification by Deep Learning Architectures. *JUCS. Journal of Universal Computer Science, 28*(9), 984–1000. DOI: 10.3897/jucs.94162

Yoon, S.. (2024). Ethical AI and academic proofs: A systematic ethical integration framework. *AI & Society, 40*(2), 56–72.

Yuan, C., Xiao, N., Pei, Y., Bu, Y., & Cai, Y. (2025). Enhancing Student Learning Outcomes through AI-Driven Educational Interventions: A Comprehensive Study of Classroom Behavior and Machine Learning Integration. *International Theory and Practice in Humanities and Social Sciences, 2*(2), 197-215. Retrieved from, https://ojs.wisvora.com/index.php/itphss/article/view/216

Yu, L., & Yu, Z. (2023). Qualitative and quantitative analyses of artificial intelligence ethics in education using VOSviewer and CitNetExplorer. *Frontiers in Psychology, 14*, 1061778. DOI: 10.3389/fpsyg.2023.1061778 PMID: 36968737

Zawacki-Richter, O., Marín, V. I., Bond, M., & Gouverneur, F. (2019). Systematic review of research on artificial intelligence applications in higher education–where are the educators? *International Journal of Educational Technology in Higher Education, 16*(1), 1–27. DOI: 10.1186/s41239-019-0171-0

Zhai, X., Chu, X., Chai, C. S., Jong, M. S. Y., Istenic, A., Spector, M., ... & Li, Y. (2021). A Review of Artificial Intelligence (AI) in Education from 2010 to 2020.

Zhai, C., Wibowo, S., & Li, L. D. (2024). The effects of over-reliance on AI dialogue systems on students' cognitive abilities: A systematic review. *Smart Learning Environments, 11*(1), 28. DOI: 10.1186/s40561-024-00316-7

Zhai, X., Chu, X., Chai, C. S., Jong, M. S. Y., Istenic, A., Spector, M., Liu, J.-B., Yuan, J., & Li, Y. (2021). A Review of Artificial Intelligence (AI) in Education from 2010 to 2020. *Complexity, 2021*(1), 8812542. DOI: 10.1155/2021/8812542

Zhang, H., Lee, I., Ali, S., DiPaola, D., Cheng, Y., & Breazeal, C. (2023). Integrating ethics and career futures with technical learning to promote AI literacy for middle school students: An exploratory study. *International Journal of Artificial Intelligence in Education*, *33*(2), 290–324. DOI: 10.1007/s40593-022-00293-3 PMID: 35573722

Zhang, K., & Aslan, A. B. (2021). AI technologies for education: Recent research & future directions. Computers and education. *Artificial Intelligence*, *2*, 100025.

Zhang, R., Zou, D., & Cheng, G. (2024). Self-regulated digital game-based vocabulary learning: Motivation, application of self-regulated learning strategies, EFL vocabulary knowledge development, and their interplay. *Computer Assisted Language Learning*, •••, 1–43. DOI: 10.1080/09588221.2024.2344555

Zhang, X., Yang, D., & Li, X. (2020). Advances in deep learning for speech recognition: A review. *IEEE Transactions on Neural Networks and Learning Systems*, *31*(7), 2458–2474.

Zidoun, Y., & El Mardi, A. (2024). Artificial Intelligence (AI)-Based Simulators Versus Simulated Patients in Undergraduate Programs: A Protocol for a Randomized Controlled Trial. *BMC Medical Education*, *24*(1260), 1260. Advance online publication. DOI: 10.1186/s12909-024-06236-x PMID: 39501219

About the Contributors

Bosede Iyiade Edwards holds PhD in Educational Technology from Universiti Teknologi Malaysia (UTM) in addition to a Master of Education in Educational Technology from the same institution. She has a strong multidisciplinary academic background, with B.Sc. (Hons) Chemistry, Masters in Organic Chemistry and a PG Diploma in Education with over 25 years of experience in teaching, training, online learning, cognitive science, and instructional design. Dr. Edwards is currently a Senior Lecturer at the Center for Instructional Technology & Multimedia (CITM), Universiti Sains Malaysia (USM). Her research focuses on emerging technologies in education and future school. She explores themes including Artificial Intelligence (AI) and immersive media applications, adaptive learning, Human–Machine Interfaces, and the broad field of technology-aided instruction. She supervises graduate and doctoral research studies in these fields and others within the instructional technology and multimedia field. Dr. Edwards has authored several journal articles, conference papers and research books. She is passionate about interdisciplinary collaborations for student development, and leveraging technology to promote equity. She invests her free time in her hobbies, writing inspirational fictions for children and counseling books for adults, and giving free consultations on international education to school leavers and guidance to budding research scholars.

Hassan Abuhassna is an associate professor at Sunway University, Malaysia's Faculty of Education, specializing in educational technology. Prior to this role, he served as an assistant professor at Universiti Teknologi Malaysia (UTM), where he also completed a postdoctoral fellowship. Dr. Abuhassna earned his Ph.D. in Educational Technology from UTM and a Master's degree from Universiti Putra Malaysia (UPM). His research focuses on online education, MOOCs, and e-learning, with numerous publications indexed in prestigious databases such as Web of Science and Scopus. Dr. Abuhassna has successfully supervised seven Master's students and is currently supervising three Ph.D. candidates in their final semester. Throughout his academic career, he has demonstrated a strong commitment to advancing the integration of technology in education, contributing significantly to both research and pedagogy. His work continues to influence the field, positioning him as a respected figure in the academic community.

Damola Olugbade earned his PhD in Educational Technology from Obafemi Awolowo University, Nigeria, in 2018. He is a Principal Research Fellow at First Technical University, Ibadan, where he leads research on learning technologies and digital pedagogy. His work centers on integrating artificial intelligence (AI), learning cognition, and innovative educational technologies to enhance educational outcomes. Dr. Olugbade has made significant contributions through publications in prominent journals like Education and Information Technologies and the African Journal of Teacher Education. He frequently presents at international conferences on topics such as AI-driven education, technology-enhanced learning, and social media in education, advancing the practical applications of educational technologies in Nigeria and beyond.

Olayinka Anthony Ojo holds PhD in Educational Technology from Obafemi Awolowo University, Ile-Ife, and has a background in Computer Science. His work experience spans both the industry and academia, and he has been extensively involved with executive training in computer applications for top management staff of various organizations. He is well-versed in computer maintenance services, and development of computer solutions for top-rated companies. Dr. Ojo has taught various computer science and educational technology courses at the University of Ilesa, University of Ibadan, and Lagos State University. He is a professional examiner for the West African Examination Council (WAEC) and a lecturer and Postgraduate research supervisor at the National Open University of Nigeria (NOUN). Dr. Ojo served as a Senior Educational Technologist at the University of Medical Sciences, Ondo, Nigeria co-ordinating technology integration and training for the university academic staff. He is a dynamic researcher with published works in educational technologies and computer science. He is currently engaged with research in computing, network security and emerging technologies at the University of Bolton, United Kingdom. His research interests are in the application of computer and mobile technologies in teaching and learning.

Wan Ahmad Jaafar Wan Yahaya has been the Director at the Centre for Instructional Technology and Multimedia (PTPM), Universiti Sains Malaysia (USM), Penang, since 2016. He also serves as the President of the Malaysian Educational Technology Association (META). He is the Chairman of the Technical Committee on Audio, Video, Information Technology, and Communication

Equipment at the Department of Standard Malaysia, Ministry of International Trade and Industry Malaysia. He holds a PhD in Multimedia Education from the University of Leeds and a Master of Education (Computer in Education) from the University of Manchester, United Kingdom. In teaching, Prof. Dr. Wan Ahmad Jaafar Wan Yahaya has been focusing on Graphic 2D, 3D & Animation, Multimedia Project Management, Multimedia in Education, and 3D Visualizations and Animations. He has graduated over 30 PhD students. Some of his innovative creations and projects have won gold awards and special recognition in International Innovation, Invention, Design, and Technology competitions in Malaysia, Indonesia, Korea, and Geneva (Switzerland). He is the recipient of the Thailand Association International Honor Award for Outstanding Contributions to the field of Educational Communications and Technology for the year 2023.

***

Mohamad Azrien Bin Mohamed Adnan obtained his Bachelor's degree from Yarmouk University in 1999. He then pursued further studies at the master's level, earning a Master of Business Administration in 2002 and a Master of Education (Arabic Language) in 2006. He continued his academic journey to the doctoral level and was awarded a Doctor of Philosophy (PhD) in 2016.

Nurul Farhana Jumaat is a senior lecturer at Universiti Teknologi Malaysia (UTM), specializing in educational technology, instructional design, online learning, and technology-enhanced learning. In her professional career, Dr. Nurul Farhana serves as an editorial board member for the Malaysian Journal of Social Sciences and Humanities and the Innovative Teaching and Learning Journal. Her scholarly work has garnered significant recognition, with her publications cited over 1,100 times, reflecting her impact in the fields of online learning, educational technology, and computer-based learning.

A.V.Senthil Kumar is working as a Professor and Director, PG and Research Department of Computer Applications, Hindusthan College of Arts & Science, Coimbatore, Tamilnadu. To his credit he has industrial experience for five years and teaching experience of 27 years. He has also received his Doctor of Science (D.Sc in Computer Science). He has to his credit 50 Book Chapters, 225 papers in International and National Journals 64 papers in International Conferences in International and National Conferences, and edited 14 books and 2 Text books. He is as Associate Editor of IEEE Access. He is an Editor-in-Chief for many journals and Key Member for India, Machine Intelligence Research Lab (MIR Labs). He is an Editorial Board Member and Reviewer for various International Journals. He is also a Committee member for various International Conferences.

Audrey Legodi serves as the Chair of the Department of Auditing at the University of South Africa (UNISA). A Ph.D. holder in Accounting Sciences and a Registered Government Auditor (RGA). Her professional background spans more than two decades and includes management, lecturing, research, external and internal audit, and finance. In some of these roles, she has held leadership and governance responsibilities. She served as Council member and a Chairperson of Audit and Risk Committee in various Higher Education Institutions. Her research interests are in Public Sector Governance, focusing on audit committees, external audit, internal audit, performance audit, anti-corruption and technology.

Oluwatoyin Ogunwale started her career as a sign language interpreter twenty five years ago. She converted to the position of Lecturer in the year 2010 as an assistant Lecturer. She rose to the level of Principal Lecturer and presently she is the Deputy Director Research and Publication, Federal College of Education Special Oyo. Her area of specialization is in Inclusive education, total communication, autism, mental health and education for learners with hearing impairment. She has contributed to reputable journals both nationally and internationally, one of which is European Journal multidisciplinary science.She has attended many conferences within and outside Nigeria,one of it is world conference on autism by US Autism and Asperger's association in Louisville, Kentucky. Oluwatoyin is an advocate for inclusion and a trainer for teachers of children with disabilities . She is a member of society for disability studies (USA), NAEC, NASET and Chairperson, society for women and Aids in Africa Nigeria,Oyo state (SWAAANOYO).

Oyeyemi Oladimeji is a multidimensional educator, researcher and lecturer at Federal College of Education (Special), Oyo, Oyo State, Nigeria. Her interest is in education of learners with intellectual disability, an area where she has published several articles in reputable journals. She had a background in English and counselling psychology which has been a source of finding her niche as a special educator and has developed her passion to see every child fulfill destiny. Her PhD thesis is on Effect of Graphic Organizers and Task Analysis Strategies on Acquisition of and Attitude towards Social Skills among Pupils with Intellectual Disability. Dr. Oladimeji has been an expert facilitator, a regular speaker at Conferences, an advocate of inclusion and trainer on Education of Persons with Special Education Needs and Disabilities (SENDs) in Collaboration with National Teachers Institute and Axiom Learn Solutions for over a decade. She is presently the Head of Department (HOD) of the Department of Education for learners with Intellectual

Disability, Federal College of Education (Special), Oyo, Oyo State, Nigeria. She is a member of Counselling Association of Nigeria, National Association of Special Education Teachers and Population Association of Nigeria (PAN) where she constantly draws her strength to forge ahead.

Index

www.ingramcontent.com/pod-product-compliance
Lightning Source LLC
LaVergne TN
LVHW081529300926
849161LV00006B/1356